MUSLIMS IN THE DIASPORA:
THE SOMALI COMMUNITIES OF
LONDON AND TORONTO

Rima Berns McGown, in interviews with over eighty Somali men, women, and children in London and Toronto, found that Somali refugees in the West have had to renegotiate their understanding of themselves as Muslims in the highly secular, Judaeo-Christian-based liberal democracies in which they newly reside, a process made more complex by the harsh realities of refugee life. They must confront the challenges of practising Islam in a non-Muslim country and transferring values to their children amid a profusion of competing belief systems.

Somalis have responded to culture clash not by assimilating, but by weaving elements of their birth and adopted cultures together. They become Western, but not Westernized, Muslims as they confront and redefine their practice of Islam and their own interpretations of what it is to be a good Muslim. Some attempt to create relative isolation, but for most, the process involves a gradual accommodation of traditional customs to those of the new society, without loss of what they consider essential to themselves as Muslims. Moreover, they have generally combined accommodation to the West with a stronger identification with Islam and 'Muslimness.'

Berns McGown contends that harmonious integration is facilitated by a political culture that creates a legitimate space for immigrants and minorities, as is revealed by a comparison of the Somali communities of London and Toronto. The flexibility and diversity of views demonstrated by Somali Muslim immigrants indicate that they will integrate over time into Western political systems and societies and that this process will be much easier if they are not marginalized and alienated.

RIMA BERNS McGOWN is a private scholar living in Toronto.

RIMA BERNS McGOWN

Muslims in the Diaspora: The Somali Communities of London and Toronto

UNIVERSITY OF TORONTO PRESS
Toronto Buffalo London

© University of Toronto Press Incorporated 1999
Toronto Buffalo London

Printed in Canada

ISBN 0-8020-4707-6 (cloth)
ISBN 0-8020-8281-5 (paper)

Printed on acid-free paper

Canadian Cataloguing in Publication Data

Berns McGown, Rima
    Muslims in the diaspora : the Somali communities of London and Toronto

    Includes bibliographical references and index.
    ISBN 0-8020-4707-6 (bound)   ISBN 0-8020-8281-5 (pbk.)

    1. Muslims – Cultural assimilation – Ontario – Toronto.   2. Muslims –
    Cultural assimilation – England – London.   3. Somalis – Cultural
    assimilation – Ontario – Toronto.   4. Somalis – Cultural assimilation –
    England – London.   I. Title

    FC3097.9.M88B47 1999   305.6'9710713541   C99-931023-2
    F1059.5.T689M88 1999

This book has been published with the help of a grant from
the Humanities and Social Sciences Federation of Canada, using funds
provided by the Social Sciences and Humanities Research Council of Canada.

The University of Toronto Press acknowledges the financial assistance
to its publishing program of the Canada Council for the Arts and
the Ontario Arts Council.

University of Toronto Press acknowledges the financial support for
its publishing activities of the Government of Canada through
the Book Publishing Industry Development Program (BPIDP).

Canadä

For two inspirational women:

Esther Jacobson
and Ruth Berns,
    née Johanna Susannah
    Jacoba Rheeder

Contents

Preface

I have always been fascinated by the interstices between cultures and how they are filled. My parents moved from South Africa to Canada when I was four in order that my brother and I would not be raised in the environment of apartheid. I was acutely conscious of being a Jewish child in a non-Jewish neighbourhood of Montreal in the 1960s and 1970s; of being the product of a British–South African household in a society of English-Canadian, American, and Québécois influences; and of the contrast in sensibilities between South Africa – where we frequently visited family – and Canada. What was my identity? Where was home?

These questions followed me through extended travels through Europe and the Middle East. It became so obvious in eastern Europe, well before the fall of the Soviet Union – in Hungary and in what was then Yugoslavia – that tribal identities were fiercely alive and that memories of perceived past injustices lurked just beneath the surface civility. Israel's social divisions appeared jagged: that between religious and non-religious Jews no less than that between Jews and Arabs.

Yet a shrinking world means that people in immigration-receiving countries – the ones to which people flee when conditions become untenable at 'home' – need to learn how to live with others. I have always been suspicious of assimilation as a way of understanding how they do this, and, beginning at graduate school at Johns Hopkins University's School of Advanced International Studies (SAIS) in Washington, DC, I sought to solve this puzzle. Muslim migration to the West has been increasing in recent years, and Muslims often find themselves misunderstood, depicted as 'Other,' with an alien value system and customs incompatible with those commonly accepted in the West. Living in Ottawa in the early 1990s, I became aware of the rapidly increasing Somali refugee community. Research for this book, which began life as a PhD thesis, quickly confirmed that the Somali communities of London, England, and Toronto, Canada, were among the largest in the West. The Somalis whom I had met struck me as forthright and sensitive and would, I guessed, be candid respondents. And so it seemed to me that this was an invaluable opportunity to understand the process of integration, enriched by the comparative perspective.

Because the communities were so new, very little research had been done on them. Background reading gave me to believe that I would find that most Somalis were Sufis if they bothered to practise at all, so I was surprised to find the kind and degree of religious observance that I encountered. Moreover, very little had been written about the Somali Islamist movements, even in newspapers. Therefore I had to undertake a dual set of interviews, one purely devoted to determining what it was that I was encountering.

In both London and Toronto, I found that Somali respondents were as candid and forthright as I had guessed (and hoped) they would be. Once they concluded that my motive was a genuine wish to comprehend the balancing act they were undertaking, and that I had an understanding of Islam and the variety of its practices, they were open, eager to put into words the dilemmas that they were facing. I am grateful for the support, in each city, of a few key people who were widely respected in the community, because doors were opened to me that might otherwise have remained guardedly shut.

A number of women invited me to meet them at their homes. I met almost all of the men in cafés or similar public places. No matter how religious they were, the men would look at me directly when they answered my questions. They told me that, as long as there was a 'business' purpose to our meeting, there was nothing untoward about it. Religious men did not offer to shake my hand in greeting, and some refused my offer of a cup of coffee, insisting on buying one for me instead. I always dressed modestly (clothing to the neck and elbows, and below the knees) but did not cover my head unless entering a mosque.

This study would not have been possible without the generosity of time and spirit of the Somalis with whom I spoke in both cities. Ultimately, they all expressed the hope that this work would assist in helping its readers understand them, and thereby diminish their feelings of apartness.

I am therefore extremely grateful for the candid cooperation and forthrightness of members of the Somali communities of London and Toronto. Our agreement to preserve their anonymity prevents my acknowledging these people by name, but I am indebted to each of them. I am also most grateful for the introductions to various members of the Somali community provided by Fred Halliday and Mohamed Abdullahi in London and by Myrna Berlin and Andy Martinson in Toronto. I am indebted to Maxamed Afrax, Omar Eno, Yousuf Garaad, and Abdurahman Sheikh Isse for their generous help and instruction.

I want particularly to thank the following people without whose help and support this project would have been difficult, if not impossible: Andy Cohen, Caren Levy, Diane Pickett, Margaret Roberts, and Nadia Taher. They put me up in their homes in the course of my field-work, provided emotional support, and picked up my children from school when I could not get home from an interview in time. Their kindness was overwhelming. I owe Caren Levy and Nadia Taher especial gratitude for their thoughtful advice, commentary, and translation. Thanks to Jamal Gabobe for his permission to quote from his poem *Dead End*.

The book is stronger for the comments of Jenny Edkins, Simon Murden, and Michael Watson of the University of Wales, Aberystwyth. I am grateful to Bhikhu Parekh for his thoughful comments. I am indebted most of all to James Piscatori, Oxford Centre for Islamic Studies, for his constant support, advice, encouragement, and mentorship. The time and attention that he devoted were truly extraordinary, and I shall always be grateful for the lessons that he imparted to me. Virgil Duff, Anne Forte, Siobhan McMenemy, and John Parry at the University of Toronto Press have made the process of publication a true pleasure.

Finally, boundless love and thanks to my family: to Gavin, Katie, Michael, and Taryn McGown; to Jean and Marc Berns; and to Esther Jacobson. And most of all to David McGown, for listening, for always being there, and for being the best of companions and the best of friends.

Glossary

In the text, the symbol ' denotes the Arabic *hamza*, or glottal stop, and the slightly different ' denotes the Arabic letter *'ayin*.

abtirsiinyo: (Somali) genealogy
ahl al-kitab: (Arabic) people of the book, especially Jews and Christians
asaasi: (Somali) fundamentalist
bida': (Arabic) Islamically suspect innovation
dar al 'ahd: (Arabic) neutral territory
dar al-da'wa: (Arabic) land of teaching or imparting Islam
dar al-harb: (Arabic) territory or land of war (hostile to Islam)
dar al-Islam: (Arabic) territory or land of Islam
dhikr: (Arabic) 'remembrance' of God; the Sufi practice of singing praise and repeating the name of God to feel closer to Allah
dugsi: (Somali) school; term often used by diaspora Somalis to refer to religious classes
fatwa: (Arabic) legal opinion or decision from recognized learned Muslim
fiqh: (Arabic) Islamic jurisprudence
gaalo: (Somali) infidel
garbasaar: (Somali) a shawl
hadith: (Arabic) reported pronouncement of the Prophet Muhammad
hajj: (Arabic) pilgrimage to Mecca. A 'hajji' (male) or 'hajja' (female) is someone who has made this pilgrimage and thereby fulfilled one of the five 'pillars,' or requirements, of the Muslim faith.
halal: (Arabic) Islamically permitted food or activity
haram: (Arabic) Islamically prohibited food or activity
hijab: (Arabic) veil or head-covering worn by some Muslim women in public; sometimes covers part of the face as well

hijra: (Arabic) migration. 'The' *Hijra*: the migration of Muhammad and his followers from Mecca to Medina in 622 CE; *hijra*: movement of Muslims from a place that is hostile to the practice of Islam to one more accepting of it

heer or *xeer*: (Somali) social contract or treaty

ijtihad: (Arabic) independent judgment; the interpretation by the lay Muslim of the Qur'an and its teachings

imam: (Arabic) religious leader

jahili: (Arabic) ignorant; term describes conditions or behaviour unenlightened by an understanding of Islam

jihad: (Arabic) struggle to defend or promote Islam; can be a holy war

jilbab (pl. *jeluabib*): (Arabic) two-piece head-and-body covering worn by many Somali women in the diaspora

makruh: (Arabic) reprehensible; in terms of *shari'a* interpretation, actions that are one step short of being absolutely forbidden

masar: (Somali) headscarf, wrapped about the head and ears; usually does not cover the neck

masjid: (Arabic) mosque

melchabad: (Somali) gauzy scarf

nikah: (Arabic) wedding contract

qaaraan: (Somali) financial aid, particularly to extended family

salafiyya: (Arabic) Islamic reform movement, centred in the Middle East at the end of the nineteenth century

salat: (Arabic) prayer; meant to be performed five times daily as one of the five pillars of Islam

salat jama'a: communal Friday noon prayer; normally at a mosque

shari'a: (Arabic) Islamic law, literally 'the straight path'

shaykh: (Arabic) tribal or Sufi leader or religious scholar, terms used by many Somalis to refer to religiously learned men and religious leaders (in place of *imam*)

Sijui: (Swahili) 'I don't know'; name for ethnic Somalis living in Kenya

siyaaro: (Somali) visit to a saint's shrine or tomb; see *ziyara*.

Sufism: Islamic mysticism

sunna: (Arabic) the Prophet Muhammad's actions and pronouncements, referred to as model behaviour by Muslims

sura: (Arabic) Qur'anic verse

'ulama (sing. *'alim*): (Arabic) Muslim learned men

umma: (Arabic) worldwide community of Muslims

ziyara: (Arabic) visit to a saint's tomb

MUSLIMS IN THE DIASPORA

Introduction:
Challenges in the Diaspora

I remember late one night the door being kicked,
a soldier yelling, 'Meeye Xunki. Halkaad ku qarinaysaa.'
And my terrified mother whimpering, 'Mooyi. Wali mu iman.'
He pushed her aside, ordered his jackbooted thugs to look everywhere,
and when they could not find me, he said:
'Next time he won't be so lucky.'
And stormed out of the house.
Home was no longer home.

In many ways though I am like everyone else.
I hold a job, go out on weekends, and love baseball
but that is not even half of it.

from *Dead End*, by Jamal Gabobe[1]

The cataclysm that was Somalia sent hundreds of thousands of its citizens, including Jamal Gabobe, into exile, most in the late 1980s and early 1990s. Like other upheavals before and since, it contributed to the global movement of peoples that the late twentieth century is witnessing on a level unprecedented in human history. Many of those people are migrating to the West, bringing with them a multitude of cultures and religions and the desire to maintain what they consider to be essential to their identities.

The questions raised by this element of migration, particularly how the refugees have redefined their identity in the course of their dislocation, and the nature of their integration into the West – including the effect on their integration of the political culture of the host society – are more timely and critical than ever. This book maintains that neither the process of integration, nor the role of the host society – as exemplified in its political culture – in affecting that integration, have been well understood. The consequences of misunderstanding for both immigrants and immigrant-receiving societies are significant. In the absence of that understanding, there is a tendency to exaggerate the inflexibility of the barriers between cultures. There is, in its absence, a tendency to conclude that some distances are too far to bridge, that essential differences separate certain cultures and religions from others, and that assimilation – the rejection of the values of one culture and their replacement with the values of another – is the only workable path to cohabitation.

People also tend, in the absence of that understanding, to miscalculate the importance of the host country's role in integration. Such was the case with the Canadian government's decision to terminate prematurely the commission of inquiry into the actions and reactions of the military in Somalia in 1993. In March of that year, the soldiers of a Canadian peacekeeping mission, belonging to the Canadian Airborne Regiment stationed in Belet Huen, first shot a teenaged Somali intruder to death and then, in a separate incident a fortnight later, beat to death a second civilian teenager in its custody. An inquiry into the incidents, established after the Liberals swept to power in 1993, was suspended in early 1997, before it had completed its work. The Canadian government believed that the perception of public justice had been served with the disbanding of the regiment that murdered Somali civilian teenagers in its custody and the court-martialling of certain of its soldiers and that there was nothing to be gained by examining the military's systemic problems in further depth.

What was not well understood was that the real issue was one of domestic politics: Canada's is in large part an immigrant population, and its political culture has been relatively successful in establishing the conditions that allow for harmonious integration of its immigrants and minorities. Actions that undermine those conditions serve also to undermine the benefits of a harmoniously integrated population. The arguments of this book examine why that is so and place Canada in contrast to Britain, a country with much in common with Canada but whose political culture is not as successful in allowing for harmonious integration of its immigrants and minorities.

The heart of *Muslims in the Diaspora* lies in the stories and in-depth interviews of over eighty Somali immigrants, the vast majority of them refugees, in Toronto, Ontario, and London, England. There exists a significant, and growing, literature on Muslims in the west, but the Somali experience has not hitherto been documented in a comprehensive way. The Somali experience provides a unique and enlightening opportunity to understand the cultural 'interface' between Islam and the West and the way in which integration works. In the first place, Somalis' strong sense of identity has perhaps attuned them particularly to confront the challenges that migration presented to that identity. The result is that questions on identity and its renegotiation did not appear to catch them, regardless of age or education, unprepared, and most of their answers were thoughtful and provocative. Second, they represent a significant non-Asian, non-Middle Eastern Muslim voice and as such have much to add to the debate over the nature of Islam and how it is interpreted. By their own admission and that of other observers, their impact on the existing Muslim communities of London and Toronto has been profound, despite the short time since their arrival and the fact that London was home to most of Britain's one to one-and-a-half million Muslims before the Somali influx. Because they are black but do not identify themselves with sub-Saharan Africans or their Caribbean or North American descendants, and because they are Muslim, but not Arab or South Asian, they demand a confrontation with much of the accepted wisdom about the nature of racism and the position of Muslims, immigrants, and non-whites in relation to the larger society, in both Britain and Canada.

Indeed, the comparison between cities is particularly illuminating here. Just as Islam is not a monolith, neither is the West. Britain and Canada are both Western liberal democracies, but they represent different examples of 'Westness.' Thus the experiences of Somali immigrants have been significantly different in each city. The comparison between them highlights the role of political culture in accommodating immigrants and ethnic minorities into a society. It is a comparison that is particularly apt in the Somali case, given the similarity in numbers and demographic structure of the two immigrant communities and the fact that they arrived in the largest city in each country during roughly the same years.

Catapulted by circumstance onto the mercy of the outside world, many Somalis found their way into the West: to Britain, Canada, the United States, and Australia, where the calamity and personal misfortune from which they ran has been compounded by the harsh realities of refugee life and its attendant cultural clash. Most particularly, Somalis have had to accustom themselves to a predominantly Judaeo-Christian and highly secular world. Islam is almost universally embraced in Somalia, albeit not with any kind of uniformity. But it is the seeming smorgasbord of values offered up by liberal Western democracies – the array of value choices, which seems so different from the 'one' truth as they saw it – that has presented Somali exiles with their greatest challenge: how to live in the West as Muslims.

This book is an exploration of the dilemmas and the choices of Somalis who have made that journey. I interviewed at length over eighty Somalis in Toronto and London; the resulting study examines the integration of Muslims into the West and compares the two sites of 'Westness' into which they are fitting themselves. It focuses on Somalis' reconciliation of Muslim practices and values with the Western values and practices of their new societies and on how they seek to forge new identities without losing anything essential of themselves and their beliefs in the process. It examines the mechanism of integration – what it is that actually happens when migrants arrive in a new land amid a new culture – from the perspective both of the immigrant and of the receiving society. Most broadly, it analyses the intersection between Islam and the West and the compatibility of the two traditions in the light of the transformation that is apparent in Islam as it is practised by diaspora Somalis.

From the perspective of the host societies, and perhaps most significantly for policy-makers, the study argues that a country's political culture is a critical determinant of the nature of integration of immigrants and minorities into its society. The process of integration and the role of political culture in affecting integration are not, however, well understood. Canada's political culture has been relatively successful at creating the conditions necessary for harmonious integration, yet these conditions are compromised and rendered fragile by that very lack of understanding.

The book maintains that integration is a gradual but inexorable process in which both the host community and the ethnic immigrant communities undergo change and some degree of convergence – change that is both superficial and over time substantial. This process becomes especially significant when the immigrant community has a framework of values and an understanding of social and political relations that is seen to differ widely from that of the host society, as Islam is frequently assumed to do. The nature of that process – whether it is harmonious or tense – is determined in large part by the political culture of the host country.

This volume explores a number of proposals for thinking about how integration occurs and its critical factors. First, it proposes that integration occurs on two levels, external and internal. The degree to which an ethnic group is *externally* integrated depends on the ability of its members to move, horizontally or vertically, within political, economic, and social spheres, and on the responsiveness of domestic institutions to a group's cultural and religious behaviour and norms. The 'mobility' of the members of an ethnic group refers to their ability to stand for and hold political office, to acquire employment and subsequent promotions, and to participate in the social and recreational life of the community, all without their ethnicity being a hindrance. 'Institutional responsiveness' refers to the flexibility of institutions such as governments, schools, hospitals, and professional associations in making procedural accommodations to ethnic and religious requirements.

Second, *internal* integration is a distinct but related process, which occurs from the moment immigrants set foot in their adopted country. It refers to the process of immigrants' weaving together their birth and their adopted cultures. No matter how similar or disparate the birth and adopted cultures, the process that occurs is integration – or cultural weaving – as opposed to assimilation – the replacement of adopted culture for home culture.

Third, as stated above, harmonious integration is facilitated by a political culture[2] that creates a legitimate space for the immigrant Other. Political cultures that allow ethnic or religious minorities to participate in society's transactions – without disadvantaging them for their ethnic or religious affiliation – will ease the process of cultural weaving for immigrants.

Fourth, over time, the dominant culture of an immigrant-receiving country will absorb and reflect aspects of the birth cultures of its immigrants. The creation of a political culture is an ongoing exercise, contributed to in varying proportions by all inhabitants of a country, as is discernible in countries such as the United States and Canada that have been receiving immigrants since their founding.

 Because Islam is not doctrinally or socially monolithic, and because therefore the definition of what is essential to being a Muslim varies with each Muslim who is asked the question, Muslims are not ideologically incapable of integration into Western liberal democracies. Islam is not a monolithic entity, either in its coherence or in terms of how its principles are interpreted by its adherents. Muslims around the world interpret Islam in a variety of ways, many of which are at variance with the multitude of Middle Eastern or Asian interpretations, and these are in turn applied differently to life in a non-Muslim environment. This ideological diversity and flexibility suggest that Muslims are not precluded from making the kinds of adjustments that entail integration into Western liberal democracies. In fact, the interviews demonstrate the emergence of an exciting phenomenon: the reinterpretation of Islam in a Western context – a phenomenon with enormous implications for both diaspora Islam and Islam as it is practised in Muslim-majority countries.

Method and Presentation

The core of this study is a series of in-depth interviews conducted with over eighty Somali men, women, and teenagers in Toronto and London between January and August 1995. These interviews cannot provide a statistically accurate representation of Somali immigrant attitudes. In keeping, however, with the idea that explorative, semi-structured interviews can provide a depth of understanding that survey research cannot,[3] I intend this study to illustrate the complexities of the process of individuals' renegotiating identity as Muslims in the West. Furthermore, the interviews reveal both the kind of accommodations that Somalis are making on moving to the West and how the environment into which they are moving affects that accommodation. While it is not possible, based on these interviews, to describe accurately the proportion of Somalis who practise their religion differently from the way they did in Somalia, it is possible to gauge the direction of Somalis' integration and the nature of the difference between host-country environments.

I present this study in such a way as to allow the reader to listen to the voices of informants prior to reading the researcher's analysis. Chapter 1 explores the nature of the Somali refugee experience and discusses the history of Islam in Somalia; it provides the context for the interviews and the analysis that follows. Chapter 2 describes and analyses the internal and external components of the process of integration of newcomers to a society. The chapters (3–6) that present the views of respondents provide some contextual information and analysis only after the reader has heard the voices of respondents. The analysis of their words, in the context of their adopted Canadian and British societies, appears predominantly in the final chapters (5–7) and in the Conclusion.

To this end, I made explorations with informants on several subjects. The first series of questions concerned religious observance and the logistics of practising Islam in the West. These were aimed at discerning how informants practise their religion in their new environment and the degree to which their practice has changed since they left their homeland. Interviews on the logistics of practising Islam in London and Toronto appear in chapter 3. This chapter also presents the advice of a number of Somali Muslim organizations on questions of practising Islam in the West and living side by side with non-Muslims.

A second series of questions concerned transference of values and aimed at deciphering what is involved in teaching children to be Muslim – or to remain Muslim – amid what is seen as a flood of competing values. This was an area of particular concern to most adult Somalis, who were accustomed to a mono-religious society. Interviews on transference of values, as well as interviews with teenagers – seen as a particularly vulnerable group – appear in chapter 4.

The third series of questions dealt with determining how respondents bridge their birth and adopted cultures. I asked questions about issues presumed to be at the core of differences between Muslim and Western value systems. These included sexuality and reproduction (birth control, abortion, and pre- and extra-marital sex) and whether respondents feel that their primary responsibility is to themselves as individuals or to their families or community. I also asked about female circumcision, an especially sensitive issue, particularly given that it is only in the diaspora that most Somalis have learned that it is not an Islamic practice. Chapter 5 presents sections of interviews concerned with values and culture-bridging.

Chapter 6 concerns the differences between London and Toronto, most particularly in terms of variances in political culture as it concerns ethnic minorities and immigrants. This chapter also presents the portions of interviews concerning Somalis' connection to their adopted lands, as well as the varying views of respondents on the case of the writer Salman Rushdie, and suggests reasons for differences encountered. It is here that the contrast between the two immigrant communities is at its strongest, and I explore the role of political culture in affecting the integration of minorities and immigrants.

The interviews, and their presentation, set the stage for the analysis of Somali integration that is presented in chapter 7. This chapter revisits the themes of chapter 2 and re-examines them in the light of the interviews.

I drew interview subjects from different socio-economic backgrounds, clans and sub-clans, ages, and degrees of religious observance, as well as equal numbers of both genders. I interviewed roughly forty people in each city, divided into four approximately equal groups: teenagers, college students and young people in their twenties, men over thirty, and women over thirty. To this end, I contacted informants through a variety of Somali organizations and via suggestions of individuals familiar with the community or parts of it.[4] I contacted young people with the assistance of two high schools in Toronto and two community organizations and a mosque in London. There were no significant differences between cities in the range of socio-economic backgrounds of interview subjects or their degrees of religious observance.

Because the Somali communities of the two cities were so new, there was little quantitative information available on their socio-economic makeup. I have referred to the few studies available, but these have been communities in transition, and a profile that indicated, for instance, high rates of unemployment or lack of English fluency in the early 1990s is in effect just a snapshot of the community rather than a definitive descriptor.

Where possible, I conducted interviews on a one-on-one basis, without an interpreter, so long as the informant was able to understand questions and respond. (Where I had doubts about comprehension I would rephrase the question until it was obvious that it was understood.) In some cases the use of an interpreter was unavoidable, and this service was provided by a friend or family member or, in the case of a group of older women in Toronto, by a couple of the young women teaching them English and a daycare supervisor.

For the most part, once they understood the nature of the questions and what I was after, the respondents were eager to participate in the interviews, which generally lasted between one and three hours. Wariness on the part of respondents generally turned to candour once they had identified me as an informed, open-minded interviewer. Whatever their socio-economic status or degree of religious observance, these were people who were eager to be understood. On a few occasions, I met with respondents a second or third time.

I usually recorded interviews using hand-written notes, which were then transcribed the same day. I used a tape recorder with some high school students, when they indicated that they were comfortable with it. On very few occasions (for instance, standing outside a doughnut shop talking to an unemployed truck driver), I made notes after the conclusion of a conversation. These occasions were rare, but in their absence a certain perspective would have been lost.

I have used pseudonyms in identifying respondents, except in the cases where the respondent was a representative of an organization. Most interviewees were willing to talk frankly, on condition that they not be identified. The Toronto high schools granted access to students on the express condition that their confidentiality be guaranteed, as did a London mosque, and most respondents indicated that they would prefer similar treatment.

It was obviously not possible to present all the interviews in their entirety, but I have tried to reproduce a full range of perspectives and to represent both genders and cities in roughly equal proportions.

Where Somalis use Arabic terminology, I offer standard Arabic transliterations. At times, both the Somali and Arabic terms appear. Somali immigrants have tended to adopt English spellings for their names (Mohamad – a name that carries a number of spellings – instead of Maxamad, the Somali orthography, for instance), and names and pseudonyms reflect this practice.

Into the Diaspora

The notion of Muslims in the diaspora evokes the two thousand years of the Wandering Jew. The evocation is deliberate. At an outdoor dinner in a suburb of north London, a Somali physicist, pondering the plight of his exiled people, waved his hand at the surrounding backyards and said, 'I look about me every day at the Jews of London. They have lived here for so long and they have not lost anything of themselves. How have they done it?'

The answer to his question would fill a library in itself, but his sentiment was revealing because, at a certain level, the comparison is apt. It is frightening to be flung adrift amid the seas of unfamiliarity. The process of integrating is the process of learning to float, and even to swim with confidence. There is a need, for those who are constrained or choose to undertake the journey, to understand the process. But that need to understand is even more imperative for the countries that receive them, because such migration is increasing. The diaspora – living anywhere that is not the mythic centre of one's culture or religion[5] – is a reality for growing numbers of peoples. Somalis were not the first to scatter into it, and they will not be the last.

1

Context

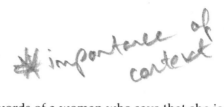 # importance of context

Any appreciation of the words of a woman who says that she is afraid of losing her children in her new city, or a man who quits a job he badly needs because his employer would not allow him to attend the communal Friday noon prayer, would well begin with an understanding of what this woman and this man have come from and what it is they have come to. This first section sketches in the background – political, social, and religious – that the Somali communities in Toronto and London drew on when answering my questions on Muslim identity. It aims to provide a context for the informants' views that follow. The first section also describes some of the significant issues of logistics and integration affecting Muslims in Canada and Britain. The second deals with clan in the Somali context and in the diaspora. The third looks at the practice of Islam in the diaspora, the fourth at Islam in Somali history, and the fifth at recent developments there and their effect on Somalis abroad.

The Somali Refugee Community

In the early 1980s, there was no Somali community to speak of in Toronto, and London's was small, composed largely of seamen and a number of political exiles from the Siad Barre dictatorship. That changed, suddenly and dramatically, in 1988, with the Barre government's bombing of Somalia's northern towns and the persecution of the Isaaq clan-family, especially those suspected of having any connection with or knowledge of the underground opposition, the Somali National Movement. The trickle of Somali exiles became a flood of refugees, first from the north of the country where the Isaaq dominate, and then, after the ousting of Barre in January 1991 and the subsequent civil war, from Mogadishu and the south.[1] By 1992, the United Nations estimated that one million Somalis (out of a total population of an estimated five to seven million[2]) were refugees, scattered in refugee camps in Kenya and Ethiopia, but also in western Europe (Holland, Italy, and Sweden, as well as the United Kingdom), the United States and Canada, Australia, and New Zealand.[3] In 1995 there were roughly 30,000 Somalis in Toronto and roughly 40,000 in London.[4]

The refugee experience has indelibly marked Somalis' encounter of the West and their self-definition and redefinition within the West as Muslims.[5] Growing within five years from a handful of individuals in Toronto, and a few hundred in London, to the size of small cities within the larger ones, the communities consist of people who have lived through war, displacement, and the loss of property and loved ones. Many were wounded or raped; many suffer from post-traumatic stress syndrome. Families were separated along the way, and their paths to their new homes were not straightforward but involved years in Kenyan refugee camps[6] or convoluted journeys via countries where they could get temporary visas. They did not so much choose Canada or the United Kingdom as estimate that their chances of rebuilding their lives or finding sanctuary were reasonable in these countries and then managed to get themselves there.

The first concern of refugees is physical safety, for themselves and their children; it is this most basic of needs that caused them to leave their homeland, and achieving it is their primary goal in finding a new home. In some cases they had friends or relatives who had already made their way to London or Toronto and were thought to be able to help. They knew that the likelihood was that they would be accepted as refugees (in Canada) or at least given temporary asylum (in the United Kingdom) having once arrived at their destination. Paradoxically, however, if officials of either country became aware (for instance, in the airport of a third country) that they intended to claim asylum on arrival, they would have been prevented from reaching their destinations.

Both Canada and the United Kingdom adhere to some extent to the United Nations Convention on Refugees, but both have none the less taken steps to limit the numbers of people who are able to apply or to remain or to benefit from social services should they do so. These steps include laws that hold airline companies responsible for transporting people with false documents. Given that genuine travel documents are impossible to obtain in a state of civil war such as Somalia's or, in the case of the Isaaq, that they were unlikely to have been granted had they been requested, it is likely that refugees will travel on false papers, which they then destroy en route before requesting asylum in the country in which they desire it. They do this because both Canada and the United Kingdom will sometimes return refugees to what is termed a safe third country, such as Kenya, if the asylum-seeker was travelling on Kenyan papers, or the United States, if that was the route by which the refugee arrived. This often takes place even though the third country may in fact be hostile to refugees or deport them to their countries of origin.[7]

Britain continues to tighten its immigration and asylum rules, most recently in efforts to extend sanctions to the Eurostar trains from Paris, where would-be refugees can board without passport checks. Regulations introduced in 1995 – and subsequently challenged by the courts – attempted to deny housing and social benefits to asylum- seekers (refugees whose status has not been determined), who are also unable to work legally. Most of those affected are thought to be from Somalia, Algeria, and Morocco.[8]

Canada's most recent measures to discourage refugees, in 1993, included application fees of $1,500 for refugee and landed-immigrant status. Repayable loans can be made to refugees who cannot afford the payment on application.

Once in London or Toronto, so that physical safety was no longer in question, refugees confronted a host of other issues, initially logistical: finding housing and social benefits, establishing children in schools, learning English, trying to find work. These tasks are difficult, affecting the sense of security with which these new members of the Canadian and British polities view their surroundings and their relationship to those surroundings.

There are significant differences between refugee experiences in the two countries. Britain has granted the majority of its Somali asylum-seekers only exceptional leave to remain, which is temporary permission to stay in the United Kingdom. It is granted for one year and may be renewed for three years and then another three, so that only after seven years may such a person apply for permanent-resident status. The implication of this arrangement is that Somalis are unable to consider themselves secure in their new homes or regard themselves as members of British society. Many of them are eager to return home, but only if home is safe and secure. They face the constant worry that Britain will consider Somalia 'safe' when in their own estimation it is not. Somali refugees to Canada did not have the same concerns, because their ability to remain in the country was secure, as most received refugee status, which is routinely converted to landed-immigrant status. However, as of 1993, refugees who arrive without valid identification cannot apply for landed-immigrant status for five years. (Until they receive such status, refugees may not apply for family reunification or be treated as residents for such purposes as calculating tuition). The less legally secure migrants are, the shakier their connection to their adopted home. This factor significantly affects their integration, and therefore their ability to be well-adjusted, contributing members of their adopted societies, as chapter 6 explores further.

The logistical issues are only a prelude to the whole series of complex questions with which this study is really concerned: the integration of Somali Muslim and Western identities. Having established themselves physically, the refugees begin to assess how they will live in their new land. How will they relate to other Somalis? To other refugees and other Muslims? To their hosts? Who are their hosts? How much of their culture, language, and religion can they retain, and in what way? What is their relationship to Somalia and to relatives, friends, and clansfolk still there?

Although ideally one needs to resolve basic logistical problems before wrestling with questions of identity, most Somalis, especially those who were parents, did not have this luxury. The refugee flood occurred with such force and rapidity that there was not a well-established Somali community able to absorb and socialize newcomers. Even in London, where Somalis had lived since the turn of the century,[9] the initial community was composed largely of men whose families were still in the homeland.[10] As a consequence, the community structure and organization that were needed to steer entire families through the logistical and emotional maze of culture shock were not in place.[11] Community organizations quickly sprang up to help their kinfolk, staffed by those who could speak English and had already established themselves to some degree, but these people had themselves been in their new homes for less than a decade, and often less than five years. In addition, children begin to adapt almost instantly to their new environments, so that their cultural integration is occurring almost before their mothers have figured out where they can obtain *halal* meat. The result is that parents confront identity questions almost immediately, because they realize that the world on the doorstep is not the world that they carry in their minds and that if they are not to 'lose their children,' as they say, they must act, somehow and quickly.

Among the particular issues that Somali parents have had to confront is the difference in parenting styles between Somalia and Canada or Britain. In Somalia, respect and obedience are expected from a child vis-à-vis anyone – parent, aunt or uncle, sibling or teacher – who is older. This respect and obedience are meant to be instantaneous and unquestioning and are reinforced with the aid of corporal punishment if need be. While this may not be radically different from the situation for Canadian and British children until recently, public debates in those two countries on the role of corporal punishment have rendered it unacceptable in most circumstances. The result is that not only have Somali parents found that the host community culture threatens their own, but they cannot enforce behaviour from their children in the way they have been taught to do. (Some daycare operators and schools have been quick to accuse Somali parents of child abuse, and children have learned that they can threaten to call police emergency numbers if their parents try to spank them.)

Thus Somali parents dealing with the trauma of having fled a war zone, recovering from physical or emotional injury or rape, trying to learn English and re-establish the logistical basics of their lives, and confronting all the difficult questions of identity – particularly religious identity – entailed in being a Muslim in the secular Judaeo-Christian West, may find the society around them questioning and thus threatening the base on which their relationships with their children are founded. To compound the stress, many families are headed by single mothers, either because the family was separated in the course of war or flight, or because stress in the new society proved too much for the marriage.

The high rate of separation and divorce among Somalis in Canada and Britain is another significant factor in their lives. Men are ordinarily considered the source of economic well-being in the Somali family – whether in traditional pastoral settings, where the women care for cattle, sheep, and goats but the men care for the camels, which form the core of a family's wealth, or in agricultural or urban environments, where again the men generally provide for the family. From this providential position flows male centrality and authority within the household, as wives traditionally respect their husbands as they expect their

high rate of divorce

children to respect them. In Canada and Britain, however, the male position of authority has been challenged, both because the relationship between men and women is perceived differently within those societies, and also because men have not necessarily continued to be the main providers for their families. For a number of reasons, chief among them sluggish economies in the host countries, the language barrier, and a disparity in qualifications, male unemployment has been high within the communities. That has meant that families have often lived on state benefits or the mother's salary alone if she, and not her husband, has managed to obtain work. Geoff Dench, in his study of Somali families in Tower Hamlets, noted that British per capita benefits were in fact higher for single-parent families than for those with two adults,[12] thereby in effect encouraging family breakups. Women sometimes see themselves better off without the man who contributes nothing to the family and is primarily a drain on its resources.

Many informants commented that in Somalia, when men were providing the family with income, it was excusable that they played no role in the running of the home or upbringing of the children, but that this failure to help was no longer seen as forgivable when they were no longer working. Moreover, neither Canadian nor British society sanctions the reinforcement of male authority by use of force, and women quickly learned that a threatened call to a police emergency number is often enough to prevent its attempt. Very many families have of course not crumbled under stress, no matter which partner was working, but the despair facing many adults in the diaspora features significantly in the comments of informants. Regardless of circumstance, a woman who sees her life's work primarily as the raising of her children still has her *raison d'être* as long as those children are with her. A man who takes his identity in significant part from his role in his family and community is bound to find things stressful when he cannot provide for his family and is not sure what role he can play in a community that he does not yet understand.

Because the Somali communities were so new, little reliable quantitative socio-economic information is available on them. Edward Opoku-Dapaah profiled the Toronto community in the early 1990s. His study, surveying 385 men and women, found that they were, for the most part, underemployed. Over 50 per cent had completed high school or college before arriving in Canada, but a lingering recession, language barriers, and a lack of recognized experience had relegated them, when they were working, to marginal work in assembly/packing industries or commercial/retail businesses.[13] The study found that only 29 per cent of those surveyed were employed.[14] Dench estimated unemployment levels to be roughly 80 per cent among Somalis in Tower Hamlets in London.[15]

Because these were very new communities in a state of rapid transition, and because no other systematic studies had been done on them, it is impossible to translate these statistics with any accuracy to the communities even a few years later. For example, a number of the present study's respondents made reference to Somali-run small businesses, all started mere months earlier. Furthermore, oft-repeated anecdotal evidence indicates that Somalis' English-language skills improved rapidly – a factor that, in combination with improving economies, would have improved job prospects.

Yet we can safely assume that the Somali communities in the late 1980s and early 1990s consisted primarily of Somalis from urban centres, many of whom had been entrepreneurs and professionals, and most of whom found themselves un- or underemployed during the period of this study. All of the subjects in Opoku-Dapaah's study were under fifty-four years of age. This book includes interviews with older women, but, as with Opoku-Dapaah, most of the respondents over thirty were in their thirties and forties. All of the older Somalis whom I encountered had migrated with their children and grandchildren.

Many men in their mid-thirties and older characterized their lives as exiled refugees as being full of despair; they did not see how they could requalify or acquire the local experience that they would require in order to work in their fields. Many became obsessed with the politics of Somalia – both those that led to the civil war and those of the anarchy that has followed.

To this anguish has been added the temptations of *qat* – *Catha edulis Forsk* – a leaf that, when chewed, offers mild stimulation well-suited to long evenings discussing politics, but then causes insomnia and lack of appetite.[16] (Qat is readily available in both Toronto and London, although Canada considers it an illegal drug.)[17] Thus, on the morrow, a man may well be disinclined to fight despair and find a job as a security guard or parking-lot attendant, especially when he is an experienced accountant or a businessman. None the less, as much as despair is a factor in the community's life, informants' answers often reveal a great deal of determination and courage, and a refusal to be bowed by inhospitable circumstances. And this is beginning to be mirrored in the small Somali-owned businesses that are increasingly in evidence, particularly in Toronto, as anarchy in Somalia continues to reign and the refugees begin to come to terms with their inability to return in the foreseeable future.

Among the many subjects of discussion for Somalis in exile is the centrality of clan politics.[18] This is the single most divisive and sensitive issue both among Somalis and between Somalis and the host community. Although discussion of clan was officially banned by Barre's government, it was under his dictatorship that the seeds of the present anarchy were sown, by the persecution of certain groups and the favouring of others.[19] There is widespread recognition that Somalia would not be in its present dire straits, nor Somalis themselves refugees, were it not for the exploitation of clan loyalties and awareness by those in authority. Many Somalis in exile had been raised in urban areas where clan affiliation was losing its potency and say that until the beginning of the hostilities they had little knowledge, and cared less, about their own clan-family background. But the tiger once roused is difficult to calm. Only the youngest children do not know someone who did not suffer purely because of the clan or sub-clan to which his or her family belonged, and suffering meant imprisonment, maiming, or death; it meant rape or the humiliation of men by the forced witnessing of the rape of their women – a particularly horrific crime in the Somali social context.[20]

The refugee communities are thus divided over whether and how to overcome clan divisions, both in the diaspora and with respect to their relations with kinfolk back home. Older Somalis who are determined to return home as soon as it is safe to do so may be more concerned with ensuring that their clan is well-positioned, but there are others who are convinced that so long as Somalis care about the relative positions of their clans, there will be no safe Somalia to which they can return. Younger Somalis who are less convinced that there will ever be a return may be more anxious to get along with all their fellow refugees in the alien environment of the schoolyard and annoyed with their mothers' rejection of their choice of a school friend merely because the family is Hawiye and the friend Darood. This is an intense topic of debate on the internet, where Somali students worldwide (particularly in the United States, Canada, and Britain) argue about the merits of clan association and such topics as whether inter-clan marriage is acceptable.

Clan in Somalia and in the Diaspora

A brief note of the clan-families, their geographical occupation of Somalia and representation in the diaspora, and some recent political history is in order here. There exist a number of clan-families in Somalia, traditionally associated with the pastoral way of life that has been the mainstay of the Somali economy and, most significantly, the society's cultural and mythic core. Despite rapid urbanization and the existence of rich agricultural lands in the south of the country, the bulk of Somalia's employment and foreign exchange was earned through the production of livestock – cattle, sheep, goats, and, most important, camels.[21] The centrality of the camel – to the country's rich poetic tradition, to the determination of a family's wealth, and to the measure of a man's worth – has been such that camel-herding was widely considered the most noble of professions. The clan-families that engaged primarily in pastoralism, including the Isaaq, the Darood, the Dir, and the Hawiye, comprised a significant proportion of the population and considered themselves 'noble.' They viewed themselves as very different from the southern 'Saab' clan-families, including the Digil and Raheenwein, or Reewin – which traditionally engaged in agriculture or some combination of agriculture and pastoralism, and which were seen to be mixed racially with the Bantu and other Africans who had formerly been slaves or 'clients' and have gradually intermarried.[22] In addition to these clan-families, there are other minority populations, including the descendants of Arab immigrants – such as the Reer Hamar (the people of Hamar, a district of Mogadishu) – who have peopled the urban areas of the Benaadir coast for a thousand years and who have helped Islamize Somalia, as is seen below, but who are frequently neglected in descriptions of the Somali body politic.[23]

Somalis are not as homogeneous a people as they have frequently been depicted, and there are significant differences in culture and even language between the northern pastoralists and the southerners, with their more mixed economy, and between the histories that have accompanied each tradition.[24] Ironically, this has perhaps become clearer since Somalia's civil breakdown, given that the disintegration of established orders has provided the impetus and opportunity for a re-creation of some of Somalia's cultural myths.[25]

Ali Mazrui has emphasized that 'the trouble with an oral tradition [such as Somalia's] is that it transmits mainly what is accepted and respected. It does not normally transmit heresies of the previous age.'[26]

The point helps explain why it is the pastoral myths, not those of the southern minorities, that have often been described as those common to Somali culture as a whole. Governance, and the bulk of Somali historical scholarship, from the time of independence in 1960 was primarily in the hands of northerners, whose story and outlook differ notably from those of the peoples of the Benaadir coast. Because the civil war has centred on a fight for control of both urban resources and the rich inter-riverine agricultural lands, much of the displacement of peoples has come from the Benaadir coast.[27] While most of the refugees in London and Toronto came initially from the four 'northern' clan-families (even though they may have been living in Mogadishu, they had often moved there as part of the governing or business class and saw themselves as having pastoral roots in the north or interior), substantial numbers of refugees are drawn from the south and its minorities, Bantu and coastal peoples.

Most of the refugees who have made their way to Toronto and London are at least recently from urban areas, such as Mogadishu and surrounding towns in the south and Hargeisa in the north. But there has also been a steady trickle of pastoralists, so that more recent arrivals in London, for instance, included refugees who had never seen a town before in their lives.[28] In Toronto, a principal who estimates her elementary-school population at between 75 and 80 per cent Somali, indicated that recent arrivals included rural children who had not had the benefit of schooling prior to their arrival in Canada.[29]

It is a mark of the divisiveness of recent Somali politics that there existed in 1995 in Toronto no fewer than thirty Somali community organizations, each dedicated to assisting the absorption and resettlement of Somali refugees, most declaring that their services are intended for all Somalis, and almost all knowing that in fact only those of a particular group or sub-clan will actually approach them. In Canada, where the public funding for these organizations is relatively centralized, coming as it does from the regional (Metropolitan) Toronto government, the province of Ontario and the federal government in Ottawa, only three received government help (thereby exacerbating divisions between the haves and have-nots). In London, in contrast, which has similar numbers of Somali community organizations, public funding for individual community associations comes primarily from the local borough, so that funding tends to depend on the vagaries of the local council. This situation causes some tension when ethnicity appears to influence local government spending.[30] Other associations in both cities are supported by volunteers and the Somali community, or more correctly communities, themselves.

In both cities individual Somalis have tended to settle alongside clan-family members. The first large wave of refugees (in the late 1980s) to London was made up mainly of Isaaqs, streaming out of the former British protectorate Somaliland, via refugee camps in Ethiopia and often thence to Djibouti and then London. Most of the seamen who already lived in London were clustered in the east end, near the docklands, and so that is where most of the Isaaq first went, to boroughs such as Tower Hamlets. Once the civil war began in earnest in the south (in early 1991), subsequent waves of immigrants tended to live in other parts of the city – north London, the west, and south of the Thames.

Toronto's first wave of refugees, in contrast, came mostly from the Majerteen sub-clan of the Darood clan-family, which was being subjected to persecution by Barre's government because a number of its members had been involved in a failed coup in 1987. (Barre was a member on his father's side of the Mareehan sub-clan, also of the Darood clan-family.) Most of the refugees who arrived from Mogadishu and its surroundings – mainly Darood and Hawiye clan-family members – tended to settle in the west of the city, initially in a cluster of apartment blocks near the airport, and gradually in less concentrated neighbourhoods. Many of the Isaaq have settled in the north (in North York) and east (in Scarborough). Toronto is of course a much smaller city than London, with a population of just over four million people, including a Muslim population of only about 100,000 and fifteen mosques.[31] This factor would have influenced decisions on where to live, in part because items such as halal meat were available only in shops in certain areas. London, in contrast, a city four times as large, holds about half of the country's one to 1.5 million Muslims[32] and hundreds of mosques, many of them purpose-built, and halal meat is abundantly available.

Islam in the Diaspora

Much has been written about the issues – political, legal, educational, and so forth – surrounding Muslims in the United Kingdom and western Europe – for example in such works as Philip Lewis's *Islamic Britain*[33] and the second edition of Nielsen's *Muslims in Western Europe*.

While there is no need to detail the discussions here, there are certain points that deserve noting (and that I address again in subsequent chapters). First, the key concern of Muslims in Britain has been and continues to be what Tariq Modood calls the need and demand 'for public space, for public respect and public resources for minority cultures and for the transmission of such cultures to the young.'[34] While this need is not singularly that of Muslims, but of minorities generally in Britain (point taken up in detail in chapter 6), it has a particular resonance for Muslims for a number of reasons.

Though a decade has passed since Lord Swann's Report, *Education for All*, declared Britain a multicultural society whose children should be educated with that fact in mind, British Muslims have repeatedly faced issues that have highlighted their insecurity about their status relative to non-Muslims.

The Salman Rushdie affair became what it did in part because of the existence of medieval blasphemy laws that are designed to protect the sanctity of the Anglican religion (and have been used as recently as 1977 for that purpose)[35] but were decreed as ineligible for use in the case of *The Satanic Verses*. Moreover, no attempt was made in the wake of the affair to extend or revise them to provide other religions with the same protection – or to abolish them altogether – which was interpreted as discriminatory by many British Muslims.

The city of Bradford was polarized when the head teacher of a local school, Ray Honeyford, published an article in a right-wing journal affirming the supremacy of Christianity in the British state and Christian education in the school system. When the Bradford Council of Mosques and a coalition of concerned groups succeeded in forcing his early retirement, the result was in part heightened concern among white parents of 'Asian takeovers' of traditionally white schools.[36]

Until January 1998, Muslim schools were continually denied voluntary-aided status, amid the hot spotlight of media focus, although this status had long been available to numerous Christian sects and Jewish schools. In the continued debate over Britishness and the place of Muslims within it, Muslims *qua* Muslims have not been able to use the anti-discrimination clauses of the Race Relations Act to find protection from the courts, because they are not defined under the act as an ethnic group.[37] This has happened partly because debate around the place of immigrants and their place in the British polity has been defined in terms of race relations and colour divisions[38] and has only just begun to change[39] to encompass a broader way of understanding the nature of participation in a society by a plurality of groups. In significant ways the debate has moved forward since the early 1980s. The content of school lunches or the ability of girls to wear the *hijab* to class are infrequently at issue. Certainly they were not problems for any of the Somali informants interviewed here, which is an indication that Muslims are beginning to have a recognizable impact on the society around them. But while British Muslims may be numerous and well organized, the central issue for them continues to be the establishment of legitimacy as a collective voice within the British polity.

Somalis entered a society in Great Britain where Islam was already an established presence, even if the legal and political role of that presence is the subject of ongoing and intense debate. By far the most numerous Muslims are South Asian, and, politically at least, Somalis have not been highly visible. Doctrinally and practically speaking, however, they claim to have had a major effect on Islam as it is practised in London, both in terms of the actual lessons being taught and in terms of the dress of Muslim women and their mosque attendance, as is discussed below.

In Toronto, however, the Somali presence has been highly visible. Somalis, said a local *imam*, 'changed the face of Islam in Toronto' when they began arriving here in the late 1980s.[40] While Canada has a history of considering itself a multicultural country, Islam has not figured prominently in the public debate on multiculturalism and its practical consequences for public policy and the Canadian identity. There are not the prominent organizations that exist in Britain to speak for the interests of Muslims. The Canadian Muslim response to the *Satanic Verses* controversy or the anti-Muslim racism that erupted in the wake of the Oklahoma City bombing in 1995, for instance, was relatively muted.

Canadian Muslims' perception is that Somalis have played a major role in how Islam is developing as a religion and an institution in Toronto and therefore in Canada. This is a particularly interesting phenomenon when one considers the course that Islam has taken in Somalia, as the next section does. But practically speaking, it has meant that whereas Arab immigrants and south Asian Muslims had already broken the ground in schools and workplaces in Britain, so that there existed policies on prayer-rooms, hijab, and halal food, this was new territory in Toronto. The Muslims already in Toronto, according to the same imam, tended to be reticent about religious demands, perhaps because they did not feel that their numbers warranted their demands, but when the Somalis arrived, notably in the schools, and began to pray in the halls because there was no prayer-room, the schools had to wrestle for the first time in earnest with meeting the needs of significant numbers of Muslims.[41]

Somalis have had to break new ground in very fundamental ways in Toronto, but at the same time, Canada's long-standing self-definition as a multicultural country with no official religion has meant that the right of minority groups to occupy public space and be taken seriously is not in question. This is a situation taken up in greater detail in chapter 6 and does not mean that there has not been serious discrimination in Canada or that the matter of its redress is a simple one. The media in both Canada and Britain, as elsewhere in the West, tend to depict Muslims as 'fundamentalist' zealots, in shrill, unflattering terms that emphasize an unwillingness to compromise and an orientation towards confrontation. The hostility of the media to Islam and Muslims was mentioned frequently on both sides of the Atlantic, but particularly often by Canadian Somalis, who feel especially visible and therefore vulnerable to verbal attack. These issues are examined in greater detail in chapters 6 and 7.

This discussion pertains to Toronto, and to a certain extent English Canada, but could not be said to apply without reservations to Quebec. The status of minorities in Quebec (not their legal status, which is the same as that in the rest of Canada, but their public legitimacy and acceptance as equal members of the polity) is very much a topic of debate, as Quebec wrestles with its status within Canada as a whole. The issue here is to what extent Quebec nationalism is based on language alone, and to what extent on 'tribalism,' or the self-conscious ethnicity of the *Québecois pur laine* ('pure' Quebecers – descendants of the original French settlers).[42] The ability of the Québecois pur laine to steer their own destiny, and what this may mean for minorities in any future separate Quebec, has been a rancorous and sensitive part of the debate over Quebec nationalism since Pierre Trudeau repatriated the constitution in 1982. Thus it is not surprising that there have been problems in Quebec with Muslim girls wishing to wear the hijab to school,[43] whereas these have had no echo in Toronto, or the rest of anglophone Canada.[44]

In both London and Toronto, Somalis appeared to cooperate with other Muslim communities, in that they shared mosques and facilities built by other groups. At the same time, community leaders spoke of the desirability of building a mosque for Somali worshippers in due course.

In summary, the importance of the differences between cities is as follows. Somalis in Britain answered questions on Muslim identity amid well-established Muslim communities whose status within the British national sense of identity is still in question. Somalis in Canada, in contrast, answered the same questions from the midst of a much smaller Muslim community, which they have been instrumental in forming, but the legitimacy of minority communities as participants in the Canadian political system (and the legitimacy of Muslims as a minority) is less questioned than in Britain. Chapter 6 returns to these issues in more detail.

Islam in Somalia: History

Virtually all Somalis are Muslims and identify themselves strongly as such. Islam has been present in Somalia from the first century after the *hijra* (622 CE), but its spread from the coastal towns into the interior is even today shrouded in conjecture and debate, where historical fact appears to collide with northern Somali clan mythology. Some maintain that Zeila, on Somalia's northern coast, was the site of refuge for Muslims fleeing persecution in Abyssinia in Islam's nascent years, but evidence to support the claim appears scanty.[45] Islam's presence in Mogadishu appears to date from the first century following the *hijra*,[46] with the significant presence of Muslim refugees during the wars of apostasy *(ridda)*.[47] There appears to have a been a strong Persian presence in both Zeila and Mogadishu for a time, and Shi'i influence can still be detected, as, in the southern Somali veneration of Fatima, the Prophet's daughter.[48] In the tenth and eleventh centuries, Zeila in the north was widely described by Arab sources as an Abyssinian Christian city,[49] but Mogadishu itself (although not its hinterlands) was noted as being Muslim by that time. Following his travels to Somalia in 1330 CE, Ibn Battuta declared Zeila to be dominated by Zaidi Shi'ites.[50] Mogadishu he described as a Sunni merchant town with a developed Islamic judicial system, where a judiciary council met weekly and emphasis was put on Muslim education.[51] In the fourteenth century and for two centuries thereafter, there is well-documented evidence of substantial immigration to the region of Hadrami and Yemeni Muslims.[52]

The question of the Islamization of the interior of Somalia is somewhat more difficult. The clan mythologies of two of the northern pastoral clan-families, the Darood and the Isaaq, both lay claim to an Arab

progenitor, and not just any Arab, but one of Muhammad's early followers. Shaykh Adburahman Ibn Ismail Jabarti, who fled his homeland after a personal argument with his uncle, married the daughter of
a local chief (the date of his arrival is argued to be between seventy-
five and four hundred years after the hijra)[53] and is said have given
rise to one of Somalia's larger clan-families, the Darood. Almost the
identical story is told of Shaykh Ishaq ibn Ahmad al-'Alawi, the supposed progenitor of the Isaaq clan-family, who is estimated to have
arrived in northern Somalia in the twelfth or thirteenth century.[54] Islam
was then believed to have spread southward as the clans began to
migrate to the south.

In fact, scholarship has indicated that Islam probably spread gradually into the interior over a period of centuries, as the result of a number of influences. These included the trade routes; the influence of the
short-lived sixteenth-century Ajuraan state in the south, a confederacy
of Hawiye clans associated closely with Islam; and the sixteenth-century *jihad* against Christian Ethiopia led by the Somali Ahmed ibn Ibrahim, or Ahmed Gurey (the left-handed one).[55]

The difficulty in establishing the historical progression of Islam in
Somalia, as with other aspects of Somali history, is that Somalia's is an
oral culture, and not until 1972, with the choice and development of an
official orthography, did Somalis begin to keep records in that language. Thence stems the power of the oral Somali creation myth,
which has had immense implications for Somali identity: northern and
central Somalis see themselves not as African, but rather as of Arab
heritage. While I.M. Lewis contends that there is ample evidence that
all six clan-families are originally of Arab heritage, the mythic strength
of the connection is strongest among the four northern pastoral clan-
families. What is more, it is a myth that appears to have been growing
in strength. Lewis describes the ongoing Islamization of traditional
ancestor cults among the Gadabuursi and the 'Iise, both members of
the Dir clan-family. As he says, the clan genealogies become 'charters
for the Islamic foundations upon which Somali culture is built, and
they also serve to express in religious terms the political prestige and
exclusiveness of large autonomous lineages.'[56]

The vaunted ability of Somalis to trace their family back patrilineally
twenty or thirty generations by memory is still in evidence, and to
Somalis this genealogy (*abtirsiinyo*) is, as I.M. Lewis has noted, an
address, an ability to place oneself in one's world.[57] Somalis traditionally use three names: an original first name is added to the names of

their father and grandfather, but these names are actually added to those of preceding patrilineal ancestors. This ancestral Rolodex allows Somalis to locate members of their extended families, which in turn indicates the level of loyalty and responsibility each has for the other, an ability that has proven as important in the refugee straits of the diaspora as it was in times of drought or competition for scarce pastoral resources. It has also meant that the ability to trace one's ancestry back to the Arabs, however mythical the connection may be, has conferred a 'nobility' on the claimant, in his eyes and those of his compatriots. This has in turn reinforced the self-perception of the four pastoral tribes as 'noble' and justified for them their scorn for the southerners, particularly as these have intermarried with Africans, whose hair and facial features are described as recognizably different from those of other Somalis. Ironically, the Benaadir coastal peoples, including those descendants of Arabs (such as the Reer Hamar) whose settlement and accumulation of Islamic culture were extremely significant in the Islamization of Somalia, have frequently been ignored in descriptions of Somalia's population.[58] Therefore any re-evaluation of Islam in Somali history and society has potentially significant consequences for Somalis' understanding of their historical identity.

Regardless of how it spread, the Islamization of the Somali interior was a long process that involved the overlay of Islam on traditional customs and beliefs, as elsewhere in Africa.[59] Rural Somalis have relied more on the body of traditional Somali customs (*xeer* or *heer*) than on the *shari'a* (Islamic religious laws) in regulating their lives.[60] In the eighteenth century, when most Somalis would have described themselves as Muslims, their religious observances combined the traditions of ancestor worship and magic with the five pillars (the most important Muslim observances) of the faith.[61] Itinerant *shaykhs* traversed internal Somalia, popularizing Islam with a combination of knowledge of Muslim law, traditional knowledge, and magic, resulting in a series of veneration cults of many of these men after their deaths. Annual pilgrimages to their tombs (*siyaaro*; Arabic, *ziyara*),[62] stories concerning their ability to perceive and even control supernatural forces, and elegiac poems were central to this veneration.[63] B.J. Andrzejewski translated a number of these poems, which were composed sometimes in Somali and sometimes in Arabic, the language of worship, but which were always written – if they were committed to paper – in Arabic. The following is attributed to a fifteenth century Somali shaykh, Abdurahman Ismaaciil:

A house does not shelter a saint of God:
He finds it detestable to possess buildings or land.
He flees from the desert to the mountains
And the desert weeps when it is deprived of his presence.
He is most patient in keeping night vigils
And in fasting at the break of day.
He says to himself, 'This is my zeal and my labour
And there is no shame in serving the Merciful One.'
He communes with his Lord, his tears flowing,
'My God, my heart is shattered and dispersed;
My God, what I ask from you is not a house
Made of rubies, where celestial maidens dwell
And not the gardens of Paradise, O my God,
And not the trees adorned with fruit,
But it is your Eternal Presence, my hope.
Grant it, for in it is glory!'[64]

The itinerant shaykhs prefigured the strong influence of Sufism and laid the groundwork for it.[65] Somali Islam has been closely associated with Sufism,[66] and over the course of the eighteenth and nineteenth centuries Sufi *tariqas* (brotherhoods) became extremely influential, especially during the colonial period and through the early part of this century.

Primary among active Sufi orders in Somalia were the Qadiriyya, the Ahmadiyya, and its offshoot, the Salihiyya. The founding of the Qadiriyya is credited to Abd al-Qadir ibn Abi Salih Jangidost[67] (1077–1166), also referred to as al-Jilani,[68]) although Trimingham and others maintain that he considered himself not a Sufi at all, but rather a strict Hanbali jurist.[69] He never dressed as a Sufi, claimed to have a path, or initiated novices in mystical teaching.[70] Gradually, however, after his death, his fame spread, and Qadiri centres were propagated in various parts of the Islamic world, including Egypt, Iraq, Somalia, Syria, and Yemen, especially during the fifteenth century.[71]

The Ahmadiyya order developed from the teachings of Sayyid Ahmad Ibn Idris al-Fasi (1760–1837) in Mecca and eventually had many branches in northeast Africa.[72] Ahmad ibn Idris was part of the reformist Sufi movement of the nineteenth century, which took its cue from the challenge of Wahhabism, the purist movement that developed during the same period and objected to what it saw as the decadence of the Sufi orders of the time.[73] Consequently, Ahmad ibn Idris reacted against the saint-veneration[74] of the Maghrib (he was born in Fez) and based his Sufism on the Qur'an and *sunna* alone. His reformism brought him the wrath of the established *'ulama* (religiously learned men), and he was forced to flee frequently, once from a charge of heresy in Mecca.[75]

Among the offshoots of Ibn Idris's teachings were orders founded by Ibrahim al-Rashid and in turn by his nephew and pupil, Muhammad ibn Salih, who founded the Salihiyya in Mecca in 1887. The Salihiyya was introduced into Somalia by Muhammad Guled, but its most famous leader was the Sayyid Mohammed Abdulle Hassan.[76]

Although not all the *tariqas* can be said to have been occupied with or even concerned with defying the colonialists,[77] the turn of the twentieth century witnessed the height of the power and influence of Sayyid Mohammed Abdulle Hassan, the 'Mad Mullah,' as he was dubbed by the British, whom he tormented for twenty-one years until his death from fever in 1920. Much has been written about this leader of the Salihiyya tariqa, but he remains a powerful figure in the Somali imagination because he managed to combine brilliance in three distinct areas much admired by Somalis but not generally expected to coexist in any one individual. He was a respected leader of a religious movement in Somalia, having received the blessing of Shaykh Muhammad Salih, the Sudanese-born founder of this Sufi tariqa, when on his *hajj*[78] between 1886 and 1889. He was a superb warrior and managed to command the loyalty of fighters from many clans, whom he remodelled as Sufi adepts. And last but not least, he was a dazzling poet in a land where mastery of this oratorical art is rewarded with awe and respect.

Mohammed Abdulle Hassan is the best known but by no means the only figure of significance from the height of Sufi influence. Shaykh Uways Bin Muhammad al-Barawi was a hugely influential leader of the Qadiriyya tariqa, who is credited with having continued to expand Islam and make it accessible to non-Arabic-speaking Somalis. From his centre in Baraawe, he adapted the Arabic alphabet and vowel signs to Somalis' needs, making it easier for them to learn the Qur'an.[79] He began religious settlements and mosque-schools, composed mystical poems in Arabic and Somali, and helped to spread Islam into Tanganyika and Zanzibar. He remains immensely popular in southern Somalia, and the annual *siyaaro* in his honour was, prior to the civil war, attended by thousands of pilgrims from Kenya as well as his native Somalia. Drums, which are culturally important to the Bantu peoples of East Africa, are used in Islamic *dhikr* (remembrances of God, and praise-singing) in the areas where the Uwaysiyya (the branch of Qadiriyya made up of followers of Shaykh Uways) was prominent outside Somalia.[80] It may have been this willingness to incorporate pre-existing customs into Islamic ones that contributed to the enmity of Mohammed Abdulle Hassan, whose adepts were ultimately responsible for Shaykh Uways's murder. Abdulle Hassan's spiritual predecessors were educated in purist Wahhabism, during the period of that reformist movement's activism,[81] and the Sayyid consequently inveighed forcefully against such Somali traditions as *qat*-chewing, which was used during meditations, and saint worship, as well as association with 'infidels.' This led him to view other Sufi orders, and their leaders, as heretical.[82] It would not have helped matters that the Uwaysiyya and Salihiyya were competing for adherents in the same region.[83]

Given that it prefigures recent Islamist movements in Somalia, there is another little-considered episode in Somali religious history that it is worth noting here: the 'Bardeere Jihad.' Bardeere was a religious community founded on the Jubba River in 1819 by Shaykh Ibrahim Hassan Jeberow. Whether it was originally a Qadiriyya or an Ahmadiyya sect to begin with, or indeed an independent religious congregation affiliated with no tariqa in particular, and whether the Bardeere Muslims were Wahhabis as claimed by some European explorers, are not clear.[84] But what is known is that the Bardeeres, who numbered some twenty thousand at their height in 1840, aimed to purify Islamic practice in Somalia. Among other things, they wanted the use of tobacco abolished, as well as dancing and male–female socializing, the ivory trade (on the grounds that the elephant was an unclean animal), and saint worship (which is how they characterized the siyaaro). Women were to veil themselves.[85]

In the mid-1830s, the community launched a jihad on the surrounding areas, attacking and forcing Looq to the north and Baraawe to the southeast, among other towns, to submit to its decrees. This success triggered a furious counter-offensive, numbering some forty thousand fighters, from Afgooye in the east, that swiftly destroyed Bardeere and put an end to the jihad. Whether because of the threat to the profitable ivory trade or the attacks on the political culture of the region (the tradition of siyaaro and mysticism), as discussed by Cassanelli,[86] the established political and religious orders were sufficiently threatened by the reformists to respond swiftly and decisively. The episode was short-lived, to be sure, and to some extent in contrast with the nature of Islam's style and practice in Somalia, and yet it was one that fore-shadows more recent developments. The movement had many charac-teristics in common with recent Islamist movements in Somalia.

Recent Islamic Developments

In Somalia

In its first years in office following the assassination of President Ali Shermarke and the military coup in 1969, Siad Barre's government allied itself with Soviet-style scientific socialism, which, given the ide-ology's hostility to religion, necessarily placed him in an uncomfort-able position on the role of Islam in Somali society.[87] While recognizing Islam as central to Somalia's identity, Barre quickly found himself at odds with it. The tariqas were tolerated, since they were seen as politi-cally neutral, but, as the dictatorship proved itself to be inhospitable to opposition of any kind, sanctions on religious expression were intro-duced and later extended. In 1975, Barre brought in a series of legal reforms, including changes to the inheritance laws, putting women on an equal footing with men. Ten imams, having expressed opposition to the changes on Islamic grounds during Friday noon prayers, were arrested and executed. Later, Islamic groups were expressly banned, and members persecuted, arrested, tortured, and killed or driven into exile.[88]

There began to grow, in the 1970s in the urban centres of Somalia, the nub of what are today sizeable Somali Islamist movements, both within the country and in the diaspora. This was in keeping with the international climate and the 'Islamic revival' that was swelling as Arabs re-examined their identities in the aftermath of the 1967 Six Day War with Israel, but it was more than an African reflection of that phe-nomenon.

Somalis had been euphoric at independence in 1960, with the reunion of the two former colonial possessions, British Somaliland and Italian Somalia, but they soon faced a crisis of identity caused by a number of factors. Somali politics fell into a morass during the 1960s, and the promise of independence appeared not to fulfill itself. Following the assassination of Shermarke and the coup, Barre fanned the flames of national fervour and irredentism by promising reclamation of the

Ogaden (that part of eastern Ethiopia inhabited by ethnic Somalis and given to Ethiopia as part of a series of deals between the Ottoman Empire and the colonial powers of northeastern Africa). Eventually, and only after much death and devastation, he failed to deliver on that promise, but Somalia was swamped by a crisis in 1974 as thousands of Somali refugees poured destitute into the country from the Ogaden. To make matters worse, Barre's allegiance switched to the United States and the West after the Soviet Union backed Ethiopia in Somalia's irredentist war, although he never formally repudiated socialism, fuelling frustration among Somalis with their government's apparent ideological confusion.

Some Somalis responded to what they saw as a growing crisis of national identity by rejecting what seemed to them to be imported ideologies and frameworks. Their aim was to find a developmental path that would work for Somalia by virtue of being truly Somali. Some of this sentiment found expression in Islamist movements,[89] which grew out of groups that had existed during the 1960s, but found a new impetus and *raison d'etre* with the political climate of the 1970s. Over time the movements crystallized into groups with somewhat differing orientations, split and in some cases reunited, and were infused by scholarship at Egyptian, Sudanese, and Saudi universities. They became, over the course of the 1980s, extremely influential in the urban areas and therefore, since these areas produce the bulk of refugees, in the diaspora as well.[90]

Shaykh Mohamed Sheikh Osman, an imam and leader of the Somali community in London, described the early days of the movements this way:

> The changes began in 1973–74, when I was about 18. I was coming from a religious background, my father was a shaykh, but at the same time some young people began to realize that Islam was not really practised in Somalia. The belief was there, people considered themselves to be Muslims; the traditions were there, but the practice of the sunna [traditions], of the Qur'an, of the *hadiths* [sayings and actions of the Prophet], the authentic practice was not there. Also at this time Siad Barre labelled people like us as colonialist sympathizers, imperialists, spies for the West, things like that. Those were the days of socialism, and you were not meant to take religion seriously.
>
> When the young started to practise Islam seriously, the question became 'what was Islam?' We began to read, and to search for the authen-

tic sources of Islam: the Qur'an, the exegesis, the commentary. We found that many in the community were Muslim by name only. They would not actually be practising at all, not praying daily: they would drink alcohol, or rob, or kill, or commit adultery, and yet they would still call themselves Muslims. This was the first shock for us. Which was the right way? So from that point we went back to the authentic references, where we started.

At the beginning no members were graduates of foreign universities. We read books, especially Sayyid Qutb. He is the mastermind; he was regarded as the father, the spiritual leader of the movement. We read news of the Nation of Islam in America, of Malcolm X. We read other scholars. Then gradually people began to go to study, first in Egypt, then later Saudi Arabia. I left Somalia in 1977 and went to Saudi Arabia to do a first degree. I graduated from Medina in 1983. I read the authentic sources there. I began to know enough to know which *hadiths* were authentic or not. I got an M.Phil. and a PhD from Birmingham in Islamic Studies. One is constantly evaluating sources and hadiths.[91]

Conflict necessarily accompanied the growth of the movements. Islamists argued over the correct path, not only which were the correct sources or how strict adherents should be, but also the best means of spreading this 'pure' Islam. They tended to be young and urban, which brought them into conflict with older Somalis and with other members of their families who did not share their approach. They destroyed some of the tombs that were points of annual pilgrimage; decried dancing and drums during *dhikr*; demanded that men and women not touch one another, even to shake hands; required that men grow beards and that women wear the *hijab* and not merely traditional flimsy headscarves. They prescribed that women wear the *jilbab*;[92] its distinguishing feature is that it is two separate pieces, a long gown of dark, opaque material, and over that a headpiece (*al-khimar*) like a nun's wimple, sometimes sweeping to mid-calf, which is meant to be able to accommodate the needs of Somali women to be active.[93]

The Islamists clashed over direction in the course of the civil war. While all Somali Islamists would like to see an Islamic state established in Somalia, some believed that advantage should be taken of anarchic post-Barre conditions to establish such a state and began by entering the fray of civil war, including an attempt to take control of the Mudug area in the northeast of Somalia in January 1991 after the ouster of Barre.[94] This group had taken on the Somali Salvation Democratic

Front (SSDF), which was manned by the fighters of the Majerteen sub-clan of the Darood clan-family, and they lost dismally, resulting in hundreds of Islamists being slain and an organization split asunder.[95]

In the 1990s, the Islamists were arrayed in two main groups. The first, Jama'at al-Islah (Society of Reform), identifies with the al-Ikwhan al-Muslimun, the Egyptian Muslim Brotherhood,[96] and is generally described as the less strict of the two. In Somalia, it sees its main work as the provision of social services – the re-establishment of hospitals and clinics, food, housing, and education – to Somalis as it gradually re-educates them. In the diaspora, members of al-Islah generally use terms such as 'aiding the integration of our community' into that of the host community, saying that compromise on strict Islamic doctrine is allowable in so far as Muslim values are not damaged in the process. What this means in practice is obviously subject to much debate.

The second group is called al-Ittihad al-Islami (Islamic Union). It is a union of two earlier groups, Jama'at Ahl al-Islam (Society of the People of Islam), or Ahli, started by Shaykh Mohamed Moallin, who was subsequently jailed for fifteen years by Barre; and the Salafiyya, begun in 1978 by a group of graduates from Saudi universities.[97] It is generally described, both by its members and by members of al-Islah, as stricter and more doctrinaire. Sometimes called Wahhabi or Salafi in their orientation,[98] adherents of al-Ittihad maintain that Islam was purest in its application during the life of the Prophet and the 220 years following the hijra,[99] and they consequently attempt to follow teachings and hadiths as rendered during that time. While al-Ittihad also works to provide social services in Somalia, and its members are divided about how to manoeuvre within a tribally divided anarchy, it reportedly issued a political manifesto in the mosques of Toronto and Ottawa in 1992, listing a series of eight objectives.[100] The objectives include: establishment of an Islamic state; rejection of *jahili* ('ignorant,' or un-Islamic) policies; attainment of Islamic justice; establishment of peace in society; a well-planned economy; propagation of Islam; war against *bida'* (innovations); and, once this is all in place, establishment of a strong army. It also rejects alliances with non-Islamic political parties.[101]

In the diaspora, al-Ittihad attempts to encourage Somalis to live an Islamic life in as 'true' a fashion as possible, making as few compromises as possible and threading a careful path through the maze of un-Islamic Western influences. One member of Ittihad described his life in an interview as a constant attempt to 'build an island of Islam' in the midst of Western secularism.[102]

Islamists have also not been able to remain free of clan pressures. Of course clan divisions are anathema to Islamic doctrine, which speaks of one Muslim *umma*, or community, but it has been impossible for the Islamists to avoid the perception from other Somalis, even from Somalis who describe themselves as Islamists or 'fundamentalists in the good sense,'[103] that, wittingly or not, clan affiliation has affected the loyalties and courses of action of the movements.[104] One educated Somali in London, sympathetic to the Islamists' goal of incorporating Islam into a reconstituted Somali government, recounted an incident that took place shortly after the fall of Barre and the subsequent declaration of Ali Mahdi that he would govern instead. The event took place during one of the weekly Sunday speeches by a Somali imam, understood to be a member of al-Ittihad, at the noon prayer. The imam was reportedly disparaging of Ali Mahdi's claim that he would lead Somalia according to the dictates of the Qur'an and declared him to be *gaalo*, an infidel.[105] The implication drawn by at least some of his listeners was that the imam was disparaging of Ali Mahdi merely because he was a member of Abgal, a Hawiye sub-clan, whereas al-Ittihad is sometimes described as predominantly Darood. At that point Ali Mahdi was only just assuming his leadership role and could not have been expected to have proven already his faithfulness to Islam.

It is possible that this story reveals more about the preconceptions of the listeners than about the imam, but in such a polarized community it is virtually impossible for any movement to avoid charges of clan favouritism. Some informants who declared themselves in interviews to be sympathetic to the doctrinal approaches of the movements none the less eschewed contact with them on the grounds that 'I am against the groups like Ittihad and Islah because they are like little parties, little factions. They are not different from tribal factions. If you have little groups, they are bound to fight. If they were one united organization, I would join them.'[106]

It is difficult to estimate the size of the Islamist movements either in Somalia or in the diaspora. They will say themselves that their influence, relative to that of other forces at play in Somalia, particularly the warlords and their factions, is negligible. And they are wary of political involvement in the midst of anarchy; they speak of a need to wait until the factions themselves have played out their fury and disorder before an Islam-oriented state can be established.

In the diaspora, however, the movements are a noticeable presence.

Al-Ittihad's annual conference in London in August 1995, for instance, was attended by roughly two thousand adults: well over a thousand men, and almost that many women, in jilbab, with children in tow. It was held at the Regent's Park mosque, a day-long affair that included guest speakers, prayer, and meals. The speakers, who regularly attend such conferences, included residents of the Middle East and North America as well as Britain. Their focus was on the preservation of Islam in the midst of Western secular culture and how this might be accomplished, but they encouraged listeners to 'show the best face of Islam' to Westerners and to live in accordance with British law. Such conferences take place regularly in Toronto and London, but there are mosques in both cities where the imams of both al-Ittihad and al-Islah are known to speak, usually on Sundays, since the Friday noon prayer is presided over by the chief imam of the mosque, who is not Somali. While the Sunday talks begin with a focus on a verse of the Qur'an, they often become political, as the discussion of Ali Mahdi's contested presidency illustrates.

In London, al-Ittihad uses the East London Mosque (also called the Whitechapel mosque), which is known as a Deobandi mosque, as opposed to the nearby Brick Lane mosque, which has Barelvi leanings.[107] Both Deobandis and Barelvis embody South Asian Muslim traditions in Britain, but the Deobandis are reformists who tend to emphasize strict Hanafi jurisprudence and to discourage popular shaykhs and shrine cults – precisely the transplanted local traditions valued by Barelvis.[108]

Mohamed Sheikh Osman maintains that in London as well Somalis – and by this he means Somali Islamists – have 'changed the face of Islam':

> This has happened in two ways. Firstly, we believe that only the authentic sources, the sunna and the Qur'an, must be followed. When I came to London there were many imams on Friday prayers who were quoting hadiths that are not authentic, following scholars who use fabricated hadiths. We challenged them. For instance, I remember one Friday when the imam was speaking about the differences between Muslims and saying these were justified by a certain hadith and I said, 'Where does this come from?' No, I showed him the correct hadith, where unity is mercy. Now in the mainstream Sunni Muslim mosques the authentic sources are used. We have made a huge impact.
>
> Secondly, the question of women. Asians did not take the hijab. You

would see the wife of an Islamic scholar who was wearing a sari, with her belly showing. Now, with the example of the Somali women, they wear the hijab, and the hijab is accepted not only all over the U.K. but all over Europe ... There is no Somali tradition of women going to the mosque. There is one small mosque in central Mogadishu for women but it was built in the mid-70s. It was unthinkable for a woman to go to the mosque, but in the days of the Prophet women went to pray in the mosques. Now this is changing, both in Somalia and here. They are starting to come to the mosques to pray and to study as well. We are trying to accommodate them but in reality we cannot change all the mosques. The Asian women are beginning to come as well. Really the Somali women are leading the community.[109]

Whether Somali women should wear the hijab and, if so, which one are contentious issues within the community. Most Somali women traditionally wore scarves and shawls (*masar* and *garbasaar*) after marriage, but this is generally described as 'culture' rather than religion. The scarves are colourful and sometimes flimsy and can be wrapped in a multitude of ways, some showing the woman's hair, not attempting to hide her neck and breastbone, and the effect is to beautify her, rather than to aim at portraying modesty. There is no tradition of seclusion in Somalia; there could not be.[110] Somali women play as active a role in pastoral life as their husbands. It is they who collapse and rebuild the portable huts after each trek and care for the group's goats, sheep, and cattle. Therefore any restrictive garment would be unsuitable. The Islamists tried to take this into account when they wrestled with the issue of women's attire; the jilbab appeared to them to provide sufficient flexibility of movement.

In the diaspora, many Somali women have consciously taken the hijab (as opposed to wearing traditional headgear), as seen below in chapter 3, for religious reasons, distinguishing between culture (how they used to dress before leaving Somalia) and religion (how they are more self-consciously Muslim in the West). Most wear short, square, opaque headscarves that are pinned at their chins. Some of them wear the jilbab. The wearing of the jilbab is in part a declaration of association with the Islamist movements, as well as an individual reorientation with regard to religion.

Debate is heated, among scholars and Muslim women alike, about the differences between religion and culture in determining the role of women in Islam.[111] Somali women in the diaspora participate vigorously in the debate, as can be seen below in the interviews. There are a number of reasons for this. First, there is the paradox of custom: traditional social inferiority in contrast to active participation in communal and economic activity. Second, in the diaspora, this has been supplemented by an increasing religious literacy and a common dominant role as head of family or its primary economic support. Third, there is an acute awareness, which demonstrated itself repeatedly in interviews, that Somalis, as Islamically literate non-Arabs, may read the same primary sources (Qur'an and hadiths) and arrive at different conclusions from their co-religionists.

The wearing of the jilbab is one of the most hotly debated topics on the Somali newsgroup on the internet, argued about by its predominantly male participants. The 'Anti-*Jelaabib* Society,' a creation of the surfers of the 'net, argues fiercely that the *jilbab* is as foreign an import as the mini-skirt, and is therefore un-Somali. Academic sources, such as Fatima Mernissi's *Beyond the Veil*, are cited as proof that such measures are not Islamically necessary. The response from the pro-Islamists is scathing: Islam is integral to Somali culture, and therefore so is modest dress; and anyway Fatima Mernissi is not a good Muslim, they claim, and misquoted the Qur'anic verses in question.[112]

One area of contentious discussion for the Islamic groups is the shari'a courts that have sprung up in various towns in Somalia following the breakup of civil order. Such courts, and their consequent harsh punishments for rape or theft, have been reported in Hargeisa in the north and in Mogadishu as well as other southern towns such as Looq.[113] Many informants who consider themselves religious, and others who would describe themselves as Islamists, denounce these courts because, they say, it is un-Islamic to put in place a system of punishment without a just society. You cannot cut off a man's hand for stealing when he has no honest way to earn his bread, they say.[114] Others contend that although there are admittedly serious problems with the courts – among them the concern that their legitimacy, and that of the judges who run them, stems from the brute power of Ali Mahdi's thugs and their guns, who are not viewed as shining examples of Islam – they are the only mechanism that has succeeded in bringing some semblance of order and peace to the chaos that had existed in those towns. Women had been unable to go to the market without being robbed: now they reportedly shop and wear their beloved gold jewellery without fear.[115]

The influence of the Islamist movements is hard to calculate, but one student who describes himself as an Islamist pointed to their impact with the following story. In keeping with Somali clan tradition, sub-clans can demand *qaaraan* from their male adult members. Qaaraan is a financial contribution, generally collected in time of trouble. This young man is a member of the Hawaardle clan of the Hawiye clan-family. At some point in the factional fighting, General Aideed's forces (Aideed was Habar Gedir, also of the Hawiye clan-family) took over the Hiraan area, which is traditionally Hawaardle. The Hawaardle wanted to retrieve control of the territory and so sent out a call to adult Hawaardle men worldwide to collect enough money to arm a suffi-cient militia to oust Aideed's forces. They were aiming for between twenty and thirty dollars per man, for a total of half a million dollars, which they wanted to collect within a fortnight.

It is considered a serious breach of the social contract to refuse to pay when it is asked of you, and community pressure to comply was intense. Yet the student maintained that of 210 Hawaardle men in Lon-don about thirty refused to pay for unknown reasons, but fully half refused to contribute because they considered it un-Islamic to pay for inter-clan bloodshed. In response, the elders at home made a video of the terrible conditions prevailing under Aideed's men, and all Hawaardle men were asked to view the video. On the strength of the video, some who had refused to pay changed their minds, and as a result of the fund-raising, a militia was created that ousted Aideed's forces, which had been in control of the area for seven months. The Hawaardle militia (under the guidance of Hawaardle elders), once back in control, responded to the incident – and their perception of the Islamic concerns of their diaspora kinsmen – by setting up shari'a courts in three main cities of the area. For the student, this was aston-ishing, considering that the elders were generally Sufi adherents who had not been supporters of Islamism.[116]

The relative strength of the Islamist movements in Somalia, in con-trast to abiding loyalty to Sufi orders, is difficult to calibrate. Interview respondents indicated that, as far as they could tell, Sufism was still a strong force in rural areas, but increasingly irrelevant within urban areas. 'Irrelevance' was not a term used to describe the Islamist move-ments. Whether they become an enduring force in Somalia's political future depends on a complex series of variables, including their ability to transcend clan differences. While the shari'a courts and advent of the jilbab may appear to be anomalous in Somalia's practice of Islam, there is a history in Somalia of reformist and revivalist Islam. In the

Somali diaspora, there is little question that the Islamist movements are significant entities, setting examples and moulding the re-creation of the Somali Muslim identity in exile.

Conclusion

This chapter has provided some explanation of the cultural and religious traditions that Somali refugees brought with them into the diaspora. It has, moreover, explored some of the salient circumstances of refugee life in London and Toronto, so that the reader is prepared for the interviews. Somalis are, by and large, people with a very strong sense of their own religious and cultural identity. They were thrust – while experiencing great personal trauma and loss – into an unfamiliar and alien world. In many cases, their socio-economic level plummeted in the transition, as many former members of Somalia's elite found themselves forced to rely on government benefits in Toronto and London. They lost status and wealth; they lost homes and family; they lost a country. They arrived in the West fearful of losing their culture and their religion. The interviews that follow explore their integration into their adoptive societies under these conditions.

2

Cultural Integration

Integration is the two-sided process of immigrants' adjustment to a new society without loss of what they consider essential to their identity (or self-definition, particularly in the sense of their religion or ethnicity) and, simultaneously, of the adoptive society's accommodation of them. Critically, integration implies that both the immigrants and the adoptive society undergo change over time. This study argues that integration is best described as a two-stage process, encompassing internal and external components, as defined in the introduction and explored in greater detail below.

Political culture plays a key role in affecting the integration of immigrants and minorities, in that it determines the level of respect – or legitimacy – that they are accorded in the host country. But it is a role that has not been well explored or well understood. The term 'political culture' refers to that portion of a society's culture that determines how its political system – the state apparatus and its procedures – actually works.

When Nathan Glazer and Daniel Patrick Moynihan set out, in the early 1960s, to test the assimilatory powers of the American 'melting pot,' they discovered that, contrary to expectation, the pot had not melted much of anything. Ethnic groups were alive and well and living in New York City, and the notion that 'the intense and unprecedented mixture of ethnic and religious groups'[1] in the United States would create a new homogeneous whole was clearly erroneous. 'The point about the melting pot ... is that it did not happen.'[2] Glazer and Moynihan noted that the Irish, Jews, and Puerto Ricans of New York were not clinging together in 'a survival from the age of mass immigration' but were in fact, 'a new social form.'[3] Their most interesting observation was that ethnic groups are constantly re-created by their experiences as immigrants, even after language and customs are 'lost.'[4]

In the decades since that study, debate has raged over the tenacity of ethnicity, a debate that reached white heat in the years following the breakup of the Soviet Union and Yugoslavia. In large part the debate concerned itself with an attempt to define ethnicity: to determine whether ethnicity is something internal, which exists organically within a group of people and in their own minds, or whether it is a definition imposed by the outside world and by the circumstances of migration. The two schools of thought have been characterized as the primordial versus the structural, and most commentators on ethnicity will position themselves somewhere along the continuum between them.

The primordial position has been articulated clearly by Harold Isaacs in *The Idols of the Tribe*, which began life as an article in a seminal collection of essays on ethnicity edited by Moynihan and Glazer in 1975, and was then expanded into book form:

> Basic group identity consists of the ready-made set of endowments and identifications which every individual shares with others from the moment of birth by the chance of the family into which he is born at that given time in that given place ...
>
> ... An individual belongs to his basic group in the deepest and most literal sense that here he is not alone, which is what all but a very few human beings most fear to be. He is not only not alone, but here, as long as he chooses to remain in and of it, he cannot be denied or rejected. It is an identity he might want to abandon, but it is the identity that no one can take away from him. It is home in the sense of Robert Frost's line, the place where, when you go there, they've got to take you in.[5]

The anthropologist Clifford Geertz emphasized how primordial attachments – including region and kin connection, religion, language, and social practices – determine a person's loyalty and behaviour. Although the strength of these bonds varies with individual, time, and society, he argued, 'for virtually every person, in every society, at almost all times, some attachments seem to flow more from a sense of natural – some would say spiritual – affinity than from social interaction.'[6]

The structuralist school, in contrast, takes as its starting point the position of Frederic Barth, whose *Ethnic Groups and Boundaries* argued that the key determinant of an ethnic group is how it relates to the larger society, because it is the differentiation that causes it to be 'an ethnic group.' The points of differentiation are the boundaries, which are determined by the larger society, not by group members, so that 'the critical focus of investigation from this point of view becomes the ethnic boundary that defines the group, not the cultural stuff that it encloses.'[7] While Barth asserted that boundaries change with circumstance and over time, it is 'the fact of continuing dichotomization between members and outsiders [that] allows us to specify the nature of continuity, and investigate the changing cultural form and content.'[8]

Wsevelod Isajiw, in establishing a workable definition for ethnicity, noted that Barth thought that people will be identified as belonging to one or another ethnic group even if they do not actively share any cultural patterns with that group, as long as others can perceive a link to the group's ancestors. It is the identification by others that triggers the indidividual's self-identification as a member of an ethnic group.[9]

This approach allows its proponents to understand the prevalence and salience of ethnic groups as elements of a puzzle when analysing such 'objective' factors as economic competition in society – an element of the puzzle, just like class, race, and gender.[10] Isajiw's working definition of an ethnic group, for instance, refers to 'an involuntary group of people who share the same culture or to descendants of such people who identify themselves and/or are identified by others as belonging to the same involuntary group.'[11] By virtue of existing primarily through the identification of others (as opposed to one's own perception), a person's membership in an ethnic group becomes yet another feature of his or her socio-economic description, to be added to class, race, and gender in laying the course for him or her in the societal maze.

To some extent the argument is in effect over the placement of the horse and its cart. Whether the ethnic group is salient because its members believe that they share an intrinsic bond, or whether it is salient because the wider society enforces it, there is little dispute that its continued existence and even its growing role are of note.

There are differing theories for this salience, of course. One view holds that redefinition of migrants into a series of interest groups seems to have occurred because ethnic groups were so much more effective as interest groups than mere class membership.[12] This assessment of ethnic-group organization is sometimes called an instrumentalist approach, because ethnic groups' cohesion is seen to coincide with a perceived greater ability to compete for resources. In the words of Daniel Bell: 'In the competition for the values of the society to be realized politically, ethnicity can become a means of claiming place or advantage.'[13] It is a view that perceives ethnicity not as a primordial phenomenon, but as a strategic choice intended to gain power and privilege.[14]

These 'ethnic mobilization' studies, as Anthony Smith commented in *The Ethnic Revival*, did not question liberal assumptions. The reasoning went as follows. Competition for resources intensifies with modernization, and ethnic groups help members achieve certain ends, but the assumption remained that with the development of 'complex industrial and postindustrial structures, the primordial dimensions of ethnicity would simply become obsolete.'[15]

This of course is precisely what has not happened. Ethnic groups are an increasingly important factor in immigrant-receiving countries, and seemingly intransigent ethnic conflicts continue to arise and to defy resolution throughout the world. John Stack has argued that it is those very postmodern, post-industrial developments that have enabled ethnic groups to become major transnational actors. He identifies the international interdependence and permeability of states; the structural inequalities between advanced industrial states and developing countries; the power of worldwide communication and transportation networks; and the interplay between states and ethnic groups on intrasocietal, state, and global levels[16] as factors that contribute to the ongoing prominence, activity, and visibility of ethnic groups.

John Porter has argued that 'the revival' of ethnicity reflects a retreat from 'the liberal notions of the unity of mankind' and underscores the failure of universalistic values to take hold or create a society of equality of opportunity.[17] Porter's comment reflects a vital link. Western immigrant-receiving countries have operated on the assumption that 'liberal notions of the unity of mankind' would dictate the disappearance of ethnicity once it was exposed to modernity. The fact that ethnic groups refused to disappear as they were intended to was related to a shocked realization in Western immigrant-receiving societies that the assimilationist model was not working.

It can be argued, however, that the assimilationist model continues to underlie most understandings of how integration works. The immigrant-receiving mythology of both the United States and Canada has long assumed that over time ethnic minorities would for the most part, and indeed should, be absorbed into the mainstream, such that their value systems and culture would be that of the majority. Their ethnic identification, to the extent that it continued to exist, would be limited to formalized customs. (There have been differences in the assimilatory approaches of the two countries, to be sure – with the United States frequently described as a 'melting pot' and Canada as a 'cultural mosaic' – but these differences may be largely superficial.[18]) This was the picture that *Beyond the Melting Pot* was beginning to shatter.

It is worth examining the history of ideas behind the assimilationist paradigm. Milton Gordon, in his 1964 book *Assimilation in American Life*,[19] paints a fascinating picture of the emergence of the assimilationist paradigm. In its first formulation, the ideology – as it could then be described – took the form of 'Anglo-conformity.' The founders of the United States were determined that, despite significant numbers of 'foreigners' in parts of their country (particularly Germans in Pennsylvania), it was important that the Anglo-Saxon speech and institutions that they envisaged be firmly entrenched. Both Washington and Jefferson were wary of encouraging immigration, not because they did not want immigrants *per se*, but because they were concerned about the ideas that immigrants would bring with them.

Jefferson, after allowing that immigrants who came with open minds (he actually wrote 'if they come of themselves ...') would be entitled to all the rights of citizenship, penned the following concerns in the early 1780s:

> It is for the happiness of those united in society to harmonize as much as possible in matters which they must of necessity transact together. Civil government being the sole object of forming societies, its administration must be conducted by common consent. Every species of government has its specific principles. Ours perhaps are more peculiar than those of any other in the universe. It is a composition of the freest principles of the English constitution, with others derived from natural right and natural reason. To these nothing can be more opposed than the maxims of absolute monarchies. Yet from such we are to expect the greatest number of emigrants. They will bring with them the principles of the governments they leave, imbibed in their early youth ... These principles, with their language, they will transmit to their children. In proportion to their numbers, they will share with us the legislation. They will infuse into it their spirit, warp and bias its directions, and render it a heterogeneous, incoherent, distracted mass.[20]

Note that Jefferson does not object to different nationalities intermingling with his American kin; it is the potentially despotic ideas that they may bring with them of which he is afraid, particularly given the newness of his own legislative project.

John Quincy Adams, in an 1818 letter written as secretary of state to Baron von Fürstenwaerther on the subject of immigrants, wrote as follows:

> They come to a life of independence, but to a life of labor – and, if they cannot accommodate themselves to the character, moral, political and physical, of this country with all its compensating balances of good and evil, the Atlantic is always open to them to return to the land of their nativity and their fathers. To one thing they must make up their minds, or they will be disappointed in every expectation of happiness as Americans. They must cast off the European skin, never to resume it. They must look forward to their posterity rather than backward to their ancestors; they must be sure that whatever their own feelings may be, those of their children will cling to the prejudices of this country.[21]

The one condition of immigration, he was saying, is that immigrants must be willing to leave their ideas behind them and be prepared to adopt the conventions that 'we,' who have founded this country, have established. Adams reflected an attitude that did not disparage immigration on the basis of nationality but was concerned primarily with the intellectual baggage that crossed the Atlantic with the immigrants. It is true that most immigrants to the United States were northern Europeans who did not challenge the Americans' religious or racial tolerance very much. None the less, two points need to be borne in mind. First, Swedes and Germans were perceived by Scots Americans and English Americans as being 'foreign'; second, regardless of degree of foreignness, what is important is the emphasis of the Americans on ideas, not on ethnicity.

The second stage in the development of the assimilation myth was born of historian Frederick Jackson Turner's seminal 1893 paper called 'The Significance of the Frontier in American History,' in which he claimed that something momentous was happening on the Midwest frontier, where Germans, Scotch-Irish, and Scandinavians were all dealing with hardship together: 'The frontier promoted the formation of a composite nationality for the American people. ... In the crucible of the frontier the immigrants were Americanized, liberated and fused into a mixed race, English in neither nationality nor characteristics ... a composite American people whose amalgamation is destined to produce a new national stock.'[22] Once again, Turner was referring to immigration from northern and western Europe, but even this intermingling seemed startling at the time, and with his essay the frontier 'melting pot' mythology was seeded.

The urban melting pot was another story, of course, since the last two decades of the nineteenth century saw a 'new' sort of immigration into the cities – large numbers of southern and eastern Europeans who could be said to have strained the limits of existing American tolerance. None the less, in 1908, only a decade before Woodrow Wilson went to Europe to sort out its borders, an English Jewish playwright, Israel Zangwill, wrote *The Melting Pot* to great popular acclaim. He portrayed the United States as 'God's crucible, the great Melting Pot where all the races of Europe are melting and re-forming.' The main character declares to immigrants on Ellis Island in New York harbour that they have come to 'the fires of God. A fig for your feuds and vendettas! Germans and Frenchmen, Irishmen and Englishmen, Jews and Russians – into the Crucible with you all! God is making the American.'[23]

Great drama it may not have been, but the play was quoted in speeches by Theodore Roosevelt and Woodrow Wilson. The concept, too, was immature, in that it was never quite clear what molten culture was supposed to emerge from this pot and whether it was something completely new or merely the assimilation of all 'other' ethnicities into the Anglo-Saxon mould. As Theodore Roosevelt (to whom the play was dedicated) is quoted: 'The crucible in which all the new types are melted into one was shaped from 1776 to 1789, and our nationality was definitely fixed in all its essentials by the men of Washington's day.'[24]

The final variation of the assimilation theme that Gordon delineates is 'cultural pluralism,' which was a term developed by the philosopher Horace Kallen in 1924. The idea was meant to describe a group of separate national cultures living peaceably side by side within the United States, all with equal access to its institutions. Kallen saw the country primed to develop into a federal republic of different nationalities, sharing common institutions, in which 'each nationality would have for its emotional and involuntary life its own particular dialect or speech, its own individual and inevitable aesthetic and intellectual forms.'[25]

Gordon argued, however, that assimilation would follow varied patterns. 'Acculturation,' which he defined as the process whereby an immigrant or ethnic group 'changes its cultural patterns to those of the host society,'[26] happened quickly and with virtually all immigrants. It was certain to be a fact by the time the second generation matured. In contrast, 'structural assimilation,' by which he meant the actual social mingling of groups, did not appear to take place much at all. The result therefore was that the United States seemed to be a society of what he called 'structural pluralism' between ethnic groups.[27] This is a notion that echoes J.S. Furnivall's analysis of a plural society, in which a number of ethnic groups function side by side but without a 'common will' or purpose to bind them.[28]

Whatever his measure of how much assimilation there had actually been, Gordon did not really question the value of the paradigm. The issue for him was what kind of assimilation had or had not occurred, not whether he had posed appropriately the question of how groups intermingle. He rejects the concept of 'integration,' which, as defined in 1956 by William Bernard, implies that 'each element has been changed by association with the other,'[29] on the grounds that the dominant Anglo-Saxon culture could not be said to have been significantly altered by association with any other.[30] Gordon was not alone in this view, since the literature scarcely mentions integration or any concept like it. I attempt in the next section to build a case that it is a useful concept in describing how ethnic groups and cultures interrelate.

The notion of acculturation, or assimilation, or incorporation of minorities into the majority value system stems directly from an assumption that immigrants, by virtue of choosing the new world over the old, were taken to be declaring a desire to adopt a new value system, the details of which they would acquire over time. The very act of immigration was essentially viewed as implying consent to adopting a new way of thinking. The immigrant was understood to be leaving history and shibboleths alike behind. The United States was a state created out of the desires of like-minded individuals, and like-mindedness – or at least an open mind – was the tacit primary requirement expected of immigrants. This in contrast to the true nation-states of Europe, such as Germany and France, where nationalism amounted to group self-expression, and therefore an accident of birth determined belonging. It can be argued that it is this assumed voluntary quality in immigrants – the assumption that they have elected to join the new state – that allows for the development of the assimilation model to describe how a growing group of 'like-minded' individuals interrelates over time. This is precisely because, having elected to belong, in time immigrants should begin to talk and behave and value ideas in the manner of the group writ large that they have elected to join. Their willingness to belong is what encourages the group to accept them and to overlook their initial differences in behaviour, speech, and values.

I would argue, however, that the assimilation model is flawed because its assumptions are misplaced. In the first place, it assumes that immigrants *elected* the new country and everything for which it stood in exchange for attachment to their native lands. They were frequently fleeing famine, poverty, and persecution of one kind or another in Europe. As many an ousted government knows, electing to rid oneself of something is not the same thing as understanding that with which one is replacing it. Most of the new world's immigrants were in fact emigrants who could imagine only that the new world could not be worse than what they were leaving, but they would not have understood the contract that John Quincy Adams was asking them to make.

Second, the model is rooted in a time when the immigrant stock did not differ much from the people who were waiting to absorb it. Northern and western Europeans, as the point has already been made, did not impose too greatly on the tolerance of the *Mayflower*'s descendants. At the time, absorbing them did seem to be a huge cultural stretch, in the same way in which the English reacted with great hostility to the first waves of Irish immigration into England in the mid-nineteenth century. Perception is one thing, but in retrospect the adjustment asked of all groups concerned in the early United States was not a great one, at least relatively speaking. Yet the notion of the possibility and desirability of assimilation did not change even when the immigrant stock began to draw large numbers of people with greater and greater religious, ethnic, and behavioural differences – differences among themselves and from the dominant American mix. By the time the play *Melting Pot* was produced, the myth was already sown, as deep a part of the American psyche as the frontier and religious freedom. It did not matter that neither the play nor the supporters of its central thesis did not, and could not, say what sort of cultural mélange was supposed to emerge from the crucible. In some fuzzy but significant way, the notion of a Blended American fitted perfectly the philosophical history that fed the American Dream, even when it was clearly growing harder to bridge the cultural distances within the confines of the model.

Hence the third erroneous assumption. John Quincy Adams and his intellectual mates did not know what they were asking. They assumed that it was possible to 'cast off the European skin,' that a promise to disavow loyalty to a monarch and learn a new language amounted to leaving one's past behind. And, of course, that did not happen. Immigration is a process of re-creation for the immigrant, as has been discussed. The initial settlers re-created themselves, but the echoes of their homelands reverberated throughout their new lives: their language, culture, religion, and values were a part of that re-creation. For the first waves of immigrants from western and northern Europe, the dominant culture was similar enough that the re-creation was accomplished without too great a disturbance; assimilation, or partial assimilation, could be seen to describe their process of adaptation. But as the immigrant stock began to be drawn increasingly from groups that did not find strong echoes of themselves in Anglo-Saxon culture, religion, or norms, the disparity between who they were and who they were expected to imitate became too great for them to ignore. Moreover, the model was never designed to encompass the incorporation of African Americans, who were seen as being outside the scope of the discussion when the melting-pot notion developed, so from its outset it was doomed to failure as an explanatory tool. Thus, for all the well-explored reasons given in the first part of the chapter, recent history has seen the stubborn refusal of 'ethnicity' to disappear.

My point here is that, certainly after the mid-nineteenth century, it was ridiculous to assume that ethnic differences could, or should, disappear, and the whole notion of assimilation as a way of understanding how diverse ethnic groups interrelate is hopelessly flawed. Yet most studies of group interrelation continue to draw on the model. A recent example of this is *Ethnic Identity and Equality: Varieties of Experience in a Canadian City,* by sociologists Breton et. al.[31] Although they use a different term, 'incorporation' into the larger society, they still seek to measure the extent to which *individual members* of various groups live without differentiation. They are successfully incorporated into society if, each and every one, they live with political, economic, and social equality. That is to say, they must be politically involved, move without difficulty in the labour market, not be residentially segregated, and intermarry with ease into the 'majority' group in order to be incorporated. In other words, successful incorporation assumes ethnic fungibility.

The study, which examined Jews, Germans, Italians, Ukrainians, Chinese, and West Indians, found that groups tended to be differently incorporated in some of these facets of life than in others, that this varied across groups, that sometimes incorporation happened with significant 'ethnic retention' and sometimes without it.[32] The 'majority Canadian' group is defined as English, Irish, or Scottish Canadians whose families have been present for at least three generations.[33] The authors acknowledge that this group is not necessarily numerically the majority and that it is not even the most powerful group in all parts of Canada. They claim that it is the 'historical collectivity that has shaped the political, economic, and socio-cultural institutions of [Toronto], and that, to a significant extent, continues to control them.'[34]

The model runs into difficulty where it includes markers such as residence and marriage choices. As I argue below, whether individuals make the choices that Breton et. al. use as markers of incorporation is irrelevant to whether the ethnic group is integrated into the adoptive society or not.[35] These markers are relevant only so long as the assumptions of the assimilationist model hold, with the assumptions being that there is a dominant group whose ideas and culture are the model of incoming groups and that the goal of the migrant group is to be able to melt into the world of the dominant group without distinction.

That the assimilationist model continues to dominate thinking about integration of immigrants is made as well by Shaheen Azmi in his article 'Canadian Social Service Provision and the Muslim Community in Metropolitan Toronto.'[36] Azmi notes that the less stigmatized term 'acculturation' has replaced 'assimilation,' but that little differentiates the two notions.[37]

The next section of this chapter proposes a way of analysing integration that may prove to be more useful for understanding the adaptation of ethnic groups to new circumstances and to each other. First, however, I want to explain my emphasis on the American experience. That experience has been critical in forming intellectual approaches to notions of migration. In many ways the Canadian and British experiences have been drastically different, yet they have emerged from the same philosophical and intellectual traditions and used the same tools, with variations, to understand the impact of immigrants on their societies. The differences between Canada, Britain, and the United States in terms of the immigration experience are discussed at length below, but it is only in recent years that the American experience has begun to be questioned as an explanatory tool. As is seen below, much of the British discussion of migration is inextricably entwined with the discussion of race relations and racism. It is worthwhile, for a number of reasons that become clear below, to disentangle the debates – the nature of integration, the role of political culture, the meaning of 'multiculturalism,' and the nature of racism – and discuss each issue in turn.

An Alternative Framework of Cultural Integration

When one wants to understand what happens to immigrant groups as they become a part of a new society, whether their 'ethnicity' melts away or is retained, and how they re-imagine themselves, it is not enough to look at the groups themselves. One must also consider 'the dominant' or 'majority' group, or, as Bhikhu Parekh prefers to call it, the 'wider society' in the midst of which migrants have arrived. A cursory look at the evidence confirms that the 'dominant group' in either the United States or Canada (to use these long-standing immigrant-receiving societies as examples) in the mid-1990s is nothing like the dominant group in either of those countries a century earlier.[38] In the time of Washington or Jefferson, the dominant group in the United States was freshly and incontrovertibly Anglo-Saxon. That was true into the twentieth century in Canada as well, with the obvious and notable exception of Quebec, whose initial colonial group was otherwise. But as wave after wave of immigration, from northern and western Europe, then from eastern and southern Europe, and finally and in greater and greater numbers, from non-European countries, brought in thousands upon thousands of new immigrants, it was less and less true. Political institutions, basic rules of law and social custom, and early mythologies were set by the predominantly British founding colonial peoples, it is true. But how those institutions have been used and interpreted and changed is a product of the people using and interpreting them.

Although it is fair to say that the 'dominant' group, in both the United States and Canada, is still made up of white Europeans, it is not true to say, Breton et. al. notwithstanding, that it is made up of white Protestants whose ancestors departed from England, Ireland, or Scotland. The United States took a Catholic for a president in the early 1960s and lionized him after his untimely death. Canadians did not think to blink at the appointment of Raymond Hnatyshn – whose ancestry was clearly not British[39] – as governor general, a post in which they invest much of their ancillary loyalism, regardless of the fact that many were not sure how to pronounce, let alone spell, his name. Canadians, who have been dividing the time in their top political office between French Catholics and English Protestants ever since Confederation, have long stopped inquiring into the religious beliefs of Supreme Court judges, ministers of the crown, provincial premiers, and powerful Ottawa bureaucrats. This mélange of people has created a constitution – in recent years – that has fundamentally altered how the law is made and interpreted at national, provincial, and local levels, in schools, workplaces, and hospitals. Washington, Ottawa, Toronto, and New York could no longer be realistically said to be dominated by Anglo-Saxon Protestants or their assimilated ideas. They are still dominated by white Europeans, but not by the people who were the majority, dominant stock in the early days of self-government in the new world. This point is made as well by Jeff Spinner when he notes that 'as the different cultural practices of ethnics are accepted in the liberal state, the dominant culture will often be reinterpreted as it incorporates different practices.'[40]

The point here is a simple but powerful one. The majority, the dominant group, the power 'centre' of a population, in the sense used by Breton et. al., is as altered over time by its immigrants as are the immigrants by their new society. The 'centre' of American, Canadian, or even British society is not today what it was a century ago, and just as this is so, so it will be yet different another half-century from now. Increasingly so, since the influences on which it draws stand in growing contrast to the homogeneity of the first settlers or the English (who themselves are an amalgamation of earlier peoples).

The process cannot be described as assimilation, since the immigrants do not passively take on the culture, norms, and behaviour of the dominant group. Nor in fact is one new people forged from the cultures of many, as in the mythical cauldron of the melting pot. What happens, it seems, is rather that ethnic groups weave – individually and collectively – their various cultures with the 'centre' of the adoptive society, in an ongoing process of cultural give and take. The real issue is the population 'centre.' The 'centre,' which is the perception of societal beliefs on which elites draw when making laws or forming public policy, however, is a coalescence at any one time of the collective imaginations of the ethnic groups that make up the whole. That coalescence clearly changes over time and is a complex combination of culture, behaviour, and norms. Moreover, it is almost impossible to define, since individuals will see different things reflected in it. It could be argued, for instance, that the dominant anglophone Canadian 'centre' in the mid-1990s is predominantly Judaeo-Christian and European, but with an expanding non-European, non-white, non–Judaeo-Christian undertone, advancing inward from the edges and demanding a central place for itself. It is my contention that that non-European, non-white, non–Judaeo-Christian undertone will gradually and increasingly become a part of the centre, never displacing the culture that first created it perhaps, but creating louder and more vibrant echoes of variations on cultural and normative themes.

What happens over time is that cultures become *integrated*. As Bernard described it in 1956, integration implies that 'each element has been changed by association with the other,'[41] which seems to be a far more realistic assessment of the process that unfolds, however gradually. Milton Gordon's contention was that the Anglo-Saxon centre of the United States had not been perceptibly altered by the enfolding of its immigrants. This, however, is demonstrably untrue, and over time the influence of non-Europeans, in addition to that of non–Anglo-Saxons, will become increasingly obvious.

But if the 'centre' is so changeable and ephemeral as to be difficult to describe at any one point, how is one to know whether a group has been integrated? If keeping one's ethnicity intact is not a sign of a failure to integrate, what is it? What are the criteria for integration?

Integration, as we saw above, occurs on two levels, external and internal. One could describe a group as being externally integrated when its members can move laterally and vertically within economic, political, and social spheres without their ethnicity being an issue and when institutions are responsive to a group's cultural and religious behaviour and norms. These are measures of institutional receptivity (in public culture and within civil society) to ethnic difference. The former consideration entails the immigrant's ability to be a full member of any part of society (become a banker, member of Parliament, doctor, engineer, or factory worker), with ethnicity being neither a negative nor a positive attribute, but rather a 'non-issue' in respect of position and advancement. The latter consideration refers to how religious requirements and cultural habits are accommodated by a society's institutions; for example, whether prayer, dress, dietary, and burial requirements are respected by schools, workplaces, social halls, hospitals, and burial grounds. Acceptance must occur in the public domain, including civil society – for Jeff Spinner, the network of formal and informal non-governmental institutions that serve the public, including the media, businesses, and community associations.[42]

A key distinction of this understanding of integration is that the personal and professional choices of individuals are irrelevant to the consideration of how the group has integrated with the larger society. External integration depends on the ability of group members to function in society without their ethnicity being a factor, but the choices of individual members of the group are irrelevant. Therefore the choice of group members to retain or discard their ethnicity has no bearing on whether the group is externally integrated or not.

The individual corollary, internal integration, is the process of weaving birth and adopted cultures that immigrants begin from the moment they set foot in their adopted lands. Children of immigrants continue the process, weaving the culture of home with the culture of school. 'Cultural weaving' refers to a process of layering the experience and meaning of immigrants' birth and adopted cultures together to create a meaningful whole. It involves a redefinition of various aspects of birth culture in the context of the adopted culture. It is not, as chapter 7 illuminates in greater detail, a process that involves replacing one culture with another, but one in which various elements of each combine together. This process will differ from individual to individual. It is affected by externalities, such as the degree of external integration of the ethnic group concerned, the political culture of the adoptive society, and the prevalence of racism in its various manifestations. However, as is shown below, while the quality of integration is thus affected, it is a process that occurs regardless of the degree of external ethnic-group integration.

Conversely, and because the concepts can be separated, it becomes possible to speak of a group's being integrated even when individuals from the group choose to emphasize their ethnic differences and isolate themselves from the wider culture. Integration does not require that the whole society and each of its constituent individuals behave in similar or predictable ways. Some immigrants may choose to emphasize whatever they perceive as the dominant culture; some may choose to intermarry; some may emphasize the distinctiveness of their ethnic customs as much as possible, by marrying someone of the same ethnicity and raising their children in as insulated a manner as possible from the cultural mélange around them; some may choose to live in neighbourhoods inhabited predominantly by members of their own particular ethnic group but to socialize outside their own groups. Similarly, individuals who see themselves as part of a dominant group may well behave in ways that are more or less tolerant of ethnic difference. If a hospital's policies are such that the needs of Muslim or Jewish dietary laws are respected, it does not matter whether the chief cardiologist marries outside his or her ethnic group. Many studies, such as Breton et. al., try to measure 'incorporation' by using indices of intermarriage or residential segregation. These are irrelevant, because they are not reflective of whether societal institutions are responsive to ethnic difference; they reflect individual choice more than they do group placement in society.

Of course, individuals do integrate into their new societies, but such integration is affected by a wealth of psychosocial factors that differ from those affecting the group. The integration of individuals will be affected, but not solely determined, by the integration achieved by the ethnic group of which they are a part. A group that moves easily in political and economic spheres but tends to be residentially segregated and tends not to intermarry (for example, Jews in Toronto) might rank fairly low on a Breton et. al. incorporation scale but higher on an integration scale where the only indices are institutional receptivity to ethnicity.

As Yasemin Nuhoglu Soysal remarks, most studies concerning the absorption of immigrants into Western liberal democracies examine, with Breton, how well immigrants adjust to the existing adoptive society.[43] Her investigation of the incorporation of migrants into western Europe, in contrast, takes a macro-level approach, emphasizing the difference in absorption made by various incorporation regimes in the different countries and the varieties of institutions – or lack of them – established in each. She argues that as internationally accepted codes of human rights and transnational concepts such as the rights of personhood gain acceptance, many rights that were reserved for citizens are now de facto granted to all residents of a nation, regardless of legal status. These factors have resulted in a variety of approaches to incorporating non-citizens into the polities of western Europe.[44]

The value of Soysal's study lies in its recognition that the relationship of migrant to nation is significantly more complex than the question of how individuals adapt to existing host cultures and institutions. The orientation of the nation-state, whether in its institutions or its political culture, is equally critical. The key is in appreciating that integration occurs at two levels and in understanding what factors are at play in both.

The Role of Political Culture

Political culture is that portion of a society's culture that determines how its political system (the state apparatus and its procedures) actually work in its own context. In other words, Canada and Britain both operate constitutional monarchies with parliamentary systems of government, but how power is shared and expressed in the two countries differs considerably, largely because of their dissimilar political cultures. Reasons for this can be traced historically in each country. That aspect of political culture that relates to the role of minorities within the political system is relevant and important, and here there are strong distinctions to be drawn.

Political culture, defined by Gabriel Almond as the 'pattern of individual attitudes and orientations towards politics,'[45] and modified by Lucian Pye as the set of 'attitudes, beliefs, and sentiments' that inform the political process and provide its underlying assumptions,[46] is upheld by a vigorous literature as a critical determinant of why political conditions differ from society to society.[47] It is cited particularly as an explanatory factor in why nations develop as they do.[48] Samuel Huntington, for instance, wrote that 'a primary place must be accorded the comparative analysis of culture' if differences in development in various developing countries are to be understood.[49]

Pye characterized political culture as 'the product of both the collective history of a political system and the life histories of the members of that system, and thus ... rooted equally in public events and private experiences.'[50] There are two implications to be drawn from this statement. First, the creation of political culture is an ongoing exercise, developing with the history of a nation or other political community. Second, if it is the life histories and private experiences of individuals that contribute so directly to their understanding of what the political system is and what to make of it, one must take into account what Clifford Geertz calls the 'givens' of social existence. These include religion, language, social relationships, and customs, all of which help to make up (to a greater or lesser degree, depending on circumstance) a sense of self and relation to others.[51]

The significance of these factors arises when one considers, as Sidney Verba has argued, that the most crucial problem of the formation of a political culture is the creation of a national identity; that societal change causes a need for a redefinition of that identity; and that identity problems can arise if some members of a cultural system are not accepted as fully participating members by the dominant culture bearers.[52] In the absence of a strong identity, he continues, nations are likely to engage in identity-creating acts – aggressions against other nations or other expressions of nationalism.[53] These considerations are helpful in analysing the relative position of immigrants in different Western liberal democracies.

It is the contention of this study that the key role of political culture in the integration of immigrants and minorities is its determination of the level of respect – or legitimacy – they are accorded in the host country. The literature on political culture is largely silent on this question, in that the link between respect, integration, and political culture has not been explored.[54] While there are a number of ways of understanding the acceptance and legitimacy of minorities within a society, one that has received a good deal of attention is multiculturalism. The word is used variously as an ideal to be worked towards, as a descriptive term, as government policy, and as short hand for a series of attitudes. As it concerns the recognition of minorities within a liberal democracy, it is the one on which I focus.

The Different Meanings of 'Multiculturalism'

In the first place, it is worth comparing various uses of the word 'multiculturalism,' a much-abused term that means different things to different commentators in various countries. In the United States, it is often taken as short hand for a view that women and minorities have been poorly served by the prevailing power elite and its reading of culture and history; that this condition should be redressed by policies of preferential treatment for previously under-represented groups; and that it requires realigning the canon of received wisdom customarily taught in liberal arts colleges, the Great Works of history and literature, written primarily by Dead White European Men.[55] The view rests on the assumption that a lack of representation, both institutionally by living human beings and on the written page in history and myth, results in a demeaned sense of self-worth for the groups who are so under-represented. It has been the subject of much controversy and sometimes thoughtful criticism, by such varied authors as the philosopher Charles Taylor and, writing more popularly, *New York Times* reporter Richard Bernstein.[56]

In Canada, multiculturalism has a dual meaning, very different from that in the United States. First and foremost, as Multiculturalism (capitalized), it is a government policy, invented by Pierre Trudeau and his Liberal government of 1971 but updated to take account of the Canadian Charter of Rights. In its most recent, 1988 version, Canada's Multiculturalism Act declares that it is 'the policy of the Government of Canada to:

> (a) recognize and promote the understanding that multiculturalism reflects the cultural and racial diversity of Canadian society and acknowledges the freedom of all members of Canadian society to preserve, enhance and share their cultural heritage;
> (b) recognize and promote the understanding that multiculturalism is a fundamental characteristic of the Canadian heritage and identity and that it provides an invaluable resource in the shaping of Canada's future;
> (c) promote the full and equitable participation of individuals and communities of all origins in the continuing evolution and shaping of all aspects of Canadian society and assist them in the elimination of any barrier to such participation.[57]

The act continues at some length in this vein. In paragraphs on its implementation, it declares that the minister shall 'encourage and assist' organizations and individuals to project the image of a multicultural Canada abroad. It does not define 'multicultural,' and although it pledges to ensure 'full participation in Canadian society, including the social and economic aspects, of individuals of all origins and their communities,' it does not explain what this means in practice. Multiculturalism as a policy has generated a significant amount of controversy, from critical academics (political scientist David Bell, sociologist Reginald Bibby) and literary authors (Neil Bissoondath) alike; a most persuasive philosophical argument in its favour is mounted by Will Kymlicka.[58] The arguments of the critics concur: Multiculturalism as a government policy tends to encourage separateness and division. Bissoondath, an immigrant from the West Indies, declares that he does not want to be a hyphenated Canadian, nor does he want to raise his daughter as one, but that Multiculturalism expects that this will be his role (both assigned and desired) in the Canadian polity. David Bell's concern is that Multiculturalism does nothing to unite a nation already struggling with a lack of clear self-definition, with strong regional, linguistic, and cultural differences. For Bell, this is of particular concern at a time when Canada faces such a clear and continuing challenge from the one part of itself that is able to articulate a strong sense of nationhood.

The issues raised by multiculturalism in terms of its being a defining characteristic of the Canadian political entity are separate from, though related to, the issues that are raised by Quebec nationalism and the possibility of accommodating it within Canadian federalism. Both deal with ethnicity and nationalism and how these are recognized within a political system, but Quebec and the rest of Canada (sometimes termed the ROC) deal with questions of ethnicity in vastly different ways, precisely because there are different elements at work in each. Similarly, a discussion of ethnicity in the United States is a different, though related discussion from one of race relations between African Americans and their white counterparts. Although in all four cases one is dealing most broadly with the place of peoples of different cultural and historical heritages within their national polities, the historical relationship between two colonial peoples (French and English) or two pioneering races (African American[59] and White) denotes a contrasting set of dance-steps from the one that involves the place of ethnic groups of more recent arrival.

Multiculturalism in Britain is a descriptive term that is significant in its newness. It is used, as by the Prince of Wales in a speech at Oxford,[60] to describe a changed population and nation, rather than an attitude or a policy per se. It is not the only term used to describe a multi-ethnic Britain. It is not necessarily the term that thinkers on the subject would like to espouse. Bhikhu Parekh, for instance, would prefer to refer to Britain as a multi-communal, or plural society.[61] Although primarily descriptive, the term evokes the mixed reactions with which Britons have watched immigration transform – or at least deeply affect – their society. These reactions are discussed in detail in chapter 6. Multiculturalism in Britain frequently refers to the kinds of policies or programs intended to address the needs of a plural society. These have been the subject of significant controversy as well, in large part because they frequently are articulated in terms of recognizing various ethnic communities, as though these communities were static, unchanging, and separate entities.[62] This is a different notion entirely from granting respect and legitimacy to members of immigrant and minority groups as fully participating members of a polity.

In the meantime, a discussion of multiculturalism in Britain is difficult to separate from one about racism, in large part because, as the point is made below, Britain has found itself confronting the two issues simultaneously. British literature on immigration has found itself concurrently confronting the question of racism, and therefore it is worth looking at that discussion.

The Concept of Racism and the Place of Minorities

It is useful at this juncture to examine the concept of racism and how it relates to the discussion of minorities. The literature on the subject is vast, in part because so many factors impinge on it: the meaning of 'race;' differences between 'race,' ethnicity, and nationalism; the legacy of colonialism; the role of capitalism and Marxist analysis; differences between 'racism' and 'race relations;' differences between concerns over immigration-sparked racism and home-grown racialization; the particular history of racism in Britain and continental Europe; and, significantly, how to account for racism that is not directed against the physically distinct.[63] While this is not the place to recapitulate the details of the ongoing debate, a number of key issues are worth noting.

For Britons, the questions of race relations and ethnicity became fused, a conceptual approach that has subsequently been questioned. This happened partly because significant numbers of post–Second World War immigrants were visibly distinct from the majority of the British population. The United Kingdom began to have to come to terms simultaneously with both the place of large numbers of ethnic immigrants within its society and the particularly significant numbers of non-white Britons among its population. The sociologist John Rex, for instance, has tended to frame the problems of immigrant absorption in terms of the institutional racism that confronts former colonials in Britain's rigid class system. The country's problem of race relations and immigration is at its root a class problem: immigrants get slotted in at the bottom end, their plight compounded by lingering colonialist attitudes towards non-whites. Some even become, to borrow from the Americans, an 'underclass.' For Rex, the British version of the underclass is the group of (non-white) immigrants not entitled to the full benefits of the welfare state.[64] Race and ethnicity are but different sides of the same coin, attributes painted by Britons to describe newcomers, Others, to their society.

Recognition that difference in culture or religion or ethnicity is not always accompanied by difference in colour, or that significant factors affecting integration may have more to do with ethnicity than with colour, have taken time to surface in public and academic discussions.[65] This was partly the result of the broadly made assumption that the large numbers of immigrants could be completely assimilated culturally, so that all that would distinguish them from other Britons was their colour.[66] The theoretical framework to which Britons first looked to understand their issues with immigrants was an American-derived one centring on race relations.[67] While it is understandable that British theorists would look to the United States, which has been dealing with race issues for over two centuries, to fathom what is, at least on a grand scale, a relatively new problem for Britain, it is also not surprising that this approach proved unsatisfying.

Race relations in the United States are not about immigrants. Whatever the difficulties with entrenched and institutional racism, with inner-city cycles of poverty and underclasses, with successful, wealthy black Americans for whom colour-racism remains a factor in their lives, there is never a question of whether African Americans are American. Their identity as Americans is not the issue, whereas the identity of black Britons, even those who are not recent immigrants, is very much the issue in Britain.[68]

Ruth Benedict, writing in 1943, defined racism as 'the dogma that one ethnic group is condemned by nature to congenital inferiority and another group is destined to congenital superiority.'[69] Racism has by and large continued to be described as a phenomenon related primarily to physical distinctions between groups of people.[70]

But the tenor of many of the most notable examples of official or public incidents of racism in recent British history has been based not on colour but rather on culture. Consider, for example, Margaret Thatcher's radio interview in 1978, in which she advocated limits on immigration in order to avoid Britons being 'swamped' by an alien culture.[71] Conservative politician Norman Tebbit's 'cricket test' remarks in 1990 questioned the loyalty and identity of immigrants to Britain. He accused them of not supporting Britain in games against their former countrymen and talked of the threat of 'the waves of newcomers intent on importing their nationality to our nation.'[72] Lord Tebbit renewed the debate in 1997, when he told a television interviewer that 'we must see if we can find a way in which Muslims can be truly British ... If one is living in a Christian country, it is Christian law that overrides [respect for Muslim law and tradition].'[73]

The *Satanic Verses* controversy itself depicts the colour–culture schism. John Patten, then minister of state at the Home Office, linked the two concepts in declaring that 'the issue of race relations has been thrown into sharp relief and all of us have had to think deeply about our objectives and priorities; about what it means to be British, and particularly what it means to be a British Muslim.'[74] He was not alone in making this linkage.[75] Yet, as Solomos and Miles both point out, many Britons of colour were reluctant to take sides in the Rushdie affair on racial grounds, because the issues at stake, as they saw them, were culturally but not racially based.[76] Tariq Modood has argued that 'colour, class and culture are ... three distinct dimensions of race' and must be taken into account separately when one is interpreting discrimination – culture no less than the other two.[77] Notions that reduce racial discrimination to colour discrimination fail 'to keep up with the socio-cultural developments that are taking place,' because much of the discrimination that Muslims face in Britain has as much to do with their culture or religion as it has to do with their colour.[78]

Then there is the question of anti-semitism. In spite of twentieth-century European history, which resulted for a time in an understanding, common in Europe in mid-century, that Judaism is 'hereditary' and 'ineradicable' and that therefore a Jewish 'race' exists and can be identified,[79] the term itself is misleading. Semites are Arabs as well as Jews, but anti-semitism is a phenomenon that does not single out Semites for derogation, but rather Jews, and it is properly understood as a cultural, rather than a racial phenomenon. As Philip Cohen points out, anti-semitism and colour prejudice are 'distinctive modalities of racism, with their own histories and structures of meaning.'[80]

A number of writers, commenting on the recent ethnic warfare in Yugoslavia and the European responses to it, have noted that old conceptions of racism, and explanations for it, are not able to describe these 'new racisms.' They argue that the creation of 'Fortress Europe' involves the promotion of culture that is white and Judaeo-Christian and that alien cultures (such as Islam) and non-whites are made unwelcome.[81] Ali Mazrui, pointing at the incongruities involved in, on the one hand, the West's firm response to Iraqi aggression ('This will not stand!'[82]) and, on the other, its willingness to see Bosnian Muslims decimated while it dithered over how to respond, wonders whether we are witnessing the birth of global apartheid, on both a colour basis and a cultural basis that includes religion.[83] 'Religion has been the fundamental divisive factor between Westerners and people of Muslim culture everywhere.'[84]

In the light of these considerations, a conception of racism that allows for cultural (or religious) racism as well as physically based racism would appear to be useful, even if the two phenomena frequently overlap. Peter Jackson's definition, which does not require a reference to physical traits, is a useful one. For him, racism 'involves the attempt by a dominant group to exclude a subordinate group from the material and symbolic rewards of status and power,' based on distinctions that need not be physical but which 'can rest on the recognition of certain "cultural" traits where these are thought to be an inherent and inviolable characteristic of particular social groups.'[85] Robert Miles's conception acknowledges that there exists frequently, but not necessarily, a physical or biological element to racism: 'Racism constructs (real or imagined) difference as natural not only in order to exclude, but additionally, in order to marginalise a social collectivity within a particular constellation of relations of domination. All racisms are instances of the ideological *marginalisation*, within a social collectivity which is thought to reproduce itself through time and space, and which has been signified as naturally different, usually (but not exclusively), by reference to real or alleged biological characteristics.'[86]

In the words of Tariq Modood, 'membership of a minority community can render one less employable on the grounds of one's dress, dietary habits, or desire to take leave from work on one's holy days.' This sort of cultural racism 'uses cultural difference to vilify or marginalise or demand cultural assimilation.'[87]

The question of how immigrant Muslims are perceived by Westerners, whether Britons or Canadians, is clearly a complex one that involves their status as members of an ethnic community, as Muslims *qua* Muslims, as immigrants, as members of a certain socio-economic class, and so forth, depending on circumstance. I consider the issue of racism below in chapter 6 and again in chapter 7. The important theoretical points are as follows. First, racism is a complex phenomenon, whose various aspects become apparent as circumstances vary. Second, an analysis of how Britain's political culture has dealt with immigrants and minorities must attempt to disentangle the various issues of integration, respect and legitimacy, and colour versus cultural racism.

Some Thoughts on the Integration of Somali Muslims into the West

Each group that immigrates will bring with it specific characteristics that will affect how it integrates with the 'host' society. These characteristics include not only the 'building blocks of ethnicity' themselves, as Manning Nash named them,[88] but how these relate to the 'centre' of the adoptive society. In other words, unilingual German immigrants to Canada will find that, particular customs aside, language is the primary hurdle that they must overcome in order to fit into an already well-integrated Canadian society (to the point of not being distinguishable from Anglo-Saxon three-generation ethnics). Russian Jews immigrating to Canada will find that they must contend with language difficulties, significant differences in their understanding of how the economics of a society function, and possible anti-semitism. None the less, they will not find themselves significantly far from the 'centre.'

In contrast, West Indian Christian immigrants to Canada or Britain might find that, although they do not have to learn a new language and do share the dominant religion, the fact of not being white puts them outside the 'centre' in a different way and is a factor in their integration.

Somali immigrants to Canada and Britain have found their integration affected by a complex set of variables. Included in this extensive list are colour, language, their status as refugees, inter-clan tensions and the persistence of homeland politics, the political culture of the host country, and the nature of existing host country institutions. All these factors needed to be circumnavigated as Somalis faced their most significant challenge – renegotiating identity as Muslims in a predominantly secular, Judaeo-Christian Western liberal democracy.

It is the purpose of this study and its in-depth interviews to examine the facets of these factors as they impinge on Muslim Somali migrants. Its central concerns are to determine whether and how Somalis are accommodating themselves to a Western adoptive society without losing what they see as essential to their identity, while simultaneously understanding the impact of what it was they were coming to – the political culture and incorporation regimes of Canada and Britain. All the study's respondents were born in Somalia; most migrated within the decade. It is clear that the answers that respondents gave in 1995 would probably not be the same ones that they would give five years later, since perceptions and experiences change over time. Yet the Somali migration represents a unique opportunity to examine the anatomy of identity in transition and, as such, the mechanism of integration.

As the discussion of chapters 6 and 7 reveals, a significant body of Western writing holds that Islam is essentially incompatible with the West and that Muslims in the West can only integrate – or be incorporated into Western liberal democracies – by forsaking certain elements of Islam. This is an idea that has gained currency in the years since the demise of the Soviet–American antagonism, perhaps because there are people determined to construct history around conflict and to believe that neither conflict nor history are, after all, at an end. Nevertheless, the notion is countered by an equally significant, and growing body of writing that asserts quite the opposite – that Islam cannot be described by reference to 'essential' characteristics and that it is capable of fostering growth in any number of directions. Similarly, this school of thought holds that Muslims do not need to reject their understandings of Islam in order to live in the West. The following pages explore these questions from the perspective of Somalis.

3

Islam in London and Toronto

Most Somalis are not Islamists, and their observance of Islam in Somalia varied widely, but moving to a largely secular Judaeo-Christian–based liberal democracy deprived them of their ability to take their identity for granted. If they had not done so before, they now had to examine what it was to be Muslim, how important their religion was to them, and how much inconvenience they were prepared to endure in order to practise it. The first two sections of this chapter illustrate how informants – adult men and adult women, respectively – answered questions on their practice of Islam in London or Toronto, and how this may differ from how they practised it in Somalia. A third section outlines the work of organizations that try to help immigrants resolve their problems 'in an Islamic manner.' These bodies, concerned about Somalis' ability to continue to practise Islam in the diaspora, are composed of Islamists and others who believe that they have a role to play in directing the religious affairs of their fellow Somali immigrants. Interviews with representatives of these organizations are interesting in themselves because they offer a sense of the different approaches and orientations within the Somali community to life in the company of non-Muslims. The fourth section offers commentary and analysis.

Because the teenagers are viewed within the community as being such a vulnerable group, their answers appear separately, in chapter 4.

Where individuals were speaking about their own lives, and in keeping with their requests, I have altered names and identifying details. Where respondents are quoted in their own words, I have edited out the small grammatical errors of new English speakers. I have not included the answers of each and every respondent, because of limited space, but I have tried to paint a full picture of the range of responses, their tone, and their complexity. I present the responses as a series of vignettes. I quote representatives of organizations under their real names, as they were speaking officially, and not about their personal lives.

Adult Men

Ismail is thirty-four and had been in Canada for ten years, during which time he has worked as an interpreter for the Refugee Board and been active in developing Somali resettlement associations. In the spring of 1995 he was completing a university degree. He had not considered himself to be a religious person when he arrived in Canada. He had been trained as an engineer in Italy and had been forced to flee Somalia after numerous detentions for publicly criticizing the government. 'Materialism in Canada ushered me back to my origins. When I first arrived, I had a temporary respect for the glitter of materialism, but gradually I came to see it as empty.'[1]

Ismail now considers himself a very religious man, who defines himself first as a Muslim, then as a Somali. He will leave a room in the middle of a lecture if need be when it is time to pray and do so in the hall. He attends not only Friday prayers at the mosque, but Somali 'study circles,' which take place regularly at a number of Toronto mosques. Ismail is bearded in the manner of the Islamists, and one of the organizations in which he is active, the Somali Islamic Society of Canada (SISCA), is commonly described as al-Ittihad's[2] organization in Toronto. He will not shake hands with women or socialize with them: 'I will help someone in class or answer a question, or talk in a group of men and women only if the subject is directly related to the academic field. I will not go to a restaurant or get together with women for "fun" ... When there is a need, there is a need; and when there is not, there is not.'[3]

Yusuf is an Islamist who does not consider himself a member of a particular movement, although he says that his sympathies lie with al-Islah and its methods. He is a community worker in his thirties, and his thinking about religion has also evolved over time, since his immigration to Canada in the late 1980s.

I was brought up in a very religious family, but I was a student during the Marxist regime of Siad Barre. I was the leader of the Somali Student Union in Mogadishu. I was taught Marxist theory at fourteen; it made sense at the time ... Over time I became disillusioned. I took the part of some students who were expelled from high school for disagreeing with the government. My actions were not appreciated ... so I left Somalia for Saudi Arabia with a forged passport and $100. I was sixteen.

I wanted to know more about Islam so I taught myself Arabic and went to school. I studied computers. In time I became disillusioned with the Arab nations. They have some of the worst brutal regimes; there is no human freedom. Islam is implemented in a narrow way ... There are many injustices there. Many people suffer in the name of God. That version of Islam is not serving the people. At that time I had no power to conclude that it was that particular version of Islam that was wrong, but the religion – Islam – is right. I began reading about widely different faiths, Judaism and Christianity and others. There was a gradual evolution in my mind. I began to read more Islamists. I read the understanding of Islam by Mawdudi [*Tafhim al-Qur'an*, Understanding the Qur'an] and the five volumes of Sayyid Qutb [*Fi Zilal al-Qur'an*, In the Shade of the Qur'an].

Now I practise a lot in the way I was taught in my childhood. The things I do are the same as the things my father did, but my reasons are different from those of my father. For instance, my father prayed five times a day because those were the instructions of God. For me, praying five times a day is a reminder of the self-discipline I must practise every day to be a good person and a good Muslim. I cannot pray and still lie or hurt other people. It makes me a kind human being ... I am convinced of the existence of God but I have no blind obedience to any authority or the translation of any group.[4]

Yusuf is married and has two small children. His wife considers herself an observant Muslim but she does not cover unless she is praying. 'This is a big source of friction for us right now,' he said.[5]

Ali is a young man of twenty-four who is a mathematics and engineering student and self-confessed internet surfer in London. He dresses in the manner of the Islamists, in loose pants rolled above the ankle, and describes himself as *asaasi* – 'a good sense of fundamentalist.' He attends the Finsbury Park mosque on Fridays, where the sermon is in Arabic (at some mosques it is in Urdu), but on Sundays he will go to the East London Mosque (also called the Whitechapel mosque) to hear the Somali sermon. Al-Ittihad's adherents congregate there – between three and four hundred on an average Sunday. He remembers being attracted to the Islamists in Mogadishu in the mid-

1980s and took up their ways, including a refusal to socialize with women or shake their hands. He says that in spite of this, he did not really know a lot about Islam until he left Somalia for Egypt in 1988. His practice of religion has not changed in London, but he confesses that it is not easy. He is constantly having to explain to women why he will not shake their hands.

> The hand-shaking is actually a big thing, because it is a test to many peo-
> ple, something that keeps coming back. It is even harder to explain to
> Somali women who are not in the hijab or *jelaabib* [plural of jilbab] than it
> is to explain to foreign women.
>   But also it's hard because I live with friends. I have one friend who
> spent fifteen years in Italy. He knows very little about Islam. He doesn't
> pray; he goes to nightclubs; I think he drinks but he doesn't talk about
> that. In Somalia it's a really bad thing to drink. I have other friends who
> have girlfriends and so on. It's one thing if people do those things some-
> where else but when they're right there it's difficult. Of course you would
> like to do those things too. I haven't been to nightclubs or been with ...
> had a girlfriend since I left Somalia. Sometimes it feels like you're the only
> person in the world not doing those things.[6]

Ahmed, an Islamist in his early thirties, lives in Toronto with his wife and pre-school son. He has held a series of jobs since arriving in 1986, including that of an apartment building watchman, a steel-fac-tory worker, and an office clerk. In each organization, Ahmed's prime concern was being able to attend Friday prayers at a mosque, which would require an absence of one to two hours, depending on the job site's proximity to a mosque. Although he would state at the interview that he did not expect to be paid for this time, he would not accept the job if he was told that he could not take the leave. If management changed and permission to leave was revoked, he would quit. Thus he was forced to decline a well-paying full-time job at City Hall when the boss would not agree to his request, although he had been valued as a part-time employee.

For Ahmed and Islamists like him, the issue of hand-shaking has also been irksome. He recounted how he and a friend had applied for a delivery job. The woman in charge of hiring told them they had won the job and stuck out her hand to congratulate them. The men responded by apologizing and saying that as Muslims they do not shake hands with women. 'She went immediately red in the face and tore up the job offer, saying if we couldn't shake her hand, we couldn't work for her.'[7] For Ahmed, self-imposed isolation from the influences of the secular Western world, to the extent possible, is the best way to live as a Muslim.

Abdulle, an Islamist and former high school teacher in his mid-forties who speaks four languages and was educated in Saudi Arabia, waits in London to be able to return to Somalia. He remembers being a high school student in the early 1970s and the public reaction to Siad Barre's style of government and his brand of scientific socialism. 'People were shocked. They went to the mosque as a reaction against it. Even colonialism never caused this kind of reaction.'[8] He has not found it difficult to 'fulfil my Islamic duty' in London, but he was denied a teaching job at a mosque there because, he says, it was controlled by al-Ittihad, and he did not have its approval.

Abdullahi and Nur are typical of men who have been influenced by the Islamists but do not belong to any of the movements because they see them as factional. Both are in their mid-thirties and describe themselves as religious. Abdullahi, the London representative of a number of Somali businesses, studied in Saudi Arabia before settling in north London in 1989. 'My knowledge increased in Saudi Arabia but my belief in God and my practice has always been there.'[9] This practice includes careful adherence to the five pillars and a conviction that 'generally, Sufism is superstition. It is not real Islam. Me, personally, I believe in the holy Qur'an and the *hadiths*, and nothing else.'

For both Abdullahi and Nur, London is not a difficult place in which to practise Islam, but the secret of success lies in the cohesiveness of the Somali community. Like Ahmed, they try to have little to do with the wider society around them. Nur said, 'There is a large Muslim community here, so you can stick with them. I used to live in Edinburgh. A group of Somalis at the university started practising together. The companionship and strength make you stronger. You can't crack this society's ways of practice. If you make yourself isolated, it can be good if you are a group and good if you have children. If you try to assimilate your kids will pick up bad things.'

On the subject of men who chew qat and do not practise Islam, Nur said, 'They will return one day [to their religion]. Every one has something that burns in him. Even if you do not practise, you know you are a creation of God. If you betray Him, your time is numbered. You will get more religious as you get weaker, and you will warn others not to follow. You will realize that only your deeds follow you after you die and that you must be good. Then you will go on the hajj.'

Hassan is a twenty-two-year-old biology student in Toronto. His parents sent him out of Qismayo, where his father was a civil servant, in 1988. He has been living with his brother since then and does not know whether his parents are alive. He says he has always been an observant Muslim and still is. He will not interrupt his classes to pray but goes to the *masjid* (the campus prayer building) after class on Fridays. If he has no classes he attends the *salat jama'a*, the collective noon prayer. He eats halal meat if he can or kosher food as a second choice. He will eat at Kentucky Fried Chicken or Burger King, but not at McDonald's, where he believes lard is used to cook the french fries. Practising Islam in Toronto is not difficult, he says, except during Ramadan, when the smell of food is everywhere. 'The only time it really bothers me to be a Muslim in a non-Muslim country is during Ramadan. Everybody is eating. It's really hard. That's the only time I'd like to go to another country for a month, and then come back.'[10]

Rashid has been in Canada since the early 1980s. A man in his forties, he works with a Toronto-area school board, solving intercultural problems between the Somali student body, their parents, and the larger community. He is from Mogadishu and a member of Reer Hamar. His family hailed originally from Yemen. He says that his father was a member of a Sufi tariqa but that he and his contemporaries never have been. On practising Islam in Toronto, he said:

I think Islam is not a strict and rigid religion. It is flexible and you can perform your obligations in any circumstances or environment so long as you understand and do your best to match the obligations with time and space – your specific circumstances. Prayers, for example. The noon prayer and the afternoon prayer fall during work time, but you can handle that such that you can do both without conflict, by doing your prayer during lunch time or dealing with your supervisor to establish that your prayer will be done during your break. You need time just to go to the washroom. You don't need the mosque. The exception, and it is difficult, is the Friday prayer, because one element of it is the congregational meeting, a chance to meet with each other and have a forum for the exchange of views. Many of us in the community have difficulties to have that privilege.

Another element is food. Even things like toothpaste. I heard that there is something like lard in there. I don't know, but the point is that you have the suspicion and it's not easy to resolve. You have to question everything. Where the preoccupation of most Canadians is fat content and cholesterol, the preoccupation of ours is to see whether the ingredients include something forbidden.[11]

Elmi was a major in Siad Barre's army and had gone to Britain on a military scholarship. He found himself stranded in London when Barre was ousted. His wife is still in Somalia; his children are in Nairobi. As a single man he is on the lowest rung of the local council's housing waiting list, so he has to make do with a room in a tumble-down bed-and-breakfast hotel on Edgeware Road. Every afternoon and evening he chews qat with his clansmen and talks anger and poli-tics until well past midnight, then he sleeps until noon. 'What would I get up for? I have nothing to do.' For him, being Muslim is part of his national identity, but not as compelling as clan. He sits in London, agi-tated and waiting. 'I am waiting for our tribe to be back in power in Somalia; then I can go home,' he said over lunch. Then he shot a glance at the other Somali with us. 'Maybe I shouldn't say that, but it is true.'[12] On Sundays he goes to the Speaker's Corner in Hyde Park and lectures whomever will listen on his version of events in Somalia. A few days after our first meeting we were due to meet again. Elmi was not at home at the appointed time. Later he called to say that he had had to take a friend to the hospital. The friend had been knifed. 'He is okay,' he said. 'What matters is that he recovers and takes his revenge for our clan.'

Elmi was relatively unusual among respondents – both because of his forthright opinions on clan politics and because of their ongoing centrality in defining his identity. Elmi does not consider himself reli-gious. Even so, he chews qat with his fellow clansmen, rather than drink alcohol.

In Toronto, some men who have not found work spend much of their time in doughnut shops, drinking coffee and talking politics. Abshir and Omar are two of them. Abshir is a former truck driver and Omar an ex-soldier. Neither worries much about practising his reli-gion, but they sit in the doughnut shops because no alcohol is served there, so they are not contravening the dictates of Islam. Their concerns with living in the West echo those of Elmi: the freedom of women, their inability to tell their wives and children what to do, and the separa-tions and divorces that consequently abound.[13] These issues are actu-ally not issues of religion. Abshir and Omar are comparing social conventions in Somalia with conditions in the West that have resulted in increased domestic power for Somali women, regardless of their degree of religious observance. (As we see below, it frequently occurs along with their increased observance of Islam.)

Abdurahman is a twenty-seven-year-old science student, who arrived in London from southern Somalia in 1992. He had spent three years in Yemen as a schoolteacher in the interim. He says that he prays, fasts, and attends the Tottenham Court mosque once a week and sometimes on Sundays. He is careful not to consume pork products and chews qat once a week or so with friends, 'but not everyday like some people do.' He does not like the Islamists: they are too strict and advise not having anything to do with non-Muslims. 'Why would they do this? Now they say have nothing to do with Christians, but this is ridiculous. You are here, living with these people, but they have taken us in, why not respect them and talk with them?' Most of Abdurahman's friends are Somali, but he has some non-Muslim friends as well. 'Just because I have a friend and he has a beer, what does that matter? He can have a beer, and I will have an orange juice. We can still sit together ... I don't go to pubs but the problem is here there are not many places to just sit and talk.'[14] Abdurahman provides a good example of how Somali immigrants are modifying the dictates of Islam as they perceive them, so as to remain true to them while accommodating the traditions of non-Somalis or non-Muslims.

Jama is a former businessman, trained as a lawyer, who escaped from Mogadishu in the midst of the fighting in 1991 with his infant son and two-year-old daughter and his mother. His wife became separated from the family during their flight and has yet to be reunited with them. Jama's path to Toronto took him through Kenya, Syria, and Moscow; he arrived in Canada in August 1994. He is desperate to bring his wife to Canada but cannot afford the processing fee required by the government on new immigrants. As a refugee, he is ineligible to bring her here under family-reunification programs that might waive the fee. He has training in mechanical and electrical skills but in the spring of 1995 had been unable to find work because all prospective employers demanded Canadian references and two years of Canadian experience. A friend had recently found him drunk and despairing on a bench outside his apartment block, where his mother looks after the children, now aged five and six. (Drinking alcohol is regarded by Somalis as a serious breach of the requirements of their religion.) None the less, Jama describes himself as 'one hundred percent Muslim.' He said that he prays and fasts and visits the Tariq Mosque every Friday, although he must take two buses and it is a long way from his home. He said that he does not practise any differently in Canada from the way he did in Somalia. His wife has taken the jilbab (she is now in Nairobi with his father), and he will encourage his daughter to do the same, although he is not a member of the Islamist movements. He says that in Somalia women did not begin to cover until they were married, but now that they understand more about their religion they begin to cover at the age of fifteen.[15] The influence of the Islamists is evident in Jama, although he does not consider himself one of them. He is learning to separate 'Somali culture' from Islam as interpreted by Somali Islamists and to attempt to counter despair with recourse to religion.

The one informant who said that he was still a Sufi was Hashi, a longtime resident of London and a man in his fifties, who 'rediscovered' Sufism in London and belongs to a Sufi group there in which he is the only Somali. He recounted his return in the summer of 1994 to the area of Somaliland on the Ethiopian border where his father had been the custodian of several venerated tombs. He returned to prepare for the annual siyaaro, in which he says four thousand people participate. Hashi has a good job as a broadcaster in London, but he said, 'The people were not surprised to see me, even after so many years. In fact, they expected me. That is what is real to them, never mind this life in London. And I will go back one day. That is my place since my father died. I don't know when, but I will go back.'[16]

There are conflicts and disagreements with the Islamists in the region, in that they vehemently oppose the siyaaro which is interpreted by them as saint worship. The Islamists do not want confrontation, so they oppose 'indirectly,' he said. They are unlikely to come and force anyone to interrupt a *dhikr* (praise-session). They had fierce arguments with Hashi when he was there, 'but I know I had the support of the people behind me, because Sufism is "grassroots".' These Islamists – they have no base, because there is no history of fundamentalism in Somalia. It has no roots.' Although this was beginning to change in the early-mid 1990s, Hashi's testimony provides evidence that Islamism was primarily an urban phenomenon. Its influence among Somalis in the West is a result in part of the fact that most migrants came from Somalia's cities.

Ibrahim is the grandson of a seaman born in Cardiff. He is in his fifties and, though born in Somalia, has lived for thirty years in London. An immigration and family counsellor who considers himself a good Muslim, Ibrahim has no time for the new-style 'extreme' Islamic groups, who in his mind have no respect for Somali traditions. With disgust, he described a wedding that he and his wife had attended the previous day. It is customary for dancing to be held following the arrangement of the *nikah*, or marriage contract, and the meal. At this wedding the mother had insisted on sending everyone home after they had finished praying. 'No dancing, no dancing, it's un-Islamic,' he quoted her as saying. Instead of dancing, there were boxfuls of Qur'ans in Arabic and Somali. 'It was awful,' he said. 'They attract all the angry young men. They are all extreme, and against anyone who isn't Muslim. That's not Islam really. Islam is tolerant to other religions, but these people are extreme.'[17]

Awes is a Londoner in his mid-twenties who left Somalia as a child and grew up in Italy and Yemen before immigrating to England as a teenager. He describes himself as 'one of the very few Christian Somalis.' His parents were both educated in mission schools in Mogadishu, and their main concern was that Awes acquire a European education. The school that he went to in Yemen was full of Christians, and he describes having gone to church on Sundays with his sport teams as a sort of social event. When he first moved to the east end of London, there were almost no other Somali teenagers. Now they have been coming in floods. 'Every time I turn around I am introduced to another cousin.' But the company has been bittersweet. When he tells them that he is not Muslim, he says that they reject him immediately. He described his mother as 'a born-again Muslim, can I put it that way?' His parents have divorced and his mother is remarried to a practising Muslim, and while she and Awes remain close, he is hurt by the way in which he has been cast out by the new community.[18] Awes holds a graduate degree in a field that allows him to work anywhere, but, not being Muslim, he lacks the primary instrument for re-creating identity used by the community of diaspora Somalis. He is thus treated as an outsider and admits to feeling himself such, as though he is missing something important in his life.

Adult Women

For women, the identity crisis that occurs in the West is more complex, because it involves the hijab. To cover oneself is to announce identity loudly and insistently. In the Somali case it is simultaneously a departure from and a reinforcement of tradition, so the decision of whether to don the hijab is not straightforward.

One of the few group interviews that I did was with a group of women in their fifties and sixties. These women were taking English classes at the Somali Women's and Children's Network, which uses portable classrooms at an elementary school in the west end of Toronto to provide day care, language instruction, and parenting classes to Somali women. When I arrived there, a few minutes before two in the afternoon, the women were just preparing to pray. They were a group of eleven, all colourfully dressed in traditional Somali robes and scarves, which they had arranged so that they did not show their hair or their throats. These were women (mostly grandmothers) who had each had small businesses before the war in Somalia. They came from Mogadishu but had not spent their lives there. In many cases they followed family to the city but had been raised in the interior, leading nomadic lives. Their path to Toronto generally led them through Kenya, and they have migrated within the last six years. The businesses that they had had were often related to clothing – tailoring or making items to sell at the market – and they missed the routine and the activity of their old lives. They spoke of still being in shock, having lost all their belongings, their homes, and, most disastrously, close members of their families. One woman had lost seven members of her immediate family, all of them drowned while trying to escape. Each aged face was etched with pain. The questions and their answers were translated by three younger women who taught the classes and ran the daycare centre.

They talked of the logistical difficulties of dressing for Canadian winters and of having to take multiple buses to obtain halal food, although an increasing number of shops carry it. They spoke of wearing the hijab and how people are constantly staring and asking questions. Some of the women said that they had been denied jobs because of their hijab, either because they wear it at all or because they have been told that they may have the job only on condition of removing it, which they would not do. In the Dixon area, where they live, people have stopped staring, but as soon as one ventures outside the neighbourhood one is subject to stares and often questions. These are often just curious, such as 'Do you wear that in the summer as well? I thought it was just for the winter, when it was cold!' Often fear or dislike is encountered, evinced by their anecdote about a tall woman in full jilbab who walked into a bank and saw all the other customers back fearfully against the walls, while no one would take their eyes off her. They found this attitude bewildering. In their minds, why would a woman who was respecting what they see as the Qur'an's decree of modesty occasion fear?

I asked why many women are more concerned to wear the hijab now that they are in Canada. In Somalia, they answered, women were all busy with businesses and their general lives, and besides, everyone was Muslim, so they did not have to think about it much. Now, they find that first of all they have no purpose aside from the bringing up of their children (and grandchildren), which means the teaching of Islam and Muslim values to them. Second, they have the time to study themselves. Finally, life in the diaspora means that Islam is not the only religion around them, so they want to understand their own beliefs, and therefore they are encouraged to study. They study every day and on weekends; they go to the mosque regularly (sitting either at the back or upstairs if there are two floors). In the course of their study, they become more religious and often, in consequence, wear the hijab when before they had been less concerned about it. One of the interpreters, a young mother in a jilbab, proposed her own reason for the increase in religious adherence among Somalis. What happened in Somalia, she said, has been interpreted by many people as a punishment for not having been good enough Muslims.[19] (This response of the Islamists echoes one of the reactions among Middle Eastern Islamists to the Arabs' defeat at Israeli hands in 1967.)

Halimo is an elderly woman living in London with her family. She is illiterate and speaks no English, and prior to her departure from Somalia she knew only the salat, the daily prayer, which she had been taught by an old shaykh whom she still reveres. But, airlifted by one of her sons out of Mogadishu at the height of the fighting and transported into a new world, she now studies the Qur'an for the first time. She goes three times a week to a local mosque with her grandchildren, wearing the hijab and learning to read Arabic.[20]

Amina, a mother of four children aged twelve through twenty years old, still trying to get her husband to Canada from Holland, began wearing the hijab after she moved to Toronto in 1991. In Somalia, she had worn the light melchabad (a gauzy scarf) after she married, 'but it was flimsy, transparent, more cultural than religious.' Once in Canada she began to take religious classes and soon came to the conclusion that 'I felt unless I wear the hijab I'm not doing anything right. I felt I should try to fulfil this requirement. Now I get all kinds of strange looks but that doesn't bother me. But often if I apply for a job I will not get it, even if I'm qualified for it. They don't actually say it's because of the hijab, but after looking for so long, I can't think what else it could be.' Amina is completely bilingual: she worked in English for the

United Nations in Mogadishu for eight years but says that even jobs with Canadian government ministries, which appeared promising when her credentials were submitted on paper, evaporated at the interview. 'I would never change my ideas about hijab now. I am a grown woman in my late thirties. Once I decided just a few years ago to cover, I am not going to change my mind just because I don't get a job. Many people have suggested I take off the hijab because of that but I won't. I believe in God; if I am meant to have a job I will get it. Otherwise I will wait.'[21]

Anab first came to England as a master's student in 1984. She works as a journalist in London.

> Personally I don't have too much trouble as a Muslim since I work for an international institution. But on the street it is a different question. After the bombing in Oklahoma City I was actually scared to walk around, and scared for my children. People looked at me strangely, because I wear the hijab, as though I was going to do something awful to them because of being Muslim. It's ridiculous.
>
> I became more religious when I moved to London. I only started to cover when I moved here. When I came here I saw many things that shocked and disturbed me: everything was so shameful. We are an educated family. My grandfather was educated at an American university; I am educated, but education doesn't spoil you or your culture. But here there was such freedom, freedom that was shocking to me. I realized that I had a good culture and a good religion and I decided to practise it more. I felt my identity very strongly. I didn't have time to study Qur'an then because I was a student and now I don't have time because I have two small children and I am divorced and have a part-time job, but I would like to study more; there is a lot I do not know.
>
> I did my master's in nature conservation but I can't get a job in my field in this country, because of my hijab. I would have to work in the countryside then, you see, and no one would hire me. It's personally okay for me in the city, because it's a cultural mix-up, but in the countryside people are so narrow and conservative, it wouldn't be possible.[22]

Deeqa, and others like her, are known among Somalis as *sijui*. She is an ethnic Somali born and raised in Kenya, who has learned to speak Somali only in Canada and still does not speak it well. *Sijui* is the Swahili word for 'I don't know,' which she says is the answer that Kenyan Somalis give when they are asked about their lineage, hence the nickname. Her father had been a shaykh and a poet, and she had worn the hijab as a child but discarded it first as a teenager and again when first she came to Canada.

> When I came to university in 1991 I took a philosophy course. We studied Plato, Aristotle, the *Leviathan*. I felt like I read them for my own mental development. I would look at the Qur'an in the light of what I was reading, and appreciate it more. My tutorial leader had a difficult time with me as the course went on. She said she thought the course would 'liberate' me from my belief in religion, and instead it was pushing me toward my religion.
>
> Then I read *On Liberty* by John Stuart Mill and I saw that for me liberty had to come through the Qur'an and not listening to others interpret it. My freedom would come through understanding the Qur'an. I took the hijab. My teaching assistant was surprised. She said, 'I expected you to be a feminist.'
>
> 'But I am a feminist,' I said. I argue with my male friends about so much. I say what does the Qur'an say on this issue? They cannot argue with the Qur'an. You get equality from applying the Qur'an, the same equality as the West. I argue with the cultural interpretations of the Qur'an, which so often spell out only the man's rights and not those of the woman ...
>
> ... For us when culture and religion coincide, that's good, but when culture contradicts religion, that's difficult, because Somali culture has become so Arabi ed. It's difficult to distinguish one from another.
>
> I hope being here makes this process easier. As a woman if you argue through Islam it's more liberating than taking a Western stand. Men can't argue with the religion, and the religion says women, as much as men, must be educated. So long as your position is in the Qur'an there is no obstacle. I hope other Muslim women read and learn to think this way.
>
> If going back to the Qur'an is fundamentalism, then I want that fundamentalism. That is different from going back to old customs.[23]

Deeqa said she must continually defend her choice to other women and other students.

> For instance, I work in a clothing store at a shopping mall. Women often come up to me and ask why I am wearing it. One woman, a social worker, came up and gave me her card. She said, 'We have shelters for people like you; we can help you.' I said, 'What do you mean? You don't know any-

thing about me.' She said, 'Oh, I know about you Somalis, you are oppressed by your husbands, but we can help you.'

At that time I was not married. I said, 'For your information, I am not married, I am not living with my family, I am living on my own. Why am I oppressed?' 'Well, you wouldn't be dressed like that if you weren't forced to wear it,' she said. I said, 'Listen, this is a choice of mine. I want to dress like this. If I am conforming to something, I am conforming to the will of God. Look at you. You are dressed in a short skirt, a jacket, stockings, high heeled shoes. You look like corporate America. You are conforming to the wishes of an adman. At least I wear what God wants. You can't judge if you don't understand.'

Once I went to a feminist meeting on campus. There was a speaker there I wanted to hear. Some woman asked me why I was there. I said, 'I'm interested in the speaker.' She said I was there to make a mockery of the meeting. I said, 'A feminist thinks she is equal to men, I think so too. I can't do everything men do, I can't be a bouncer, for instance, but if I'm looking for the same pay at work as a man, that's equality.' She said, 'You are an embarrassment to us in your veil.' But I would not wear a veil if a man wanted me to. I wear it because it is important to me. As far as I'm concerned, the Qur'an was not written by man, but by God.[24]

Deeqa is a striking example of a woman using *ijtihad* – her independent interpretation of the Qur'an – to guide her life and winning support from her religious husband and imam for doing it.

Hibaq is twenty-nine and has not lived in Somalia since the age of eleven, when she was sent to India to be educated. She later joined her family in Qatar, where her father lives, and she moved to London in 1985 to study. At first, Hibaq wanted only to be accepted by her classmates and British society. She had been covering herself in the Middle East, but she stopped when she came. She neither prayed nor fasted, and she went to pubs and nightclubs with her new friends, but she says she was soon 'shocked' at the racism that she discovered here. First a classmate of hers said to her: 'Hibaq, you are so nice, I find it hard to believe you are black.' And once, at the end of a long day, when she was very tired, Hibaq was sitting on a crowded bus when an elderly white woman got on. Although she had been raised always to stand for an older person, Hibaq hesitated that day because she was so tired, but in the end her upbringing got the better of her exhaustion and she offered the old woman her seat. To her shock, what she got in return was an angry, 'Oh, don't speak to me! Why don't you go back where you came from?!' Hibaq said after those two incidents she became far more guarded and reserved. She realized that she would never 'fit in to British society, and so I returned to my community,' which was not easy, because there were few women and children; most Somalis in London were seamen or young men who had left Somalia for political reasons.

Hibaq began to cover herself again and returned to practising Islam when her mother and sisters arrived in London five years ago. They were dismayed to find that she did not pray or rinse when she went to the bathroom. Hibaq began to practise Islam initially in order not to hurt her mother, but then she found there were many benefits from returning to the practice. In the first place, she said, she began to value the peace and strength that she found by spending a few minutes at prayer five times a day, and, like many other Somali women, she began to cover herself although she was not yet married. 'When you are living in a hostile community, you become more introverted, and Islam gives you strength to cope with not being accepted.'[25]

Hibaq always takes her hijab off when she goes for job interviews, because, she said, she knows that if she wears it people will see nothing but the scarf. Once she has the job, she will work for a week or so and then begin to wear the scarf. Some of her friends say that she is not being true to her beliefs, but she said that if she does not do that she will not get the job, but once she has the job and has proved herself and people know her, they will not fire her for wearing the hijab. 'Sometimes you have to compromise,' she said, adding that, for the same reason, she and her husband have taken a mortgage, something that some Muslims will not do. 'Otherwise I would not have my own house.' Hibaq's 'compromises' are her way of retaining her practice of her religion while redefining what she views as acceptable in an observant Muslim.

Ayaan does not wear the hijab but considers herself reasonably religious. She is twenty-three and arrived in London in 1988 to study English; she wanted to work as an air hostess. While she was there the war started and she was unable to return. Her father was dead (of natural causes), and she wanted to bring her family to safety, so she began to work at a local grocery store and was eventually promoted to assistant manager. She worked there every day from 9 a.m. to 6 p.m. and at another food store evenings from 7 to 11 and weekends. She did this for a year, during which time she had not one single day off. She saved US$11,000, enough to bring her three youngest siblings to London. At the time, the boys were twelve and ten, and the little girl five. The mother had taken them to Nairobi. They arranged for a Somali woman with a British passport to bring them on the airline to Heathrow, where she left them in the Immigration queue and continued through without them. The children had no identification or documents. They told the authorities that they were all alone (they would not say who had brought them there) and then said that they had an older sister in London. When contacted, Ayaan could not (or would not) say who had brought them, but she was working and could support them, so they were allowed to stay. Then, given that she had a job and three small children to look after, she applied to bring her mother and older sister to Britain under a family-reunification program.

Three months after arriving in London, Ayaan was taken by a friend to a nightclub. She said that the experience transformed her. Although she had been brought up in a religious family she herself was not religious and had never prayed, but she so disliked what she saw at the nightclub that she had nightmares when she got home, dreams of wretchedness and evil and something gripping her throat. She recounted that she did not sleep the rest of the night but got up and prayed the morning prayer. Since then she has prayed five times daily and now considers herself to be religious. 'I was afraid the West would change me. If you follow the culture here and feel free it is not nice, not part of my culture. Being religious keeps me safe. In Islam your religion doesn't stop you from doing nice things. My culture is sweet, my religion is sweet. I didn't want to forget that.'[26]

When Ayaan's young siblings arrived in London, she signed them up for school and classes at the local Somali community centre to 'learn religion and Somali language and culture.' Her mother, who had only ever worn the traditional *garbasaar* before arriving in London, now wears the jilbab and 'became very religious' when she arrived. Ayaan's youngest sister, aged nine, wears a headscarf. In the summer of 1995, Ayaan married a white Briton who had converted to Islam because she told him that she would not marry him otherwise. None the less, she does not cover herself, although her mother, brothers, and sister 'are constantly telling me to wear the hijab. But right now I don't want to, and I don't know if I ever will. I feel good as I am.'

Nura is a tall, big-boned woman, in London since 1986 and a mother of three. She has a paid job at a local community centre; her husband does not work. Her refusal to wear the hijab causes her constant trouble within the community. She says that she 'believes in religion' but does not cover herself or pray regularly. She fasts and prays during Ramadan and proudly displays her copy of the Qur'an, in Somali and Arabic, in her living room. Her children attend Qur'anic school on weekends. Nevertheless Nura, a former member of Somalia's women's basketball team, wants to practise Islam in the way she always has.

> But most Somali women are more religious. I feel ashamed not covering when I pass people on the street. I am emotional about it. I never felt like this in Somalia. People see me, they say 'salam alaykum' to me and I am so embarrassed. I feel I should cover but I have never covered. I have three kids and I don't cover; my husband has never pushed me to do that. I didn't do it there; why should I do it here? But I feel that I should now. People see me at work and they say, 'Nura, Nura, why don't you cover? You should cover,' and I am ashamed. But I knew some of these women in Somalia; they never used to cover there either. They push me every day to cover, but back home they never wore the hijab or even long clothes. But now that they're here they want people to know they are Muslim and not Christian.[27]

Farhia lives in Toronto with her family and had just graduated from university with a degree in chemistry. On the day she met me, she was wearing a long skirt with a headscarf, but she told me that she often wears jeans and the hijab together. Farhia attends a Somali study circle, fasts, and prays, 'although I drift a bit sometimes. Everyone in my family believes, but the environment here doesn't allow you to do it unless you're really into it. My mom is really into it. The others are off and on.'

> For most people back home Islam wasn't really important. They didn't pray or wear Islamic clothes. Now we observe it. It's like it's a new religion. Back home everybody was Muslim. You don't need to worry about the food; it's your culture, it's all around. Here you can only eat certain foods. Back home the shaykh calls you for prayers; here you have to have a schedule or you forget. You are more aware of it here, you don't take it for granted. You have to think about what you wear, what you eat.
>
> I loved learning the Qur'an in Arabic when I was little. I was in love with the Qur'an. I love poetry, and the Qur'an is poetry. When I came here I wanted to learn but I wasn't practising. I had to put this on [the hijab] in Saudi Arabia. After a year in Toronto I went to a study circle with Muslims and put this on. That first year I didn't go to the mosque or even

fast. I thought Islam was in my heart and what was on my hair was irrelevant. But one day I put it on and my sister said it looked good. It felt
good, so I kept it. That was in 1990. My parents encouraged me not to put
it on. That was during the Gulf War and they were afraid of me going way
down to Weston Road where I was volunteering twice a week; they were
afraid that I would be threatened by somebody if they knew I was Muslim. But I wanted to wear it, so I did.[28]

Saida is thirty-four. She arrived in London on a graduate scholarship
in 1989 and, unable to return home, was subsequently joined by her
three children. Her husband is still in Kenya, and Saida is trying – via
the family reunification program – to have him join the family. Saida
lives in Sudbury Town, a middle-class neighbourhood in northwest
London. She was dressed in *masar* (a colourful scarf wrapped only
around her hair) and a long, simple Somali robe. A friend, visiting
from Sweden, was quick to cover her hair when a male visitor entered
the house, but Saida did not. She does not think that covering is essential. 'There is religion on the one hand, and culture on the other. Religion must be stronger than culture. In the middle is African culture.
We have all three.[29] Saida prays, fasts, eats only halal food, and
observes Ramadan. Although she goes to the mosque only during
Ramadan, she takes the children to Qur'an school on weekends.

Saida accompanied her father on the hajj in 1988 because he had no
sons and wanted a companion. She described it as a moving experience, 'but it depends on you as an individual. If you go you will get the
name of *hajji* or *hajja*, and so once you go you should always be in a
good way of thinking; you should set an example.' She says that there
has been no change in her practice of Islam since arriving in London.

Samira is a master's student in her final year at the University of
London's Institute of Legal Studies. The first female human rights lawyer in Somalia, she worked in Mogadishu for the release of prisoners
improperly arrested and held under the Barre government. She faced a
dual challenge – the difficulty of the work itself and the fact that she
was continually mistaken for a secretary of a law firm. As a woman,
she could not find work with an established firm and had to start her
own, but at first no Somalis would engage her. She recounted how she
managed to rescue one man from certain execution, and to secure his
release, only to find that he was insulted that he owed his life to a
woman. Another man, after she got him released, was full only of his
own bravado at having allowed a woman to defend him. But gradu-

ally she earned respect and a reputation as a formidable lawyer: 'It was interesting to me that in time the Muslim society did accept that women can work defending people.'[30] Eventually the political situation became too difficult for her to stay. By 1991, once Barre had been deposed and the civil war began growing in intensity, neither she nor her daughter dared sleep at home, for fear of being raped or arrested in the middle of the night.

Samira and her family – her husband, their five children, and two other children for whom she cares – left for Italy in 1991. They had hoped to stay only a few months, but the fighting only got worse, so they made their way to London. She would like to return to Somalia to help put the country to rights. In Samira's estimation, the conflict had transposed into one between two cultures, the rural and the urban. Many nomads had been called by their clan elders to come to Mogadishu to help in the civil war and, once there, grew bitter at the stark contrast between rural and urban environments. 'All they want is revenge. They are bandits, camel-raiders come to claim their entitlements after they freed the urban dwellers from the regime.'

Samira said that she would have returned to Somalia to negotiate with the elders on how to convince the nomads to leave the city, but as a woman she has no credibility in the pastoral elder culture. She does not see a future for herself in London; having been given only exceptional leave to remain, she has no certainty that she will be permitted to build a permanent life in Britain. 'My dream of returning is becoming a myth,' she said, so she is planning to look for work in an international organization or in the field of women's rights. 'I would prefer a Third World country because of the conflict of culture I see here and the impact on my children of raising them in a Western society. It is definitely negative. I am afraid my children would dissociate themselves from their roots. That is worrying me.'

Samira 'runs a Muslim home.' She takes the children to the mosque on Eid, the holiday that celebrates the end of Ramadan. She herself prays and encourages her children to pray: 'What I think is that my religion is the link between me and God. I am accountable to God. I try to explain this to the children. The youngest pray with me sometimes. The eldest did for a bit, but he stopped. The children know that to be a good Muslim they must pray.' She notices that the children are reacting to racial prejudice that they encounter at school, which is affecting the way in which they view fellow Muslims: 'There is a link of blackness in the schools. They stick together, the black kids, when they are attacked by white kids. My son found the black kids were sticking up for him when the Arabs were not. So he is closer to the Jamaicans or Nigerians than to the Iranians or the Turks who are the same religion as he is.'

Samira is a tall, striking woman. She was wearing a long, traditional Somali dress, her hair tied back in the *melchabad*, although her ears and a band of hair were visible, as well as her throat. She commented on the social pressure on women within the Somali diaspora community. 'I have a problem. I like to swim but I can't wear a swimsuit here. It is not just Islamic teaching not to expose the body; it is the social control within the Somali community. Most women here will not wear jeans, and most cover their hair. In Italy I never wore a scarf, but here there is the social control to wear the scarf and not to expose your body. I do what is practical for me. My daughters don't cover. I know I am contravening conformity, but I suppose I am more liberal.'

None the less, Samira says that she is more religious than she was in Somalia.

> At home I never cared about religion. I just took it for granted. Here I have to be more concerned, because it seems that otherwise something is slipping away in the long run, so I wake the kids at six to pray with me. Another factor is that I am relying on the religion because of what we suffered and experienced – all the atrocities. If there are not logical reasons for this, then I look for supernatural reasons. There must be reasons for what happened. I am trying to find the justification for what happened.
>
> I know I should be thankful to God that I was saved and my family was saved. When I arrived here I went to a psychiatrist for three months because I was crying all day, every day. I was questioning. Why did this happen? How did it happen? Why not me or my children? Why did these people deserve such treatment? Referring to Allah is self-help for me. I reali e this. You question yourself constantly. You think of your neighbour, the shop-owner, the driver, people you spent your life with. You wonder, why them? Why not you? I think survivors of the Holocaust went through this, too.

Fadumo, a woman in her late forties, who has lived in Italy, Yemen, and Britain, has found that she has latterly become more religious. She says that this is true of most of the Somali community but that the increased religiosity is of two kinds:

> You have to understand what these poor Somali people have been

through. They have suffered so much. They have gone through so much trauma. These people lost everything, all their possessions and their homes. They were often professionals or government workers or wealthy businessmen, and now they have nothing, no position, no money, nothing to do. And on top of that they lost members of their families, sometimes three or four. And then it was so hard to get here, going through the Middle East or Ethiopia or Kenya, where it was so difficult for them and they never knew whether they would manage to get here with their families. And finally they are here and they encounter every day so much hostility. How many times you hear, every day, on the bus, 'Oh, you bloody foreigners, go back where you came from.' And everybody is unfriendly, staring at you and making you feel that you have no right to be here, that you are here to take their jobs and bleed them dry and live in their homes, and they act as if they can't wait to get rid of you. Then it's so hard to get the minimum of things you need to survive – a roof over your head and food. And you want to work, but many people can't find work. Everything is so hard; you realize that material things are not permanent, because you lost those. And even human beings are not permanent, because you have lost so many members of your family, so you turn to God for strength. Your faith becomes what keeps you going. It becomes your strength. This is the gentle way of turning to Islam. Still you respect other people and their right to believe what they want, whether they are Christian or Jewish.

But some people, especially the young people, they go to school and they walk down the street, and they are made to feel unwelcome here and as though they do not fit in. They become so angry, so they turn to Islam in anger, and these people are al-Wahada [members of the Islamist movements].[31] They have a growing appeal for people who are frustrated and angry.[32]

The Islamic Organizations

Both London and Toronto have a series of organizations whose purpose is to help Somalis live a Muslim life amid the pressures of the West. They will field telephone calls from people asking how to deal with prayer and work issues and counsel couples and families on how to resolve their difficulties in an Islamic manner. Obviously, the advice given depends on the outlook of the organization, and what follows below is a picture of three different organizations.

The Somali Islamic Society of Canada (SISCA) is often described by

Somalis as the organization of al-Ittihad in Toronto. This claim is refuted, however, by its director, Aden Ibrahim, who maintains that while SISCA's members may support the ideas and goals of al-Ittihad, its role in Toronto is limited. 'Our role is to ensure that Muslims live an Islamic life here, to ensure that they abstain from drugs, alcohol or corruption and so on, and to provide religious support for Muslims.' Al-Ittihad seeks to establish an Islamic state in Somalia, he says, something that cannot be done in Toronto. 'Here it is already a sophisticated system, a whole society. We can't make any changes here. You have to "love it or leave it," as they say. We are really having difficulties to live in this country and maintain our religion.'[33]

Among the kinds of guidelines that SISCA dispenses are the following. Muslims should not:

- shake hands, socialize, or work with a member of the opposite sex;
- work in an establishment that sells anything *haram* (such as Loblaws, a major grocery chain, which sells products containing alcohol and pork);
- have anything to do with a financial institution that uses interest; or
- assist anyone to consume alcohol (so that a Muslim taxi driver should refuse to transport a passenger carrying beer or wine).[34]

SISCA counsels women to wear the hijab, preferably the jilbab. It says that they may work, though not with men, but it counsels them to allow men to be the main providers for the family, where possible, as this gives them a sense of responsibility and place. It recognizes that where women are single mothers they will have to support their families and that this will often entail their working with men. This is unavoidable, though Islamically undesirable, as is much else that Muslims encounter in Toronto.

SISCA tends to advise wariness of contact with Canadians and their values. In the words of Aden Ibrahim: 'Muslims will never be part of Western society, even if they try. As a Muslim you cannot adopt the Western system.'

SISCA's main challenge, according to its director, is to convince members of the community not to despair, not to chew qat, but to work and become productive and active and to maintain their religion. It has plans for a mosque and Islamic centre, but for the moment there is no money; the community is preoccupied with the plight of Somalia and relatives in need. In the meantime, it offers study circles and Qur'anic classes in Somali at an existing mosque and conducts a series of seminars and conferences that feature Somali speakers from the Middle East, the United States, and the United Kingdom. In addition, it publishes a monthly newsletter, in English, entitled *Codka Jaaliyadda* (Community Voice), which includes interviews with visiting imams, stories about the life of the Prophet's companions, and notices of upcoming Islamic conferences. There are editorials on current affairs in Somalia and Bosnia and commentaries on such as issues as the Canadian media portrayal of the Somali Islamic courts.[35] The newsletter is distributed free of charge in halal food stores and other places where Somalis are likely to gather.

Hassan 'Jami' Ali Mohamud is the president of the Somali Youth Association of Toronto (SOYAT), and one of its founding members. SOYAT was formed in 1992 by a group of young Somalis who were concerned that their elders risked transposing Somalia's clan-based problems onto the diaspora community. SOYAT's aims are twofold: to unite all Somali youth members in Canada (to overcome clan factionalism) and to help Somali youth integrate positively into Canadian life.[36] The president, Hassan Mohamud, who considers himself an Islamist,[37] said:

> I had been in Canada a year by then [1992] and had already gained much experience working with Canadians. I speak four languages; I had earned a diploma in social services. I saw we Somalis can integrate positively into the Canadian lifestyle. I reali ed people can live together with their differences. There is a verse in the Qur'an that says that if you are not fighting with the people you live with, you can live with what you believe and what they believe. You can live with them peacefully, justly, and as brothers.
>
> Another Islamic principle is that a custom is okay to adopt if it does not contradict an Islamic custom. So there are many ways of achieving the same end, many doors you can go in.[38]

The organization provides heritage classes – including religion, language, and culture – for Somali children, which include discussions on practising Islam and preserving Somali culture in a Canadian context. SOYAT offers summer school in order to help immigrant children who need extra help with their studies and runs periodic cultural events and year-round sports leagues in basketball and soccer.

Hassan Mohamud, trained as a lawyer in Somalia, also holds the equivalent of a master's degree from Cairo's graduate institute for Islamic studies, al-Mahad al-'Ala Li'l-Dirasat al-Islamiyya, and is completing a degree in social work at York University. His family counselling has two dominant themes: teaching parents new ways of relating to their children and helping husbands and wives resolve their differences short of separation and divorce. He recounted the story of a girl who left home because her parents wanted to force her to wear the hijab. (He had a call from her school telling him that it would avoid calling the Children's Aid Society if he could resolve the problem.) He met the parents and the girl separately. He told the parents that they had to learn to convince their children what is right, rather than simply assuming that they can impose their will and backing it up by force if need be. He then told the daughter that no one would impose anything on her against her will and went on to ask her whether she considers herself Muslim and whether would she wear the hijab if she understood that it is a part of being Muslim and why. He said that her parents would in future give her the freedom to choose once she understood their point of view, which they would explain, not impose. The girl reportedly returned home and now wears the hijab.

Hassan Mohamud maintains that the problems with most marriages can be traced to qat chewing. The husband arrives in Canada, accustomed to being the main breadwinner, cannot find a job, loses hope, and chews qat, which exacerbates his problem because he is not employed but neither is he contributing to the work of the home. He does not help with the running of the home or with the children's homework, which is all the more problematic in cases where the mother is illiterate. After some months of this situation, the wife is distressed and wants him out of the house. In such cases, counsellors will try, first, to convince the husband to stop chewing qat, and second, to help the wife understand his difficult predicament and encourage her to help convince him that what he is doing is not according to Islam. (Often she is the more religious of the two and is the reason they are going to the counsellor at all.) Marriage counselling by outsiders is virtually unknown in Somalia, where problems at home are normally resolved by a series of relatives and, if necessary, clan elders.

Hassan Mohamud's belief is that 'Islamically and culturally, integration can happen. The only way to retain our heritage is to have a strong community ... As a Muslim, I say that Islam is a religion that delivers a message in a peaceful way. We think the right way to deliver the message is through a group like SOYAT, building our culture and building relationships with Canadians.'

Nur ul-Islam (Light of Islam) in London provides Islamic advice and counselling from an Ittihad perspective.[39] From a small office near the Whitechapel mosque in the east end, Ibrahim Sheikh Mohamed talked of the challenges facing the organization:

> There are all kinds of difficulties for people. You know, we never heard about suicides in Somalia. We have had twelve to eighteen suicides over the last year and a half. Just yesterday I went to a funeral for a boy in his early twenties who threw himself in front of a tube train. There are difficulties here because of the stress of the different culture, and all the things that happened to people during the civil war – their families destroyed, the rapes, the killings, all the terrible things they saw. So there is a lot of mental illness. Recently in Cardiff another woman drowned herself in the sea.
>
> People do different things when they face a change in culture – racial hatred, no jobs, and so on. Some people look for counselling from religion; others chew qat or get drugs or alcohol. There is a group of five to seven Somali boys who sit outside the Whitechapel tube station drinking alcohol. I spoke to them, 'Why do you do this?' One of them said, 'I lost my whole family in the war, I have nothing here, what else is there, what does it matter?'[40]

In response, Nur ul-Islam tries to encourage Somalis to find support from Islam and to find Islamic solutions to family disputes, including appealing to elders for help in resolving marital disputes before resorting to divorce. It dispenses advice daily to individuals wanting to know the correct response to a particular dilemma. One family called to ask what the proper burial procedure should be for a four-month-old miscarried fetus, for instance.[41] One of the particular objections of Nur ul-Islam is the exposure of young people in British schools to sex education and dancing, from which parents have been unable to withdraw their children.

Nur ul-Islam runs a Qur'anic school and of course the Sunday programme at the Whitechapel mosque, where people speak on the Qur'an and on Somali and Islamic history and give detailed reports on what is happening in the country and so forth. There are conferences and seminars to which the organization tries to attract as wide an audience as possible.

We are trying to make people Muslims to safeguard their own way of life ... People find the West outrageous, compared with Somalia, where there is respect for the family and the importance of the family being together. The importance of this has disappeared in the West because of individual independence. In the West you have adultery, and all this new sex – gays and lesbians. All the things that are bad in Somalia are seen as good or okay here. People fear that their kids will have this immorality; they fear their kids will see these things as good: everybody has his own freedom here. Everybody is free. Sometimes Westerners ask ladies in the hijab why someone is making them wear hijab here, but that is ridiculous. Everybody is free here. No one can make anyone do anything here.

In spite of the exposure to Western society, Ibrahim Sheikh Mohamed sees no difficulty in being able to lead an Islamic life in London: 'There is no *dar al-Islam* [the juridical concept of 'land of Islam'] in this world. London is better than Saudi Arabia, because there is more freedom to do what you want here. Nobody asks how you worship or whether you worship. As long as you obey the laws of the country you are fine. My obligation is to attract other people to Islam, to tell them of the history and so on, and to help them to be good Muslims wherever they are.'

Mohamed's comment is fascinating. Not only is it an indication of how Muslims are adapting to life in a non-Muslim country, but it indicates a preference – on Islamic grounds – for living in the West, precisely because of the freedom to practise as desired. This position is in effect an inversion of the traditional doctrinal notion of *hijra*, which assumes that migration from non-Muslim lands to Muslim ones is ideal, so that one can practise Islam unhindered. While I discuss this point further in chapter 7, it is a reflection of how adaptation and integration occur and, together with the other interviews presented here, shows how Muslim immigrants are weaving the obligations of their birth cultures with the realities of their new lives in the diaspora.

Analysis and Commentary

The interviews of this chapter illustrate how most of the adults interviewed have a heightened awareness of their religion, regardless of how positive or negative they feel about their existence as refugees and immigrants. They are determined not to lose their religion and most frequently demonstrate their adherence to it in a more self-conscious way than they were accustomed to doing in Somalia. Prior to their emigration, their religious and cultural identity was something that they could take for granted and not pay much attention to. After emigration, it has become a focal point in their lives. Far from contemplating 'assimilation,' they tend to take steps to make religion – as opposed to Somali nationalism or even clan loyalty – the primary material of their identities. Many have begun to study the Qur'an, in a way that they never would have done in Somalia, in order to apply it to their current lives. Many women newly wear the hijab, and women frequently spoke of community pressure to dress in a 'Muslim' fashion, which they had not felt in Somalia. The Islamist movements assist Somali resettlement and adjustment to the West, and their influence appears to be felt by many who would not claim to be members. However, this increased religiosity, as will be seen below, is not merely *more* of what would have occurred in Somalia. It is in fact the basis for a transformation of the practice of Islam, as immigrants redefine it in a Western context. This will become clearer as we explore how Somalis deal with issues of social interaction, including sexuality and reproduction, in chapter 5 and as we analyse the subject in chapter 7 and the Conclusion.

Removed from the battles and politics of Somalia, Islamists are proving to be greatly influential as moral leaders within the diaspora community. Some Islamists advocate isolation from mainstream society; others believe that a Muslim life can be built without that distancing. This difference is an indicator of the diversity of views and philosophies even within Islamist circles, which stands in sharp contrast to the essentialist Western view that holds that Islam and Muslims demonstrate inflexibility in their inter-cultural relationships. This point I explore more thoroughly in chapter 7.

The Islamist groups, however they might refer to themselves within Somalia, are careful to discourage use of the term 'fundamentalist.' Somali Islamist groups object to the word because of its equation with terrorism in Western news media. And in their London and Toronto contexts, at least, they do not have the expressly political agenda that Bhikhu Parekh has described as an integral part of the definition of a fundamentalist movement.[42] This is not to say that they do not have a political program; they clearly do, in Somalia, as chapter 1 has shown. But, as they themselves point out, this agenda has little relevance in the diaspora. In fact, detachment from local politics appears to give them moral weight within the community. Respondents appeared to feel free to look up to them as models of religious observance without feeling compelled to accept their particular interpretation of the Qur'an or its injunctions, paradoxically strengthening their position within the community because their apolitical stance has seemingly contained their power.

Somalis have been characterized, by observers such as Ibn Battuta and I.M. Lewis, as an intensely proud people with a strong sense of identity. This sense of self runs like a thick current through the interviews. Somalis' response to their cultural dilemma was not to dilute their religious identity but to strengthen it, albeit in a redefined fashion. Faced with a cultural challenge that prevented them from taking their culture for granted, they undertook to re-examine it. They then separated, in many cases, religion from cultural habit (especially where the two were in conflict) and sought to understand more about their religion, precisely in order to define themselves in a part of the world where to be Muslim is to stand apart from most other parts of society.

There are many and complex reasons for Somalis' increased religiosity, some of which receive elaboration below. Sometimes this happens in reaction to the perceived hostility of the wider society (one of the subjects of chapter 6), and one sees a difference in the responses here of respondents in London and in Toronto, but that is only one explanation for the trend. As the respondents themselves said, theirs was sometimes a reaction to the tragedy and chaos that surrounded their departure from their homeland.

Furthermore, as Parekh notes, secular Western societies still rely on Judaeo-Christianity as a major source of their values and 'are constantly nurtured and sustained by a deep religious undercurrent.'[43] The encounter with highly individualistic, secular societies that are none the less informed deeply by a religious tradition alien to them forced a 'crisis of identity.' As Parekh describes it, such a crisis occurs when the identity of a community of religious adherents and what is expected of them by their religion are no longer clear.[44] In effect, the move to the West had just such an effect, obliterating the ability of migrant Somalis to take their identity and religion for granted. The encounter therefore, forced a re-evaluation of religious identity among Somali immigrants. Whether they came of their own free will or were refugees who had no choice, they still found themselves having to deal with this crisis of identity, which forced a rearticulation and reconsideration of their relationship with their own religion and resulted for the most part in an increased observance of it.

At yet another level, their religion became an anchor for them. It provided an oasis of tranquillity amid the dislocation of refugee straits and the turmoil of adjusting to a new culture, trying to learn a new language, and attempting to find jobs. It was, at this psychological level, an invaluable reducer of stress at a time of immense anxiety. What was valuable about it was the very ritual of stepping outside the daily struggle, five times over the course of the day, to concentrate on the prayers that never alter, in rhythmic language that linked them to a community of believers that was theirs no matter where in the world they were.

And finally and most important, it seemed a crucial step if they were not to lose their children to an alien culture.

Their increased religiosity did not take the nostalgic form of a return to the religion as practised by their parents or grandparents – Sufism. This bears out what respondents repeatedly related, which is that Sufism was no longer a vital force in Somalia, at least in its urban areas. Only one respondent (Hashi) in over eighty said that Sufism was important in his life. For the others, increased religiosity took the form of a return to the Qur'an and the hadiths. Even here, however, it is not a return to the memory–work of the Qur'an school of their childhood days. Rather, it is an active reading of the Qur'an and frequently involves – whether they would call it by this name or not – their exercise of ijtihad, independent judgment, or the determination by the lay Muslim of whether actions are Islamically correct or not. They do not examine the Qur'an in a vacuum, but with the intention of working it into the context of their new lives. Deeqa's case is a particularly strong example of this, as she argues for a feminist interpretation of the Qur'an. I place this issue in a wider context and take it up in more detail in chapter 7.

These active readings of the Qur'an are accompanied by a constant, conscious, attempt to reunderstand Islam as Somalis practise it in the context of their new society. This might involve worrying about the ingredients in toothpaste or which fast food chain uses lard. It might consist of determining where to live or work (within a certain transportation radius of a mosque) or how to make allowances for prayer (whether to pray wherever one is or to 'save prayers up' until one is back in an Islamic environment such as the home). It involves the question of dress and how this relates to school and work.

What emerges strongly is that Somali immigrants have not tended to shy away from their religion in an attempt to fit into Western culture.

In some cases, they have wanted to continue to be Muslim without fan-fare, as they consider they did back home (see Nura, for example), which they say community pressure in the diaspora makes it difficult to do, but the desire to abandon Islam, or even to submerge it under a Somali nationalism, is rare.

As chapter 7 shows, it is their Muslimness, as opposed to their Somaliness, that immigrants have chosen to emphasize in the course of their self-redefinition. The issue of clan remains an extraordinarily sen-sitive one for the community. It quickly became apparent that I could not ask respondents directly which clan or sub-clan they belonged to, and I could not approach the subject at all until the very end of the interview, after I had established a trust relationship and had dis-cussed questions of religion and identity. In part, this is because the pain of the clan-based war was still so raw for them (if I had asked which clan they belonged to, they would have wondered why I wanted to know, and on whose behalf), and in part it is because the community is deeply divided over how to deal with clan in the diaspora. Many immigrant-help groups are clan-based (although they claim not to be), and most sub-clans still collect money to help their community in Somalia, but a significant proportion of the diaspora community believes it critical that clan issues be overcome. Given the prevalence and strength of these sentiments, it is all the more striking that the redefinition of identity has taken a predominantly religious, and not clan-based or nationalist, form.

Although the observations and interview extracts of chapters 4 and 5 are helpful in tying the theory to the respondents' comments, some preliminary comments are in order. Internal integration – the cultural weaving of birth and adopted cultures – is in evidence in the adapta-tion of religious practices to the circumstances of the new, Western society. And although this process is described in greater detail in chapter 7, the reader can observe how Somali immigrants, rather than slipping away from their religious roots, are redefining them in the context of their new environments and are in the process becoming Western (as opposed to Westernized) Muslims. The distinction is important, both because they are no longer the same Muslim practitio-ners with the same understanding of their religion as they had prior to leaving Somalia and because their observance of their religion has not been diluted by exposure to different religions and perceived values. Rather, they have redefined their understanding and practice of Islam in a new context that has made them more consciously aware of it than they were before their arrival in the West. As is shown in chapter 7, this raising of consciousness has huge implications for the evolution and practice of Islam as a religion and for the diversity and flexibility of the religion and its practitioners.

One of the fascinating observations to be made concerns Somali women. Given their critical role in child-rearing, and particularly given the number of single-parent homes run by women in Western communities, their position within the community has strengthened considerably, in significant part because of their increased religiosity. As the observations of Hassan Mohamud show, as well as the women's responses themselves, women are often at the forefront of a family's increased religious observance. This has the effect of giving them stronger moral leadership, which is heightened by the fact that circumstance dictates that they are as likely as men to be the working partner in a family, or indeed the single working parent.

Many women indicated that their religious concerns stem from an awareness of their responsibilities for the transfer of values to the next generation. They view their children as vulnerable to the lure of a foreign culture in a way that they feel they are not. The next chapter explores the adjustment of teenagers, who find themselves having to balance the fears and increased religiosity of their parents, on the one hand, with the new world that they encounter on the street and in the schoolyard, on the other hand.

4

Transfer of Values

Mommy, our God is not here.

Five-year-old Somali girl on seeing her first Canadian snowstorm

The single greatest fear expressed by Somalis in both London and Toronto was a concern that they would be unable to teach Islam, and an
Islamic value system, effectively to their children in a Western environment – with its multiplicity of choices and its seemingly endless smorgasbord of competing values. Even Somalis who were confident in
their own ability to straddle two value systems were concerned about
how to impart a solid grounding in Islam, because it is a minority religion and because so much of what competes for their offspring's attention is so very alien. There were those, however, who did not evince
this fear, who felt that traditional methods of teaching must change,
but that the values of Islam are strong enough to withstand the competition of the Western marketplace of ideas.

Among the issues raised in this context is the question of schools
and whether children should or can be sent to Muslim schools.[1] While
not all Muslim parents think separate schools a good idea, many
would like to send their children to Muslim schools if they could afford
to do so, which most of them cannot. In both Canada and Britain, Muslim schools are private institutions, few in number and expensive.[2] The
issue was complicated in Britain throughout the last decade – and during the period of the interviews – by the fact that many Christian and
Jewish private schools, but no Muslim schools, had been granted voluntary-aided status and in return for following the national curriculum receive state support. Voluntary-aided schools were established

by the Education Act of 1944. There are roughly four thousand of them: about two thousand each are Church of England and Roman Catholic; a handful are Jewish and Methodist.[3] Although Muslim schools had been trying for years to be granted this status, notably Yusuf Islam's (formerly pop singer Cat Stevens) Islamiah School in London, their requests had been consistently denied. In the 1980s, five schools in Bradford had applied for this status, all unsuccessfully. Two applications by the Islamiah School, in 1990 and 1993, were both denied by the education secretaries of the day. Feversham College (formerly the Muslim Girls' Community School) in Bradford had its application rejected in February 1995. The decisions were carefully watched by Muslims and non-Muslims alike. An editorial in *The Times* prior to the second Islamiah decision urged the approval of the application.[4] Public scrutiny added a political dimension to the question, amid charges of discrimination and hypocrisy on the part of politicians.[5] Tony Blair's Labour government, with the strong personal support of the prime minister, finally granted state support to two Muslim schools – the Islamiah school and Al Furqan school in Birmingham – in early January 1998.[6]

Most provinces in Canada have no equivalent to voluntary-aided status. Provision was provided in 1867 by the British North America Act for government funding for denominational schooling as it existed at the time of Confederation, and this constitutional situation remains largely unchanged.[7] In Ontario, the Protestant school boards have evolved into those meeting the needs of the non–Roman Catholic population and do not teach or preach any one religion. Roman Catholic schools continue to provide Roman Catholic religious education. Ontario has been reluctant to provide public funds for denominational schooling, beyond what is constitutionally obligated, on the grounds that the school system is a key integrationist institution and that what is given to one religious group would have to be given equally to all.

Among the other significant differences between education in Canada and Britain is how religion is treated in the classroom. Education is a provincial responsibility under the Canadian constitution, so the approach differs from province to province. Ontario classrooms take a secular approach to religion. The current Education Act stipulates that elementary and secondary schools be opened or closed each day with religious exercises consisting of 'readings of the Scriptures or other suitable readings and the repeating of the Lord's Prayer or other suitable prayers,'[8] but this is broadly interpreted. Readings from a variety of beliefs – including 'secular humanism' – are considered to meet the requirements of the act,[9] and many schools do not have the readings performed on a daily basis. Ontario courts have held that public schools should not be used to promote the faith of any one group,[10] nor should government funds be used to pay for religious independent schools, a stance that was upheld by the Supreme Court of Canada in 1996.[11] Holidays such as Easter and Christmas are generally taught as festivals celebrated by most, but not all, of the school's population. Emphasis is placed on customs as opposed to religious significance. Similarly, Jewish and Muslim holidays may be discussed in the classroom, but it is their customary and not their religious significance that will be stressed.

In Britain, in contrast, religious instruction is seen as an important part of the school curriculum. The Education Acts of 1944 and 1988 both require religious education and assembly, which 'shall be wholly or mainly of a broadly Christian character.'[12] Children may be withdrawn from the daily assembly by their parents for religious reasons,[13] or the school may make alternate arrangements for its non-Christian pupils. In schools where a majority of pupils are non-Christians, an application can be made to lift the requirement for Christian collective worship.[14] Christian religious education has been augmented by religious education in other faiths as well.[15] Muslim leaders' criticism of the approach of the Education Acts and Lord Swann's defining 1985 report, *Education for All*, have centred on the perception that the resultant banquet of religious instruction either leaves the impression on the student that all religions are equally valid[16] or that continued emphasis on Christianity gives that religious denomination 'a very privileged place while marginalising other faith communities.'[17]

For these reasons, at the beginning of the 1996 winter school term, fifteen hundred Muslim pupils were withdrawn *en masse* from religious education (RE) in Batley, West Yorkshire, as a result of a coordinated campaign among parents.[18] Shortly thereafter, the parents of five hundred Muslim pupils, who account for 70 per cent of the population at a Birmingham primary school, convinced the school to replace the regular RE syllabus – for the Muslim children – with lessons taught by a Muslim and qualified RE teacher, Maulana Imran Mogram.[19]

Many parents see education as a critical issue because they recognize that the home plays a limited role in transmitting values to children, and they are unwilling to have religion limited to the private domain. For them, education is where private and public domains interact. This intersection – what Jeff Spinner refers to as part of civil society[20] – is a critical arena in which public culture is defined as accepting – or not – of cultural difference. (See chapter 6.) It is not enough, in the eyes of these parents, to restrict religious education to home and the Qur'an school (also called *dugsi* in Somali).

Many families recognize Qur'an school as a crucial element of value transfer and community socialization.[21] Somali teenagers and adults talk of their Somali schooldays being divided between hours spent at the *dugsi* and hours at school. Many teenagers remarked that it was strange to them not to have religious (Qur'anic) education incorporated into their regular school day. The idea that religion was extraneous to education, and had to be worked into extracurricular time much like sports or games, was to them a peculiar arrangement. For many diaspora Somalis, Qur'anic education in Somali becomes an important part of a child's education.

People have devised a number of solutions to the problem, not all equally successful. In some cases, classes are given on afternoons or weekends in existing mosques, whose premises are shared with other Muslim groups. In other cases, classes are set up in private houses on weekends. Some parents employ private tutors for their children. Because the Somali diaspora community is made up largely of refugees there are not always internal resources to rent space, buy materials, and so forth. Qur'ans are widely available in a Somali/Arabic edition (printed in Medina, they are distributed by the boxful at venues like weddings), but this solves only part of the financial problem. This is the genesis of concerns such as those of Fathia, quoted below.

Other school issues that emerged concern compulsory classes in fine arts, performing arts, and sex education. All three of these pose problems for some Muslim students and their parents. The concern with respect to art class is with representations of the human form;[22] with music, the creation of an 'unhealthy' environment;[23] and with drama class the need to perform in close contact with members of the opposite sex.[24] Sex education – including information on AIDS and its avoidance – is compulsory in British and Ontario schools and is problematic for Muslims both because of the content of the programs and the public location of the discussion, a matter taken up at greater length in chapter 6. The British Education Act of 1993 does allow parents to withdraw their children from some aspects of sex education,[25] but in order to take advantage of this proviso Somali students would have to discuss the issue and what is learned in class with their parents, something they are extremely reluctant to do.[26]

None of the Somali parents or children interviewed complained about either their daughters' ability to wear the hijab to school or the content of school lunches. Additionally, high schools with significant numbers of Muslim students appeared to have made provision for prayer facilities. The fact that these questions have largely been resolved in London[27] and Toronto[28] indicates that the host societies are responding to at least some of the needs of the Muslim communities in their midst.

Both parents and teenagers frequently referred to the rapid eruption of the urban myth of '911' or '999' within the Somali community. Because parenting styles are different in North America and Britain from those in Somalia, and because these involve elements of persuasion and not simply imposition of will, parents often expressed a fear of being unable to discipline their children at all. The concern was that children would threaten to call police emergency numbers (911 in Canada or 999 in Britain) if parents in any way infringed on their freedom, even to insist on a verbal demand.

This chapter presents first the range and texture of adult concerns on these matters, of both those who are parents and those who are not, and second, the sense of Islamic practice and identity as expressed by the teenagers interviewed in London and Toronto. This group is particularly interesting because by and large its members have been out of Somalia for at most seven years. Chameleon-like, they adapt to new environments and new peer pressures. They seek to understand how best to survive and flourish in their new worlds, and thus they live, simultaneously and bewilderingly, in the Western environment of the school and in the refugee or immigrant milieu of home. Their balancing act is at once tenuous and insecure, improvised and brashly self-assured. A section of analysis and commentary forms the final section of the chapter.

Adult Concerns

The women of the Somali Women's and Children's Network in Toronto expressed a uniform fear that they are 'losing their children.' Their concerns were that they have no control over their children, that the children are becoming what they see as Canadian – losing their values and religion, that they are disrespectful, and that mothers cannot discipline their children without fear of the government taking them away if they call 911. Even elementary school children talked about using 911 at home, they complained. Government schools not only do not provide Muslim teaching or values, which they would not expect, but actually undermine what the parents try to instill at home. One woman, for instance, said that she does not mind countering Christmas trees and the Easter Bunny – she would not expect anything different, but she does mind when her children are given condoms along with their sex education classes in middle and high school. 'This is going too far,' she declared. Other women said that they *did* mind Christmas trees and the Easter Bunny, because in their minds there is implicit religious instruction in the assumption that everyone should celebrate in the common classroom, even if Jesus is not discussed directly.

The main concerns, however, were the related issues of discipline, respect, and control. Unwittingly, they believe, Western values and society have resulted in a 'war against parents' who have consequently no way of enforcing their views and are therefore bound to lose their children. Islamic school is not an option because it is too expensive, and even then it does not solve the problems of life outside school. For instance, the influence of television is pervasive, and mothers often do not know what it is their children are watching. 'The kids are free to do whatever they want here, and society agrees with them, so as a parent you stand alone.'[29]

Although discipline of children reaches beyond religious issues, it is these that are frequently the source of tension between parents and children. Kalima, working with a Somali resettlement agency, was given a government grant to train thirty-six women and youth volunteers from within the community, to help resolve intergenerational difficulties. In a typical instance, she recounted the story of a Somali woman in a shelter for abused women, whence she had gone with her nine-year-old daughter to escape physical abuse from her husband. The daughter went on summer excursions arranged by the shelter and after a time began wearing shorts and refusing to pray with her mother. The mother, who was deeply religious, was upset and after an argument slapped the daughter, who promptly reported her to the shelter personnel. By the time Kalima was called to mediate the dispute, the mother's blood pressure was dangerously high and she was close to a breakdown, incapable of understanding why her daughter could 'spy' on her.[30]

Rashid, the outreach worker who solves intercultural disputes between Somali parents and Toronto schools, spoke as follows:

Upbringing and raising children is a big challenge for Somali parents today because we are in a transition period. Things are changing rapidly. So it is important for us as parents to set limits for everything; how much we want our children to preserve and how much they will abandon. It is important because peer pressure is so strong; the media and environment is very influential. What we need is to know in advance what will arise, be more curious about Canadian culture, explore everything so as to teach kids when it does arise, be able to explain to them when they do. For instance, things that arise at school: Christmas, Chanukah, Easter. The resurrection of Jesus. For us, Jesus was a prophet but there could be no resurrection.

The schools' approach [to teach not religion, but customs] is a positive step forward, but the Easter Bunny is still part of an alien culture, and it is connected to religion. It is not part of a Somali parent's tradition, so the parent needs to learn in order to teach.

Of course there are compromises – for example, birthday parties. These are not an Islamic tradition, but given that it's just a party to have fun, people are doing it. But when a conflict of belief arises, you need to explain to them and give them the arguments they need to defend their own traditions.

The resettlement period is one of transition. People are not settled, but the children's lives are going on. Imagine a single mom, with all sorts of kids, the father not here, she's not settled, she doesn't understand Canadian culture, she doesn't speak English: the coincidence of transformation with settlement can be traumatic for someone like this.

For us from the time a child is born until adulthood he is under the care of a parent. This is a libertarian society, but it is traumatic to hear that a child is eighteen and he can do whatever he wants, he has his own rights, can do things his own way. We understand a person to be a man or a woman at puberty, but we also have the tradition that you are still your mother's child at forty, and the two concepts are in conflict.

This society has seen a breakdown in the family system. We don't have the tradition of a Children's Aid Society. This is an alien system. In Somalia if you abuse your kids, society will alienate you. This is a terrible sanction, so the system corrects for people who would hurt their kids. Some kids use this system [in Canada] to gain additional freedom. The major thing is if the institution is there for the kids' welfare, and the parents are there for the kids' welfare, there is one objective, so the major thing is to mediate misunderstandings between parents and institutions.

The thing is, parents who have taken their kids 20,000 miles from a war-torn country will never hurt their kids. Parents who have had to face danger – hunger, lions, fear, uncertainty, murder, the trauma of leaving everything behind and braving immigration to a new country – these people have faced things that social workers in Canada will never begin to understand – all to keep their children safe. Why would they then hurt their children? Of course they would not.[31]

Osob, a single mother in Toronto, left her husband once she discovered, after their marriage, that he drinks: 'I wanted him to be a person my son will look up to. He will ask who his father is, but if he is drinking people will talk behind his back. They will say he is a bad man; he drinks. I don't want my son to have a father who people talk about behind his back. Also, if he sees his father drinking he won't accept that this is something wrong in our religion. He will say if it's good enough for his father he won't see it as wrong. He can't learn if we don't show him.'[32]

Osob has been distressed by the number of times her three-year-old son's daycare personnel have questioned her about bruises that he gets playing or from minor household accidents. 'I think they think that because we're from Somalia, men abuse women; women and men abuse children. It's not true. Sometimes children are spanked, but I'm afraid to touch my child. I'm afraid he could be taken away from me. I am always feeling that eyes are looking behind me, interfering, telling me how to be with my children.'

Osob had sought counselling to help her overcome her fears of parenting, but she looked ahead to her son's adolescence with apprehension:

Children go to school from eight to four, then they do their homework and go to bed. The influence from outside will be more than yours. That's okay if you're in an Arab country or at home, where the outside mentality is a lot like yours. But here it is completely different. For instance, for us, men cannot wear earrings. My stepson came to visit when I was living with my uncle; he said he wanted an earring. My uncle said that is not for Muslims. Boys do not wear earrings, but he sees other kids and he just wants to be like them. And girls will see their girlfriends with boyfriends; they will not understand why it's okay for the friends but not for them ... That is why I will try to find work in an Arab country after I finish studying; at least until my son is fifteen or sixteen and understands more of what is wrong and right ... You can't force your kids. They will be con-

fused between what you tell them and what they see. They will take the
easy way out – doing what they see outside. We have a saying that it's
easy to make a sin; it's much harder to do the right thing. Like girls in
those tight spandex tops; that's not right, but how can you tell a girl she
shouldn't dress like that? The chances are 70 per cent that they won't listen to you. That's a big chance. I don't know if I want to take that chance.
In an Arab country at least everywhere the influences would be the same.

Ahmed, an Islamist, was unsure how to protect his four-year-old son
from values that he does not want the child to learn. The boy was still
home with his mother, but that would change shortly when the time
came for school. Ideally, he would like to place his child in an Islamic
school, but there are few of these in Toronto, and they are expensive.
The family has no television set. It had owned one but got rid of it
'because it was a waste of time and also because it was full of non-
Islamic values': 'If you can have an island of Islam in Canada, then that
is a good choice, and if you can't, then you have to leave ... But I don't
think I can leave, and most Somalis cannot go back, so we have no
choice but to make an island of Islam.'[33]
For Rashid, Islamic schools are not the answer: 'No one can live in
isolation. Going to Islamic schools will not solve your problems. The
education of a child does not end with Islamic school. During a critical
age, children should have more influence from parents than from
school. They spend more time outside school. Between their peers, TV,
and so on, kids absorb so much other information. Parents can do what
is needed without Islamic schools; they need to instill a sense of self,
right versus wrong and so on.'[34]
Roda agreed. A young woman who grew up in London, she 'rediscovered' her religion and her culture at university, after a teenaged
rebellion in which she rejected her parents' values. She was on the
verge of a marriage to a religious Somali in the summer of 1995 and
had fasted during Ramadan for the past two years. 'I have come back
to the atmosphere [of Islam], and I have a desire to study. I have been
reading about women in Islam.' Roda worries about her younger siblings, who are adolescents, especially the younger ones, who 'have no
Muslim friends.' But she said that she would not send her own children to Islamic schools: 'Isolation doesn't work. They must be
equipped to live in this society, but I would want them to be aware of
their culture and religion. I would teach my kids the Qur'an. I would
also make a big effort for Eid. Christmas is such a big deal at school. I

would give gifts at Eid but would keep openness for other religions. I think it's important to respect other religions. Openness is a positive element in anyone's life.'[35]

For Anab, it is the discipline of British private schools that is attractive:

> My big worry is my children. In Somalia you are not allowed to have boyfriends, but here they start as early as eight. I want my children to grow up modern but protected, educated but protected. I always advise them. I try to explain everything to them. On Saturdays I take them to the Arabic cultural school so they can learn the Qur'an and Arabic, at least the girl; the boy is a bit too young. During the week they go to the state school. If I could afford it I would send them to a private school. I wouldn't care if it were Christian or Muslim or Jewish, as long as it has the discipline; that is what I want. Yes, the big worry is the children. You had them, they are now your responsibility. You have to make sure you do a good job.
>
> The problem is if you live in a deprived area. If you have a good income you can live in a good area. But if you are on income support you live in a poor area and the people around do not always have good values which they teach your kids. The other kids affect your kids. For example, Hackney is one of the worst areas in England. There is no good education there, no encouragement for the kids outside the home or from other kids. Many Somalis were wealthy in Somalia, ministers of government or something, and now here they are on income support and in a three-bedroom council flat. And the worst thing is they can't get jobs, so they can't do anything about it.[36]

Her concerns are echoed by Fathia, living in New Ham in London's east end, a borough whose council had thus far not granted funds to help the Somali community organize cultural or religious instruction for their children:

> 'The kids are at home most of the time. Their schooling is terrible. They are put in school according to their age, no matter whether they have ever been in school before and even if they can't read or write. Then they come home and stay inside. This is true on weekends as well. There are no Qur'anic schools to send them to, nowhere to go. The local council won't give money for facilities because they are all Asians and the money all goes to Asian facilities and programmes.'[37]
>
> We moved here to New Ham borough in 1990. Ever since then we have

been trying to get a small place to meet – single mothers and elders. We haven't been able to succeed. There is no one in the local council office to support us.

I am worried about the education of my kids. The education system is in a bad state. These kids need help. They don't get help with English or with being behind in their work. Often they come at fourteen and get put into school, sometimes for the first time in their lives. At sixteen they are told they have graduated, even if they can't read. They are told to go to college if they want more education, but what good will that do? When they go to college they sit with older people who can't read either. It's free, but you don't learn anything. So there is no future for them. You won't find more than a handful of kids who have passed their A-levels. Kids can't possibly pass because they didn't get the education they needed when they were small.

Kids are depressed. They can see there is no future for them so they go around town and become gangs. We never had this in our community before.

It's very frightening and depressing. I don't have the money to send my kids to private schools. It's worrying me very much.[38]

Abdullahi, the religious Londoner who would be part of an Islamic movement if he did not see the various groups as Somali political factions, said that there are some advantages to the 'conservatism' of British society, which he described as the unwillingness of the British to welcome strangers in their midst:

It's difficult not living in a Muslim country, but here in Britain my kids go after school every day to the mosque. Maybe it's better than other places in Europe; there are lots of Muslims here. My kids are lucky to be in a school which is 60 per cent Muslim, in North London. When they grow up, they will probably feel fifty percent less than what I feel about being Muslim and Somali, because society is influencing the other 50 per cent, while I am 100 per cent. The conservatism of this country is probably good because it helps us keep our culture. If the neighbours and other people were friendly, there would be more cultural interaction, so the unfriendliness is good for our culture. This country is made up of so many little communities all sticking together.[39]

His companion, Nur, was vehement about his choice: 'I am thirty-six and I am not married, and I have no children. Why? Because I will never have children here. It is 100 per cent sure that I will go back. The individualization in this country would never work in our culture. I won't have children here because I don't want them to be lost. My children would be lost here.'[40]

Daud is a Bantu Somali, in Toronto for seven years. For him, the immigrant experience is 'a replica of my life in Somalia,' where the Bantu were unrecognized minorities whose 'tradition was eradicated by the Somali system.' Educating children in Canada is therefore to some extent a variation on the theme that he would have played in Somalia had the family remained there.

As a Muslim, well, it is hard, but I am here. I can't change a society that was here before me. I have to find a way, use my brains, so as to avoid a dilemma for my children. I explain that Santa Claus and Christmas is not our holiday, but I will buy my kids a gift so they don't feel out of place; we will buy a gift for their friend Beatrice, because it is her holiday.

The problem with Somalis is that they don't communicate with their kids; they try to impose everything on them. That doesn't work. For example, recently I had a friend over, and my daughter came to me. She was having trouble tying her shoe, so I bent and showed her how to do it. When we had finished, my daughter said, 'Good man, Daddy,' before she went off. If we were in Mogadishu, she would have been sent away. Men don't stop entertaining a friend in order to help their children with their shoes. My friend said, 'I like this, Daud. I wish every Somali was like this. That kid will come to you, bring her problems to you, make you part of her life.'[41]

In Golder's Green, a middle-class section of London, Aden and his wife have five children, the eldest of whom is fourteen and the youngest five months. They do not like what they see happening to children of friends, how they drift away from their parents' values and religion, so they said that they teach their children absolute respect. The children must show respect to everyone even a year older than they are; when called they must come immediately and not answer from another room. He and his wife expect their children to come straight home from school and not dawdle or chat with friends. They expected them all to live at home until they have finished university. On weekends they go to Qur'anic school. Aden looked hard to find a school where the children would not be 'brainwashed' by rigid extreme religionists. He says that he is determined that no matter how long the family lives in England, his children will consider themselves as 'one hundred percent Somali'.[42]

Yusuf sends his children to public schools in Toronto because the Islamic ones are financially out of reach. Although he feels strongly about teaching his children Muslim values, he said that it is important not to denigrate those of his non-Muslim neighbours. He related the story of how his four-year-old had called the Christmas tree at a day-care centre 'sick,' something that he had learned from his neighbours. Yusuf had told him that even though the Christmas tree was not his tradition, he must respect it for others. 'If you become a victim of bias and prejudice, you don't want to carry it in your own heart. It is a bitter pill, and you don't want to spread it,' he said.[43]

Farhia, the young Toronto woman who often wears jeans and hijab together, expressed the uncertainty of some young people who do not yet have children of their own: 'I don't see staying here. Society is corrupted; things are out of hand. I want to bring up my kids back in Somalia. Also I am black but not black American; I am Somali. But Canada is different from any other European country; I love Canada and feel Canadian, but Islamically I would want to raise my kids in an Islamic environment. I could do it here, but it would be harder. I wouldn't go to the Middle East; that would be worse than anything. If I couldn't go to Somalia I would stay here. I don't believe in isolation; I believe it's good to mix in, but I think it's important for a person to know who they are.'[44]

Samira, in London, is worried about both her teenagers and her young primary-school children: 'Teenagers are vulnerable. The education policy here seems to be to assimilate ethnic groups into the mainstream – not to acknowledge their ethnic differences, language or religion. There is also a pathological stereotyping of blacks as being difficult to teach. I notice an ignoring, or a reluctance to acknowledge, the presence of large numbers of children with different ethnic backgrounds in the classroom. It is particularly apparent in history or social studies classes, which is why the Somali kids tend not to like those classes.'

Her concern with the primary school has to do with religious education.

I am especially unhappy with the youngest kids' school. It is a denominational school, church-owned, which I did not know when I registered them. It is the closest one to home, but I didn't realize when I registered them that they would be given a strong Christian education. I didn't want them taught this, but the school told me it is a church school, so the only choice I have is to move them. I have been trying to do that, but I haven't been able to secure them a place in another school, so I have not been able to move them. The school would not excuse them from collective worship; they are forced to sing Christmas carols and learn all about Christmas and Easter and so forth. I have an open mind and full respect for other religions, but this indoctrination of my children hurts me. I complained to the authorities, and all they said was they teach other Muslim kids. In fact 40 per cent of the kids at the school are Bangladeshi Muslims, but the parents are not aware that this is going on. It's deceptive. The parents have the idea that it is safe for their kids to go to school. So now I belong to a group lobbying for space in a creche to have time on Saturdays to teach Somali kids about their religion and language and culture. There are not enough Qur'anic schools to send kids to. The community to this point has not been very organi ed at setting up facilities to educate their children in language, culture, religion, and so forth.[45]

Saida, whose children are in public schools in another part of London, has no such concerns about religious education in the classroom. In her children's primary school, the non-Christian children are separated for religious education, so they do not have Christian RE. The school even provides space for the community to teach Qur'anic classes on the weekends, but Saida prefers sending her children to the mosque classes so that they will also learn how to pray. This does not stop her anxiety about her children, however: 'I am so worried about their growing up. Their thoughts as they grow are different from mine. Even television is a lesson for them, although I control what they watch. But their whole environment is a lesson in culture.'[46]

Adolescents

Asha is fifteen and considers herself to be very religious. She came to the interview with her best friend, who was wearing a jilbab. Asha herself wore what she called 'the little hijab,' a headscarf. Asha had been in Canada for less than a year. She and her mother had escaped to Kenya, and after a year an uncle gave her the money to come to her older married sister (who does not cover herself). Their mother was still in Kenya. Asha said she prays regularly, fasts, and has no trouble obtaining halal food. She will leave class when it is time to pray and, although there is a prayer room at her high school, will often just pray in the hall if it is faster. Her friends are Somali religious girls only. On weekends, she studies Qur'an with 'a lot of people' at a private house. She said that there is no difference between how she practises Islam in Toronto with how she used to do so in Somalia. Her only two problems at school are with the enforced physical education class of grade nine and the sex education given in health class. 'I won't listen or look; I try to study something else. So I got zero in my first semester. The teacher told me I have to study this semester or I won't pass. Then they'll make me take it next year. I don't want to have to take it again, so I have no choice; I will study.'

She is disapproving of the choices of many Somali girls at her high school: 'Most Somalis here don't wear hijab, and their mother told them to, but they say, "You can't tell me what to do, this is my life." I don't try to argue with them because I know they would just say it is my problem ... When I was a child I wore it because my mother wanted me to, but now I know it is my religion.'[47]

Hamda, nineteen, has lived with her family in north London for nine years. She is a college student who donned hijab three years earlier, while still in high school, when a boy, a convert to Islam, asked her why she would not cover herself always if she covers herself when she prays. At first her friends did not understand what she was doing. They assumed that it was merely a phase or asked her whether she had tried to dye her hair and made a mess of it, but eventually they got used to it. She said that high school was 'not great' for Muslims, because there was no chance to learn about Islam. There were no gatherings of Muslims. College has been 'liberating' because there are many Muslims; imams come to talk; there are open talks and conversations. She said that she often finds herself in arguments with non-Muslims about Islam. She goes to very few movies and will not go to parties at all. 'Parents have reasonable fears about losing their kids because the schooling here is different from what they received and the influences are different; you could lose your identity. But in my case they have nothing to fear.'[48]

Layla, eighteen, is living in the north of London with her mother and five siblings. Layla's father was a prominent political prisoner during the Barre years, but has been unable to obtain a visa to enter Britain. Her mother became religious when the father was jailed, and, in the year after he was released and before the family left Somalia, the father would wake all the children for the pre-dawn prayer. Layla remembers him reading the Qur'an with them until it was time to go to school. Her mother continues to be religious in London, as are Layla's older sisters. Even her younger sisters pray with their mother and wear hijab.

Layla herself stopped praying and wearing hijab in January 1995, a few months after she started college. In high school there were many Muslims, and she used to go home at lunch and pray, but once she got to college she found that she was one of only two women wearing hijab. 'I used to wear hijab because my mom brought me up to wear it. But as I grew up I didn't feel like I'm up to wearing it. My mom was forcing me to wear it, but I began to think I shouldn't wear it because I'm scared of my mom, but because I'm scared of God. I should wear it when I mean it, when I'm up to it, when I'm ready. I want to go back to it one day, but I'm not ready now. I couldn't explain it to my mom because I don't think she would understand, but she accepted my decision. She was very upset. But you can't make someone do what you want them to. They have to do what they think is right.'[49]

Layla still fasts on Ramadan and eats halal meat when she can. She will eat chicken sandwiches at McDonald's, but 'I don't eat and I never will eat pork stuff.' She works part-time at a local fast-food restaurant: 'This is my first job, which I got in January. I looked for fast-food jobs before I took off the hijab, but they would never hire me. They just said no. And you can't work in supermarkets because they sell alcohol there. Most places won't hire you if you wear hijab. There are a few companies that don't mind; I've seen people working at Marks and Spencers, but there aren't many of those.'

Layla's mother interrupted the interview to ask me why I was questioning Layla, given that she could not possibly know anything about Islam. 'She has lived here so long, she has lost her identity,' she said. 'She knows nothing of her culture or her country.'

None the less, Layla's attitudes belie her Western exterior.

I don't like parties, they're not my 'thing.' I didn't go when I wore hijab, because it wasn't right, and now I've been to one or two, but I don't really like them.

My friends at work often go out to pubs. One day they asked me to go with them. I couldn't say no and I couldn't say yes, but I went and it was horrible. People were loud and laughing and drunk. My friends were drinking, but I said I wanted orange juice. I wasn't there five minutes. I left as soon as I drank it. I said 'Sorry, I don't like this place.' I experienced it. It's not my type of thing – so many people laughing and acting mad. I felt uncomfortable.

Sex education. Yes. When I first heard it I didn't know the meaning of the word 'sex.' My mother had never told me. It's hard to talk about when you're Muslim. Most Muslim parents think it's disgusting. In science we watched videos of a baby being born. I was shocked. I didn't know how babies got born. They showed us pictures of men and women and how they are different. I never mentioned it to my mom. I once said something to her about condoms, and she said, 'How do you know about such things!' It's hard to talk to parents about these things. I just accepted that my mom wouldn't talk about it. I would feel uncomfortable talking to her about these things. My mom would go mad if she found out that kids have sex at sixteen.

It didn't bother me to learn these things. I needed to know the other side of life. Some girls didn't go to class, but if I didn't go, how would I learn these things for when I was older? At first I couldn't watch the videos. I would turn my face away as I had been taught to do when things like this come on the TV, but then I learned this is part of life and it didn't bother me. Now I can talk about it with Christian girls but not with Muslim girls. It's disgusting to talk about it if you're Muslim.

There's a girl I work with, she was telling me about her new boyfriend. She's saying 'Tony this' and 'Tony that,' and I reali ed she's sleeping with him, even though she's only been going with him for a week. I acted like I know what she's talking about and experiencing, because she'd think I was stupid if she thought I was shocked. I tell her be careful, give her advice. But this is when I reali ed that I am so completely different from her, because in my religion Allah doesn't allow me to do that, and I don't think her religion allows her to do that either, but I don't know. But then you know this person is completely different from you. You may talk and act like she does, but you know you're a completely different person.

As is clear from Layla's comments, and as chapter 5 explores further, sex and related issues are extremely sensitive for Somali girls and women. Layla had said nothing while her mother was in the room. When she left, she said:

My mom is really stressed because my dad couldn't get a visa. My mom has been a single parent looking after six kids for almost eight years. She has been a mom and a dad to us. She's a strong lady, but she's going mad, cra y, with missing my dad.

What my mom sees is that I used to wear hijab and now I don't, and maybe I go out a bit late, and she wants to know everything, but no matter what I say she doesn't really believe me about what I've been doing. She thinks I've lost my identity, but I know where I've been and I know what I've been doing and I know I'd never hurt my mom or my religion. She thinks I've lost my religion, but I'm still holding my religion. Parents might think that if their children change their views they've changed them to the views of other kids, but you never change your feelings about your religion.

I don't think my feelings about my religion will ever change. I feel so guilty when I see someone wearing hijab walking in the street. My big sisters are really into religion. They always advise me to be more religious. I feel guilty when I go to visit them. But then I see my friends again, and my friends make me feel something else, just feel right. I don't go out and go with boys, or anything. I just go out with a group of girls. I just want to be with my friends.

In a way I think it's important to marry a Somali so I won't change my culture. If I marry a black or a white man it would change my culture, and that would bother my mother, but it wouldn't bother me if he was a good person, so long as he is Muslim. That is important. But it would be easier if I married a Somali. He would understand me and my mom.

I think I can bring up my kids with a Muslim culture here. My mom had her troubles. I will do things differently from her. I will *understand* my kids, talk to them. I don't think my mom did that. I would be comfortable with them, give them some freedom, mainly trust them. If you trust them, they will trust you. I would be open to them. Most Somali ladies don't understand that. And most importantly, I would teach them religion. But I wouldn't force them to do what they don't want to do.

Layla's comment that finding a Muslim mate would be crucial to her is a typical one. Contrary to her mother's view, she sees herself as strongly Muslim, even though she has decided not to cover her hair or pray regularly.

Sahra, eighteen, came to her interview with her long hair in dozens of thin braids under a Nike ball cap worn backward, with three earrings in one ear and chipped red nail polish, jeans, and a tee-shirt. Both her mother and grandmother, with whom she lives in Toronto, wear the 'little hijab.' Her father is still in Somalia. Sahra has a part-time job at a bank branch and contributes her pay to family earnings, part of which are sent each month to help her father. When Sahra is at home, and an uncle or male relative stops by the apartment, Sahra too will don a headscarf. The family eats halal food and observes the Eid festivals. In Somalia, Sahra went to Qur'an school daily before regular school, but she does not study it in Toronto at all.

> I don't pray, but I used to pray before I came. I want to pray; I'd love to, but it's not like you can do it sometimes. If you start you have to always do it, you have to do it from the start to the end, you have to do it at school and at work, you know? so I would love to, but ...
>
> My grandmother would like me to cover. My mother would like that too, but it is hard, because if you go to school and you didn't when you started, then everybody would ask, 'Why are you doing that?' It is hard to change.
>
> I don't go to mosque because I would have to wear hijab and everything. I would love to. It makes me guilty, because every country is different from every other country, and you have to do what people are doing in the country where you are. So when I was in my country I used to go every single day; I used to go to the mosque and Islamic school and pray, myself, you know, but now I don't go because when I was in my country I didn't go to work. But in this country you work and you learn English. I go to school and I work ... It's not that it's bad to pray at your house. If you can't go to the *masjid* [mosque] you can pray at your house. But you have to do it every single day, five times, right?
>
> I don't know, something changed me. [Sahra suddenly appeared dejected and spoke sadly.] I feel different because I don't pray. It bothers me. I could pray, but every single time I try, every time when I go to bed I think about praying, I say, okay Sahra, you're going to start tomorrow, start tomorrow, start tomorrow, but ... if you're going to pray, you can't care about your friends, you have to be serious for Allah. If I want to pray then I don't care about what my friends say. I would say, listen I don't care, I am still the same for you guys. But when I see my friends, well, not my friends, the girls of my country, when I see them pray, and they go to the masjid, and they do all these Muslim things ... But it's not just saying the things that makes you Muslim, you know? It's not hard to say the things, but it's the way you say it. I'm a Muslim, but I don't do the things I'm supposed to do. I want to pray and I want to do everything Allah's way, but I'm trying still ... Nothing makes it hard but everything makes me the way I am now because I go to work, and I would have to pray every single time, but if you tell that to your manager that you want to go pray he's going to give you a hard time. You have to wash your hands,

and your face, your feet, everything, then you have to pray. It takes more than five minutes. You would be fired if you came back too late.[50]

Despite her ambivalence about praying, Sahra is very clear about where she stands on other issues.

I go to dances and parties, but I never drink alcohol. I just say I don't drink when people try to give it to me. No, they don't always understand. Some people are surprised that I don't drink at all. I say it doesn't matter how old I am, I just don't drink. I have a friend, right? She asked me what kind of drink I want, I said I want pop,[51] because it's the only thing I drink. So she goes 'Okay,' and then she went into the kitchen and she poured me a beer. Beer is not like alcohol, but it's a little bit alcohol, right? It's not like water. But I was looking at her. She didn't think I was looking at her. She gave it to me. I told her, 'That is bad if you give me alcohol, right, because you lied to me. And if I am your friend it is not good to lie to me, 'cause I told you I don't drink. If you give it to me and I didn't know it was alcohol it's not a sin. But God knows that you gave it to me when I asked you not to. It's not good to lie.' She didn't understand. She said, 'But when I go to your house you'll order a pi   a if I'm there so why won't you try to drink?' I said, 'Look, sweetie, I don't drink and I don't eat pork, at my house or at your house. That doesn't mean that I don't want to eat anything from you.' So then she understood.

Well, God knows what is going to happen to me, whether I am going to drink alcohol or be a bad person, but I try to be a good person.

It's okay to dance with boys. I don't have a boyfriend now, but I did. He was a Christian boy. It doesn't bother me as long as you love the person. Still, it is not important to marry a Somali, but it's good, because we can understand each other, we wouldn't have to explain things in English or another language. I would love my husband to be a Muslim if he is the right man. But if I love him and I am Muslim and he is Christian, then that would be okay if we love each other. He doesn't have to come to my religion, and I don't have to come to his.

For Sahra, having a boyfriend does not mean sleeping together. Sahra expressly said it is important not to have sex before marriage.[52] When Sahra says it is all right to marry a non-Muslim, she is not speaking doctrinally. Doctrinally, she is incorrect. While it is permissible for a Muslim man to marry a monotheist – a Christian or a Jew (people of the Book, *ahl al-kitab*), Muslim women may marry only non-Muslim men if they first convert to Islam.[53] Under the assumption that children will tend to adopt the religion of their father, this injunction is intended to ensure that the children will be raised Muslim.

Khatara is sixteen. She left Burama in northern Somalia in 1991 with her older married sister and travelled to London through Ethiopia. She entered grade nine in north London. At that time there were no Somalis in her class, although there were some in the school. She intends to study medicine when she finishes high school and then to return to her family in Somalia.

Khatara was wearing khaki pants and a knitted short-sleeved top. Her short hair was pulled back into a pony tail. Her married sister, with whom she still lives, wears the hijab and would like Khatara to cover herself as well, but Khatara is not ready to take that step. 'I say when I want to wear it, I will, maybe when I am twenty or when I get married. I think your religion is in your heart, not how you dress.'[54] Other than wearing the hijab, she considers herself religious: she prays five times daily, fasts at Ramadan, and eats halal food only. She attends Qur'anic classes at the mosque on Saturdays.

School is 'alright.' There is room to pray, and although she attends Christian religious instruction, she says, 'I just write it down, but I don't pay any attention to it.' Occasionally she is asked to do school-work with a boy at school. 'I don't like it, but there's not much I can do, is there?' Khatara condones neither having a boyfriend at any time before marriage nor the use of birth control after it.

Aman and Hawa are best friends and cousins. They arrived in Toronto in 1992 within months of one another. Their mothers began to wear the jilbab once in Toronto and press them to cover themselves as well, although they do not, and they pray, but not always five times daily. Their fathers were still in Somalia in the spring of 1995.

Aman: I don't pray every day; I don't know, I find it hard. I didn't use to pray, even in Somalia, but my mom does. Sometimes I start, but after a week I just get tired of it, maybe because I didn't get used to it before I came, that's why.

Hawa: Yeah, because when we were in Somalia, we were young, and when you are under the age of, let's say, ten or eleven, you don't have to pray, it's not something you have to do yet. You just practise. We came here and we're still practising, I guess.

Even in Somalia our parents didn't use to practise the way they practise now, because they didn't think it was dangerous for us in Somalia [in terms of losing our religion] because we were in a society where every-body was Muslim. But now they wear the hijab and they are learning more about the Qur'an because of us, because they think we are in danger of not being Muslim. They think they have to show us the way ... In Somalia they used to cover their hair with the *melchabad* only.

Aman: Our moms would like us to wear the hijab because they think it would be safer for us in this society. Because when you are wearing hijab, every time you try to do something which is not good you will remember yourself. You will remember that you are Muslim and what God told us not to do.

I hope that I will wear the hijab sometime, but I don't know when. That's my dream actually. I don't know why I don't. I will decide some day ... Most of the people I know who wear hijab, they don't have as many problems as we do in society.

Hawa: The thing is that when you're wearing hijab, you're gonna act dif-ferently than when you're not, because when you're wearing it you're gonna refuse to go to movies and stuff like that, and you can follow the rules. But if you're not, as we are, you're gonna act like you're non-Mus-lim. You're gonna do the things that Muslims are not usually allowed to do, and that's gonna affect you. And other Muslims are going to say, 'Why are you doing this and that?' and that's hard.

Occasionally their teachers ask them to do things in class – such as hold hands with boys – that as teenaged Muslim girls they do not think they should be doing.

Aman: Sometimes I even forget, and I just hold hands with a boy. Because I'm not wearing hijab, I forget. That's the reason I would like to wear hijab, because I forget. After a while I remember and I think, 'Why were you holding hands?'

Hawa: It's hard. You can't go to the teacher and say, 'I can't hold hands.' He's going to ask you why, and you'll say, 'Because I'm Muslim.' But you don't have the symbol to show it, the hijab. You feel ashamed that you don't wear hijab then.

Aman and Hawa have chosen not to don the hijab, yet they see it as having value as a symbol of dedication to Islam – both for the wearer (in reminding her of 'proper' behaviour) and to justify certain behav-iour in the eyes of non-Muslims. Hawa is implying that refusing to comply with a teacher's request to hold a boy's hand is easier to justify if the symbol of religious observance is in place. Aman 'forgets' that holding a boy's hand is not proper behaviour because she is clearly struggling with her personal ideas of what is and what is not acceptable for her as a Muslim teenager. She has been told that holding a boy's hand is not acceptable but perhaps is not quite convinced of it. Indeed, the girls say that they are sometimes afraid that they will unwittingly begin to act in an un-Islamic way.

> *Aman*: Because someone is doing something wrong, they don't see themselves as doing something wrong. Sometimes I think that what if I do something wrong and I don't see it; I'm kind of worried about it.
>
> *Hawa*: For example, if you want to go to a movie, you might know it's wrong, but you'll say, just today, just once, and then it will be another day and you'll say, just one more day, and it's gonna get worse. Movies are not so serious but they're an example ... , there are other things.
>
> *Aman*: Or dancing. It depends how you dance. Slow dancing is really wrong. Fast dancing is okay because you're not touching.
>
> *Hawa*: I have to ask why our religion says you're not allowed to do something, because there must be something God is trying to protect you from. So you have to ask yourself that question. You see them dancing and you say it's nothing, but I don't know, you get closer to a boy, you're gonna get ... you're gonna have feelings, you know, and that is what God is trying to protect you from. And then you're gonna do things that ...

They say that they protect each other.

> *Hawa*: If I see her doing something wrong I'm gonna just go to her and talk to her without her even asking me if she's doing something wrong. We keep an eye on each other.
>
> *Aman*: I let her know whatever I'm doing, and she's the same with me.[55]

Sadia, in her last year of high school, had been in Toronto for four years. Her father holds a good job and a professional degree from an American university, so Sadia suffered relatively little dislocation in her move from a Mogadishu private school. She was fashionably dressed, with her hair carefully styled. In her mind, there is a significant difference between the practice of Islam in Canada and that in Somalia. 'For one thing, everybody wore hijab. I used to wear it. But here it's totally different. I mean when you don't have your religion all around you, you don't have time to go to Islamic school, you don't have time to pray, everything changes. I stopped wearing it the first month. My aunts were here before us. They were dressing normally. They became my role models. They were wearing jeans, pants. They're not strict. You forget about religion.'[56]

At school, Sadia found that she had more in common with the students who did not dress in hijab than with those who did: 'My parents don't mind if I don't wear it. They tell me to wear it, but they think I'm old enough to make up my mind. My mother wears it. Even back home some people are stricter than others. We're kind of in the middle. We're not too strict but we haven't forgotten about the religion.'

None the less, Sadia prays daily, fasts, and is careful to eat halal food when she can and to shun pork. She does not mind wearing shorts during physical education, nor does she find sex education troubling. 'That's why you're here, to study, to learn.'

> I go to parties, but I won't drink. My friends understand. Dancing is okay. It's not something I should be doing, but I do it anyway. I don't consider myself to be fully Muslim because I do some things I shouldn't be doing ... I worry about it. Sometimes I think I should stop, things like wearing pants, but I think it's going to take time before I decide to do it. I see myself one day doing all the things I'm supposed to do but it will be hard in Canada, because if you wear hijab and you're travelling on the bus people will come up to you and ask you questions like 'Why are you wearing this,' and so on. And if you wear the long hijab people will look at you differently. You might feel too different.
>
> It's okay to have a boyfriend. You just can't have sex with them until you're married. But you have to have a boyfriend, otherwise you won't know what men are like. But some people who are really strict don't even see their future husband or wife until the night before the wedding, even here.
>
> It's not okay to have sex before marriage. Whatever you believe, the religion says it's not okay. This is not the same as not wearing hijab; this is a serious sin ... I know I think differently from my non-Muslim friends about this.
>
> It's important that I marry someone Muslim but not that he be Somali. But I could marry a Christian if he does not interfere with my religion. Kids would be a problem then.

Mubarek, eighteen, had lived in the St John's Wood area of London for six years and had just finished high school. He had begun to pray regularly two months previously. He said that he has fasted (and prayed) during Ramadan for years. He attended the Sunday Somali Qur'anic lessons at the Regent's Park mosque. His family, he says, is observant, and its practice of Islam has not changed since it arrived in Britain. His school was a mixture of religions, and his friends there were mostly Christian. Nevertheless, 'I don't go to parties except birthday parties or weddings. It's against my religion,' he said.

He started to pray regularly because 'I was afraid of losing my religion. Watching TV, the environment, the culture, how people dress. I don't want to be losing my religion. I want to be the same religion I was growing up with. It was my own idea to start to pray. My parents advised me to pray, they pushed me a little bit, but I don't want to be like Christians, even though I can be good friends with them ... Now I am not afraid of losing my religion. Some people lose their religion when they come here, they start to drink beer and go to discos, stuff like that.'[57]

Mubarek said that he does not feel that Britain is his country now: 'Naaah! Well, just a little bit. It's important to be in your own country, where you're born. But it's not good there now. Maybe when the war finishes. I will stay in Britain if the war is not over. There is some racism, mainly the media, which shows some programs which are racist. At white schools it would be a problem for me, but I go to a mixed school in St John's Wood, a mixed area, so it's okay.'

He said that he was not worried about being surrounded by Western values. He did not see the need to have a girlfriend. 'Maybe when I grow up more, when I choose someone to marry, not at this time.' He was convinced that if he stayed in Britain he would eventually keep his elderly relatives at home. 'You should keep the old people, parents together with the family. The girls usually keep the family together and look after them, but it's everyone's responsibility to share.'

Living in an expensive country like Britain, however, had changed Mubarek's mind about contraception: 'Birth control is okay. Some do, some don't. I don't want a big family. In this country the houses are too small. Maybe you could have five or six kids, not twelve.'

Abdikarim was eighteen and a high school student in Toronto. One day when he was fourteen his mother sent him to get groceries in Mogadishu. When he returned, the house had been destroyed and his family was nowhere to be found. He ran to his grandmother's house in Qismayo, and after a couple of days she gave him some money and secured a place for him on a convoy to Kenya. He was taken safely to

Mombasa, but on its next trip the convoy was caught and all its pas-
sengers were shot. After he had spent a couple of years in Mombasa,
Abdikarim's grandmother paid a family to take him to New York, and
he crossed the border to Canada on his own. Abdikarim lived with
some distant relatives for a year, but by March 1995 was living on his
own.

Abdikarim attends a public high school in Toronto's west end. When
Somali children first arrived in Toronto, and all left the classrooms at
once when they considered it time for prayer, the schools consulted
with local Islamic leaders. The imams suggested to the teenagers that,
as long as their prayers were made within a certain time period, they
were still valid and could therefore be made either before or after class,
during a suitable break.[58]

I'm okay now. I forgot all about that stuff. I'm glad to be in Canada and
have a better life. I'm going to go to college next year, so my life's going
okay.

I want to learn accounting. I spoke English when I got here because I
went to private school in Mogadishu. I was born there and stayed there
my whole life. My dad was in marketing, a businessman. He had a few
companies. He used to travel a lot.

I pray five times a day. I read the Qur'an; I fast on Ramadan. I do follow the steps of Islam. In Somalia I studied the Qur'an; I studied and
memori ed the whole Qur'an. I go to the mosque and go to lectures, and I
volunteer in the Somali community, at SOYAT. I go there and talk to people about Islamic issues and give lectures, about the Qur'an and things. If
we have knowledge we should share it. I go to the masjid, the Tariq
mosque.

On Fridays while we are in school we pray together, the *salat jama'a*. We
all pray. First we prepare a speech and talk to people, and then we ask
God to give us blessings, and then we pray. We do it in a classroom, about
twenty, twenty-five of us, mostly males, and then some females who sit at
the back. We take turns giving the talk. We eat our lunch, and then we
come to the classroom.

Sometimes we ask the teacher to leave class to pray, like if the time
changes. If the teacher doesn't let us leave we do it after school or at break
time. It only takes five minutes. We have a place to pray, but you could
pray anywhere, on the stairs or somewhere, as long as it is clean and dry.

Back home I used to study my religion most of the time. In Canada, I
don't get much time. I spend most of my time in the classroom. We come

here at 9; we leave at 3; back home we left at 1 and the rest of the time read the Qur'an, study, or attend a lecture. I am a strong believer; my family taught me to do everything. I do these things for my God; if you want to be a Muslim you have to do these things for yourself. On the day of judgment God will want to know you did these things for yourself.

I sociali e with everyone who wants to learn; I don't discriminate against people. I talk to everyone. I don't go to parties, because it's not good. It's good to have fun, but dancing is a waste of time, you spend hours and hours. People that usually come to dance are not strong believers, so it's hard for me to communicate with them.

I do have friends who are not Muslims. Some students call me strange when I say I don't want to go to parties and things; they ask me why I don't want to have fun. I say that God told me, in the Qur'an, to talk to the person and try to tell them good things about Islam. If they don't listen to you, there's nothing you can do. I like people, and I like to talk to them, so sometimes I try to explain things to them. It's hard for me sometimes. It's not against the religion to go to parties and talk, you know, it's just that there are different parties. There are parties where you go and dance, and there are pubs, and that's not good for us. They are a waste of time.

We have a lot of halal grocery stores. At a friend's house I wouldn't eat pork. I would eat the other food, but not the pork. I would just explain to them. I try to explain what is good and what is not good. Some people understand, and some don't.

There's nothing I can do about sex education at school. I have to go to school. I can't tell the school what to teach. We only have one Qur'an, but there are other books, the hadiths, that tell you everything. I think that's enough knowledge. I don't think you need details on everything, like sex. In our religion it is forbidden unless you are married.

I won't have a girlfriend until I am married. It would cause many problems. I don't think it's a good idea to have boys and girls mixed together, because they don't have ... they have different feelings, because one is male and one is female. The main thing is it's not good to contact a person like that. You could go to restaurants and eat, you know, as long as it had something to do with the subject you are studying, but not as a relationship. I know a lot of people who are not strong believers who have girlfriends and it causes a lot of problems. But when I go to them, I don't give them pressure, I don't tell them, 'that's not good for you'; I try to help them, I try to give them a chance to figure out what's wrong.

I do watch TV. I like to watch movies, the news, anything, but sometimes on movies there are things that are not good. It's not good for kids, and it's not good for believers. I turn the channel, and when that part is gone I go back.

Gym class with girls doesn't bother me. I figure if she's a female, she wants to learn, you know. I just say, let's put the girls on the other side. It's a different society; it's not the same as where we used to live. I just do what I'm supposed to do. I do the gym thing, I study for my tests. If a girl comes and asks me a question, I answer it. It doesn't bother me that much, but sometimes when we do physical things a girl will fall down, and it's not good for you to stay there and watch. I just turn my face.

It's not important to marry a Somali person. You could even marry a Christian. I think it's better to marry a person who will understand you. Maybe a Christian could communicate better than a Somali girl with you, could understand each other. It really depends on the person you marry.

It's not important for me if she covers. But God told us that it's better for females, that they should cover their hair, and only show it to the person they marry, but it depends on the person. If a person wants to do that, they have to do it, and if they don't, it's up to God, you know?

In saying that marriage to a Christian is permissible, Abdikarim is speaking as a man.

Abdikarim spoke and sat calmly, unlike many of the young men his age who crouched tense on their chairs, like overwound clock springs. His eyes were serious, but his smile was broad and sweet. He shrugged and smiled his generous smile when asked how he copes with his memories. 'I live on my own. My strength comes. God told us if we follow him and study Islam and help everyone, then God will give us a hand, a light, you won't feel alone.'[59]

Warsame has lived with his uncle and nephew in Toronto for two years. Shortly after he arrived in the city, his father, a former supreme court judge, was murdered. When he relates this event his voice chokes and he swipes at his eyes. His mother refuses to leave Kenya for Canada because she does not want to move to a non-Muslim country. Warsame always wears a *kufi* (a small cap) and prays wherever he happens to be when it is prayer time.

When I was back home, I went to school for the Qur'an. I have to pray five times a day. I do it every day; I go to the mosque on Fridays; I fast on Ramadan; I pray here, even when I'm in school. In class, when it's time to pray, I go out of class. Sometimes when I go downtown and it's time to pray, I do, and nobody gives me a hard time. I pray wherever there is space, where people aren't walking, where it's nice. I put newspapers there and I pray. Sometimes in the subway, wherever I am. Nobody attacked me ever. People go around me, nobody ever gives me a hard time. People respect me; it's a nice respect. Some people ask me what I'm doing; it's nice. I respect other religions, and they respect me. It's nice to respect each other.

When I was in the subway praying, two weeks ago, a lady was asking me, 'What are you doing?' I said, 'I'm a Muslim and I'm praying.' I gave her a little card. I said my English is very poor; I can't explain everything well. But I find in Canada people from different countries live here, and they respect each other and their differences. As well I see that in Montreal there was a Muslim woman wearing hijab and they told her to go home from school; that seems to me ... maybe they don't understand Muslims and the Muslim situation ... I haven't heard that in Toronto; people seem to respect Muslims here.[60]

Warsame's uncle and nephew would prefer that he not mix with non-Muslims, for fear that he will be influenced by them. This was the cause of many good-natured but serious discussions, during which Warsame says that he argued that a good Christian, one who does not smoke or drink, is a far better influence than a Somali who has strayed from Islam. None the less, he was wrestling with the temptation provided by different social standards in Canada and finding one situation in particular somewhat stressful:

It is actually not permitted to take a girlfriend the way the Christians do it, but it's okay to have a girlfriend. You shouldn't sleep with her or kiss her or touch her, but you have to know each other. You can talk to her, to tell her all your secrets, do your homework. Right now we are friends. She's a Christian girl, but I would like to make her a girlfriend my way. We are friends. We talk, sometimes we go out to eat, but sometimes she wants to touch my hand. I pull away and say, 'No, don't touch me.' She says, 'Why not?' Sometimes I hold her hand, it's a mistake but you know ... Sometimes she says, 'You want your own way, that's not good, sometimes you have to go my way.' I say 'Okay,' but you know, it's very very very tough; very tough. I don't know. It's hard. There are Somalis who have girlfriends. They don't go to movies, but they go out, they do homework together. It's very nice, that's the way to feel. But the bad part is, I like this girl, but she is Christian. She likes what I am doing. She respects my religion. She phoned me at home at Ramadan and told me when it was time for me to stop my fast. 'It's 6:30, you're going to eat breakfast now, great!' And for example at lunchtime she went out to eat lunch; she wouldn't eat in front of me; very respectful. Now she is learning about Islam. But I don't know what will be the end. It's a very tough situation ... She tried a lot of times to kiss me. I said no way, a kiss would be the end!

Farah is a seventeen-year-old basketball player at a Toronto high school. He lives with his mother and brothers and arrived in Canada in 1993 after a three-year-stay in Kenya. His mother is religious, but Farah wants only to play ball and hang out with his friends.

> In Somalia, if you want to pray or do something, you can hear the people say, 'Come, come let's go pray.' They call from the minarets, but if you're here you can't hear that so you have to remember yourself, and it's hard to do that. There everybody does it, so you do it too, but here it's not like that.
>
> My mom wears hijab and studies the Qur'an. She would like me to study. She talks to me every day. She asks me if I prayed. Last night she asked me if I was studying Qur'an. I told her I was half-studying, I was trying. She would like me to study at home, when I have a chance. I tell her I try, a little bit. It's hard though, to have the time.
>
> It's hard to be a Muslim in Canada, big-time hard. It's hard to remember to pray. If you could hear the mue   in you would remember. Also it's big-time hard to fast during Ramadan when you see your friends are eating; you want to eat with them too.[61]

Farah goes to school dances and parties. 'My religion says it's not okay to dance with girls, but I think it's all right.' None the less, even then he will not drink, even when his friends pressure him. 'I say, "No, I'm sorry, I don't drink." They say, "Come on, come on," but I don't listen to them.' Moreover, he said, it is okay to have a girlfriend and hold hands, but no kissing and no sex.

Amir lives in foster care in London. He has been there for two years. His story is similar to Abdikarim's: he arrived home one day to find that his family had fled. A relative took him to the Kenyan border and put him on a boat for Nairobi, where he stayed for eight months before being sent on to London. He has since determined that his family is safe, but it prefers that he stay in London while Somalia is unstable. Amir spent a year in the children's home; he now lives in foster care with a West Indian family from Jamaica. The family is Christian, but there is another Somali boy in foster care with them.

Because schools in Mogadishu collapsed in 1991, Amir missed two years of education. He had just graduated from high school. He had been put in the class commensurate with his age group and given extra English lessons, but the same work as everyone else in his class (no remedial lessons). He said that after six months he could manage. He learned English quickly and began to interpret for others, for teachers and new students. He feels that he caught up. In September he planned to go to college in Brixton to study business.

Amir prays, fasts during Ramadan, and attends the Regent Street mosque every Friday. The family prepares halal food for him, because he told his social worker that this was important. He has been praying regularly since the age of thirteen. He said that the biggest difference between Somalia and Britain is that in Somalia there were always shaykhs around who would explain the Qur'an, who knew everything. 'People were talking twenty-four hours a day about religion. Here I have not so much contact with shaykhs.' 'I am more religious here than I was in Somalia because when I see the people who are in this country who are not interested in religion I feel scared, the way they treat our religion, because they are Christians. In Somalia most people are Muslim. Here they drink beer and eat pork and don't fast. People here don't have religion. That makes me feel more strongly about my religion.'[62]

Amir will not go to parties but has many non-Muslim friends with whom he plays football, basketball, and computer games. Once they asked him to come for a beer. 'I told them I won't have things like beer because I'm Muslim, and they never asked again. They know me. I'm strong. And then they didn't bother me any more. Somali kids like me are mostly not following Christian kids. We do have girlfriends; most of them are Somali. English girls always want me to buy them a beer. I tell them the doctor said I can't drink; it's not good for my stomach, I mustn't have acids. It's easier to tell them that than to say I am a Muslim, but even so if I don't drink they don't stick around long. Sometimes I do buy them a drink, though.' The girls are 'just friends.' There is no touching, no sex before marriage. 'I have made a group of my friends like me, who also have no family. At first I felt bad when I came here alone. After a couple of months I got used to it. I will never change. We keep in touch all the time, me and my Somali friends. I have the other guy I live with, my friends, I run to the mosque. I don't go to parties or clubs. I have lots of Muslims around me. I don't have to worry. I feel the same as before.'

Abdi is also living in foster care with a Christian West Indian family in London, but he is more concerned with fitting in with his new friends than in practising Islam. He dresses fashionably, smokes, and does not care whether he eats halal food or not: 'It's different here. Everyone changes here. People act like Christians. Even some Muslims are drinking. I do everything I want here. I feel less Muslim; it doesn't bother me.'[63]

Abdi attends college, where he studies English as a second language and computers. He would like to move closer to the college and his friends in Lambeth because when he stays out late he frequently misses the last 'tube' (subway) home. He said that he goes to nightclubs but that he does not drink there. He said that he does not care whether he marries either a Muslim or a Somali. 'I like it here. People are free. In Muslim countries everyone is talking rubbish. Here everyone wants to enjoy himself, to go with girls, to go and dance.' Abdi said that his parents, in Kenya, are religious, and would probably not like the fact that he is living with a Christian family, but he does not talk to them about it.

These young people are, above all else, almost painfully courageous. They met my eyes with theirs; they spoke thoughtfully and frankly, even of events and emotions that were unresolved and obviously still tormenting them. With their lives shattered, separated at a vulnerable time of their development from parents or siblings, often unable to absorb the fact of the violent deaths of their loved ones, they nevertheless grabbed on to their new lives with a fierceness, with a determination to find a workable path, with indomitable spirit. They were intent on surviving, and surviving well, remaining true to themselves and their culture, but not by forgoing the exploration of the life that was opening to them. For all they had been through, their eyes were not dull or despairing. Some were hurt by rejection or racism, or confused by it; many carried the burden of memories too agonizing to relate, but they did not give the impression of people who could no longer love, or hope.

Analysis and Commentary

The teenagers provide excellent examples of the cultural weaving of internal integration. They are combining the religious practices of their birth culture with their experiences of their adopted culture and in the process redefining what they understand to be acceptable behaviour for a good Muslim. This is a subject of constant renegotiation, and intergenerational conflict arises most often when the parents' redefinition does not coincide with that of their teenagers. This might happen over the suitability of movies or television, appropriate friendships and curfews, and, significantly for girls, the question of dress.

Contrary to the parents' fears, however, these teenagers are in no way drifting away from Islam. Like their parents, they are almost fiercely proud of their heritage and identity. They do not see themselves as being vulnerable to being swept away by a tide of secularism, Christianity, or freedoms that are in seeming conflict with Islam, as their parents fear. Rather, they are engaged in precisely the same sort of balancing act as their parents are, but rather than try to accommodate work and prayer, they are working to reconcile the life of a peer-pressure-conscious, Western teenager with the demands of their religion.

Each has found a different balance, which will undoubtedly evolve over time. It is as though they have each determined their own baselines (hijab or no hijab; parties but no drinking or dancing; dancing but no drinking; no parties except on special occasions; boyfriends or girlfriends but no sex; no boyfriends or girlfriends, and so on), and everything else is up for negotiation. Their environments are different from those of their parents. They do not want to cause more pain to these people who have seen so much of it, yet they must experiment with their practice of their religion.

It is clear that they are much more tentative in their redefinitions than young people in their early twenties. Hawa and Aman, for instance, speak of needing to bring each other up short when one or the other engages in questionable behaviour, and both believe that wearing the hijab would serve as a reminder to them to continue to behave in an Islamically correct way, although neither believes that as a teenager she should be required to wear it. Sahra is painfully ambivalent about praying (which she does not do because she feels that she is not serious enough, although she claims to desire to be in the future). But even this experimentation does not come at the price of the loss of a Muslim sensibility. Hawa and Aman do watch out for each other, and Sahra ferociously defends her right to be who she is when non-Muslim friends try to alter her behaviour (such as when a friend tried to trick her into drinking a beer).

The difference in political culture between Toronto and London, which is fully explored in chapter 6, is apparent in the differences in how religion is viewed within the schools, in particular the requirement of RE in Britain and the dominance of Christian religious education, as well as in parents' perceptions of the resources available to their children as non-English-speaking immigrants. These children have faced formidable educational barriers: in both Toronto and London, they are put in classes commensurate with their age level, not their educational background. The war and their multi-stage refugee journey, often including long stays in refugee camps, meant that they frequently missed years of schooling. In some cases they were learning to read and to speak English simultaneously, and there is often no parent at home capable of helping them with their studies. Parents in London complained more frequently that classes in English as a second language and general remedial resources were not sufficient to enable their children to succeed prior to finishing secondary school.

Attitudinal differences in teenagers are most strongly visible when the students are asked questions concerning their attachment to their adopted countries and concerning the Salman Rushdie affair (and the issue of respect), as becomes clear below.

The fact that the practice of religion is redefined, and that the cultural weaving continues despite strong attitudinal differences concerning host-country attachment and all that that implies, is a strong indication that integration is best analysed as a two-part process. Internal integration, as the answers to these questions demonstrate, proceeds regardless of how externally integrated a minority group is, particularly in this very flexible age group. Even here, it is possible to discern the differences, an indication that the quality of internal integration is affected by differing political cultures. In London, there is a defiance in Abdi's rejection of his culture and religion, and Layla said that she stopped wearing her hijab because she was made to feel embarrassed. One boy, interviewed at a London mosque, was so fearful of the negative perception of Muslims by non-Muslims that he refused to give me his real name, even when assured that he would be identified only by a pseudonym. Among my informants, there was no London equivalent of Warsame, who is proudly Muslim and has found Christian friends – and even a Christian girlfriend – who are supportive of his practice of his religion. Nor was there a London teenager who spoke of societal acceptance of praying as Warsame did: 'Sometimes when I go downtown and it's time to pray, I do, and nobody gives me a hard time. I pray wherever there is space, where people aren't walking, where it's nice. I put newspapers there, and I pray. Sometimes in the subway, wherever I am. Nobody attacked me ever. People go around me, nobody ever gives me a hard time. People respect me; it's a nice respect. Some people ask me what I'm doing; it's nice. I respect other religions, and they respect me. It's nice to respect each other.' Chapter 6 explores fully the question of political culture and manifestations of difference in the two cities.

Abdi is unusual, in that most Somali teenagers appear to demonstrate a pride in their heritage, religion, and culture that results in a determination to remain true to themselves, no matter what the pressures to conform to Western peers. Despite the fears of parents that their children are being 'lost' to Western culture and values, the interviews indicate that most teenagers feel strongly Muslim. Conscious that they are charting a course between their parents' stronger identification with Islam, on the one hand, and the relative freedom of their Western peers, on the other hand, they have each developed their own blueprint for acceptable behaviour. Teenagers, like their parents, redefine what is acceptable Muslim behaviour as they do this. They do not act with the assurance of young people in their twenties, but it is an ongoing process, explored further in the next chapter. The interviews further reveal that while the education of their children is a major source of anxiety for Somali parents, the school systems in both London and Toronto are responding to the needs of Muslim children with respect to clothing, diet, and prayer facilities, which is an indication of the wider society's beginning to take institutional account of its inhabitants. This point, too, is discussed in further detail below.

To this point, it is mostly Somalis' practice of Islam that has been described. The next chapters examine Somalis' confrontation with issues that seemingly engage the very values of their culture and contrast them with the perceived values of the adoptive society. Chapter 5 describes how respondents deal with such issues and with their perception of the differences between the values of Somali/Muslim culture and those of the West. It provides further demonstrations of the redefining of their practice of Islam. Chapter 6 explores how the Western political culture affects the integration of immigrants and minorities and explains how the environment of the wider society – as exemplified by its political culture – affects even the most personal religious decisions.

5

Bridging Two Worlds: Weaving Two Cultures

No matter how long they have been in the West – though bearing in mind that the same individual's attitudes will change over time – all the persons interviewed had come to certain conclusions, whether consciously or subconsciously, about how to reconcile the values and practices of Islam with those of their new societies. Most informants saw the schism as one between a value system (both Somali and Muslim) that stressed responsibility to family and another that emphasized freedom and individualism. Asked to encapsulate their sense of the difference between Somali/Muslim values and those of the West, they frequently spoke of family consciousness on the one hand and 'selfish' freedom on the other. For many, that freedom was frightening, and yet, as has already become apparent in their descriptions of how they express and practise Islam, they were finding ways to balance the identity with which they arrived with a new identity reflective of a new environment.

This chapter presents first the informants' comments on a number of topics at the heart of this self-identification, including way of life, sexuality and reproduction, and responsibility to elderly parents. Second, female circumcision is discussed in a separate section. The chapter concludes with analysis and commentary.

Perceptions of Value Systems

When asked to define the differences between the Somali/Islamic value system (the two are often seen as intrinsic to one another) and that of the West, Somalis often speak of the divergent expectations of the individual: responsibility to one's family in contrast to 'absolute' freedom. In a Somali framework, the individual is seen as responsible for his own actions before God, where they concern religion; but also to his family and relations, particularly when they are in need. The Somali kinship ties – the clan network, with its increasing levels of responsibility to close blood-relations – reinforce and are reinforced by those teachings and injunctions of Islam that emphasize structure and the place of family relationships. Somalis often view with fear the threat to these structures that the individualism of the West seems to present.

Said holds a doctorate from an American university. He is in his forties and has been in Canada since 1983. 'This is the hardest part. How can I assure my kids will adopt this, the essence of Somali culture, the most important part? I tell you if Somalia had had a Western culture during the civil war, most Somalis would not have survived. The fact that so many survived is because we are compelled to help each other. You know, my mother's father went to the hajj in 1945. He had nothing, no money at all. He walked to Zayla, took a boat to Mecca, and came back, not worried about finding food or shelter or people to guide him. This could only happen in Somalia, in such a helping culture. That's the culture I want my kids to adopt in addition to Western culture.'[1]

Yusuf, thirty-four, is a religious Torontonian who lived in the Middle East before immigrating to Toronto.

> My community has been important to me all my life. I always think of my group. I cannot imagine living for myself; it contradicts all the things I believe in. When my friend phoned me from overseas to say he wanted to come but had no money, I sent him the money, even though I had very little and it was 50 per cent of my savings. It is a constant cultural clash, living here. I think those of us who have strong convictions of the faith will live with them. Our personalities were formed in Somalia. But here different things will be imbedded in our children. All I can do is give my children training. They will be bicultural. I am under no illusion that I can create a mould of the child I want. But what I can do is give them information so they can make informed decisions and hope that they choose what I think is right.[2]

Safiya, thirty-five, runs the Somali Women's and Children's Support Network. She was translating for a dozen older women, indicating that on this point they concurred. 'There are no rules here! Everything is freedom! What does freedom mean? Freedom to be gay or take drugs or whatever?!'[3]

Amina, who is in her late thirties, began to wear hijab only after she arrived in Canada. She would prefer to return to Somalia, but her children will not hear of it. 'There is selfishness in this country. In our culture we support whomever needs us for as long as they need support. We are always giving and helping family who need us. We can teach that to our children, but will their children have that feeling if they are raised here? I do not know.'[4]

Hibaq, twenty-nine, is married to a Briton who converted to Islam. She has lived in London for a decade.

> The elders are afraid of growing old here and being stuck like other old people into an old age home. It's horrible how they treat old people here – stuffing them into old age homes where they are stuck in front of TVs from morning to night. In Somalia it's not like that at all; everybody helps out. All the neighbours will drop by to chat for a few minutes during the day to make sure no one is lonely or forgotten. Here they sit like vegetables. The older people fear getting old here terribly.
>
> In Somalia, the idea that everybody helps out is so strong. I remember when I was nine I used to go to school from seven until one, and I always got home at the hottest part of the day when I was exhausted and hungry and hot and all I wanted to do was lie down. But my neighbour always made a lunch box for her parents, who lived fifteen minutes' walk away up at the top of a hill. I would walk there with their lunch every day, even though I didn't feel like it. If ever I complained, my mother would say, 'Come now, how would you like it if you were old and there was no one who bothered to bring you your lunch?'
>
> The West is so selfish. I have had an Irish friend for five years, and now she is moving to Ireland, and she asked my husband whether he would help her pack. She said she would pay him. I was shocked. It's ridiculous. Why are we friends if she has to pay us? I would take five days off work if she needed me to help her. If she wants to pay she could get a moving company! I don't understand this way of looking at things at all![5]

Nura steadfastly refuses to wear hijab in spite of community pressure. In her thirties, she supports her husband and three young children in London. 'Everyone considers themselves to be free here, you can't do anything or they will call 999. Even the wife, the way she can treat her husband here; they have more power than their husbands.'[6]

Nura's comment may be a reaction to the frustration that her husband feels at his inability to find a job. A strong woman who appears to be thriving in the diaspora, she is keenly aware, however, of the dislocation occasioned by the sudden reversal of gender roles in her family.

Roda, twenty-five, is rediscovering her Islamic identity, having spent most of her life in Britain. She is engaged to a Somali from a religious home and had begun to study the Qur'an but does not veil herself. 'I feel in-between. I believe in the value of the community, but when I compare myself to my cousins I am not that committed to my extended family, especially now. My father's second cousin will call and want serious money from me, like £300–£400, just because I'm working. I get so angry but I have no choice but to give it to him. The thing is that the extended family is the social security system of Somalia. It will break down with financial independence. When people need each other they provide, but as they become self-sufficient those feelings will fade. I will make sure my child is as independent as possible, so that he or she will be the helper, not the needy.'[7] Roda's story about her father's second cousin indicates that she at least views his request as an imposition. It is a sign that the clan network is losing salience in the diaspora, whereas for her and others religion has gained in signficance.

Warsame, eighteen, is in high school in Toronto. He is religious but was interested in befriending a Christian girl. His uncle, who cares for him, was trying to dissuade him from pursuing the friendship.

It's hard to explain. This is what I'm always talking about with my uncle. He says you're looking to be Muslim and democratic. It's really difficult. He says you want to go with Christian people; you want to have a Christian girlfriend, and do your job as a Muslim. He says you can't be a democratic Muslim, because a Muslim is a Muslim. But for me I want to make friends with Muslims and non-Muslims, it doesn't matter if a person is black or white, all people are the same. It doesn't matter if I have a Somali girlfriend, or a Christian girlfriend. But they say she must be a Muslim, because there is an article in the Qur'an that says that if you are with someone you will become like them. But there are a lot of Christians who are very nice. They are not drinking; they go to pray on Sundays, so it is a little bit difficult. If I was in Somalia it would not be difficult, but when I came here I met a lot of people who are nice and who respect you, so if a person respects me and my religion I like to respect them. I'm trying to find my own way, but my uncle and nephew say it is bad. But I am not doing anything bad. Sometimes my Christian friends come with me to the mosque to see what is going on there, and I went two days to the church to see what it was like. My uncle has nothing to worry about. We are friends; he can't force me to become Christian. I can't force him to become Muslim. Friends is friends; religion is religion; it's a matter of respect.[8]

The comments of Warsame's uncle reflect the concern of many Somali parents that mixing with non-Muslims will result in their children's drifting away from Islam and its values. He is not, in this context, declaring that democracy and Islam are inherently incompatible, but saying that it will be hard for him to retain his faith amid a tide of secular non-believers. Warsame counters this concern by emphasizing the similar values and beliefs that he has found with Christians.

Rashid works as an intercultural mediator at a Toronto high school. He is in his forties and he always tried to see both sides of every dilemma.

The balance is in the middle. A focus only on the individual will have a negative impact, as we can see by looking around here. A focus only on being part of a collective family also will undermine the responsibility of the individual too. You have to draw the line between religion and tradition. The Muslim world tradition is this sense of collective group, where your action reflects on the community. But the religion says that everyone is responsible for his own actions. Some *sura* [Qur'anic chapters] says that on Judgment Day you cannot resort to the actions of your mother or father or anyone else. You will be judged for your own deeds. So the religion speaks clearly. There is responsibility for the individual even though responsibility for family and the umma is also there. You need a good balance.

What I'm teaching my son is these are your responsibilities and you will have a problem if you fail to do them. If you do meet them, you will not have a problem and you will also have honoured your family. He must be aware of that. If you fail in school, you are the one who will have a problem, but also you will not honour your family who gave you every opportunity to succeed. Your failure affects you primarily, but also your family.[9]

Nasra, twenty-nine, dresses fashionably and does not consider herself religious. She left Somalia in 1984 to study in India, where she learned Hindi and English. In 1989 the war started, so rather than return home, she immigrated to Toronto, where she owns a small business.

It's important to me to marry a Somali, not a Muslim. I don't care so much about the religion, but I worry about tradition and culture. We take care of each other, so if my mom's had a hard time and she wants to come over, I want her to do that without having to explain everything to him. We have our own social services thing; like if your cousin is broke, you would help her out. I don't want to have to explain to anyone why I'm doing this.

At the same time, it bugs me; it drives me cra y. When my family first came here I had to take care of them. I had two jobs to support them. I had expectations that after a while they'd support themselves and I would be able to take care of myself, but my family still wants me there all the time. They want me to live there; they want me to support them. Sometimes I think I want to escape from them and live anywhere else and not have this responsibility.[10]

Nasra was rare among respondents in stressing her Somali cultural – as opposed to religious – identification. Yet she, like Roda, sees traditional family dependence relationships and expectations as a burden and something increasingly out of the ordinary.

Farhia, twenty-three, was a graduating student who began to wear the hijab while in university in Toronto. She lives with her family. 'People changed when they came here. In that sense I guess I'm Westernized; I think everybody has to work. I will help someone with their schoolwork or so on, but I won't give someone money to be a bum. That togetherness makes society more lazy. If I believe someone is working hard I will help them in any way, but not if I don't.'[11]

Anab, who is in her thirties, holds a master's degree from a British university. She wore a long robe and the hijab. 'This is not affecting our generation, but it will arrive when our kids grow up to be teenagers. We will feel this conflict of values then. It is shocking, the most difficult thing, especially in a large city like London. It is not so bad for the generations of seamen, who are ignorant and quite isolated in places like Cardiff. Their isolation keeps them safe from this. But for we who are more educated and sophisticated it is hard. The teenagers who have come now have chucked their own culture, and they are floating somewhere in the middle, because they haven't quite grabbed onto British culture yet. Many are lost and confused. This is the most vulnerable age.[12]

Layla, eighteen, is a London college student who had recently stopped praying daily and wearing the hijab, much to her mother's consternation. 'We never had gays or lesbians or AIDS in Somalia. When you see two women together it is so disgusting. I saw a show on

TV about two women getting married. I would have done something bad to them. It's disgusting. It just makes me sick. If I see them in the street, holding hands, it makes me want to go home, but you can't go home and you can't ignore it. Things are different and new and horrible here.'[13]

Shifting Perceptions of Sexuality and Reproduction?

The areas of sexuality and reproduction are particularly stark markers of cultural difference in the Somali context. Acceptable behaviour is strictly defined. Taboos are clear, and the consequences of breaking them severe. Until the shari'a courts made their recent appearance, Somalia had not had a history of submitting adulterers to *hudud* (prescribed Qur'anic) punishments, but babies born out of wedlock are shunned as having no father, and therefore no heritage. Questions of sexuality are complicated by the tradition of female circumcision and infibulation, almost universally practised in Somalia, about which more is said below. Girls were traditionally inspected by the female relatives of the bridegroom immediately prior to the wedding ceremony and would be rejected by the family if the infibulation scar were not intact. It is with regard to the virginity of their daughters at marriage that mothers expressed the most poignant fears about culture clash.

I asked respondents questions about birth control, abortion, extramarital and premarital sex, and the practice of female circumcision.

Birth control, or family planning, is not viewed uniformly by Muslim jurists. Although large families have traditionally been encouraged in order to ensure a strong Muslim community, economic and development issues have prompted legal positions that allowed for family planning in many Muslim countries. The only birth control mentioned in the hadiths is 'azl (coitus interruptus), which was frequently frowned on in *fiqh* (jurisprudence) literature because it was seen to be detrimental to the woman.[14] However, Basim Musallam maintains that there is significant juridical support for birth control, based on hadiths which indicate the Prophet's tolerance of the practice and on the writings of such respected jurists as al-Ghazali.[15] Many contemporary *'ulama* rule that the use of contraceptives is permissible as long as both husband and wife agree to it, and a number of Muslim countries have national family planning programs. Yet many Islamists discourage the use of birth control on the grounds that it contributes to immoral behaviour such as pre- and extramarital sexual activity.[16]

Respondents' opinions on whether birth control is permissible were evenly split. Nur ul-Islam, the Islamist organization in London, advises women that it is good to space children out by two or three years but that this is best done by breast-feeding and without the use of contraceptives.[17] The use of contraceptives had begun to increase in urban centres in Somalia in recent years, although in rural areas large numbers of children are seen as an asset, as their labour is important to the pastoral life and infant mortality rates remain high. Reaction to the issue was mixed. Some women, such as Fawziya in London, said hesitantly that contraceptives could be used for two or three years, but 'not for too long.'[18] Strong opponents said that birth control was 'like killing the baby.' Others, including Abdurahman, a well-educated twenty-seven-year-old Londoner, said, 'No, Somalis like many children,'[19] or, like Ayaan, the newly married twenty-three-year-old in London, 'You should be thankful for what God gives you.'[20]

On the other side of the argument, perhaps along with an understanding of the financial repercussions of supporting children in large Western cities, came the following:

> It's okay. You can't even have normal deliveries here; Somali women all have cesareans,[21] and babies are difficult to have. I have a friend who got married the same time as me. She already has six kids and she's pregnant again. In Somalia it's not okay to use birth control, but this society pushes you to use it. You can't afford to have so many kids.[22]

> Birth control is ok. My older sister was eighteen when she got married. Three weeks ago she had her third child. She is twenty-three. She doesn't speak English, she never really had a chance to learn. I feel so sorry for her when she goes out because she can't speak to anyone, and she can't speak to the doctor when she takes her baby to see him. Now she doesn't want any more kids. She's at home taking care of them all by herself; her husband is off at university. It's awful. I would use birth control if I were her.[23]

Opinions on birth control were given by men and women of all ages and degrees of religious observance. (Many argued that Islam sanctions its use for a few years, since having children too close together is unhealthy.) This was one area where opinion was split along gender lines. Most of those who argued against the use of contraceptives were men, and most of those who argued in their favour were women.

Virtually everyone who answered questions on the acceptability of abortion, however, answered categorically: Abortion is murder, unless the life of the mother is in danger.[24] Only three respondents argued that it was acceptable, and one of these said that she favoured the idea of choice but that she would not be able to go through with it herself.

Most respondents discussed the issue of premarital or extramarital sex. It was a difficult topic for almost everybody. What follows conveys the flavour of their reactions.

The Islamist Ismail (thirty-four, Toronto) described a lecture that he had attended on J.S. Mill and freedom. A discussion ensued in which it was being argued that society did not have the right to comment on that private decision. 'But I said yes, it does, because their actions may have consequences outside the bedroom. What about the illegitimate child that results from the union and nobody wants? Who is to take responsibility for it?'[25]

Ahmed, thirty-four, considers himself to be an Islamist: 'In our community we have to tell them to stop [an unmarried couple engaging in sex] but there is no Islamic government to punish them. In our community it is difficult to continue something like this. Everybody will tell them to stop and make their lives miserable. So they will have to stop or not be happy to live in the community.'[26]

'Society will cast out' offenders who engage in sex outside marriage, said Fathia (late thirties, London),[27] echoed by Nura (thirties, London): 'It's a big bad thing. Even with all the single women, it's not okay. Many people will stop talking to someone if they are doing this and are not married.'[28]

Fawziya is a mother at home with two young daughters in London, who is most concerned about her ability to bring them up according to traditional values. 'This is very difficult. It is forbidden, but here ... I will teach my daughters their religion, their culture, and tell them about how I was when I was young, but if I see that is not working I will try to go to Somalia or some other Muslim country. I will try to advise them on a better way, the way of our culture. But if it is not working I would leave with my daughters.'[29]

Sahra, eighteen, is a Toronto high school student, in baseball cap and painted nails, who felt ambiguous about her own observance of her religion.

Some people just do what they want to do. I don't want to do sex before I am married because it's not good to lose your virginity if you don't know that other person is going to be there for you. If he's not going to be here for you like your husband, then you don't have to lose your virginity. If I want to do that then I need to make sure that person is going to be there, is going to marry me. It's better to keep yourself, because that's the most important thing in your life – to be a virgin when you get married. I don't talk about that with my friends, but sometimes if you have a best friend, a really best friend, they will say if they slept with their boyfriend or if they had sex. But if she tells me that I'm going to get mad, 'cause I'm gonna feel sorry for her; she loses her virginity and she doesn't know this person. She doesn't know if he's going to be here for her life, to be a serious person.[30]

Aman and Hawa did not care for the sex education classes they were forced to attend at high school.

Hawa: We have to earn the credit, that's why we sit there and listen, but no other reason. You know we're not going to go out and get pregnant because ...
Aman: We don't really need to learn those things because we're not going to do that.
Hawa: Besides, birth control is not allowed in our religion, at all, even when you're married. Because you're not allowing what God decides to have happen.
Aman: God will decide how many children you have, not you. It's kind of like you kill the child if you use birth control.[31]

It was not only teenage girls who took a dim view of sex before marriage. Osman, seventeen, did not consider himself particularly observant. His family had not been religious until his father was killed; then his mother donned hijab and enjoined her sons to pray daily with her, but Osman said that they had not thus far followed her example. 'Sex before marriage is not okay for the religion; and if I break her virginity, it is like murdering someone, for the religion. It's very serious.'[32]

One Somali Londoner has supported himself in part by interpreting when needed at the Old Bailey Courts. He described a case he had attended in which a twenty-one-year-old Somali man was on trial for murdering his wife. The man was religious, and in the course of the fighting in Mogadishu had seen his family completely destroyed, the women raped and then killed, the men tortured and murdered, not even children spared. The only person left alive in his family, he had left Mogadishu for Kenya, where he became active in the Muslim community in Mombasa. After a time, he married the daughter of a local notable, whom he took with him to London in 1991. They had a daughter. He remained religious, but, to his distress, his wife began to take on Western ways – no longer praying or dressing modestly, going out to nightclubs with friends. In time he began to suspect her of having an affair. They separated and reunited but continued to quarrel. One evening, a strange man telephoned to speak with her. The husband, angered, began to argue with the stranger, who evidently declared that he was the wife's lover. In fury, the husband killed his wife, for which the judge gave him a sentence of life imprisonment. The Londoner who recounted the story commented, 'Of course it was terrible what he did. But he had seen so much and been pushed so far. His wife's betrayal was the crushing of everything he believed in. It was the last straw.'[33]

The majority of informants took the view that sex outside of marriage is unacceptable. Many did not elaborate but were emphatic. There were, however, a few who either acknowledged that this view was beginning to alter, slowly and covertly, or who had personally changed their opinions on the matter. 'For Somalis it's absolutely forbidden. People shouldn't be doing it outside marriage. Publicly no one will be soft on it, but practically, it happens in any society. We are human beings. There is a difference between theory and practice. The generation born in this society will have different values, but now people are not comfortable with the idea of their daughter or son or relatives having premarital sex, especially where women are concerned. There is more concern with girls. Unwanted children are considered an insult.'[34]

Osob, thirty-two, considers herself quite religious. She does not wear the hijab but will not even sit at a table with someone who is drinking alcohol. 'Many people do this now. Many women have boyfriends. If you tell them they shouldn't, if you tell them it's not right, they say "You're a nomad. You don't know anything about this life!"'[35]

Roda, twenty-five, had rediscovered her religion, but that did not cause her to change her opinion about premarital sex: 'If two people are having sex and they're married to other people, well, if it was a close friend of the family I would try to stop it. The community should and will be involved in such things. If it's premarital, well, I have a hazy opinion. If it's a secure relationship, I know it's a sin, it's wrong, but if someone loves someone and it's a secure relationship, then it's okay.'[36]

Kalima, in her late thirties, covers her hair and is observant but prides herself on not having become ostentatiously religious since immigrating to Canada in 1989: 'I would like to bring up my children as I was brought up, with Muslim values but not isolated from Canadian society ... I would even encourage my daughters to sleep with a man they are considering marrying, in order to make sure he is a good man and to get to know him better.'[37]

Jewahir, twenty-five, is a university student who prays daily and observes Ramadan but who does not wear the hijab:

Virginity at marriage is no longer important to me. It was important when I first arrived in Canada, and until about two years ago. Since then, I changed my mind (don't tell my mother!) because of society ... the people I hang around with ... I can't hang around with typical Somali men who have just arrived here. I talk about a lot of things – issues – I read a lot, and I have nothing to say to them. So I hang around with 'Sijuis' – Somali men who have grown up out of the country, in East Africa maybe, and have been here in Canada for a while. They don't value those things ... I've had some bad relationships. For two years I went out with a guy. We had no sex. We had a promise that he would wait until I graduated and then we would get married. The sex issue was a big thing. He wanted to. I wouldn't. Eventually he broke up with me and started going out with somebody else. He wouldn't wait. He was Somali, but educated. He grew up in Tan ania. The idea of virginity at marriage wasn't important to him.

So then I started thinking about this whole thing. I thought that the issue would continue to come up ... My mother's ideas are very strong – they are that you are like a piece of meat, hanging from a tree, and the men are like lions. It sounds silly, but she would just say, 'Don't let yourself fall from the tree' ... But I was thinking, the world has changed. Is it only me who has not changed? I had girlfriends (Somali girls) who changed their minds ... And I met a Somali guy who would not go out with Somali women. He said, 'You go out with them for six months and finally they give in, and then you have intercourse, and then you have to court them all over again so they don't feel bad that they've had sex with you. It's too big a deal, too much.'

But then I start feeling that my mother has been through a lot, and she has given me a lot of trust. Sometimes I wonder whether I am using that trust badly. So there's guilt ... I talk to my doctor about it. I could never talk to my mother.[38]

Nasra does not consider herself religious and said she is not concerned that she marry a Muslim but added that she would prefer her future husband to be Somali.

> We can't have sex until we're married. I don't know if a non-Somali would understand that. He might have expectations that I would sleep with him; he wouldn't understand this is how we were brought up. Some girls do and some girls don't, but I can't explain it to someone.
>
> Once I went out with a non-Somali guy; it lasted three nights. He tried to talk me into sex and one night he tried to force me; it really scared me ...
>
> Also we're circumcised. Only a Somali would understand that. Even some Somali guys, it drives me cra y when they try to talk me into having sex with them. They say we're in North America now, it's okay to have sex. But not every girl will do it. It drives me cra y. I say, look, in the first place circumcision was men's idea, to keep us virgins. They're the ones who said this is tradition and religion and it's a good thing to do. Then they're here five years and all of a sudden they want to have sex and change everything? It drives me cra y. It doesn't work that way. You can't change people's ideas overnight.
>
> I had my circumcision reversed last year. They told me not to have sex for six weeks. I said I don't even have a boyfriend. I thought I'd leave it two months and then it would be ok, I'd try sex, but I couldn't. I still haven't had sex. It's something inside me, and a fear maybe something would go wrong. You've been hearing this all your life, that you shouldn't do this.[39]

Female Circumcision

I asked almost all respondents about their views on female circumcision, or female genital mutilation (FGM). Both terms are problematic, because both are value-laden: the first implying an operation that is as neutral, simple, and lacking in complications as its male counterpart, which it is not; the second implying an intention to harm on the part of the perpetrator, which is inaccurate. Almost all girls in Somalia are circumcised (a 1985 study put the proportion of circumcised women at 99.3 per cent),[40] the vast majority of them undergoing infibulation, which involves the amputation, partial or total, of the clitoris, the excision of the labia minora and the inner walls of the labia majora, and the sewing closed of the surrounding flesh, leaving only a matchstick-sized opening for urination and expulsion of menstrual blood.[41] Infibulation is the most extreme form of circumcision, with the mildest in contrast being the *sunna*, which involves excision of the tip of the clitoris. Much has been written on the practice and reasons for it, which differ, along with its symbolism and meaning for the women involved, from country to country.[42] As immigration from countries with a tradition of female circumcision to the West has increased, so has concern in the latter countries about how to approach the practice.[43] Female circumcision has been expressly outlawed in Britain since 1985, and Canada took this step in 1995. In 1994, for the first time, a Somali woman was granted refugee status in Canada because of her fear that her daughter would be infibulated were she to return to her homeland.[44] For Somalis, the particular issue is that in their oral Muslim society, infibulation was historically understood to be a requirement of being a good Muslim woman.

Circumcision is not practised in most of the Muslim world, and it is not an Islamic requirement. The desirability of the sunna form of the operation continues to be debated in Egypt, where clitoral amputation is widely practised. Shaykh Gad al-Haq Ali Gad al-Haq, then the rector of al-Azhar, issued a *fatwa* (legal opinion) around the time of the Cairo conference on population in October 1994, declaring that the practice of circumcision is mandatory for both Muslim boys and girls, for which the Egyptian Human Rights Organization sued him in 1995.[45] Gad al-Haq was not the only Egyptian Muslim leader to support the practice. During October 1994, the popular Shaykh Muhammad Mutawalli Sha'rawi declared during his Friday speech that although female circumcision is not mandatory, it is still a laudatory practice, as it preserves the dignity of women.[46] More recently, as part of an ongoing tussle for credibility within that country, some Islamists, under the leadership of Shaykh Muhammad Yusif al-Badri, took the government to court for banning the procedure in hospitals and won their 1997 case in a Cairo administrative court.[47] The current shaykh of Al-Azhar, Muhammad Sayyid al-Tantawi, continued to affirm his support for the government's ban,[48] although Dar al-Ifta, the formal legal institution delivering fatwas, encourages circumcision.[49] Egypt's Supreme Administrative Court in December 1997, overturning the lower court finding in al-Badri's favour, ruled that the procedure is not an Islamic one and that the ban therefore is legal.[50] This debate complicates the question for Somalis as they wrestle with the tradition of infibulation.

The core of the issue, as Somalis in the diaspora discover – whether because of increased health education or because they have become more religious and better doctrinally educated – is that infibulation is not an Islamic requirement. The question becomes whether to cease the practice or continue it in spite of its illegality, the fact that it is anathema to Western values, and the physical and mental problems that it causes its victims.

In her book *Infibulation*, Esther Hicks posits that the practice, which anti-dated Islam, served as a mechanism to ensure virginity among unmarried girls in pastoral societies. Unable to separate the girls physically from possible violation, the societies developed a physical chastity belt that was meant to perform the same function as seclusion. The importance of virginity and chastity outside marriage, the maintenance of family honour, and the perpetuation of patrilineal lineage were all values that found a solid echo in Islam when the religion was adopted. As a result, the practice was maintained and reinforced,[51] even once the societies evolved into agricultural or otherwise settled communities. In closed pastoral-originated societies, she argues, there has been little reason for change.

What has happened in the context of the Somali refugees is that a relatively closed society has opened, rapidly. Of course exposure to education and literacy was increasing within the country even prior to the civil war and exodus, particularly in the urban centres, but the move to the West has speeded the process and removed Somali women from an environment in which there exists a wide conviction that infibulation is 'normal.'

A number of factors are at play, however. Chief among them, of course, is the increased religious education and observance among Somalis generally, particularly women, which results in their understanding of the practice as 'tradition' or 'culture,' as opposed to 'religion.' However, Somali mothers fear the seemingly untrammelled freedom of the West and worry that, first, they cannot control their children, and second, that teenage girls are particularly vulnerable to 'foreign' values. Additionally, the issue has sometimes been sensationally and insensitively dealt with by Western media, which have dubbed it, and by inference its practitioners, as 'barbaric,'[52] as it does seem to most Westerners, although harm is not intended by the procedure. These latter factors have resulted in some degree of cultural backlash and a minority of immigrants declaring that, Islamic or not, the practice is Somali, and it is none of the business of Westerners to decide how or when it should cease.

These attitudes are represented in the comments of informants, but fifty-two out of sixty respondents argued that the practice was a misguided one and that as it is not Islamic and should be stopped. Eight respondents argued that it should be continued, either as infibulation or in a modified sunna form.

Hibaq, twenty-nine, has been in London for a decade and attended university there. 'It is deeply imbedded in people's psyche. Even now I find it shocking to hear people who say they won't do it. I would have done it if it weren't for Islam and that I know it is not Islamic and therefore taking away something God gave women.'[53] Roda, twenty-five, has spent most of her life in London. 'So much of it depends on people's social and education background. Women who are educated and not traditional are learning not to do it. Mine is the first generation who had some sunna done. Someone educated, like my mother, would do nothing to her daughters here. My younger sister is not circumcised at all. My older sister and I were circumcised – just the sunna – by an aunt without my parents' knowledge. But my mother wasn't upset when she found out.'[54]

Ayaan, twenty-three, had been horrified by her first visit to a night-club when she immigrated to London. The experience was the beginning of her return to religion. None the less, she was dressed in a fashionable Western dress and does not cover her hair. 'I believe it is culture, not religion. It is not right. If you are a girl you can control yourself and how you behave; the operation won't stop you. I won't do it to my daughters. Most Somalis feel like me, except the old people. You can't talk to the old people; they always think they are right.'[55]

Fawziya and Kinsi are two mothers at home with young children in London. Fawziya spoke, and Kinsi nodded agreement: 'It is not a Muslim thing to do. Our mothers didn't have enough education to know that, but for our generation we will not do this to our daughters. If we were in Somalia it would be difficult. Your mothers and other women put pressure on you to do it, and there is so much pressure that you give in. But she is not here so it's not a problem.'[56]

Ibrahim Sheikh Mohamed was speaking as a member of Nur ul-Islam, the London organization that advises Somalis on proper Islamic behaviour: 'Islamists do not circumcise their daughters, not even sunna. Eighty per cent do not. In Somalia there was pressure from others in society to keep doing it for fear the girls would not be able to marry, but here they do not. The Islamist women know this and do not do it, but the others? Who knows?'[57]

Saida had gone to London to do graduate work in 1989 and subsequently brought her children to join her.

Female circumcision is sunna;[58] so there is no punishment if it is not done. But in England it is a criminal offence. My family told me to circumcise my daughter before she left Somalia, and I said no; send her as she is. I wanted to get a sunna circumcision here; not cut her but just a prick to make it bleed a little. But when she was here I found that even that is a criminal offence. I asked many people, even at the masjid. The imams said female circumcision is sunna and that sunna can be inside, just having thought it is good. So if you put it in your mind, the sunna is done.

I know a woman in Ealing who circumcised her daughters, just a little bleeding, not the big cutting. She was critici ed by her mother-in-law for how it was done, because it was just a little bleeding, and she told her mother-in-law that it was a criminal offence here and you could be put in jail for doing it, and two weeks later the man who had done it was shown on a TV crime program.[59]

Zeinab teaches Islamic classes to women in Toronto. 'Some people like my mother don't want it to stop, but the educating is continuing. Over time people are stopping.[60]

Said does not intend to have his daughters circumcised. 'Female circumcision persisted thousands of years; it will not die easily. Somalis thought it was an Islamic custom, but now when they realize it is not, people are changing their minds and stopping. It is not something done by men – this is a misconception that you hear again and again. Men have been fighting against it. Some people say, 'This is my culture,' but there are changes. It happens slowly.[61]

Anab holds a professional job in London and dresses in a long robe and the hijab. 'I forgive my mother, but no way will I do it to my daughters. The younger educated generation will not do it, no way, to their daughters, but the problem is that many women are illiterate and do not know or don't listen to people saying it is not Islamic, so they take the girls back to Djibouti or other places in Africa to have it done. Not here because it is a criminal offence, but they take them out of the country. It depends who the mother is.'[62]

Fathia has lived in London since 1987 with her husband and four children.

It's difficult because some women are willing to accept the practice should be abolished since it is not Islamic; but others protest strongly that their daughters will not find husbands or that it is an important part of Somali culture. I try to convince them that it is a bad part of Somali culture: it does no good at all, and causes a great deal of pain and hardship. It prevents a woman from enjoying her life with her husband, when Islam specifically encourages her to enjoy sex within marriage.

I remember how much I suffered and what I went through. I look at my daughter enjoying her life and playing and think, 'How could I do that to her?'

I never knew it was not Islamic until I went to Abu Dhabi. There I met other Muslim women who were not circumcised. 'How can this be?' I asked myself.[63]

Sadia, nineteen, like other Somali youngsters, has been exposed to health classes on the issue in a Toronto high school. 'I was surprised. I thought it was part of our religion, and I just found out it was not our religion; it was our culture. A group of Somali doctors and nurses came to speak at our school last year. Actually my mom never did it to me or my sister because she knew the problems she faced when she had it done. She had a big fight with her mom who said, "You have to do this to your daughters." She said, "I'm not going to."'[64]

Qassim, seventeen, is an Islamist who says that he tries to convince fellow Muslim high school students to behave in an Islamic manner. 'Actually what they are doing is wrong. It is not a good thing for a woman. It is not Muslim. It is not important for me to marry a woman who is like that. Some people do not know the Qur'an.'[65]

Amina began to study the Qur'an and wear the hijab when she moved to Toronto from northern Somalia. 'Even before we came here many of us did not do it; understanding of this has increased since 1970. Many girls born since 1970 did not have this done. Girls talk about it among themselves. My little one came home and asked me about it. She said, "What is this thing they are talking about?" I said it was a bad thing that used to be done to girls. But even when I was young even if the parents did not bring it up the girls would ask for it; they thought it was a good thing. They would say, "Why not me?"'[66]

Jewahir, twenty-five, is a Toronto university student: 'I know it is still going on here. I was circumcised myself, but I will never allow it to be done to my daughters. I asked my grandmother if she would have allowed it to be done if she had known it is not in the Qur'an. She said, never. She thought it was in the Qur'an. Now that she knows better, she would never have allowed it to be done.'[67]

Farhia, twenty-three, is graduating with a chemistry degree from a Toronto university: 'Most women are stopping. Some keep doing it because they are afraid their daughters would be outcast. My mom didn't want to do it to us, but we begged her to. My sister was eleven, I was seven. We begged her to because we wanted to be accepted. Our friends wouldn't play with us; they laughed at us. Finally she gave in. There was a huge party. I don't blame them for doing it; I wanted it. My youngest sister is now sixteen; she is not circumcised. I don't think people should say it's barbaric and all that. No one intended to do anyone harm, the problem was who would stop first. When my parents were debating it, it would have helped if lots of people had stopped.'[68]

Warsame, eighteen, is trying to balance his friendship with a Christian girl with his strong Muslim beliefs and the concern of his uncle. 'No, it's a bad thing to do this one. But the religion says sunna is good; not what they do in Somalia and Sudan. The sunna is OK, but in Somalia and the Sudan they do it very badly. I decided not to do it at all to my daughters; that is my judgment.'[69]

The translator, after discussing the issue with the older women of the Somali Women's and Children's Network, said: 'Now that they study, they know it is not an Islamic custom, and 99 per cent of the women do not believe it should be continued.'[70]

The discussion had been voluble and animated, but this was a particularly interesting comment, given that, to the extent that female circumcision is practised in the West, it is generally attributed to the desires of elderly women to see it perpetuated.

Osob is a young single mother. 'I think it is wrong. It makes no sense. It is not Muslim. If God had wanted me to be different he would have made me different to begin with. My mother and father decided not to do it, although my mother was infibulated. My grandmother and my mother's family was incensed. Once when my father was away they ganged up on her and said she was ruining us, so she gave in and had the sunna done. Only the sunna, but she was sorry about it afterwards. She said she didn't want us to be different from other girls. She wanted us to be able to be married and live normal lives, so she had it done.'[71]

Some respondents were ambiguous about the practice. Others had a variety of reasons for believing that the sunna form of circumcision would be desirable or acceptable in certain circumstances.

Sahra, eighteen, is keen to fit in with her friends, Somali and non-Somali, but believes that it is important not to engage in premarital sex. Ambiguity surfaces again here, as it did in her consideration of dress and prayer (see her comments in chapter 4).

You don't have to be circumcised, but it's good. Some things about it are bad, some things are good. The things that are not good are like when you get pregnant, and the baby can't come out because it's too small. And where it's good is because it keeps you hard and clean. It reminds you of what you are a woman for: to be a good mother, to be a good wife. You're not going to have sex just like that. You feel like you want to have sex but you won't. I have friends who are not circumcised, and they feel good how they are and I feel good how I am.

But, no, I will not have my daughters circumcised, because it's really hard, you know how it makes you feel when you're dead, so if you have a daughter it's not good to do 'cause you know how it is to be circumcised. I won't do it because it's hard. I would do it if everyone did it, but I won't because it's hard. People did it to other people but it was a mistake, so I won't do it.[72]

As Sahra spoke, her voice hardened abruptly and her face darkened when she spoke of the pain of circumcision and said, 'you know how it makes you feel when you're dead.'

Mubarek, eighteen, indicated that he would follow custom wherever he was. He did not seem aware that female circumcision is not condoned in most of the Muslim world. 'I don't care if my wife is not circumcised. I would not do it in a Western country to my daughters, but I would if I lived in an Arab country, where people do it.'[73]

Abdikarim, a high school student, lives alone in Toronto, having lost his entire family in the civil war. He considers himself very religious. 'I won't do it the way Somali people do because they do it the wrong way. A long time ago the Muslim people, they used to only scratch, just the sunna, not cut the whole thing. Because if you cut the whole thing the woman won't have feelings, and that's not good. I know some Muslim sisters who have problems when they go to the washroom, or when they have their period. It's just a traditional thing they do as Somalis, but if you want to have circumcision, you should do what they used to do in Islam. Some people don't have the knowledge. I don't think that's right.'[74]

Like Mubarek, Amir, seventeen, seemed unaware of Islamic doctrine. Like Abdikarim, he lost touch with his entire family at the age of fourteen, and made his way alone to London, where he lives with a foster family: 'Muslim people circumcise girls and boys. I will do it, yes.'[75]

Nur, thirty-six, is a self-declared Somali nationalist living in London. He was unhappy with the West's intervention in Somali affairs. 'Somalis will stop this when the time is right, not because of outside intervention. Even if it is barbaric, it is hard for an ancient culture to die. It is not Islamic, but it is a cultural thing. It was practised before Islam. It is a matter for Somalis. A woman inherits this from her mother and her grandmother. In Somalia if a lady is not circumcised there will be no room for her in society ... If I have daughters I will leave the decision about circumcision to the women. It is the decision of the women. The change must come from Somali women.'[76]

A science student at a London university, Abdurahman, twenty-seven, is not religious. In spite of his belief, female circumcision is not practised in Saudi Arabia. '[Infibulation is] not Islamic. Women get problems when they are virgins or when they have a baby; it is not good. The good system is like the Saudis, where they just have the sunna. Just a small cut, otherwise women will be nymphomaniacs. But the traditional way is torture; it is too much really. I would just do the sunna on my daughters.'[77]

Layla, eighteen, is a college student in London who had recently stopped wearing hijab and praying but still considers herself to hold strongly different values from non-Muslim friends. 'There are two kinds, the sunna, which is just a bit of blood, which the Prophet said was okay, and the traditional Somali way, which is totally out of order. It destroys the whole female's life. My mom had just the sunna done on me and it is nothing; it doesn't feel like anything. I would do the sunna on my children, which is not painful. But my half-sister had the traditional way done on her. My mom didn't want it but her granddad did it. It was horrible.'[78]

Ismail, thirty-four, left Somalia as a political dissident and became an Islamist on immigrating to Toronto in 1995. 'The Somali community is traumatised by the treatment of this issue in the West, the media attacks and so on. From the early seventies, mosques in Somalia dealt with the issue, the first organized groups to do so, emphasizing that it is not a Muslim requirement ... The sunna is the compromise; it is a slight cut that does not result in health problems or lack of sensation in the woman and is not even required ... Somalis are not intimidated by being told that something is contrary to Canadian law. That will only anger them.'[79]

Analysis and Commentary

The comments of respondents on these issues provide further evidence of how cultural weaving and the process of internal integration works. Beyond the practice of Islam per se, Somali immigrants are redefining what it is to be a good Muslim in the context of their new environments. As their perceptions of responsibility to family members or their judgment of the rightness or wrongness of various aspects of sexuality and reproduction shift, they do not retreat from belief. On the contrary, as we have seen, the same people whose attitudes on various value questions are shifting are also increasingly aware of, and observant of, their religion. What is happening is that their definition of what comprises a good Muslim is shifting as well.

The clearest example of this concerns female genital mutilation. Within a Somali context, being circumcised is an inextricable part of being seen as a good Muslim woman. Once in the West, having discovered that in fact circumcision is not mandated by Islam, Somalis are for the most part disentangling religious from cultural custom and deciding to adhere to the religious. In the process, they have reconfigured the meaning of Good Muslim Woman. It is particularly interesting that this process has happened precisely as and because their religiosity and religious knowledge increased with their move to the West.

The redefinition of acceptable Muslim behaviour and belief is also evident in shifts in perception of the admissibility of birth control and even, to a lesser extent, in an increased tolerance of extra- and premarital sex. People who indicated that they would accept these things had not drifted from a practice of their religion or experienced an ebb in belief. Jewahir, for instance, a woman in her mid-twenties and a university student, considers herself deeply religious. For her, being a good Muslim required her to pray and fast but not to cover her head. Nor did it preclude her engaging in premarital sex. Kalima, a mother in her late thirties who does wear the hijab and is very concerned to bring up her daughters as observant Muslims, said that she would encourage them to have sex with their boyfriends if they were considering marriage.

At the same time, it was crucial to women and men that their daughters marry within the faith. There was particular concern not that prospective partners be Somali, only that they be Muslim. Men are doctrinally permitted to marry Christian or Jewish women providing that the children are brought up to be Muslim, and respondents were aware of that, yet the clear and strong preference was for all offspring to marry Muslims. Moreover, when asked what they considered their community to be, almost all respondents answered Muslims, not Somalis in particular.

They do continue to feel particular connection and responsibility to members of their extended family and sub-clan, as their comments indicate. Here, too, it is possible to discern a shift, however, as where Nasra or Roda evince impatience with their families' ready willingness to ask money from them rather than working harder to find it themselves.

Although intergenerational rifts were clearly apparent over the practice of Islam, as has been noted in previous chapters, the education and destiny of daughters did not appear to be an issue. Parents interviewed wanted the best secular education they could get for all their children; no teenagers or young women in the twenties reported a difference between what they wanted for themselves and what their parents wanted for them. Women do not traditionally play a significant economic role in Somalia, although they have always worked (having primary responsibility for the smaller animals and the moving of accommodation in pastoral settings and often having small, market-related businesses in the city). Here as well it is possible to detect the increased significance of women in the diaspora community. Girls did not appear to be discouraged from obtaining education, training, and jobs. Certain of the Islamist organizations spoke of the desirability of women not working or, if they must, of working only with other women, but this did not appear to be an issue in any of the interviews with parents, teenagers, or young adults.

Some intergenerational disagreement is apparent with respect to the permissibility of association with non-Muslims. Clearly, not all adults view non-Muslims as unsuitable companions. Many quoted the verse of the Qur'an that maintains that Allah created different tribes, or ethnicities, so that people could become acquainted with one another. And I was told that as long as it did not interfere with their practice of Islam, there was no reason not to befriend non-Muslims. However, not all respondents felt that way (Nur, in London, for example, and certain Islamists who believe that Muslims can retain their faith only in isolation). Moreover, the intergenerational conflicts are connected with the view of parents and guardians that their youths are particularly vulnerable to the lures of non-Muslim ways.

One strong example of such a conflict is Warsame's disagreement with his uncle over the suitability of his Christian friends. Warsame had a Christian girlfriend, which was causing him a great deal of joy and angst, because, as respectful of his religion as she was, she kept trying to hold hands and kiss him, which, he acknowledged, would be 'the end' of him. Of as much concern to his uncle, however, were his other non-Muslim friends. Warsame's phrasing is that his uncle claimed that he was trying to be 'Muslim and democratic' and that it was not possible to be a good Muslim and have Christian friends and a Christian girlfriend. He seems to use the word 'democratic' in the sense of being all things to all people. 'You can't be a democratic Muslim, because a Muslim is a Muslim', Warsame quotes the uncle as saying. But Warsame disagrees. As far as he is concerned, as long as he understands who he is (and he said that he prays, fasts during Ramadan, is careful to wear only loose clothing, and always wears a kufi as a sign of his religion), he can continue to befriend non-Muslims who are respectful of him. This is another instance, as with matters of religious practice, of differing redefinitions of what is permitted a good Muslim, but it is not a sign that Warsame considers himself to be less of a Muslim than his uncle.

In the comments of respondents on various questions, it is possible to discern how people, without abandoning their values and beliefs, adjust to new environments. They do not consider themselves less Muslim and more Westernized as this occurs, nor do they consider that their core values (consideration for family and communal responsibilities, adherence to Islamic beliefs as they interpret them) are compromised. Yet they take new circumstances into account as they determine what behaviour allows them to conform to those values, even in such sensitive areas as sexuality and reproduction. People are therefore not assimilating – trading one culture for another – but rather integrating their own beliefs into new circumstances. This analysis is taken up further in chapter 7.

6

London and Toronto

One of the major contentions of this study is that political culture pro-
foundly affects the integration of immigrants and minorities. More
specifically, a political culture that emphasizes the ability of immigrants and minorities to participate in society as full members of it,
and that accords them respect as political and social actors, facilitates
harmonious integration of immigrants and minorities.

Political culture is apparent in almost every aspect of immigrants'
are minorities' encounter with the society around them. It is apparent
in the public pronouncements of public figures – politicians, whether
members of the government or not; judges; media, sports, and enter-
tainment personalities, among others – as well as in public reaction to
those pronouncements. It is evident in media coverage of issues affecting immigrants and minorities and in media sensitivity to the reaction
of the immigrant and minority groups concerned. It is reflected in
immigration and refugee law and in all aspects of law as immigrants
and minorities encounter it. It is apparent in the school system and in
decisions about which schools receive state funding and why. It can be
seen in the decisions of municipal planning officials and the public
reaction to these. It is apparent on the street: on public transportation
and in shops and in the hiring decisions of private businesses.

More important than the attitudes or pronouncements of any single
individual is the public reaction to them. In the early 1980s, a Canadian
anglophone politician ran for leader of the federal Conservative party.[1]
When criticized for not speaking French, he quipped that he did not
speak German either. He would not have been the first prime minister
to speak only one of Canada's official languages, but the fact that his
insensitivity doomed his election bid spoke volumes. No politician

with prime ministerial aspirations has since dared to appear on the national stage without some degree of bilingualism. Even the leader of the western-based Reform party, which has campaigned on a refusal to give Quebec special status within Confederation, learned French before making any serious attempt at national status.

This incident demonstrates another key characteristic of political cultures, which is that they are in constant flux. This chapter argues that at present Canadian political culture has been more successful, and British political culture less so, in creating an environment of legitimacy and respect for immigrants and minorities. But these situations are in flux, and it is possible to point to examples of change. An interesting one concerns British Conservative politician Norman Tebbit, who has on at least two occasions made headlines with intolerant comments about the suitability of South Asian immigrants as British citizens. The first time, in 1990, he got himself in trouble with the immigrants in question. The second time, in late 1997, his party leader publicly denounced him and distanced his party from the comments. This sort of sanction is enormously powerful, indicating that such comments are no longer acceptable. It is a major step in the alteration of public attitudes.

The first two section of this chapter draw on the theory as outlined in chapter 2, and describe Canadian and British political cultures, respectively, as they differ concerning immigrants and minorities. It next illustrates how Somali immigrants – both as visible minorities and as Muslims – experienced these differences, most particularly in their reaction to the Salman Rushdie affair (third section) and in terms of their description of their connection to their two host countries (fourth and fifth sections). The sixth section compares and contrasts Somalis' experience in Canada and Britain, and the seventh considers the results of these differences. The Rushdie affair is often described as an issue of freedom of speech. This study maintains that the issue, while exceedingly complex, was for many Muslims rather about respect and as such worth considering in this discussion.

It is worthwhile to bear a number of points in mind. First, I refer to British versus Canadian political culture, because I maintain strongly that the critical structures are set in place, and the tone set, at a national level. Yet obviously cities have political cultures too, and these will differ within the nation. It is for this reason that I chose Toronto and London as cities of comparison, although there are sizeable Somali populations in smaller British cities, such as Cardiff. London and Toronto are the two largest and most central cities in their respective nations. Toronto is significantly smaller than London, but recent census results indicate that fully 32 per cent, or a third, of its population is made up of visible minorities.[2] While it is impossible to find two cities in different countries that differ only in terms of their national political cultures, the differences in Canadian and British political culture in this area are particularly striking precisely because of their similarities in other respects. Moreover, whereas both Britain and Canada have internal political units that would dispute the central government's ability to speak on their behalf, this is less of an issue in London and Toronto than it might be in Cardiff or Montreal, Glasgow or Vancouver. It would be difficult therefore to extrapolate from the study and assume that Somalis' answers in Cardiff or Montreal would be the same as those in London and Toronto, at least without certain qualifications. Cardiff and Montreal clearly have Welsh and Quebec political cultures as well as the national ones. However, as the largest and most central cities in Britain and Canada, and whatever their inevitable differences as cities with municipal political cultures of their own, London and Toronto could be argued to exemplify their respective national political cultures.

The Place of Immigrants and Minorities in Canada

Among the reasons that Multiculturalism (the policy) has attracted criticism in Canada is that Canadians, a people of strong yet understated myths, have been forced by recent events to re-examine their national identity. Most notable among these events have been the public debate over a Free Trade Agreement (FTA) with the United States, concluded in 1988, and an ongoing debate over the place of Quebec and Quebec nationalism with the Canadian federation. Quebec's sense of itself is very strong, both because it concerns itself with *la survivance* of its language and culture as an island of French in a predominantly anglophone continent and because that language and culture take as their core the ethnicity of the descendants of the original French settlers of New France. Those Québécois, conquered on the Plains of Abraham in 1759 by the English – a traumatic, myth-engendering event – none the less found their religion, culture, and language preserved first by their English conquerors, supported by the Roman Catholic church, and then by the tenacity and anger of a people made Other by their English neighbours both within and outside Quebec. The political cul-

ture of the rest of Canada – a vast tract of thinly populate land – is usually credited with having originated in the particular circumstances of
the United Empire Loyalists[3] who created English Canada as a reaction
to the American Revolution and out of loyalty to the British Crown.[4]

Throughout the late nineteenth and early twentieth centuries, waves
of immigration from Europe passed through the central Canada on
their way to the prairies and the west coast of British Columbia. But
there were other immigration waves as well, coming east from China
and Japan, and layered atop more recently from east, west, and south
with immigrants from Africa, Asia, and Latin America. Quebec aside,
the rest of Canada has often defined itself negatively. It is not American; this it has long asserted. Ardent anti-Americanism existed from
the time of the Loyalists. Loyalty to Britain and its empire helped
define identity, but gradually diminished following Canadian military
successes and casualties during the First World War – a cataclysmic
struggle on foreign soil. Yet the parliamentary debates in the 1960s
over whether Canada, long independent from Britain, should have a
distinctively Canadian flag and an anthem of its own were rancorous
and bitter.

Canada developed into a nation less because of a driving ideal or set
of shared ideals, as in the American case, or because of a shared sense
of ethnicity, as in the European model, than as a group of peoples sharing and dealing with a northern land-mass. Unlike the United States,
with its strong set of defining myths (the settler conquering the elements, the drive westward, the achievability of liberty, happiness, and
wealth through dedication and perseverance), and unlike Britain with
its strong sense of history, culture, and empire, Canada has been less
assertive about, even wary of, defining myths. These are often manu-
factured in the crucible of history, and Canada has seen neither a war
of independence, nor a civil war, nor a crown a thousand years old.

The free trade debate, while unremarkable for its economic complexity, was a fascinating exercise in what it revealed about the Canadian
sense of self. Opposition to the agreement centred on concern that a
ratified FTA would further the seemingly inexorable process of Ameri-
canizing Canada. Some critics seemed to propose that handguns
would suddenly appear in the streets of Moose Jaw (a midsize town in
Saskatchewan), and universal medical care vanish, as though the definition between countries is determined in major part by the stoutness
of their barriers to trade. It is my contention that in the presence of a
stronger sense of identity, opposition to the FTA would have taken a

different form and would have been based on an economic, not cultural, rationale. In such a culture as English Canada's, the myths that have captured the public imagination are clung to with particular fervour. Among the most important of these are the nation as middle power, as conciliator, as peacekeeper, following the role that Canada developed on the world stage with Lester B. Pearson at the helm; the 'sacred trust' of universality of health care and a generous social safety net; and the myth of Canada as a tolerant nation.[5]

Tolerance does not have a particularly long history in Canada. While British North America may have been a land of immigrants, tolerance was extended generally only to northern Europeans, much as in the American case. The first, nineteenth-century, Chinese immigrants to Canada were badly treated, and laws were passed excluding their immigration in 1923.[6] Japanese Canadians were interned and their property confiscated during the Second World War. Canada turned away a boatload of Jewish refugees and admitted only 5,000 Jews between 1933 and 1945, (where Britain took in 70,000 and the United States 200,000), because of overt and covert anti-semitism in the country, especially in Quebec.[7] In the nineteen-twenties and thirties, when Canada's anglophone business elite was still centred in St James Street in Montreal, McGill University limited its enrolment of Jews precisely in order to minimize Jewish entry into the business world.[8] Quebec nationalism was fuelled by anti-French bigotry. The list could continue. None the less, the vision of Canada developed by Pierre Trudeau (an anti–ethnic-nationalist) as an antidote to the 'Two Solitudes'[9] vision of the Quebec nationalists, was a Canada in which both languages and cultures could flourish and that accepted and accommodated all the ethnic threads in the population tapestry. Acceptance of the first part of the vision, in both Quebec and the rest of Canada, has not been overwhelming; there have been two inconclusive referenda in Quebec and a painful ongoing constitutional debate, but the effect on the Canadian psyche of the vision's second part has been in fact tremendous.

As it has developed, Multiculturalism is, at its simplest level, a series of government grants whereby public funds are given to ethnic groups to stage dances and food festivals, to teach third languages to children, and to sustain ethnocultural attractions and organizations. But symbolically, Multiculturalism has transformed the Canadian mosaic (an ethnic patchwork intended to be seen as distinct from the American melting pot) into a Myth of Tolerance. Canadians believe themselves to be more open to ethnic, cultural, and religious difference than Americans.[10] They believe themselves to be less racist, and that any pockets of racism that exist are indeed that – pockets, isolated and lacking public sympathy. As Reitz and Breton maintain, these are debatable contentions,[11] but I argue that the very existence of the Myth creates, as myths do, a singular and ineffable factor in the Canadian political landscape. In Benedict Anderson's famous phrase, to the Canadian 'imagined community,' the Myth of Tolerance is critical indeed.[12]

Literary author Neil Bissoondath's point is that forcing recognition of him as a hyphenated Canadian impedes his ability to renegotiate his own identity as he wills it, so that Multiculturalism is, at one level, a constricting force, and an alienating one. He resents the Canadian government's implication that the preservation of elements of his birth-culture are and should be important to him, when perhaps his choice may be to eat nothing but poutine and tortière[13] for the rest of his days and to attend only quiet dinner parties where Mozart and Bach are played discreetly in the background. He resents the mould that he sees forced on his daughter in school, affixed with a hyphen because of her brown skin, although she is Canadian-born and no closer to the Caribbean in her outlook than to the Arctic. He charges not that the hyphen comes with a lack of respect but that perhaps she does not desire the hyphen at all and should not have it forced on her.

Bissoondath's points are well taken on an individual level, although Reitz and Breton's study would appear to argue that Multiculturalism has little if any impact on immigrants' retention of their birth culture. I would argue that what Multiculturalism, or the Myth of Tolerance, has significantly done is to create a space in the Canadian public imagination, and therefore in its political culture, for the acceptance of the legitimacy of the voice of Others, be they ethnic groups per se, or religions, or people of colour.

Hannah Arendt, in *The Human Condition*, writes of the public realm that it contains what is accessible to every and any member of society and, furthermore, that the very fact of being common, or commonly available, renders it substantively different from matters that are private or intimate. Acceptance in the public realm constitutes a kind of legitimacy.[14] In modern, complex, technologically sophisticated societies, there is tremendous scope for both official public culture (validations of the established order) and unofficial public cultures ('disruptive cults in the shadow of the temples' and other eruptions of the shared imagination) to 'desacralize' the official public culture and share that public realm.[15]

Furthermore, as Jeff Spinner contends, public culture should change as a polity's membership changes. He defines public culture as the 'standards of acceptable behaviour and appearance in public, public celebrations, the pronouncements made by public officials about the identity of the country, and the history and values taught to its children by the political community.'[16]

Canadian public culture, both official and, to a large extent, unofficial, has created an imagined community in which there is space for ethnic minorities to play a legitimate role in public life. It is a space whose dimensions are fluid and whose meaning is not always clear. (For instance, when a zoning permit is temporarily denied in East York, a borough of Toronto, for the building of a mosque, on the pretext that there is insufficient parking for the facility,[17] it becomes apparent that the theory of multicultural acceptance is being tested in the reality of mosque-building. The boundaries of legitimacy must constantly be redefined as practical situations force the myth-holders to confront the myth head on.) Nor does it eradicate racism in Canada. In fact, Canadians find it difficult to discuss racism, given their need to believe it is so minimal. Witness, for instance, the insistence within the sovereigntist camp that the drive for Quebec's independence has nothing to do with ethnicity, although Premier Jacques Parizeau blamed the loss of the October 1995 referendum[18] on 'money and the ethnic vote' and was promptly supported by his immigration minister, if reviled publicly by other sovereigntists. Witness, in English Canada, the difficulty of the Royal Ontario Museum, and Toronto's media, in understanding the concerns of African Canadians with respect to the context of a 1990 exhibit that presented a colonial view of Africa in the nineteenth century but did not address racism and inequality in contemporary Canadian society.[19]

But, just as *habeas corpus* is a critical element of a state's commitment to due process in the pursuit of justice, so this public acknowledgment of Multiculturalism (the existence of a plurality of ethnic groups) as a 'fundamental characteristic' and 'invaluable resource' of the Canadian polity denotes respect by virtue of its existence.[20] Moreover, examples are plentiful of institutional receptivity to Muslim needs, such as the Toronto hospital that organized awareness seminars to limit cultural misunderstandings with Somali patients,[21] the Etobicoke School Board's meetings with local *'ulama* when confronted with large numbers of Somali children, or the stocking of halal meat by a province-wide supermarket chain.

One of the chief reasons that the Meech Lake Accord[22] was seen to fail was that it was the closed-door agreement of 'eleven white men.'[23] In other words, the constitutional implications of the accord had been agreed to by representatives only of the perceived ruling elite, and not by representatives of Aboriginal peoples, women, or minorities, all of whom were recognized to be significant constituencies. A royal commission (the Spicer Commission) was hurriedly composed, whose mission it was to listen to 'ordinary' Canadians. The Charlottetown Accord, into which the Spicer Commission fed its results, also failed to be ratified in a national referendum, but the legitimacy of the voice of minorities in the creation of important Canadian policy was widely recognized.

Canadians may be motivated more by a need for differentiating and defining myths than an altruistic acceptance of ethnic difference, and the political process may not always accept the arguments of the voice making them, but its legitimacy to participate in the public discourse is not in question.[24]

The Place of Immigrants and Minorities in Britain

This situation contrasts sharply with Britain, a nation with a strong sense of self and culture, with centuries on centuries of history, literature, and imposing architecture to bolster its residents' understanding of Britishness.[25] (It is understood that Britishness carries variations on a theme, depending on which part of the Isles one hails from. It is also understood that the definitions of Britishness vary with social class and that the perceived threat to identity is often triggered by a threat to socio-economic position.)[26] Although a central, English definition of Britishness would be contested by the Scots, Welsh, and Irish, it is the large numbers of recent postwar waves of immigration, bringing people who in many cases were tinged by Britishness and empire before they ever reached London, who have primarily triggered a national debate over the meaning of Britishness and British identity. For the most part, these people drew their identities from lands with strong cultures of their own, cultures that they did not see as dispensable or inferior to that of their new land. In part because they could not, and did not want to, leave their birth cultures on the boats and planes that brought them; in part because Britons would not let them (by continuing to demarcate them as 'Other'); and in significant part because sheer numbers made it impossible to ignore them, the postwar immigrants have forced an ongoing, national discussion about the meaning of being British.

The classist nature of British society may have tended to obfuscate the problem for a time, given that less well-off immigrants are inclined to begin their British lives in traditional working class areas, such as northern industrial towns or the east end of London, where their problems and existence become confused with those of the lower classes: poverty, lack of representation or opportunity, and so forth. But not all immigrants are poor, and even in a strongly classist society there is movement into the middle and professional classes. Although they may not yet have houses in the country, the numbers and presence of immigrants and their British-born children are such that it is no longer quite so clear what it is to be British.

The Prince of Wales's speech, in which he acknowledged that 'Britain is a multi-racial and multi-cultural society,' is a significant marker of that public conversation.[27] So, too, are a myriad other events, including the Honeyford Affair[28] and ministerial concerns over the loyalty of cricket fans, but also including the increasing sensitivity of schools to the religious and cultural diversity of their students and 'ethnic awareness' courses intended to increase judges' sensitivity.[29] As is shown below, the main underlying theme of the Rushdie affair for British Muslims was a cry for respect.

Bhikhu Parekh, noting that assimilation did not (indeed, could not) work in absorbing the postwar waves of immigrants, argues for an 'alternate' public vision of cultural differences that recognizes them as a 'valuable national asset.' He presents a vision in which 'cultural diversity should be given public status and dignity'; in which minorities accept (and are in return granted) the full obligations of British citizenship, involving 'allegiance and loyalty to British society, and sensitivity to its values, fears and dilemmas'; and in which minority communities are permitted to develop and adapt to British society in their own way and in their own time. These communities need to know that they have the respect of the wider society, the confidence that they are valued, and the sense that British society is not hostile to them.[30] He notes finally that 'a plural view of British identity' does not entail understanding Britishness as a particular view of history or as something that Britons possess but rather postulates that being British 'means learning the grammar, vocabulary and syntax of the prevailing form of life and knowing how to participate in its ongoing dialogue intelligently and intelligibly.'[31]

John Rex contends that Britain has tried to deal with its multicultural society by relegating minority cultures to the '"private" domain of the family and community' but that this does not work well because there is no clear demarcation line between private and public domains in such critical areas as education and religion. What is required therefore is a complete 'renegotiation of the political culture of the public domain.'[32] In Jeff Spinner's terms, it is crucial that civil society – which he defines as institutions and associations that are not controlled by the state but that serve the public, such as media, stores, factories, and corporations, as well as schools and cinemas – accord equal respect to ethnic communities.[33] This is unlikely to happen if Britain's public culture allows for the exclusion of certain of its groups. Spinner quotes Margaret Thatcher, as prime minister, announcing in a speech to the General Assembly of the Church of Scotland that 'the Christian religion – which, of course, embodies many of the great spritual and moral truths of Judaism – is a fundamental part of our national heritage.' People of 'other faiths and cultures' are welcome in Britain, she continued, and will be treated equally and with respect. 'There is absolutely nothing incompatible between this and our desire to maintain the essence of our own identity. There is no place for racial or religious intolerance in our creed.' The problem with this stance, as Spinner notes, is that even while holding out the olive branch of toleration, Thatcher excludes Muslims and other non-Judaeo-Christians from 'the essence of our identity.' She, as Britain's leader, continued to define Britain in its essence as a tolerant, Christian nation.[34]

Another example of this kind of exclusionary thinking occurred in 1994 when a Conservative councillor in Havering, Essex, objected to his council's grant of £200 to the Essex Islamic Educational Trust to purchase copies of the Qur'an, stating, 'The United Kingdom is a Christian country and local government policy should reflect this in every way.'[35]

However, there are statements to be found in British leaders' speeches that speak of change. Important among these are the televised comments of the Prince of Wales in 1994, speaking of his becoming 'defender of faith,' as opposed to 'defender of *the* faith.' (His statement was greeted with substantial opposition from the established Church of England.)[36] When Lord Tebbit made televised comments in October 1997 exhorting Muslims to be 'truly British,' he was publicly repudiated by William Hague, the new Conservative party leader, as well as by the queen, in Pakistan on a state visit at the time.

'A distinctive new identity – that of British Muslim – has emerged. I find that healthy and welcome,' she said in a speech.[37]

Also in this inclusive vein, a 1995 British submission to the United Nations stated the following: 'It is a fundamental objective of the United Kingdom Government to enable members of ethnic minorities to participate freely and fully in the economic, social and public life of the nation, with all the benefits and responsibilities which that entails, while still being able to maintain their own culture, traditions, language and values. Government action is directed towards addressing problems which prevent members of ethnic minorities from fulfilling their potential as full members of British society.[38]

Additionally, there are examples to be found in recent British events of public culture and civil society beginning to reflect a willingness to accommodate diverse practices. Among these are the Royal Bank of Scotland's decision to commission a new set of uniforms for employees in a variety of styles, including a *sari*, and *shalwar* and *kameez*;[39] the London boroughs of Healing and Hillingdon granting permission to Muslims to bury their dead in a shroud, not in a coffin;[40] and hospitals in Bolton as well as the Manchester airport ensuring that halal food would always be available.[41]

Britain's ambivalence over accepting the pluralist nature of its population, and over granting that plural population legitimacy, is neatly illustrated by the 1997 dilemma of the Oxford Centre for Islamic Studies. The centre, having outgrown its old quarters, intended to move to a 1.66-acre site in the midst of Oxford. It applied, with the blessing of the Prince of Wales, for planning permission to build its new centre – including a 108-foot minaret and 75-foot-high dome, designed by a noted architect and intended to blend Western and Islamic styles of architecture – and immediately met with national controversy and intense opposition from officials at a number of Oxford colleges who resented the intrusion of a minaret in the midst of the city's historic 'dreaming spires.'[42]

Part of the trouble with public culture in Britain, and its relation to its ethnic communities, lies in how they have been viewed in law. Robert Miles has made the point that the very fact that British law, in its Race Relations Act, defines a race as 'a group of persons defined by reference to colour, race, nationality or ethnic or national origins' is problematic because it 'legitimates the belief in the existence of "races" in an attempt to eliminate ... discrimination.'[43] Moreover, with race thus defined, the law offers no protection for those who consider themselves to have been discriminated against on religious or cultural grounds, as opposed to racial or ethnic grounds, which became a point of contention for Muslims during the Rushdie affair.[44] Therefore, as constructed, the Race Relations Act has the double disadvantage of artificially dividing the population and providing protection from only some, but not all, kinds of racist or discriminatory treatment. What it does not do is create a participatory legitimacy or a legitimacy of identity for immigrant or minority Britons. The ongoing difficulty with this legislation has recently prompted the Commission for Racial Equality to begin recording complaints of religious discrimination, in part because the Home Office would not consider passing legislation outlawing religious discrimination until it has been proved that this exists to a significant extent.[45] It is to determine the extent of religious discrimination against Muslims that the Runnymede Trust created a commission to study British Muslims. Its first consultation paper discussing the phenomenon was released in February 1997,[46] and its full report, *Islamophobia: A Challenge for Us All*, was published at the close of that year. One of its recommendations called specifically for the outlawing of religious discrimination. The Home Office had begun considering such legislation in the summer of 1997,[47] but Home Secretary Jack Straw would not commit himself to more than that after the report's release.[48]

One of the points made about political culture by Sidney Verba is that tension will be created if there is a disjunction between legal norms and other markers of identity – cultural, linguistic, religious, or ethnic.[49] If a society's laws do not create the conditions that allow for the respect of a group of its citizens by the wider society, some disjunction exists and will manifest itself as societal tension.

Bhikhu Parekh has written a thoughtful article, which is relevant for this discussion, on how societies might best deal with minority practices.[50] He suggests that all societies develop what he calls operative public values. These are the 'minimum body of values and practices' that the members of a society share. They are a part of its 'moral structure, and are embodied in its major social, economic, political and other institutions.'[51] Moreover, they are constantly changing 'in response to changes in society's circumstances and self-understanding.'[52] They are often contested and need to be periodically reassessed, such as when confronted with minority practices that the wider society considers offensive. Parekh goes on to describe how societies need in such cases to engage in a dialogue with the minority group in question, eventually changing the laws to accommodate the practice, or not. The point is not that laws that do not accommodate minority practices are always wrong, but that society has a duty to engage in a dialogue with minority groups where disharmony exists. I would maintain that this is true whether the disharmony exists over a minority practice or over the larger question of the status of the minority group within the wider society.

Perhaps the clearest recent illustration of this lies in the way the Salman Rushdie affair played itself out in Britain.

The Salman Rushdie Affair: Freedom of Speech or Respect and Legitimacy

In the autumn of 1988, protests erupted in Pakistan over the publication of *The Satanic Verses*,[53] a novel by Salman Rushdie, born a Muslim in India, whose epic novels of India (*Midnight's Children*, winner of Britain's premier literary prize, the Booker) and Pakistan (*Shame*, shortlisted for the Booker Prize) portrayed – often with humour and satire at the expense of the powerful – the emergence of these nations after empire. His more recent *The Moor's Last Sigh*, also shortlisted for the Booker, dealt with Spain's rich culture of Jews, Christians, and Moors before Ferdinand and Isabella.

The Satanic Verses, also a work of fiction, contained segments that many Muslims found offensive when they heard about them, chief among them a dream sequence that depicted the Prophet Muhammad and his wives as despicable characters. The Pakistani protests quickly found strong echoes in Bradford, calling for the banning of the book in Britain. In February 1989, the Ayatullah Khomeini of Iran was moved to place a death sentence on the head of Salman Rushdie, accompanied by a hefty reward to anyone who carried it out. Six years later, when the interviews were conducted, the author was still living under police protection, his name still reverberating among Muslims in Canada and Britain. The affair generated a publication mini-industry, particularly in Britain, where it was one in a series of incidents involving relations between British Muslims and non-Muslims. Significantly, British authorities refused Muslim requests to use blasphemy laws to prosecute the book's authors and publishers, although they had been successfully used in 1977 to prosecute the publishers of a poem deemed insulting to Jesus Christ. This latter point is important because the affair in Britain had more to do with the legitimacy of Muslims – their ability to occupy public space, to command public respect, to have their sensibilities publicly recognized – than with freedom of speech or the sanctity of the Prophet or the death sentence made by the head of one state against a private citizen of another.[54]

The Rushdie affair was, of course, about all those things as well, but one of the reasons that it continued to rankle years afterward was that discussing it was a little like the group of blind men trying to describe an elephant after each has touched only one part of the beast.

As James Piscatori has written, there was much going on simultaneously.[55] Salman Rushdie was working at establishing an alternate view of religion, playing with the language of Islam and at '[offering] himself as an arbiter of Islamic belief' in order to challenge some of the religion's accepted wisdom.[56] Piscatori emphasizes that Islam has an extensive history of 'change through tradition' – where metaphor pushes thinking along new paths and permits an evolution in Islamic thought precisely because it appears to be compatible with high tradition and therefore allows for the 'pious fiction of a seamless Islam.'[57] However, Rushdie's lack of subtlety in this effort resulted in the predictable antipathy of those who believe themselves in a position to speak for Islam. What is interesting is the variety of responses from different international quarters and their lack of unity.[58] The meaning of the Salman Rushdie affair depended very much on the point of view of the observer, or participant, because it had many meanings, depending on one's particular perspective.

For many Westerners, the central issue was the sanctity of freedom of speech, which was being dangerously threatened, not in a remote dictatorship on another continent, but in the heart of a major liberal democracy. Indeed, as John Horton points out, the Ayatullah's intervention served to polarize much of the liberal and writing community, many of whom felt that a death sentence was an extreme sanction for what they had previously reproved Rushdie for publishing because it was likely to have an adverse effect on race relations in Britain.[59] Freedom of speech was held to be the very cornerstone of a liberal democracy, and Muslims would just have to learn to take it, if they were going to live in Western liberal democracies.[60] One academic wrote, in defence of freedom of speech as it pertained to this issue, that the logic of liberal philosophy denotes that although people should be free to form and pursue their own beliefs, they may have to endure challenges to those beliefs by others engaged in the same process. They cannot and should not be protected from offence. Of course, these challenges should be presented in a way that respects the 'decencies of controversy,' but liberal governments should not legislate them invalid. In Peter Jones's view, 'legally, people should be entitled to do what, morally, they may be unjustified in doing.'[61] Gratuitous vilification of someone else's cherished beliefs is not right, but it should not be illegal, he writes. At the same time, authors who do this should not 'expect to be spared the vigorous protests of those who strongly object to their works,' short of threats to their physical safety.[62]

But for many Muslims, freedom of speech was not the issue at all.[63] Rather, it was the preservation of the sanctity of their religion, something that they regularly feel is under attack. As Tariq Modood writes in a companion article, the issue was about *imani ghairat* – the quality of a Muslim's pride in or love for the Prophet and his religion.[64] The honour of the Prophet, he argues, 'is as central to the Muslim psyche as the Holocaust and racial slavery is to others.'[65] Therefore a book that attacks the honour of the Prophet, and which is then hailed as a literary masterpiece, is also a book that attacks the very core of what it is to be Muslim, and therefore the legitimacy of being Muslim in society. The *Satanic Verses* crisis, he writes, was 'an attempt by Muslims, however inept in terms of public relations, and callous as regards the author of that book, to press their claim to be recognised as an oppressed group in British society, as a group whose essential dignity must be respected by the rest of society.'[66]

One of Modood's main concerns with respect to British anti-racism laws is that they are extended to groups that identify themselves by colour or race, but not religion. Therefore, Muslims as a group are not protected under these laws. Modood argues that an attack on the honour of the Prophet was perceived as an attack on all Muslims, the way a refusal to acknowledge the numbers of Jews killed in the Holocaust is perceived as broad anti-semitism. British law, however, offers no recourse to such a perception, since Muslims are not defined in law as belonging to a race, per se.

It may well be argued that the core of the issue for British Muslims was not even the insult to the Prophet, but their perception of their place in British society. It is impossible to understand censorship decisions and the reactions they engender without considering the political and public opinion that surrounds them. The fusses over *Lady Chatterley's Lover* in the early 1960s, or *Ulysses* in the 1920s, illustrate the point. Public notions of propriety were evolving, and in that context these books seemed threatening to those who feared the direction it was taking. In the context of a time of widespread Muslim migration into the West, and the insecurity felt by many Muslims over their legitimacy within Western society, a book that appears to attack the very foundation of their belief also appears to be particularly threatening. Such a situation is exacerbated when Westerners appear to misunderstand completely the basis of Muslim fears, dismiss them, and consider the reaction of many Muslims to be an attack on Western values. This situation was particularly true of Britain.

A significant difference between Britain and some other European countries, notably Germany, is that most Muslims are citizens in Britain, and have been almost since their arrival in the country – and increasingly, because of birth there – and by virtue of this fact have been promised equality of treatment and place.[67] This chapter argues that Britain has been less than successful at following through on this promise. *The Satanic Verses* controversy in Britain was perhaps more a demonstration of this state of affairs than it was anything else.

In Canada, however, laws do exist that forbid the incitement of hatred against any race or religious group, yet these were not employed to limit the availability of the book. The Canadian Society of Muslims (CSM) proclaimed the book 'an obnoxious piece of hate literature' in a 1989 declaration and wanted it banned. (Having said this, however, the CSM declaration went on to regret the Ayatullah's *fatwa*, and most particularly the introduction of a bounty.)[68] However, outside the Muslim community, it was not perceived as a broad attack on Muslims, partly because non-Muslims do not widely understand Modood's point about *imani ghairat*. In this way, it was viewed as being different from Jim Keegstra's attack on the veracity of Holocaust numbers,[69] since the broad public perception is that such a position is equivalent to an attack against Jews as a people. If non-Muslims do not read *The Satanic Verses* as a broad attack on Muslims, then while it may be offensive, it is not understood to be an incitement to hatred. In a world of widespread ignorance of Islam, however, Muslims may well perceive that any material that does not depict Islam in a favourable light contributes to anti-Muslim racism.

There are a number of possible reasons for the comparatively subdued reaction of Canadian Muslims to *The Satanic Verses*. The first is structural: the political cultures of Canada and Britain are significantly different as concerns the place of immigrants and ethnic minorities, and this affects the sense of legitimacy that members of various communities experience as citizens. For these very reasons, Muslims in

Canada did not need to engage to the same degree in the same tussle for public space and 'essential dignity' that Modood argues was at the heart of the controversy in Britain. Second, demographics may have played a role: there were fewer Muslims in Canada, and they were not overwhelmingly members of a particular community. Gilles Kepel has argued that the nature of the protest in Britain resulted from the fact that the British Muslim population was predominantly South Asian and that the political relationship between community and state had therefore been formed, prior to immigration, in the days of the British Raj.[70] Moreover, as Piscatori notes, most British Muslims, within memory's grasp of their peasant origins in the subcontinent, are particularly sensitive to issues of honour and tradition,[71] along the lines that Modood emphasizes.

Finally, there is the question of transnational connections. While one has to be careful not to overemphasize the degree of transnational coherence and organization in discussing Islamic movements or connections, the Jama'at-i Islami – the group founded in Pakistan in 1941 by the enormously influential thinker Maulana Mawdudi – has been instrumental in determining the structure and ideological outlook of British Muslim organizations. Key among these are the Islamic Foundation and the UK Islamic Mission, which orchestrated much of the British protest during the Rushdie affair.[72]

I asked respondents, in these interviews, what they thought of the freedom-of-speech argument in the Salman Rushdie instance. The issue resonated with almost each and every respondent in both Canada and Britain, although there were significant differences in the quality of that resonance. Only a handful of teenagers could not place Rushdie at all. Most informants knew he had written 'something against Islam'; few knew precisely what it was that had been troublesome about the book. Most could name the book, but none had read it. Some did not realize that Rushdie was a Muslim himself. The following paragraphs present a sample of the comments that the question elicited. The vast majority of respondents expressed a belief that freedom of speech must have limits in any society where people hold different beliefs and that freedom, whether of speech or of action, should stop short of injury to others. Religion, in particular, was a topic where it was felt that particular care needed to be taken not to cause pain. For many people, it appeared that the Rushdie case was yet one more example of non-Muslim intolerance and prejudice, alongside continual media misinterpretation and depiction of Muslims as alien Others. The anger in the words of some respondents was echoed in their tone of voice.

A few respondents did not feel that Rushdie had transgressed Muslim societal norms. Both Farhia and Saida consider themselves reasonably observant. 'I understand both sides. I don't think it would have bothered me to read *The Satanic Verses*. I have my opinions; let others have theirs.'[73] 'The religion says you can criticize but not in a written form. Really the Iranians made too much of a fuss over nothing. Freedom of speech is important. Everybody has to be able to express what they want.'[74]

Some respondents emphasized the importance of using free speech judiciously, in such a fashion that it does not injure others. 'Freedom of speech doesn't mean hurting someone or someone's religion. I can't say anything bad about Judaism or Christianity or Buddhism. Freedom of speech means the freedom to have your own religion or criticize the government, but not to insult someone else. Rushdie meant to hurt people. That was not good.'[75]

> Freedom of speech is fine, but you must have knowledge of the consequences of your exercising it. If I say certain things that hurt the community as a whole, is that the right thing to do? What is the end result? For instance, broadcasting the technology of how anyone can make a bomb on the radio is not a smart thing to do. Who knows how that information will be used? I believe in responsible speech. It can be done in many ways. In a society which holds lots of preconceived notions, you must think of the possible results of what you say and the connotations that will be out there as a result of the words you use. For instance, the American Senator D'Amato on a U.S. talk show recently was simulating a Japanese accent when he was talking about Judge Ito [the judge who presided over the O.J. Simpson case]. In a society full of stereotypes and stigmas about race, why add to it? Just because you can speak and are free to speak?[76]

Someone else observed: 'Freedom of speech is fine, but not for religion.'[77]

Nasra does not consider herself religious, and did not realize that Rushdie is Muslim, but responded to the injury perceived by the community, as did Ismail and others who are religious.

> I understand freedom of speech, but what I don't understand is how

someone can write or say something that's not true about another religion. I was hurt. I don't think he should be killed, but I don't know why he had to do this. It's like that crazy guy in the States, Farrakhan, saying that all white people are devils. It's not true, and it's hurtful and he shouldn't say it. That's just the way I see it.[78]

Rushdie showed no sense of self-regulating behaviour. He did not take into account the injury his words would cause to his own community. There can be no freedom without responsibility.[79]

Even in the West, freedom of speech is not freedom of speech when it hurts someone. You have no constitutional guarantee of a right to hurt someone.[80]

Every religion deserves respect. If someone is disrespectful it's not freedom of speech. He's hurt people and devalued their faith. Anyone would be upset if that happened to them.[81]

I did not read his book, so I can't really say, but I think people should respect each religion. We respect other religions; so should others. No one knows which religion is the best or telling the truth.[82]

I feel solidarity with my fellow Muslims. One has obligations. Freedom of speech is all very well, but people must be accountable for what they do. Every person gets what they do or say returned to them. If you do good you will receive good in return, and the opposite. The community rewards him today, but he faces God tomorrow. People are born into certain values. Society gives them teachings of norms, traditions, formally and informally. You cannot blame people for how they behaved.[83]

At first I thought Khomeini was a lunatic. I used to say that Rushdie only wrote a book, he didn't kill anyone. Then I realized what he had written from what I read in the papers. I think Rushdie was wrong to write what he did. When you treasure something and someone else attacks it, of course you are hurt and you are justified in your hurt. Their reaction was extreme. Still, there's a limit to everything. He pushed the Muslims too far.[84]

High school students such as Farah were children in 1989, yet the furore over the book had an impact on them as well. 'Freedom of speech is okay for here, but not for Muslims. You can say whatever you want, but you can't say anything about Allah or the Prophet. They shouldn't be talking about the religion. They can hurt people or politicians with what they say, but not the religion or God.'[85]

Warsame was convinced that mistrust and ignorance were at the root of the problem for both Muslims and non-Muslims. 'Yes, I was really upset when I heard, in Somalia, but still I have not seen that book. I want to see what he said. I know it's bad, but I want to see what it was. Lots of Muslims have never seen Christians or white people; they just know Christians are bad. You can say what you want, but religion ... you can't insult it, it is different, it is special.'[86]

Some respondents saw the widespread Western support for Rushdie as the real injury. Some echoed Ali Mazrui, who pointed out that the American company PBS, in rebroadcasting a British television series that he had written and narrated, deleted a phrase referring to Karl Marx as the 'last of the great Jewish prophets' in order not to offend Jewish viewers. Mazrui, in a commentary on the Rushdie affair, noted the hypocrisy: no American journalist defended his right to freedom of speech in this instance.[87]

It was irresponsible for him to write that collection of insults ... I think that the West allows religion to be insulted, but the reaction of the West was a calculated effort to malign Islam. The other thing is that even though the West believes in freedom of speech, hate propaganda is prohibited. This caused hate and the loss of life. The intervention of Khomeini hurt Western interests, and the West considered that anything to do with the Ayatullah was a devil-thing, a bad thing.[88]

I don't know about Khomeini; we have different ways, Shi'a and Sunni. And Rushdie is an individual ... But what is unforgivable to me is the West. Why did they have to jump to be on his side? He insulted us. If he is hurting us, what kind of freedom is that? ... It is the lack of respect for Muslim feelings that the West showed that bothered me, not everyone, but the majority of people.[89]

My view has changed just in the last week. I was against the *fatwa*, but now I look at the hypocrisy of the West. Rushdie committed a crime against Islam. The Ayatullah was crazy, but Rushdie was wrong.[90]

A few respondents spoke vindictively about Rushdie himself.

What he did was totally wrong. If the religion agrees to kill him I'm 100 per cent behind it. Freedom of speech is okay, but keep it at home. In public it is not right to insult someone who is without sin like the Prophet. In the West you cannot speak for communism – they will stop you. So there is a limit. It is the same with this.[91]

People can write books, but they should be careful when writing about religion. They must not jeer at religion. Salman Rushdie is a criminal.[92]

Salman Rushdie deserves his fate. He has no right to offend Islam.[93]

He is a bastard. If I saw him I would fight with him. I don't care how criminal it is, if I see him I would kill him. He said lies about my Prophet, lies about my religion. He said rubbish.[94]

He was wrong and should be punished. There is no freedom of speech in the West. If something is in favour of the West, it's called 'free.' If Rushdie had written anti-Western things, he would not have been supported.[95]

If I see him, I will kill him.[96]

He is a lying man.[97]

There is no correlation between the informants' degree of religious observance and their condemnation of Rushdie. Among those who expressed the greatest vehemence towards him were people who described themselves as only moderately religious, while many Islamists, while disapproving of his work, were equally disapproving of the Ayatullah's reaction to it. There is, however, some relationship to be discerned between reaction to Rushdie and a feeling of disconnection with the wider society.

It is not surprising, given the foregoing discussion, that the most striking difference between the interviews conducted in London and Toronto consisted in the quality of the connection that the Somali immigrants felt towards their new homes. Most adult Somalis, not having left their native land out of choice, indicated that they would rather be living happily in Somalia, but by 1995 they had begun to realize that their predicament, if not permanent, was long-term and that their children, growing up in other countries, did not share their fervour to return. They had begun to face the possibility of permanent exile. Respondents were asked about the connection they felt to their adopted lands. The following provides a portrait of their responses.

The Connection to Canada: Responses in Toronto

Rashid, an educator in his forties, was torn between concern for the welfare of his family and his guilt at being part of the brain drain that will make rebuilding Somalia so much more difficult.

> It is the dream of many Somalis of my generation to go back. There is a bond with home; it means something. This is less and less true for people the younger they were when they left. It is unfortunate that much of Somalia's elite and talent are sitting in Toronto and other foreign cities. The brain drain is tragic, and there is guilt associated with it. You know it's your home; you know you could make a difference and affect your people and your country. Without the ability to do that you feel helpless. And also I had a family to think about. A lot of us talk about if we were there, maybe ... But there are these waves of violence, and you might die before you did anything; that too has happened to a lot of people. And ultimately you also have a responsibility to your family and to protect them. It's a difficult dilemma.[98]

Yusuf, thirty-four, called Canada 'tolerant' despite having experienced racism in the country. He was once attacked and beaten by what he described as a group of street thugs for being black, but he was more concerned about the anti-Muslim racism that he detected even at university. 'Canada is a most tolerant society. It is second to none but far from perfect. Racism is alive and well here. Even things that Canadians take for granted are more difficult for me. If I call to get my cable installed, my accent says I am a foreigner and it will take longer for me than for other people. I got higher marks in university if I wrote my initials on an exam, so people didn't know I was a Muslim. Anti-Muslim racism is worse than colour racism here. Still, Canada is home. I'm here to stay and very proud to be Canadian.'[99]

Zeinab, a woman in her fifties who taught Islamic classes to women and considers herself deeply religious, had been in Toronto for six years. 'Life here is not liveable. No matter how hard you try, you are seen here as someone who will never amount to anything. People see Somalis as people who can't do anything. When we explain the difficulties, in finding work and so on, they respond, well, why don't you change the way you dress?'[100]

Nasra, twenty-nine, does not consider herself to be religious and identifies herself as a Somali first and only incidentally as a Muslim.

> Canada is tolerant compared with other places, but not 100 per cent the way they think. When I first came here I didn't see the racism, but slowly I began to see it, like, I went to rent an apartment. Over the phone they told me there was room but when I got there they said it was taken. I told my friend at work, who was white. She went over, and it was still for rent. So I went back to see if I could rent it, and there was another woman there. She got on the phone to the owner and spoke in Hindi, she didn't think I could speak Hindi, and she said there's someone here but she's black and she's young. After speaking to him she said no. My friend was really upset and wanted to go to the Human Rights Tribunal, but I said no. I couldn't live in a place where someone didn't want me because of my colour. I don't want the government to fight this battle for me.[101]

Nasra speaks Hindi because she was educated in India. The incident concerns racism on the part of another immigrant. Nasra is saying that, while Canadians would like to believe that there is no racism in Canada, it clearly does exist, even between immigrant groups.

Sahra, eighteen, a Toronto high school student, had been in the country for three years. 'Yes, I want to stay here. I can do everything that I want; I can talk to everybody that I want. I would like to go and visit my country and visit my people. I would keep my baby here and go back by myself.'[102]

The translator was speaking here on behalf of a dozen women, whose prime concerns were their ability to ensure the Muslim identity of their children and grandchildren: 'Canada is a good country. They see themselves settling and staying here. For one thing, this is home to the children, who were born here or left Somalia when they were young. Although they have problems, they think they can live here and make a new environment for Islam in Canada.'[103]

Hassan, twenty-two, was a biology student at university, who wanted to study medicine. He had been in Canada for seven years. 'Canada is definitely home now. I want to stay here. But it is hard to be a Muslim here. You tend to forget what time to pray. You have to decide whether you should go to clubs. I do it, but I don't drink. Every day I have to think about it.'[104]

Farah, seventeen, a high school student, had been in the country for two years. 'I think Canada is tolerant. I have had good experiences here. I've been in Kenya, you know, but they don't like Somalis there. We look a bit different from them, you know, and so they look at us and say, 'You're different; we don't want you here.' People would say that on the street. I didn't feel good there. Here I don't find that; it's OK … Canada is home; I would like to stay and have kids here. I might want to visit Somalia if the war is over; my big brother and my mother's family is still there.'[105]

Jama, a Somali-trained lawyer in his forties who had not succeeded in finding work in Canada, was caring for his mother and two young children alone throughout his multi-country refugee odyssey. He had been unable to bring his wife to join him in Toronto. 'Life is better here in Canada than all I have seen. In Nairobi I couldn't put my kids in school, not even in Qur'anic school, and it was the same in Syria and Moscow. Here I have health care, schools, a home. It is difficult, but much better than elsewhere. I am comfortable. Canada is tolerant in comparison with the rest of the world.'[106]

Daud's analysis is based on his relative experiences as a member of a minority population group in Somalia. He was a man in his forties: 'I have security here. I did not have security in Somalia. I could be thrown in prison just for being Bantu.'[107]

Nasir, nineteen, a high school student in Canada for one year, considered himself to be very religious. 'Canada is tolerant, yes, and respectful. I was afraid before I came that people would try to change my religion, but I've never seen anything like that here. Even when I want to pray and the door to the room is locked, and I go and say why has this happened? They will say, Oh, Nasir, sorry. Everyone is very respectful of me and my religion.'[108]

Hassan Ali Mohamud, counsellor of the Somali Youth Assocation of Toronto, considered himself to be a religious Muslim. SOYAT teaches that Muslims' needs can be met in a Canadian context. 'Most of the kids I talk to say, "We're Canadian; we're not going anywhere." Most people will stay because they're accepted as Canadians. They will go back to Somalia to visit, but they see this as another alternative land where they can live.'[109]

The Connection to Britain: Responses in London

Samira, a woman in her forties, was a lawyer who had been in London for four years and had returned to university. She expressly commented on the difference between her experience and that of her brothers in Canada.

> The whole community in London is consumed with uncertainty; you can't settle like in Canada. In Canada you can plan as a Canadian to integrate, get a passport and so on, but here that's impossible. Since 1991 in Britain you can only get exceptional leave to be here, so your status is in limbo. I am not officially recognized as a refugee. I'm allowed to stay only 'til 1997. So which is better, to integrate or not to integrate? I think not. It's better in these circumstances to keep your identity and pride ...
>
> For instance, I have no interest in British politics; they mean nothing to me. My brothers in Canada talk to me about Kim Campbell, the former prime minister, and other Canadian political events. I ask them, 'Why do you care?' They tell me, because these are *their* politics, too. I was amazed. I have no such connection to Britain.[110]

Fawziya, in her thirties and at home with two toddlers, had been in London for four years: 'I am not comfortable here. I am always feeling lonely, and I feel different. My culture is different, and I feel different, but I do not know whether we will stay or go. That depends on [my husband] and if he gets a job somewhere else when he finishes studying.'[111]

Layla, eighteen, was a teenager who had recently stopped praying and wearing the hijab, to her mother's distress. 'I don't feel British. If I was white I would, but these people are different. They make me feel different. College is allright, but at school the kids would say things, talk behind your back, make you feel uncomfortable. If Somalia was on the TV they would say, 'Is that your country? Disgusting, you're this, you're that.' This is home to me now, I can see staying here, but it isn't back home the way my country is. I would love to go back if I could.'[112]

Amir, seventeen, a high school student, had been in Britain for two years. 'I am Somali. I don't feel I am British because I am not. I don't get what British people get – a passport and everything. They are a lot different from us. I don't feel this is home. Of course I would like to go back to Somalia if there is peace there. I will stay here until there is peace in our country, when war is finished. I am getting an education in this country.'[113]

Nura, a mother of three in her thirties, did not consider herself religious and resented the fact that she was frowned on by fellow Somalis for not wearing the hijab, when this would not have been expected of her back home. 'Nobody treats me British; they treat me like I'm Somali. Being here is better than being in Somalia now, but if it were peaceful there I would prefer to be there.'[114]

Ayaan, twenty-three, was newly married to a white Briton who converted to Islam in order to wed her. She had been in London for seven years and had succeeded in bringing her mother and siblings to join her. 'I don't feel British. I'm Somali. Even if I have ten children with him I won't feel British. I will stay here now. I have no choice now that I've married him. I think we will all stay here except for my mother. I will not let my brothers and sister go back until they have their education, but my mother would like to go back when she can.'[115]

Fathia, a mother with four school-aged children, had been in London for eight years. She was most concerned with the quality of their education and the racial hostility and violence that she saw as widespread in the neighbourhood: 'I can't wait to go back to Somalia. My children and I, we have no future here.'[116]

Hibaq, twenty-nine, in London for ten years, described herself as rebuffed in her initial attempts to be accepted by British society. 'Shocked' by the racism that she encountered, she 'returned' to her community, becoming more religious and associating predominantly with Somalis: 'Even though I am married to a British man, I want to leave the UK and go to a Muslim country or Somalia both because it is safe there and also because living here is like being in a home where you have not been invited. You are made to feel unwelcome, and it makes you want to leave quickly.'[117]

Khatara, sixteen, a high school student, had been in London with an older sister for four years. Her intention was to study medicine. 'I would like to go back to my country. I am not comfortable here. Mostly it is because you should be with your parents and your grandparents. I miss them. I haven't seen them in so long. I should be living with them. But also there is lots of racism here in England and Europe. People smile but they don't mean it. They see you as black, and they don't like you. If you want a job they will see you're black, and not give it to you. They'll tell you the position is full even if it is not.'[118]

Abdullahi considered himself very religious. A man in his mid-thirties, he had his family with him in London. He was employed as the London representative of a number of Nairobi-based companies. 'I have been in this country for six years. I feel as isolated as if I were in prison. Maybe I visit friends or they visit me, but the rest of society leaves me out. In this kind of situation some people solve the problem by trying to assimilate – drinking or finding pleasure. Some people want to go back.'[119]

Roda, twenty-five, had arrived in London as a child of eleven. She was engaged to a Somali man.

> London is the only home I know. My memories of Somalia are fuzzier and fuzzier, but it's stressful to be in this country. My ideal would be to live both here and there. Here you can make a good salary and pay the mortgage and so on, but big ambitions can only be realized at home. My boyfriend is a chemistry student. He would like to work in the Middle East and save money, or work ten years either in the West or Middle East, and then set up a business in Somalia. I see myself as an international person. Once you know who you are, you can live anywhere. I want to travel and live in different countries for a while. In a way England will always be home for me. My boyfriend is afraid he would always be a second-class citizen. But at the end of the day, if someone asks me who I am, I still feel Somali.[120]

Saida, thirty-four, a former university lecturer in Somalia, had been in London since 1989. Her children had joined her, but her husband was still in Kenya. She considered herself a practising Muslim: 'It is acceptable here, compared with other places like Germany. There, there is a lot of racism. Here I don't feel anything like that. It is comfortable here. I didn't expect to find it to be so good here. I came from a Muslim world; this is a Christian world, but I'm so happy with how it is. I was expecting it to be more difficult. They help us here as a humanitarian, not caring if we are Muslim and they are Christian. They respect us. It is not hard to lead a Muslim life here.'[121]

Anab, in her mid-thirties, was professionally employed and had been in London since 1984. 'Of course I would like to go back to Somalia if I could. The reason is that no matter how long you stay here you are still a foreigner, regardless of what your passport says. The English still see you as a stranger. This is their land. They own it. Not everyone is an immigrant here, and they make you feel that you are. So I do not have here what I want to make my life good, and of course I would go back if I could. Maybe it would be different in Canada or America. Everyone is an immigrant there.'[122]

Contrasts and Comparisons

The differences in the quotations are striking. Marginalization and differentiation from what they see as mainstream Britain are constant themes running through the comments of London Somalis: 'The English still see you as a stranger. This is their land. They own it. Not everyone is an immigrant here, and they make you feel that you are.' 'Living here is like being in a home where you have not been invited.' 'My brothers in Canada talk to me about ... Canadian political events ... because these are *their* politics too. I was amazed. I have no such connection to Britain.' 'I don't feel I'm British. I'm Somali,' – repeated again and again. In contrast, as unhappy as many Toronto Somalis may be as they deal with culture clash, loss, and unemployment, it is rare for them to use the language of alienation. In all the interviews conducted in Toronto, only Zeinab, quoted above, spoke in terms of life being 'unliveable here.'

Racism, of both the colour and anti-Muslim varieties, clearly exists in both Toronto and London.[123] Moreover, the inference to be drawn from the quotations and commentary is not that Somalis in Toronto are happy and well-adjusted and Somalis in London are not. Yet the Toronto interviews suggest that Somalis there felt that the wider society was inclined to accept them, whereas the London community felt ghettoized. External boundaries, in other words, were much more clearly demarcated in London than in Toronto. Two reasons can be suggested for the difference – legal status and political culture.

Legal Status

In Canada, the vast majority of Somalis have been granted full refugee status and thus begin a future with a reasonable assurance that they will be able to build it in their adopted country. Refugee status can be converted to landed immigrant status in Canada, provided that the applicant has proof of identification, the purpose of which is ostensibly to prevent the entry into Canada of war or common criminals. Prior to the passage of Bill C-86 in 1992, an affidavit of relatives and acquaintances was sufficient to testify to a refugee's identity, but the identification requirement was introduced – suspiciously, as far as many Somalis are concerned – coincident with the arrival of the waves of fleeing Somalis. In November 1996 the government decreed that Somalis who arrived without identification would have to reside in Canada for five years before being able to apply for landed immigrant status.[124] Being a landed immigrant confers the ability to sponsor relatives – clearly the issue of most concern to Somalis – and after three years can itself be converted to full citizenship. None the less, refugee status denotes ability to work and access to the full range of social services available to Canadian citizens, as well as the assurance of remaining in the country.

In contrast, the vast majority of Somali refugees in Britain have been granted not full refugee status, but rather exceptional leave to remain (ELR). ELR may be commuted to permanent residence, but only after seven years, which is a long time to live in limbo. It comes up for renewal twice in that period. ELR does not give the right to education for anyone over the age of sixteen; nor does it allow for family reunification for a four-year period. Although asylum-seekers holding ELR have not generally been forced to leave the country when the time came to renew their applications, they have in recent years been required to restate their cases for asylum.[125] Interviews with Somalis in London indicated that the very fact of holding ELR status, and not refugee status, gave them the sense that British society was holding them at arm's length.

Political Culture

The second reason for the difference concerns the legitimacy of immigrants and ethnic minorities in the wider society. Although shopkeepers and kindergarten teachers do not talk in such terms, the culture of Multiculturalism has permeated the Canadian psyche and has become such a part of the political culture of the country that it is widely reflected. Clearly this is aided by Canada's consciousness of its newness as a nation, the sense that even the Fathers of Confederation – the signatories of the 1867 British North America Act – were of immigrant stock. Canada's is an entirely immigrant population, with the exception of its Aboriginal population. I would suggest that this could be (and was) overlooked in previous decades, but that one of the side effects of Multiculturalism as official policy has been the recognition that an immigrant's head start of a couple of hundred years does not grant his descendants a greater legitimacy in the public or political order.

This is an important point for the subsequent chapter, for what follows from it is an understanding, confirming Lucian Pye's analysis,[126] that the making of political culture is an ongoing exercise. All participants in it are collectively responsible for its creation, and it is, at any one time, the combination of all the elements of the various traditions of its creators, though clearly not in equal proportions. For Hannah Arendt as well, as Bhikhu Parekh has emphasized, a true understanding of politics concerns the participation in the polity of its citizens. The notion is that it is not accurate to describe people as being ruled by their governments. Rather, they 'empower' leaders to exercise authority on their behalf.[127] It is through the political community that individuals acquire a public identity.[128] Through public speeches and actions, a society's collectivity of individuals in turn shapes the political community that it comprises.

Canada has been relatively successful at creating the conditions that allow for the inclusion of all of its resident voices – including those of recent immigrants and minorities – in that process. This is precisely what Parekh refers to when he exhorts Britons to a redefinition of nationhood – one that acknowledges as a matter of course that 'a Briton is not by definition white but could be black, brown or yellow, that he might speak Swahili, Mandarin or Hindustani as his first and English as his second language, and that his "kith and kin" might be found in Bombay, Barbados and Ibadan as well as in Salisbury and Wellington.' Only then 'can the non-white minority feel as authentically British as the native, and can be so accepted by the latter.'[129]

The legitimacy that Canadian political culture accords immigrants and ethnic minorities is less visible in Britain. British political culture, in contrast, is relatively hostile to its immigrants and ethnic minorities, tending to alienate and ghettoize them. Yet the role of political culture in the process of integrating immigrants and minorities is not well understood, so that the fabric of legitimacy that it has created in Canada is tenuous and fragile.

The Role of Political Culture Not Well Understood

It is the contention of this study that, although political culture is a critical determinant of the harmonious integration of immigrants and minorities, it is a role that is not widely understood, by either academics or policy-makers. The following example, concerning the Canadian military's conduct in Somalia and the subsequent reaction of the Canadian government, will illustrates the point.

In March 1993, the soldiers of a Canadian peacekeeping mission, belonging to the Canadian Airborne Regiment stationed in Belet Huen, first shot a Somali teenaged intruder to death and then, in a separate incident a fortnight later, beat a second civilian teenager in its custody to death. In the aftermath of the publication of these events, the regiment was disbanded, certain of its members were court-martialled, and senior military officers were reassigned. The newly elected Liberal government, sweeping into office in November of that year, ordered a commission of inquiry to examine the circumstances surrounding the military's behaviour and its reaction to the deaths.

The interviews presented in this study were conducted in the first eight months of 1995. While many respondents noted the lack of success of Operation Restore Hope and regretted what was characterized as the West's unhelpful intervention in Somalia, no respondent in either London or Toronto chastised the Canadian military for its conduct. The only mention of the specific incident was in the Londoner Samira's reference to the fact that her brothers in Canada felt involved in Canadian politics and considered Canadian politicians to be 'their' politicians too. The implications is that what was important about the incidents to Canadian Somalis was less what happened in Somalia than how official Canada responded. At the time of the interviews, official Canada was responding sharply to the unacceptable behaviour of its forces. This response symbolized the respect and legitimacy that Canadian public policy promises to accord – and to a large degree, its political culture succeeds in according – to its immigrant and minority populations.

In early 1997, prior to a further election and when the commission of inquiry's investigations appeared to point to an alleged cover-up of the incidents within the highest echelons of the military and in ministers' offices, the government abruptly curtailed the commission, accusing it of cost over-runs. It was forced by the courts to rewrite, in a more limited fashion, the commission's terms of reference. The commission's truncated report, entitled *Dishonoured Legacy* and released in the summer of 1997, was none the less a scathing indictment of the military's preparation for, involvement in, and subsequent treatment of, its own mission in Somalia. It declared pointedly that 'left uncorrected, the problems that surfaced in the desert in Somalia and in the boardrooms at National Defence Headquarters will continue to spawn military ignominy. The victim will be Canada and its international reputation.'[130] The minister of defence, followed by the prime minister, dismissed the report as 'excessively critical.'[131]

Most Canadian Somalis were publicly quiet following the release of the report, which may have encouraged the government in its belief that no disadvantages attended the inquiry's truncated mandate. On the contrary, however, what the incident demonstrates is how little understood is the role of political culture in allowing for the harmonious integration of immigrants and minorities. No single incident per se will prevent that harmonious integration from occurring in a country such as Canada, which is relatively successful at creating a legitimacy for its immigrants and minorities. This is particularly true when the initial official reactions were swift and uncompromisingly unsympathetic towards the deeds' perpetrators. However, the political culture of acceptance – and all the benefits for the state that accrue from a well-integrated immigrant population – are undermined by such events, if only because they highlight how ill-understood it is and indicate that further policy decisions may be made that erode it.

The Canadian government believed that the perception of public justice had been served with the disbanding of the regiment that murdered Somali civilian teenagers in its custody and the court-martialling of certain of its soldiers and that there was no value to be gained by examining the military's systemic problems in further depth. What was not well understood was that the real issue was one of domestic politics: the premature closure of the inquiry carried the message that in fact the lives of Somalis are not as valuable as those of Canadians, because the government does not care to ascertain what the systemic failures were that led to the loss of those lives or the belief that it would be acceptable to pretend that they had not been lost at the hands of Canadian soldiers. It is a directly contradictory message to the one sent by the disbanding of the regiment, and it may, in the long term, be the more significant.

A Further Note Concerning Racism

The reader should not misunderstand the intentions of these comments. The point is not that racism does not exist in Canada. Racism appears to be more subtle in Canada than in Britain. It is hidden, and rarely overt.[132] (This is even more true in urban English Canada than in Quebec, for the reasons spelled out elsewhere.) Although fully one-third of Toronto's residents are members of visible minorities, there is little racial tension in the city. While the occasional confrontation arises between police and the black community over whether a crime suspect was treated particularly harshly because of his skin colour, black writers admit to having trouble getting racism acknowledged as a factor of any significance in Canadian life.[133] In part this is because of English

Canadians' need to believe in the Myth of Tolerance, as discussed else-where, and in part it is because racism is a more subtle creature in its Canadian formation. M. Nourbese Philip and other writers maintain that it exists in a systemic way, in the same way that gender discrimi-nation does, so that people of colour are not given public arts grants, or promoted, the same way that white people are.[134]

In spite of this, however, or rather, alongside this, there exist the con-ditions – political, historical, cultural, and otherwise – that grant immi-grants and minorities a legitimacy of voice. It is this respect and inclusion that Toronto Somalis refer to when they call Canada a toler-ant place and say that they feel Canadian. It can be argued that in order for these conditions to hold, it is not necessary for a society to be com-pletely without racism; it is only necessary that it not be characterized by overt racism and public hostility. The eradication of systemic racism is a longer, gradual exercise. Obviously, its existence at any level will temper the legitimacy of which we have spoken. But just as anti-semit-ism has all but disappeared as a factor of any significance in English-Canadian society, the eradication of all kinds of racism begins with their social unacceptability in any overt form. To borrow from *Islamo-phobia*, attitudes of the wider society change only once it is understood that holding racist viewpoints – and understanding what these are – is not 'normal.'[135]

Manifestations of Difference

The variant societal orientations of Canada and Britain produce clearly different results in their respective Somali immigrant populations. In the first place, as demonstrated by the quotations above, the quality of the connection to the wider society is vastly different as expressed by Canadian and British respondents. Toronto Somalis speak of a sense of belonging, of acceptance, and of legitimacy in their adopted country. London Somalis continually speak of the distance that is placed between themselves and British society, of a sense that they are never permitted to forget that they are intruders.

This overwhelming difference necessarily affects the quality of the integration that Somalis undergo as they learn to accommodate them-selves to their new environments. In both cities, Somalis must learn to live in what they perceive as an alien culture that is individualistic and secular. In both cities they have had to adjust to new logistical demands and the rigours of transferring values in a multi-religious environment. In both cities they have encountered the widespread condoning of alcohol consumption, of pre- and extramarital sex, of birth control and abortion. They have encountered condemnation of the traditional practice of female circumcision. In both cities, as chapter 7 discusses in detail, they have made accommodations to these factors in their own way. In both cities, the dominant trend has been for Somali immigrants to become more, not less religious. Yet there is a striking difference in how they have made these adjustments.

The argument has been made that the distinction between 'public' and 'private' life is hard to draw, because so much of what is generally considered private – the family, for instance – has its unmistakably public aspect.[136] The argument is valid for two reasons. Firstly, as Arendt made clear in her historical considerations of the human condition,[137] the contextual definition of what is public and private, and how these interconnect, changes over time. Societies are continually renegotiating, or re-evaluating, what falls into either realm. The question of domestic violence, for instance, is an area where what was once considered, and not very long ago, to be purely in the private realm is now regarded as a matter of public concern if certain boundaries (those of physical safety and integrity, in particular) are crossed. And second, as Eickelman and Piscatori explain, even the most personal and private sides of life have their public – and political – angles.[138]

Somali immigrants have encountered this juncture of the public and the private where female circumcision and other sexual matters are concerned. Subjects that many Somali women would have found difficult to discuss in the privacy of their own living rooms are suddenly the focus of classroom lectures and public health campaigns. As Shabbir Akhtar points out with respect to the negative reception of many Muslim parents to the sexual education of their children, it is not only the question of content that is at issue, but indeed the location of the discussion. Sexual education might be viewed by many parents as an issue for private, home discussion between mothers and their daughters, and fathers and their sons.[139] In both Canada and Britain, however, the view is taken that the societal consequences of sexual ignorance (in terms of disease and unwanted pregnancies) are such that sexual education is a public requirement. Similarly, female circumcision, which is regarded with horror by Western legislators, feminists, human rights activists, and the media alike, has become a very political issue, no longer the private concern of mothers and grandmothers. (It could be argued that even in a traditional Somali context, female circumcision was never really a private matter, because there were immense societal repercussions for a girl who was not circumcised.)

The point is that virtually every aspect of life has its public and therefore potentially political facet. Decisions to avoid all physical contact with members of the other gender, or to avoid all contact with alcohol, or to cover one's head with a scarf are all ostensibly personal decisions with tremendous public, and sometimes political repercussions.

This interplay and overlap between the public and the private become particularly salient for immigrants and ethnic minorities when the political culture in which they function is considered. As argued above, Britain's relatively hostile political culture translates into a sense of alienation and ghettoization for London Somalis. This alienation in turn is incorporated in some measure into every aspect of their lives precisely because there is no clear distinction between the public and private and because even the most private concerns have their public angles. Therefore, all conscious or subconscious decisions of the Londoners, with respect to integration, somehow incorporate the cultural isolation that they feel is forced on them.

This phenomenon is most vividly apparent where the question under consideration is explicitly public. The connection that respondents felt with their adopted country is an example of this, but that is not the end of it. Respondents on both sides of the Atlantic held a similar range of opinions, in roughly the same proportions, about female circumcision. British respondents, however, frequently noted that they had encountered, in awareness seminars or on the street, women who reacted strongly to what they saw as outsiders meddling in their culture. Their reaction was to counter that female circumcision is a Somali custom and no one else's business, and it became irrelevant whether the custom was Islamically sanctioned. In the absence of such outsiders' interference, the issue of Islamic sanction would have been significant. Although similar health campaigns have been run in Canada, and the practice is illegal in both countries, only once did a Canadian respondent note that outsiders' obsession with the issue was unhelpful.

It is not surprising, given this analysis, that London Somalis tended to be more emotional and angry as they discussed the case of Salman Rushdie. But even when they discussed how and why their practice of their religion had changed since migrating, it is obvious that political culture was intruding on personal decisions. Canadian Somalis explained their increased religious observance by talking about a new need to understand better their religion and transmit it to their children. They spoke of a reaction against what they saw as the excessive individualism of Western secular culture. British Somalis spoke of all these things but, in addition, of the alienation that they experience in London. Hibaq 'returned' to her culture – and became highly observant for the first time in her life – after she had been rebuffed by British society.[140] Abdullahi spoke of how the compartmentalization of British society, and the fact that Somalis felt uncomfortable, were useful in terms of helping them retain their culture. For him, enforced distance helped him bolster in his children the need for cultural and religious retention.[141] Faduma spoke explicitly of how the racism and rejection of London society had caused the angry embrace of Islamism by significant numbers of young Somalis.[142] These sentiments were repeated, in one form or another, in interview after interview.

Conclusion

This chapter has thus argued that integration is fundamentally affected by political culture – including legal norms and the climate that they engender. Harmonious integration – both external and internal – will be facilitated by a political culture that creates a legitimate space for the immigrant Other.[143] Essentially, political culture determines the degree to which the inhabitants of an imagined community are willing to share the shaping of that collective imagination with the Other. Integration therefore occurs more fluidly when immigrants are not made to feel that their identity – however they define it – is at odds with the society around them.

This chapter has demonstrated that Canada is more willing, and Britain thus far more resistant, to drawing ethnic minorities into that process. Resistance itself does not prevent the participation from occurring, but it occurs with an edge and a consciousness among immigrants of having had to fight for a voice, which is absent in a more pliant society. It is possible, however, to see the beginnings of societal accommodation to Muslim communities in London as well as in Toronto. While it may be more overt in Toronto, examples can be found in both countries of institutions, such as the Royal Bank of Scotland and the Bolton and Etobicoke hospitals, becoming more sensitive to Muslim employees, clients, and patients. These are signs, however embryonic, that the host societies are beginning to enfold awareness of Muslim needs into the larger culture.

The next chapter turns to an analysis of integration itself. It re-examines the mechanism of integration as discussed in chapter 2, analysing in that context the views and outlook of Somalis in London and Toronto.

7

Integration

This chapter reiterates and re-examines the process of integration – how it is that immigrants 'renegotiate' their identity; how they retain part of their birth-culture and graft onto it a new culture, and what they end up with; what their children, born in the new land, retain of their parents' heritage that is theirs as well, and how they stitch the home-world onto that of their schoolmates; and what society makes of the hybrid-citizens that it nurtures.

The chapter is divided into three sections. The first re-examines the process of integration itself, both at the level of the individual and then at the level of political society. The second section looks at the answers of Somalis, particularly where they responded to the questions of how they bridge two worlds, to illustrate the explications of part I. The third section discusses one of the central issues of this book: the nature of the meeting of Islam and the West and whether they are essentially and necessarily Other to each other or whether that is an illusion and a mis-perception.

Integration

The process of integration, for an immigrant-receiving society, is best described as one in which both the stream of immigrants, and the society into which it moves, take something from each other. Over time they begin to reflect one another, however dimly this may happen at first. Neither the United States nor Canada, for example, both immigrant-receiving societies from their inception, has in fact *assimilated* its immigrants. Assimilation implies the replacement of birth-culture by that of the new land, which is a false understanding of what happens to immigrants.[1]

What the United States and Canada have done is to integrate their immigrant stock into their culture and political culture, so that the mainstream United States and mainstream Canada, and the government procedures and policies that each country produces, reflect to a great and increasing extent the diversity of their populations. As for the immigrants, they too have learned the dominant language(s) and have adopted many of the ways and beliefs of their new land, but 'assimilation' is the wrong word to describe what has happened to them. Even Cajuns[2] did not assimilate, although for the most part they lost their language. The reason that no one will ever mistake New Orleans, Louisiana, for Atlanta, Georgia, is largely that the Cajuns have retained a large part of whatever it was that made them French New Worlders. They have not assimilated; rather, they have *integrated*. They took from their new society, and they gave in kind, and New Orleans retains their reflection.

Integration has a wide spectrum, and at a macro-, societal level, it does not matter whether individuals insist on calling themselves hyphenated nationals or simply nationals of the new land. Cajun descendants are not recognized as being separate from other Americans for the purposes of economic, social, or political activity, so that they can be said to be externally integrated into American society. But it may be that some individuals feel strongly about their French history, roots, and language, that they take pride in this heritage, and that it plays a significant role in family dynamics. It may be that other Cajuns do not, that they are Americans or southerners first, and that their name with its French derivation is merely an amusing dinner anecdote. It does not matter. They were not assimilated. Their cultural influence may have been localized and limited, but it remains perceptible centuries after their forced removal from British North America. This story, repeated across immigrant groups again and again, has in its totality created two nations in Canada and the United States whose political culture, whose sense of nationhood, is inextricably bound up with the varied cultural influences.

The individual immigrants arrive with their birth-culture – an amalgam of their language, religion, beliefs, customs, and experiences. But from the moment they arrive in their adopted land, the influences they are surrounded by are different. Even for those whose birth-cultures have a lot in common with their adopted cultures – for instance, South Africans in Britain or Americans in Canada – this process occurs. It may be a question of accent or the way a phrase is used, the fact that climatic differences temper the way in which people live and dress, a political system with different nuances, a difference in how religion or nationalism is observed in the schools, a difference in how formally or informally business is conducted, but the adopted culture is not the same. After a number of years amid the adopted culture, immigrants who return 'home' will feel the difference. They are not the people they would have been had they not varied their experiences. They have different perspectives, see their old towns and companions with a new distance. And time has not stood still in the old country, either. Things have moved on, and they have not been a part of them, which increases the sense of distance. Our immigrants are no longer a product only of their birth-cultures, nor do they belong entirely to their adopted cultures. They have become something else.

The fewer the differences, the more subtle the nuances of distance, between the birth- and adopted cultures, the more easily immigrants may bridge the two. The accent of South Africans in London may change; they will adjust their turns of phrase so as not to be misunderstood, accustom themselves to the rain, learn to understand the new politics. Americans in Canada will adjust to changes even more subtle: a broader political spectrum in which 'socialist' is not a dirty word; a greater tolerance for government intervention in the lives of ordinary citizens; people who apologize when it is their toes that were stepped on. In such cases, where the birth- and adopted cultures are so close that the adjustment is almost unnoticeable, it is easy to talk of assimilation. Immigrants appear to have adopted completely the culture of their new country; they have become one of 'us.'

In fact, however, the process that occurs is different only in degree, but not in kind, from that which occurs when the birth-culture and adopted culture are farther removed from one another. South Africans in London may retain a taste for spicy food or endless sunny days or the open veld. They may find the monarchy either quaint or ridiculous, in contrast to their British friends, and have difficulty treating it as a serious institution. Depending on their political persuasion and the reasons they had for leaving South Africa, they may find British society too liberal or not liberal enough. Americans in Canada may find Canadians impossibly passive in their business dealings and may never understand their tolerance for provincial peevishness or the long-distance monarchy. These attitudes of our fictitious immigrants (and of course not all South Africans in Britain or Americans in Canada will share the same ones) will then be folded into the attitudes of

Canadians or Britons, because that is what the immigrants have become.

The farther apart the birth- and adopted cultures, the less likely an immigrant's process of adjustment is to be described as assimilation. Immigrants who hail from a country with a different language, or whose religion differs from the dominant one, or where social customs or beliefs about family dynamics or the relative roles of men and women are different will have a greater adjustment to make. The bridge spanning their two cultures is more complex. Perhaps there is more than one bridge, some stronger and more easily constructed, others tentative and fragile. Nevertheless, for these immigrants, as well, the adopted culture, layered over the birth-culture, leaves them creatures of neither one nor of the other culture, but something else. The immigrants will retain some, reject some, moderate some, combine their two cultures. The people they become can never go back unchanged; they are products of their experiences, after all. To alter a saying of Gertrude Stein, there is no longer any there there. And if they stay in their new land, they cannot erase what they brought with them. They can moderate beliefs or change their minds about some, but it is part of a process of adaptation. It is important to reiterate that what is happening is exactly what happens to immigrants with similar birth- and adopted cultures, only more so.

To what extent is colour a factor in all of this? Colour is a factor only in so far as it is a visible mark of difference that is recognized as such by the adopted culture. In other words, white South African immigrants with a good ear may be able, over a period of years, to obliterate their accents and stop complaining about the weather enough to pass as non-immigrant, non-minority citizens. It is much more difficult for black South African immigrants to do that, not because they cannot obliterate their accents, but because their colour marks them as minority members of society. The case of Somalis is interesting here. For a number of reasons discussed in chapter 2, Somalis frequently do not consider themselves African. Mythically and otherwise, they consider themselves closer to Arabs than to Africans. In their determining their own sense of self, their skin colour is not the significant factor. Therefore it has been shocking to many Somali immigrants to be assumed by most Britons and Canadians, without question, to be African like all other sub-Saharan Africans. Canadians and Britons do not generally differentiate between Somalis and other Africans racially. They see them all as black. Many Somalis are shocked and sometimes dismayed by this, since, before emigrating, they did not see themselves as being any more African than a Scot. This is an example of an ethnicity boundary, imposed externally by the adopted culture, around which Somalis are then forced to negotiate in their new environment.

Thus far I have argued that immigrants become hybrids of their birth- and adopted cultures, in greater or lesser amounts, depending on their individual circumstances, personalities, and experiences, as well as the age at which they immigrated. What about their children? Children of immigrants are hybrid creatures, too. Depending on the nature of the differences between the parents' birth- and adopted cultures, there will be differences between the home environment, or the home culture, and the environment and culture of the outside world. In their own way, immigrants' children will have their own bridges to build, their own accommodations to make between what they learn at home and what they absorb from school, television, street, and playground. They will cast off some of their home beliefs, and customs will fade; they will retain some, as will their children in turn.

An ethnic group can be said to be *externally* integrated when an individual member's social, economic, or political mobility is not affected by his or her ethnic status. This might be true for Germans or Italians, Roman Catholics, and Jews. However, it might not be true for Asians, Africans, or Jews (depending on where and what social, economic or political arena they are attempting to enter). Where it is not true, society has erected boundaries that define ethnicity, usually negatively, for the purpose of movement in social, economic, or political circles. It may be said therefore that this sort of integration is marked externally, by factors beyond the control of individuals within the ethnic group.

External integration is something that individuals cannot control. Their internal integration – how they relate to the 'primordial' aspects of their ethnicity – is something else. Unless they are marked by externally recognized boundaries, immigrants and their descendants may choose to live in the outside culture alone, ignoring as much as they can of the home culture. The children of white South African immigrants do not have as much as an accent to surmount, and, if they choose to have it that way, they can quickly make an Afrikaans surname nothing but a spelling obstacle and a dinner anecdote, as with the French surnames of New Orleans's Cajuns. The children of black South African immigrants may not find it as easy to ignore their parents' past; similarly for the Muslim child named Muhammad or the Jewish child whose last name is Cohen. These people, whose external markers identify them as 'ethnic,' must constantly work their ethnic identities into their lives at a conscious level. To the extent that those markers affect their mobility socially, economically, or politically, they are less than fully integrated. In contrast, South Africans who are 'coloured' but whose skin is light; white South Africans; the Muslim named Leila; the Jew named Porter – these people may choose to 'pass' and thus circumvent the boundaries that society has erected for them. Or they may choose to identify strongly with their home culture, their ethnic group, in both the public and the private spheres, in defiance of those very external boundaries or because they prefer the intrinsic value of the 'home culture.' Again, the choices of individuals on any level – public or private – are irrelevant to whether the ethnic group can be said to be externally integrated at any level – economic, political, or social.

Political societies are the products of the collectivity of individuals who make them up. When a society is a conglomeration of individuals who come from a variety of backgrounds, and when that society functions as a liberal democracy, it will tend to reflect, in its political structures, the procedures, decisions, and interests of that broad conglomeration. Where it does not reflect the interests of the migrants in its midst, they will exert pressure on the system to change. The United States does not adequately reflect the interests of its large African-American population; the kind of tension apparent during the Los Angeles riots or the O.J. Simpson trial simmers constantly beneath the surface of American life. Canada has not found a way to accommodate adequately the interests of a large self-consciously ethnic minority (the Québécois) without in turn damaging the interests of the minorities (the anglophones and ethnic communities) of the province of Quebec or the perceived interests of the other provinces; the result resembles what former Premier Jacques Parizeau called 'an endless trip to the dentist.' Britain is struggling to understand and accommodate the interests of its large influx of immigrants, many of whom are non-white and non-Christian. Whether in the form of urban violence or the organized reaction to the Rushdie novel, tension is apparent there, too.

The previous chapter argued that what Canadian political culture has succeeded in doing is recognizing that immigrants' head start of a couple of hundred years does not grant their descendants a greater legitimacy in the public or political order. Again, what follows from that recognition is an understanding that the making of political culture is an ongoing exercise, that all participants in it are collectively responsible for its creation, and that it is, at any one time, the combination of all the elements of the various traditions of its creators, though clearly not in equal proportions. Chapter 6 also argued that Britain has not yet been able to find a way to make such an accommodation, even in theory, but it is easier to achieve in the case of a country barely a century and a quarter old than in one with the weight of history – including, significantly, the legacy of colonialism – that Britain bears. When 'we' barely know who 'We' are – that is, when our collective self-understanding is not well entrenched – it is harder to distinguish 'Us' from 'Them.' Put another way, the more 'neutral' the territory, the easier it is to be generous about sharing the myth-making.

External and Internal Integration for Somalis

External integration and internal integration are two distinct but related processes; there is a connection between them. Immigrants will undergo internal integration – or cultural weaving – even in a hostile environment, but the quality of that integration will be affected by the hostility. Internal integration carries an inner dynamic that sets the process in motion and propels it onward. In the very act of living, immigrants make daily choices based on influences and experiences (current and past), and that process becomes one of weaving together birth- and adopted cultures. However, because even the most private of those daily choices has its public aspect, the ambient political culture impinges on the process of internal integration.

Political culture clearly and directly determines the degree to which external integration can occur. Although it does not cause internal integration to occur or not, it does affect the *quality* of that integration. As chapter 6 argued, the lack of distinction between private and public spheres of life means that even the most private decisions have some element of 'public' intrusion into them. A woman deciding whether to wear the hijab is aware that she will be regarded differently on Oxford Street or Yonge Street if she does so. It is political culture that helps determine the reaction that she will get. Anticipation of a hostile reaction – as opposed to an indifferent one – will affect the process of internal integration. It will not necessarily be the most significant factor in determining an individual's choices, but it will be an element in the process. The woman may decide to don the hijab regardless of the anticipation of hostility, or precisely because of the anticipation of hostility, but it will be a different kind of decision than if she anticipated indifference or the occasional curious glance.

External Integration

In terms of my working definition of external integration, there is no question that Somalis are less than fully integrated. There are a number of barriers that stand between them, as an ethnic group, and ready mobility in social, economic, and political fields. These include language, education, and professional qualifications, and colour and religion to the extent that racism exists. I deal with each factor in turn, giving special attention to religion.

Language is the most fundamental barrier to integration, both 'external' and 'internal,' although anecdotal evidence would suggest that Somalis are acquiring English-language skills rapidly. Somalis in both Canada and Britain advanced a number of explanations for the phenomenon. Some said that it is because Somalis have historically learned language, genealogy, poetry, and history via oral as opposed to written means, which lends itself to the absorption of new sounds, regardless of literacy. Others credited their legendary independence and their consequent unwillingness to have to rely on friends and relatives to translate for them. Still others supposed that it resulted from the flexibility that comes with a nomadic, pastoral way of life, even one that is now merely family history. One woman, who has been working at an East London hospital as a translator for Somalis requiring health services, said that she is planning to leave her job because she has so little to do. In 1989, when she started, she could not keep up with the demand. But although use of the health care system by Somalis has increased, she says, the need for translation is fast disappearing. A Toronto woman who runs a language school mentioned that the Somalis in her English classes are extraordinarily quick students, as did the principals of two high schools who noted that the Somali students had learned English and integrated into school activities more quickly than any immigrant group they had witnessed.

The problem with unrecognized professional and educational qualifications, which has resulted in doctors driving taxis and engineers working as security guards, is not one that afflicts Somalis alone. The problem affects immigrants from many countries and points to the inefficiencies that result when international standards have not been worked out between educational and professional organizations worldwide. As migration grows, so will the pressing nature of this issue. While it has begun to be addressed in negotiations in international trade discussions concerning services, it remains a barrier for immigrants to industrial countries from the developing world.

Colour, as discussed above, is a barrier to entry and movement in so far as it is seen to be so by Britons and Canadians; for Somalis, it is a particularly galling one.

Cultural Racism

Religion is also a barrier to entry and movement when it is regarded with prejudice by British or Canadian society, or when Somalis disqualify themselves from certain jobs or activities for religious reasons (for example, they would be unable to attend Friday prayers or would be required to sell or carry alcohol).

As we saw in chapter 6, religion is one of Clifford Geertz's cultural 'givens'[3] of birth. Although individuals may in adulthood rethink or reject all or some of the religious ideas of the culture into which they were born, religion is often an integral part of their identities. Even if they reject its practice or ideas, people may consider themselves culturally Jewish, Muslim, Hindu, or Eastern Orthodox Christian. When people are marginalized or excluded because of their religious beliefs or cultural adherence, this too is racism.[4] Somalis, particularly in Canada, differentiated between colour and religious racism, because they frequently found that while they were accepted as new immigrants, and colour discrimination was not widespread, prejudice directed at their religion and religious practices was far more prevalent. 'Cultural racism' is perhaps a more accurate term than 'religious racism,' because it is broader and describes racism on the basis of cultural practices as well as the ideas or practice of religion per se.

Cultural racism is apparent when a Somali woman in the hijab, for instance, finds that prospective employers continually reject her on sight but has no trouble finding work when her head is uncovered. It is similarly evident in the experiences of white British women who have converted to Islam in order to marry and have found that societal doors are suddenly shut to them, as long as there are obvious signs of their conversion, such as the hijab. It appears as well in the stories of men denied work because they refused to shake the hand of the female employer who offered the job or in stories of examinations continually returned with higher grades when an initial is used to identify the writer, instead of an obviously Muslim name. The Runnymede Trust, in its recent monograph on religious discrimination against Muslims in

Britain, called the phenomenon 'Islamophobia.'[5] In particular, it describes what *Islamophobia* calls a 'closed' view of Islam: a view of the religion as a 'single, monolithic bloc,' holding values that are 'separate and other' and have nothing in common with those of the West. This closed view sees Islam as inferior to the West, violent and aggressive, a political ideology with no constructive criticism to offer of the West. Those who hold such a hostile view of Islam tend to use it as a justification for discrmination against Muslims, which they further view as 'natural' and 'normal.'[6]

Internal Integration

Let us look at how Somalis are dealing with balancing their birth-culture with their adopted cultures – the process of internal integration. In turn, we examine practice, transfer of values, and the values themselves.

Virtually the entire Somali population of Toronto and Britain, with the exception of a small core of Londoners, is composed of immigrants so new that they are still struggling to re-establish their lives and their families. Even so, the process of integration – of bridging old and new cultures – begins almost immediately after their arrival.

Practising Islam in the Diaspora

There is a significant and growing literature on how immigrant Muslims are adapting to life in various Western countries. Adaptation is affected by how Islam was practised in the countries from which the immigrants hail and the peculiarities of the host country.[7] Turks in Germany, Algerians in France, and South Asians in Britain all face particular circumstances that arise from both the traditions that they brought to their new homes and the legal structures and political cultures that they encountered when they arrived. Germany, for instance, still considers its Turkish immigrants to be guest workers, and calls them such, even though children and grandchildren have been born in Germany. The rate of naturalization of non-Germans is extremely slow, in large part because of Germany's conception of what a nation is and who deserves membership within it.[8]

In France, a strong political tradition of cultural uniformity has dictated a policy of attempted *intégration* of Muslim immigrants. *Intégration* is better translated as assimilation, since its intended result, according to Gilles Kepel, is the 'absorption, individual by individual, of people of Muslim origin into French society. They would be able to practise their religion in a fashion acceptable to a secular state .... This process of *intégration* implies, over time, the dissolution and weakening ... of community ties.'[9] However, Kepel believes that the crucible of the 1989 headscarf affair, during which three college students were prevented from wearing the hijab to school, in combination with political developments in the former French colony of Algeria and the kinds of ties that exist between residents of France and the Maghreb, have strengthened community ties, as French Muslims persist in practising their religion in the way that makes sense to them and not to their secular hosts.[10]

Indians, Pakistanis, and Bangladeshis, who together make up the vast majority of Britain's Muslims, have created a vibrant series of organizations whose structure and beliefs are in large part a reflection of the Asian subcontinent.[11] Politically and culturally, they have set the tone of the debate about the place of Muslims in British society.[12]

The place of Muslims in American life is complicated by the domestic dimension: the role and significance of African-American Islam. African Americans make up the largest single community of Muslims in the United States, but they are by no means the only one, and here as well diversity in origin is as significant as host community in determining the dynamics of the relationship.[13]

While the issues faced by any community of Muslims in the West are as varied as the communities themselves, there are some common threads. The continued emphasis on community, for instance (whatever the desire of the French Republic to be 'une et indivisible'[14]), and the importation of custom and organization from home make up one trend. It is not unusual, moreover, to encounter the phenomenon of a heightened sense of religious awareness, such as that stressed by many Somali respondents. Among the most notable examples of this is that of Sayyid Qutb, the Muslim Brotherhood writer whose visit to the United States inspired much of his subsequent writing.[15]

Most adult Somalis appear to have become more, not less, religious on moving to London and Toronto. They did this for a number of reasons. Many had lived through a time of terrible trauma, both in Somalia and during their flight. In many cases they found themselves reduced to poverty from lives that had been quite comfortable. They lost friends, influence, money, familiarity, home, and family. As they fled from the comfortable and familiar into the unknown and the inhospitable, religion was the one thing that came with them and that the civil war could not take away.

Like the fable of the sun and the wind which vie with one another to part a traveller from his cloak, inhospitable conditions (weather, people, foreign-ness – whichever and however they discovered it) tends to cause people to tug the warm and familiar closer to themselves. The interviews were full of stories of young adults who left home quite happy to embrace the ways of the West and, frightened or repulsed by what they saw, returned to their religion, sometimes with an intensity that they had never felt before. In the case of London Somalis, as described in chapter 6, the perceived hostility of the wider society augmented this sentiment.

Almost the overwhelming response of mothers was to become significantly more religious, in large part because of a perceived need to protect their children from foreign values and set an example and also because they needed the support that it gave them. People spoke about a sense of peace and security amid the tumult of their refugee lives: the rhythm of prayer, the solidity of the Qur'an and hadiths, the companionability of Friday prayer. For some of these reasons, many women – who would never have dreamt of going to communal prayer in Somalia – do so in Toronto and London. Or they get together for study, not just to learn the Qur'an by heart, but to understand it and apply it to their lives. Even women whose tendency has not been to become more religious have found their behaviour regulated by community members who have done so and have commented on how communal standards are significantly stricter than they used to be in Somalia.

Men have predominantly had one of two responses to exile: they have tended to become disillusioned and depressed by their powerlessness – their inability to find work commensurate with their experience, or to find work at all, and to languish. Or they too have taken strength from religion. Many Somalis, men and women, have become more religious because they believe that religion is what will provide a political answer for a home country that has tried a number of forms of government that have thus far proven unworkable.

Not all who have become religious have become Islamists (self-consciously reverting to what they consider first principles, using the Qur'an and hadiths to guide most of their actions, following the dictates of certain teachers in preference to others, explicitly endorsing the need for political action to set Somali society back on the 'straight path' of Islam), but many have been influenced by them. The people who consider themselves Islamists may be relatively few, but the number of people whose practice of Islam has been affected by the Islamist movements is significantly larger, in both London and Toronto.

Many of the Islamists' concerns, particularly within organizations, continue to centre around life in Somalia and how to advance the cause of Islam in any emergent political system there. But most of their time is taken with the problem of integration, however they conceive of it. For adherents of al-Ittihad's philosophy, integration is a nasty word. The key for survival is to be found in isolation. These are the adherents of the construction of the 'island of Islam,' and their aim is to be left in peace to do so. Elsewhere on the spectrum are groups such as the Somali Youth Association of Toronto (SOYAT), which believes that only solutions that are acceptable to both Western and Islamic value systems make the future of Islam secure in the West. While many Somalis consciously espoused one or another of these viewpoints, others did not. But everyone was finding his or her own way through the maze.

For the isolationists, acceptability might include defining what jobs may or may not be taken, what restaurants may be eaten in, and where food may be bought. It would include being vigilant about each and every activity of the day. A taxi driver would need to learn how to explain to an obviously liquor-toting client that he cannot transport him or her. If television is permitted in the home, isolationists must decide which programs are acceptable and which are not. If Islamic school is not financially viable, they must determine how to counter the non-Islamic (or what might be considered anti-Islamic) teachings that children receive. The isolationist may quit a job that does not allow for Friday communal prayer.

The consciously integrationist Muslim might not feel that Islamic school is necessary or even desirable if school is supplemented by religious instruction. Social separation from non-Muslims may not be thought to be necessary or desirable either. It might not be worth losing a job over a handshake or quitting a job if Friday prayers are a problem.

As they become more confident in negotiating their practice, people tend to learn to find their way around individual problems. Deeqa (Toronto), who got a job in a clothing store despite wearing the hijab, has found an argument that she can use when non-Muslim feminists question her wearing a headscarf. Hibaq (London) takes off her hijab when she goes for job interviews and replaces it after she has the position. Ismail, a self-described Islamist in Toronto, once avoided restaurants but now enters without fear, having decided to take the approach of inquiring about all the ingredients in each dish that he orders. His sister, for whom he cares, attends a public high school, but he made himself an adviser to the school and the school board on Muslim affairs and is vocal about incidents that he or his sister finds offensive. Warsame (Toronto) prays wherever he happens to be when it is time to pray, even if that is a subway station, smiling and handing a card explaining that he is a Muslim to anyone who asks. Hamud (London) does not stop what he is doing to pray and sometimes misses prayers, but his children attend Qur'anic school, Qur'anic values are emphasized at home, and his elderly mother is studying the Qur'an for the first time in her life.

Although the interviews recorded plenty of complaints about the inconveniences of practising Islam in Toronto and London, most respondents concluded that Islam could be practised without obstruction in both cities. The two significant exceptions to this were time off work for the Friday communal prayer and dress for women, since women in the hijab suffer continual harassment, through comments, hostile looks, or exclusion from a portion of the job market. In part, it could be argued that the problem over Friday prayer involves a lack of imagination on the part of employers. The same way that employers are increasingly varying work arrangements to accommodate parents of small children, they could do so around an extended Friday lunch hour. The reason that this has not happened, however, is perhaps the same reason that women in the hijab suffer discrimination on the job market: cultural racism, addressed again in the final section of the chapter.

Transfer of Values

The most startling change to which parents have had to accommodate themselves on leaving Somalia is that their Muslim identities, and those of their children, can no longer be taken for granted. They now live in a world of competing religions, which translates into competing frameworks of behaviour, or competing value systems. Though the value systems advocated by Christianity or Judaism may not differ substantively from that of Islam, the value system that is seen to be embraced by the secular West appears to be frighteningly at variance with their own beliefs and traditions, as discussed in chapter 4. The fear and concern of Somali parents have been whether it is possible to instil Muslim values and traditions in their children in this multi-religious and secular world.

From their perspective, their inability to apply Somali parenting styles (authoritative, unquestioned, if necessary backed by corporal punishment) in the West has deprived them of control over their children. This has happened precisely as non-Muslim influences over their children have burgeoned. In this environment, parents have confronted two issues: how most effectively to influence children at home and what to do about competing influences. In answer to the first question, many parents have become more overtly religious, and more conscious of fulfilling the daily requirements and of demonstrating the importance of such events as Ramadan and Eid. Some have advocated, or participated in, workshops in alternative parenting styles. In answer to the second, parents debate the worth of isolation versus social interaction. They must decide whether children are better prepared to live in a multi-religious world if they are cloistered as much as possible with their own or, rather, if they are taught how to engage and counter other influences.

Many parents assume that their teenaged children are 'lost,' because they see them experiment with styles of socialization, clothing, and hair and bring home the habits and vocabulary of their new environments. It could even be argued that the teenagers as a group are more 'conservative' than those in their twenties. They seem unwilling to part with home culture, beliefs, and traditions as their parents define them. Insecure in their new environment, attempting to balance the culture of home and that of their school, teens are keenly aware of the distress through which their parents have lived and do not want to cause further pain. They themselves have been through distress and turmoil and need the love and support of their parents. They also need to figure out how to live in their new world, and it is not immediately obvious to them that they cannot be Muslims and still socialize in a Canadian or British way. They see that their non-immigrant friends have a different kind of rapport with their parents from what they had been taught was the way children should relate to elders. This rapport involves a type of give and take that is not traditional in Somali families. The teens, drawn into their new world much more quickly than their parents in many cases, learning English, soaking in the new culture like sponges, feel that they have as much to teach their parents as they have to learn from them, so are often unwilling to accept traditional Somali parenting.

None the less, the interviews with Somali teenagers show that children tend to hold strongly to the values their parents are so frightened about their losing. Although the teens make compromises in style, their understanding of what is right and wrong, and why, is unshaken. Each young person has decided for himself or herself how far down the road of compromise he or she is prepared to go. For some, parties and dances are unacceptable. For others, it is acceptable to attend but not to dance with the opposite sex. For yet others, dancing is permissible, but drinking alcohol is not. For each of them, it is a matter of deciding what they are prepared to live with and what they are not. Some said that they feel guilty because as 'good' Muslims they think that they should be praying five times daily, or wearing the hijab, or not going to parties. Some pointed out that in Somalia parental pressure to conform to tradition would not have been so strong; it would have been accepted that they are still young and 'practising' to perform their religious requirements.

While the teenagers' appearance may have changed, at their core they did not consider themselves less Muslim than their parents. Their balancing act may have expressed itself differently, but it was the same one in which their elders were engaged.

Values

Overall, the position of teenagers tended to be more hesitant because they were not sure of themselves and because they felt caught between their parents and their new world, not yet sure what they themselves wanted. Somalis in their twenties, in contrast, tended to be less hesitant about redefining for themselves what made them 'good' Muslims. If they did not wear the hijab or attend Friday prayers or even pray daily, they did not make apologies for it. They indicated that while they may change their minds, for now they felt comfortable doing a or b and believing x or y. In some cases, these people had left the parental home once in the diaspora; in others they had immigrated without parents.

In many cases they had been through an odyssey of sorts. Their personal identification with their religion – how they wanted to practise it; how and whether they identify themselves as Muslims – had altered significantly as they came to terms with their new lives. Their experiences continued to modify their attitudes. While this is true of all the immigrants, it appeared more marked with this age group, in part because its members are not yet encased in families of their own, and it is perhaps easier for them to reshape themselves. No adolescents, for instance, declared themselves to be comfortable with the idea of sex before marriage. In contrast, a number of twenty-to-thirty-year-olds said that sex before marriage, while not sanctioned by their religion, did not detract from their sense of themselves as believing Muslims, even as increasingly religious Muslims.

Among older Somalis, virginity at marriage, particularly for girls, was seen to continue to be of paramount importance. However, a number were pragmatic about extramarital sex, particularly if neither partner commits adultery. It happens, many felt, whether or not it is sanctioned, and in times of turmoil for large numbers of single adults it may happen with particular frequency. Many of those who accepted it as a given also identified themselves as practising Muslims and did not deny the status of believer to those engaging in extramarital sex.

The use of birth control is likewise revealing. While use of contraceptives may be discouraged by many imams, many people who considered themselves religious evinced the view that in expensive, industrial societies such as Canada's or Britain's, where the cost of raising a child is significant and living space limited and expensive, contraceptives are permissible. Their use was not felt to diminish the value of a person's belief or her status as a Muslim. (Notably, this particular accommodation tended to be gender-based, made predominantly by women.)

Most Somalis, from teenagers to grandparents, were dismayed by the individualism that they saw as central to Western life, which translates in their minds to selfishness and disregard for other people. Most of them did not separate Muslim from Somali traditions in emphasizing, as they saw it, a value system that encourages precisely the opposite: an ethic of sharing and of caring for the community. The community, when they were asked to define it, was generally described as all Muslims, whether Somali or not. They did not want to lose, or to have their children lose, this sense of responsibility for others, which they saw as being in conflict with the total freedom that they believe comes with Western individualism.

The interviews did show evidence of some unhappiness with the tradition of unquestioned financial aid to close sub-clan members. A few working young people expressed annoyance with older extended family members whom they saw as not pulling their weight and yet still expecting generous financial support. It might be expected that most young people, along with the impatience that they feel for the clan sensibilities of their elders, might redefine the group to which they feel obliged to give loyalty unquestioningly. One young Canadian woman, for instance, was startled to find a stranger insisting on hosting a graduation party for her when she finished university, merely because they were of the same sub-clan. Another student was upset to learn that her mother in Toronto had been upbraided by a distant relative in Kenya, whom the student had never met, because the Somali in Kenya had heard indirectly that the student was dating a young man from another clan and told her mother, 'We don't like [this situation]'. Young people find this meddling irritating and anachronistic, particularly since they blame clan tensions for Somalia's downfall. The process of moving away from clan affiliation – and therefore obligation – was occurring in Somalia's urban centres before the civil war, according to many commentators. The compelling reasons for clan identity tend to fall away in an urban environment.

This tendency will probably be exaggerated in the diaspora, because it is not difficult to move out of the 'village' if one is unhappy within it. One young woman explained that while she and her husband had been grateful for the resettlement help when they first arrived in Toronto, after a couple of years the nosy interference of their clansfolk in their married life became more aggravating than helpful; they thus moved to a suburb of the city.

But redefining the inner circle – who is a family member deserving of unquestioned support and who is not – is not the same thing as abandoning feelings of strong emotional and financial obligation. While Roda may not continue to give 'serious money' to any needy relative of her father's who asks for it, it does not mean that she will put her mother in an old age home and never visit her. Of course, Somalis' definition of what is selfish and uncaring may change with time. They may come to believe, as do many families of elderly in facilities, that they are best caring for their aged parents by entrusting them to professional care outside the home.

Throughout the interviews it is apparent that Somalis in both Canada and Britain are doing two things. First, they are reacting to the differences that they encounter between their birth- and adopted cultures and analysing how they are different, and second, they are beginning to accommodate themselves to the new realities that they encounter, which is what internal integration is all about.

Different individuals are adapting at different speeds, partly because of who they are, and partly because of the experiences that they have. Some are doing so as little as possible, like two Londoners: Elmi, the ex-soldier, who chews qat, sleeps, and plots revenge while he waits to return; and Nur, the Somali nationalist who says that he will never marry or have children until he can return to Somalia. Some are adapting in spite of themselves. Like Ahmed, they may be working to build islands of Islam. For Zeinab, who professes deep unhappiness in her new life, it is a matter of teaching other women to study the Qur'an, of showing them that Islam can be studied, and practised, anywhere. Most, however, are discovering that they can practise Islam in the West, and that even though they may find that their attitudes have changed on sexuality or reproduction or on how obligated they ought to be to distant relatives, it does not change their identity as Muslims.

Somali immigrants are not becoming less Muslim in the process of integrating. If anything, many are stronger believers and more self-conscious practitioners than they had been. Though some are frightened of losing their religion, or of their children being less Muslim, their comments do not show that this is what is occurring.

Their way of dealing with female circumcision is illustrative of how they have chosen to identify themselves in the diaspora. By and large, they have separated culture from religion where there is demonstrably a conflict, and the identity that they have chosen to emphasize is Muslim, as opposed to Somali nationalism. Thus when they learn, as most of them have for the first time, that female circumcision is a traditional Somali, but not Muslim, practice, they have abandoned/rejected the practice. There has been some Somali nationalist reaction that has led to a tenacious hold on the practice; some insistence on its validity as a means of protecting virginity in a frightening environment; and some movement towards the 'compromise' position of clitoridectomy. But by far the strongest tendency has been to abandon the practice altogether, given its mental and physical health–related problems, and given that it is not doctrinally prescribed.

The Somalis interviewed, when asked to define the 'group' to which they feel loyalty and responsibility, almost always answered 'Muslims,' not 'Somalis' or other clan or sub-clan members. Many of them differentiated, however, between the way in which Islam is practised in Somalia and the cultural attributes of Islam in the Middle East, with particular reference to the place of women. This has exciting implications for the future of Islam in the West.

The significant difference between the two cities therefore is not that one set of respondents integrated and the other did not but rather involves the quality of the integration. As argued above, London's Somalis continually calibrated the hostility of British political culture and its alienating effect, in addition to the variant values that they were balancing. Canadian political culture has created a more neutral environment for immigrants and ethnic minorities, though not one that is completely accommodating.

A Word about Choice

Almost all recent Somali migrants to the West have been refugees and have not left their homeland voluntarily. Often they had little choice in their destination. Clearly the question of choice affects integration, particularly its internal aspects. Refugees who hope to be able to return home will invest less energy in renegotiating their birth-cultures with that of their adopted society. They are more likely to attempt to retain their birth-culture in as pure a form as possible and to regard what accommodations they do make as temporary. Respondents such as Nur and Abdullahi in London are examples of this. But, as most respondents indicated, the dream of return has tended to exist along-side a pragmatic realization that that dream may never realize itself and that, even if it does, life has to be lived in the meantime. Children are maturing whose experiences consist mainly or only of this existence on the border between cultures, and their elders must adapt along with them. Therefore the involuntary nature of refugee migration may temper, but not generally prevent, the process of integration.

Islam and the West

A number of points suggest themselves from the theoretical approach pursued in these pages, and the interviews, concerning Islam in the West. Islam, and Muslims, are frequently portrayed as essentially Other in both academic journals and popular journalism, a depiction that serves as a backdrop for much of the cultural or religious prejudice that Muslims encounter in the West. While colour racism is increasingly regarded as a problem to be overcome by a society, institutional cultural racism, or anti-Islam racism, receives subtle encouragement from writings that emphasize essential differences, and therefore an implied adversarial relationship, between Islam and the West. A few notable examples will suffice to illustrate the point that Islam is generally presented, according to this view, as a monolithic entity whose adherents are essentially hostile to the West and its values. While the adversarial relationship has seemed to become pressing in the wake of Communism's collapse, Middle East scholar Daniel Pipes warned of the Islamic threat in 1980, following the Iranian revolution, the seizure of the American embassy in Teheran, violence in Mecca, and the Soviet invasion of Afghanistan: 'Suddenly, for the first time in modern history, the Muslim world emerged as a unit in international relations. Attempts to forge it into a bloc appear doomed to failure, but Muslim countries can still cooperate on numerous issues with real effectiveness. Prompted by their new power and wealth, encouraged by Saudi Arabia and Libya, inspired by Khomeini, Muslims will continue to act for Islam.'[16]

More recent examples of the essentialist school include Bernard Lewis's contributions to the *Atlantic Monthly*, including 'The Roots of Muslim Rage' in September 1990, in which he wrote: 'The struggle between Islam and the West has now lasted 14 centuries. It has consisted of a long series of attacks and counterattacks, jihads and crusades, conquests and reconquests. Today much of the Muslim world is seized by an intense – and violent – resentment of the West. Suddenly, America has become the archenemy, the incarnation of evil, the diabolic opponent of all that is good, and specifically, for Muslims, of Islam.'

It is a quotation that the *New York Times* saw fit to reproduce in whole six years later in its story entitled 'The Red Menace Is Gone. But Here's Islam.'[17] The story is subtitled 'A Heated Debate Is Raging: How Dangerous Is the "Green Menace" of Fundamentalism?' It reads in part: 'But one threat has resonated in the public mind: Islamic holy war.' Above the story is a detail of a poster portraying Ayatullah Khomeini – a close-up only of his eyes, which makes them appear dark and menacing.

The depiction of Islam in the mainstream media as the religion of fanatics and suppressors of women's rights and freedom of speech, as a narrow confrontational vision, with violent tendencies, pitted inevitably against the West's liberal democratic tradition, gains a level of credence among even high-brow thinkers by such articles as Harvard professor Samuel Huntington's 'Clash of Civilizations?'[18] The article asserts that the Muslim and Orthodox peoples in southeastern Europe seem 'much less likely to develop stable democratic political systems. The Velvet Curtain of culture has replaced the Iron Curtain of ideology as the most significant dividing line in Europe.'[19] Moreover, he claims: 'Western concepts differ fundamentally from those prevalent in other civilizations. Western ideas of individualism, liberalism, constitutionalism, human rights, equality, liberty, the rule of law, democracy, free markets, the separation of church and state, often have little resonance in Islamic, Confucian, Japanese, Hindu, Buddhist or Orthodox cultures.'[20]

The history of Western academic attacks on Islam is not limited to the late twentieth century. Albert Hourani has traced the history of academic European consideration of Islam, much of it an attempt to justify Christianity as the superior faith, and Christians as superior people. Pascal, for instance, entitled his Seventeenth Pensée 'Against Muhammad.'[21] Friedrich Schleiermacher (1768–1834) wrote that the attitude of Christianity as against all other faiths, including Islam, should be that of the 'true towards the false.'[22] Ernest Renan (1823–1892) wrote that 'Everyone who has been in the Orient or in Africa will have been struck by the kind of iron circle in which the believer's head is enclosed, making him absolutely closed to science, and incapable of opening himself to anything new.'[23]

Significantly less nuanced, but no less influential, are the attacks of the popular press. Notable examples include a 1994 American television documentary, *Jihad in America*, which warned of the increasing presence of Islamic fundamentalist groups on American soil. *Newsweek*'s cover story of 29 May 1995 was entitled 'Muslim Europe: How Will a Rising Islamic Population Change the Continent?' The *New Yorker*'s article of 30 January 1995 on Naguib Mahfouz's troubles with Islamists was entitled 'The Battle for Cairo: The Mysterious Stabbing of Egypt's Nobel Novelist, and the War between Mubarak's State and Sheikh Omar's Militant Followers.'[24]

The *Globe and Mail*'s (Toronto) feature story on the growth of the 'Islamic movement' began with a half-page story of a crowd of men in face-masks, one wielding an axe, in front of a minaret. It was headlined, 'The Children of Allah: What Has Drawn So Many People Together under the Islamic Banner and Led So Many to Use Violence to Pursue the Aims, Even at the Cost of Their Own Lives?'[25] Noting that NATO Secretary-General Willy Claes had recently described 'the radical Islamic movement' as 'the greatest threat to the West since Communism,' the story continued ominously: 'The Islamic movement, however, isn't just a few suicide bombers seeking to overturn a military regime. The movement has a tremendous amount of popular support.'

While the occasional dissenting voice is heard (the *New York Times Magazine* published a story in November 1993 by Edward Said called 'The Phony Islamic Threat'),[26] it is drowned out by presentation, by the media, of the cataclysm-warnings of the alarmists. John Esposito, whose book *The Islamic Threat: Myth or Reality* questions the premise of the alarmists, was quoted in the *Times*'s 'Here's Islam' article. However, the story goes on to reproduce the charges of the *Jihad in America* journalist (that the influence of Islamic fundamentalists can be found in the very bastions of the institutional United States) without any attempt at independent verification. Such a lapse in journalistic integrity on the part of the American newspaper of record would have been unthinkable were public acceptance of the charges unlikely to be high.[27]

There are other voices that argue that Islam has as complex a heritage as any other religion and, with Fred Halliday, that 'the broader issue of Islamism's relationship to the contemporary world and its supposed opposition to modern and secular forms of thinking' is 'not so much a clash of cultures or civilizations as the pursuit of power, political and social, in the conditions of the late twentieth century.'[28] But these voices do not make headlines. The result is that the 'debate,' as far as the media are concerned, sounds rather one-sided.

Halliday argues that anti-Muslimism, as he calls it, is a complex phenomenon that is actually different things in different places.[29] In the United States, it is primarily fear of terrorism and inter-state political confrontation; in Europe, it is predominantly fear for European identity and the matter of how to deal with massive immigration in a time of economic recession. It is as dependent on context as it is multidimensional. Yet the consumers of anti-Muslim literature – whether in *Foreign Affairs* or the *Sunday Telegraph* or the *Globe and Mail* – do not always stop to analyse the context of the writer's perspective.

Halliday's point – that it is politics or general xenophobia or economics that more often determine anti-Muslimism, not dislike for the religion or its practitioners per se – is indeed well-taken. Yet the essentialist view of Islam, which portrays the religion and its doctrines as inflexible and monolithic, goes further than a critique of specific regimes or their human rights records or the way in which Qur'anic verses on the position of women are interpreted in a given society.[30] Its implications are that Islam is incapable of producing different kinds of societies than those that abuse human rights and that Muslims can adapt to Western societies only by leaving their religion behind them.[31]

Moreover, the particular nefariousness of the contributions to the essentialist view of such academics as Huntington is that they lend a cloak of high-end academic respectability to more blatant prejudice.

This study argues that the confrontational portrayal fails to take into account the internal cultural and theological differences that characterize Islam as much as any other religion. Moreover, it is a portrayal that fails to deal with the mechanism of integration and how that works to soften the edges of interaction between any two cultures and any two, or more, religions.

A telling example is the question of hijra. Hijra means to migrate, abandon, or withdraw. The Hijra, in Islam, refers to the exodus of Muhammad and his followers from Mecca to Medina in 622, which dates the beginning of the Islamic calendar,[32] but its connotation for Muslims is broader than that. Hijra is the believer's physical removal, where possible, from a place where Islam is persecuted to an environment more conducive to its practice. Over the fifteen centuries since that first exodus, the term has been interpreted by Muslim jurists in a variety of ways. Questions of territory and obligation have been discussed and disputed. When is a territory *dar al-kufr* (land of unbelief) or *dar al-harb* (land of war) and when is it *dar al-Islam* (the land of Islam)? Do the inheritance laws of Islam apply to Muslims living in dar al-kufr? When is it incumbent on Muslims living outside dar al-Islam to migrate, and when might they remain?

According to Bernard Lewis, all Muslim jurists 'agree that it is a bad thing for Muslims to remain under non-Muslim rule, the principal disagreement being whether such an action falls under the heading of disapproved or forbidden or ... whether emigration is commanded or merely recommended.'[33] He goes on to say that jurists have not considered the predicament of Muslims involved in large-scale migration to non-Muslim countries and wonders whether the new Muslim immigrants to the West – 'many of them of limited education' – are aware of the juridical arguments.[34]

A different perspective is offered by Muhammud Khalid Masud. Noting the various definitions of dar al-Islam that have been formulated over the years, including the Hanafi majority view that if Friday and the religious holidays can be observed, a land is deemed to be dar al-Islam,[35] he goes on to describe the new dimension of hijra that emerged during the nineteenth century. Scholars began to allow for a reverse hijra, from a land of disease and financial insecurity to a better place; for the purpose of propagation of Islam; or to obtain education and training in modern science and technology.[36] Finally, he cites 'Abd al-'Aziz al-Siddiq, who argues that the conditions for the practice and propagation of one's religion are in fact better in Europe and America than in most Muslim countries and that Western countries which have made pacts and treaties with Muslim ones are no longer dar al-kufr.[37] The Lebanese scholar Shaykh Faisal Malawi has added the concept of *dar al-da'wa* (territory of preaching) to the traditional categories, in order to describe Muslim-minority countries where Islam can be practised without interference.[38]

Indeed, I asked Somali respondents specifically about the doctrinal permissibility of their remaining in Britain or Canada. Most of them appeared to be aware of the doctrine of hijra, answering that ideally they would return to a Muslim land. However, as this was not possible for the short term, and possibly for the duration of their lifetimes, they could stay in the West as long as they could practise their religion, which they then said they could do. Some said that it was incumbent on them to educate non-Muslims about Islam. Some said that they were actually better Muslims for practising Islam in non-Muslim countries. And occasionally an answer echoed al-Siddiq: 'There is no dar al-Islam in this world. London is better than Saudi Arabia because there is more freedom to do what you want here. Nobody asks how you worship or whether you worship. As long as you obey the laws of the country you are fine. My obligation is to attract other people to Islam, to tell them of the history and so on, and to help them to be good Muslims wherever they are.'[39]

For these people, not only does necessity leave them with no alternative but to remain in non-Muslim lands, but they feel doctrinally justified in doing so. The point here is that doctrine, and its interpretation, are far more flexible than they are frequently thought to be.

As individual Muslims learn to live with the West and in the West, without losing their Islam and yet making accommodations on the most superficial logistical level and at other, more significant levels, they become *Western* Muslims. Western Muslims are not 'Westernized' Muslims or assimilated Muslims, Muslims who have traded their value system for a foreign one. Somalis after a decade in Britain or Canada are no longer the Somalis they were when they left home. They are no longer people who have only ever lived among Muslims. They have lived in multi-religious societies and have neither lost their values nor remained impervious to the societies around them. They have affected, in profound ways, the way Islam is practised in both London and Toronto, and they have added a non-Asian, non-Middle Eastern voice to the debate of what Islam is and how it is best practised.

Their strongest sense of the difference between a Somali/Islamic value system and that of the West consists of the dichotomy that they see between emphasis on responsibility to the group versus satisfying the desires of the individual. But as each immigrant, or daughter or son of an immigrant, attempts to evaluate for himself or herself what that really means, there are ways to remain true to one's interpretation of a Somali/Islamic value system while making the choices societally available. After all, Westerners would not categorize their value system (which they see more accurately as a series of value systems, competing for adherence) as 'selfish' and discouraging of responsibility to other people, but perhaps as a series of principles, each of which is debatable in and of itself. The notion that individuals have the right and responsibility to make informed choices about the way they live their lives is perhaps one that is common to Western liberal democracies. It does not follow that the choices all individuals make will be the ones that offend Muslim sensibilities, although some undoubtedly will.

This is why the Salman Rushdie affair was quite as intriguing – and as maddeningly difficult to interpret – as it was. Perhaps if Muslims had felt more confident about their public space, it would have been possible for the various issues to have been clarified. As it was, the cacophony was too loud for much to be clarified. The point that was made in interview after interview was that if people of different religions are going to live together, it is important that the cardinal rule of the relationship be mutual respect. Rushdie's right to free speech was less the issue for them than the fact that, within an environment in which they had to struggle for public respect, Rushdie's book appeared to them to deprive them of it further by reinforcing a negative view of Muslims and Islam. Many of the commentators in *Liberalism, Multiculturalism and Toleration*, in talking of the seminal need for a free and honest exchange of views in a liberal democracy (without which individuals cannot make their own informed choices), mentioned the 'civilized' manner in which these exchanges should take place. The trouble with the Rushdie case, which non-Muslims found difficult to understand, was that because public respect could not be taken for granted, and was frequently not granted at all, the manner was the message, and it was clear: this is why you do not deserve respect. For those who view the written word as the most civilized form of exchanging views, and for those, like Peter Jones, who maintain that in a liberal democracy one must be prepared to have one's ideas challenged, and therefore to be offended from time to time, the reaction to the book appeared anti-liberal and anti-democratic.

Western observers implicitly established a test – of whether Muslims could accept fundamental Western values (freedom of speech).[40] Muslims seemed to fail the test, but only because the game was not played on the proverbial level playing field. Britain's Muslims – as immigrants or people of colour and/or of a minority religion – felt marginalized and alienated by the society of which they were a part, a society that had promised them equal treatment and had then reneged on that promise. The Somalis who responded to questions about the Rushdie case, many of whom were still in Somalia in 1989 during the furore and few of whom knew exactly what had been written, interpreted what had happened as a lack of respect shown by a major writer, who was supported in that lack of respect by non-Muslim countries.

It is easy to interpret the Rushdie affair as an example of why the West and Islam will always be at loggerheads. It is easy to say that it is impossible for Muslims to understand that freedom of speech is a cornerstone of Western liberal democracies and that this issue goes to the very heart of the essential differences between a religion that demands deference at the price of critical individual argument and the freedom of choice and argument that is at the core of liberal society. But that would be a misinterpretation of the problem and its potential solutions.[41]

In an environment of respect and understanding, where Muslims were not assumed to be confrontational and adversarial, where their mode of dress – if they choose to wear the hijab – were not seen as threatening, where they are not assumed to be Other or to hold values inimical to those of the West; in this environment, the story might well have played itself out differently and hold different lessons. In such an environment, the reaction to the book might have been more muted and less public. It might have been denounced at Friday communal prayers and in Muslim publications, but otherwise ignored. Without the outpouring of frustration and anger evinced by British Muslims, the Ayatullah might not have found it politically advantageous to hang a death threat on Rushdie. This would have avoided the polarization of the debate among the Western intelligentsia,[42] which would in turn have avoided much of the consequent sense of Muslims in Canada and Britain that the West and its public opinion were arrayed against them.

Islam, like any other religion, might better be described as a set of principles, the interpretation of which is not immutable,[43] and which therefore does not preclude the integration of Muslims, like any other ethnic group, into Western countries. The creation of a society, its culture and political culture, is an ongoing exercise, contributed to by all the people who live within it. As Afrikaaners have at last been forced to realize, the presence or contribution of a people cannot be legislated away, but immense destructive pressures within the political system are inevitably created in the attempt. A liberal democracy, if it is to remain true to its definition, must allow for the recognition and legitimacy of all its members. The fear that Muslims cannot adapt to a liberal democratic tradition is in part what lies behind the ongoing cultural racism, but there is no evidence that this is justified.

The Somali case demonstrates a number of interpretations of Islam. These differ among themselves and from the interpretations of other cultures and Muslim countries. Among the issues that are seen from variant points of view are the societal role of women, their mode of dress, whether Muslims can live as good practitioners of the faith in countries governed predominantly by non-Muslims, and whether they can socialize without constraint with their non-Muslim neighbours. On none of these questions do Somalis as a group have doctrinaire answers.

As discussed above, the specific role of women as understood by the Somali community is undergoing significant change amid the realities of life in the diaspora and under the influence of the Islamists. Women were traditionally accustomed to participating in the social and economic life of the community, in both its urban and its pastoral forms. The veil was never, and is not now, a substitute for seclusion. (Even the Islamists who declare themselves followers of al-Ittihad encourage women to attend the Friday communal prayer, albeit separated from men when they are there. This in itself is a tremendous departure from traditional Somali practice.) Women who take the hijab or the jilbab in the diaspora do so as a sign of their Muslim identity and of their increased adherence to their religion. Not one woman interviewed said that she had decided to wear the hijab because it was asked of her by fathers or husbands. Many women wore the hijab for the first time in the diaspora; in each case it was her own decision. Nor is it insignificant that many Somali diaspora households are headed by single women, who thus have religious authority and economic centrality – at least within the family – thrust on them.

In many cases, the decision to don the hijab is accompanied by increased understanding of the Qur'an and hadiths, which gives women the sense that they can make decisions about their lives based in part on their own understanding of religious teachings. A number of women spoke confidently about their ability to refashion their Muslim identity as they saw fit, based on their own ability to read and understand the Qur'an.

While the connection to the Arab world was strong in Somali mythology, the civil war experience has destroyed some of its attraction for diaspora Somalis. Many expressed disillusionment with Arab countries; they expected to have been welcomed with open arms, and they found that they were not. One woman described how her mother had died while on the hajj; she had been hit by a car while walking on the side of the road. The woman, a student in Germany at the time, was not given permission by the Saudi government to attend her mother's funeral.[44] This lack of responsiveness to members of the umma causes many Somalis to question Saudi – and Arab – religious leadership. The conclusion reached is that Arab Muslims, once perceived perhaps as moral leaders, scarcely possess a monopoly on Islamic virtue and teachings and that they – diaspora Somalis – have as much right to determine doctrinal interpretations as other Muslims. Somali women are, in their own right, critical in terms of the renegotiation of the Somali Muslim identity in the diaspora.

What is in the process of happening is a part of what Eickelman and Piscatori have called 'objectification' among Muslims.[45] Objectification is the self-conscious understanding, in this case by Muslims, of their religion as they answer for themselves questions concerning what Islam is and what it means for them and of how the answers to those questions regulate their conduct. Eickelman and Piscatori maintain that these queries – the kind that can be made only in a modern world where one is aware that alternative belief systems exist – were being explored in all social classes across the Muslim world by the late 1980s.[46] The phenomenon of objectification, in combination with mass education, increased access to technology, and the explosion of ideas that accompanies travel and the return of travellers, has had immense implications for how Muslims consider and act on Islam.

In tandem with objectification, therefore, the Muslim world has witnessed an increasing fragmentation of authority.[47] Whatever monopoly the `ulama may have had on sacred authority, it is long gone, replaced by a plethora of competing voices, including Sufi shaykhs, intellectuals who have often not received a traditional religious education,[48] and even women. Eickelman and Piscatori note: 'Because Muslims around the world possess an intensified awareness of Islamic ideas and practices, they are more assertive in their judgements of what constitutes proper Islamic conduct and who is a true believer.'[49] This phenomenon can only be enhanced in the Muslim diaspora, where Somalis and other Muslims are contending with particular circumstances and reinventing traditions, as it were, in new contexts.[50] It is witnessed in the influence of the Somali Islamist groups, whether isolationist or consciously integrationist, in both London and Toronto. But it is also evident in the comments of respondents such as Deeqa, quoted above, who wears the hijab and considers herself religious:

I argue with my male friends about so much. I say, 'What does the Qur'an say on this issue?' They cannot argue with the Qur'an. You get equality from applying the Qur'an, the same equality as the West. I argue with the cultural interpretations of the Qur'an, which so often spell out only the man's rights and not those of the woman.

It was so difficult for us to work this out as a couple before we got married. I wanted to interview the shaykh before we got married. I needed to know where I stood. Finally my husband said, 'You make a lot of sense.' You see, I see marriage as a joint partnership. That's what God said, not the domination of one person over another. The shaykh also was very liberal. We had a small ceremony. He talked about equality, how you treat one another in a marriage. He gave me his card. 'In case he gives you trouble,' he said. He is not Somali; he is from Guyana. He was traditional but forward-looking, not in terms of Westernizing Islam but in terms of looking to the roots, educating Muslim sisters. He agreed that usually the position of women is not emphasized.

For us when culture and religion coincide, that's good, but when culture contradicts religion, that's difficult, because Somali culture has become so Arabized. It's difficult to distinguish one from another.

I hope being here makes this process easier. As a woman if you argue through Islam it's more liberating than taking a Western stand. Men can't argue with the religion. And the religion says women, as much as men, must be educated. So long as your position is in the Qur'an, there is no obstacle. I hope other Muslim women read and learn to think this way.[51]

Deeqa's comments are a pertinent illustration of what Eickelman and Piscatori describe. The fact of migrating and confronting Western culture has caused Deeqa to re-evaluate her understanding of her own religion, but she is not content with traditional interpretations. Rather, she is using the Qur'an (obviously emphasizing some suras and de-emphasizing others) to reinterpret orthodoxy. Moreover, she has won the support of both her husband and a local imam for her efforts.

Deeqa and other Somali immigrants are accommodating themselves to life in London and Toronto while retaining their Islam and their 'Muslimness' – becoming Western Muslims without becoming West-ernized Muslims. Their integration serves as an illustration of the idea that there is nothing intrinsically inimical about Islam – as a religion or a framework for a value system – vis-à-vis Western liberal democracy. Rather, the mechanism of integration serves to blur the edges of ostensibly radically disparate cultures. It can furthermore, in the appropriate political culture, encourage the flexibility – and not the rigidity – of a religion and a culture such as Islam.

Conclusion:
Transformative Islam

The lives and experiences of Somalis in Toronto and London are illustrative of a number of striking developments within Islam. As portentous as Martin Luther's Wittenberg launch of the Reformation, these developments point to the evolution of the practice of Islam in the diaspora in a way that is bound to affect it as well in the very heart of the Muslim world. These developments are neither absolute nor universal among diaspora Somalis, but they are clearly discernible, and they are profound.

As diaspora Somalis establish themselves in the West, they identify themselves primarily as Muslims. Fading is the territorial identity that anchored them – as pastoralists, farmers, or even new urbanites – in their homeland. In its place, diaspora Somalis have developed a strong consciousness of identity through religion, in order to place themselves in a new society that is predominantly non-Muslim, and indeed to assert themselves within it. This religious consciousness is apparent at all ages, although it is expressed differently by different individuals, and differently again by teenagers or unmarried adults than by their elders.

Their religious consciousness, moreover, has not merely strengthened. It is not, in other words, *more* of what it used to be in Somalia. It has been redefined. Each individual, and therefore the community as a whole, has reshaped the practice of Islam. Neither is this exercise an imitation of the practice of other communities. It is the evolution of what *was* in the context of what *is*.

In this context, the Islamists have acquired a moral leadership beyond the circle of those willing to identify themselves as such. Their credibility, and therefore their influence, is increased in the diaspora precisely because they are not perceived to be primarily political. Within Somalia itself, where al-Ittihad actually holds territory and repels attack from Ethiopian invaders or clan-based militias, its religious credibility is diluted and diffused by the web of political intrigue. But in the West those factors are less prominent. The Islamists – al-Islah and al-Ittihad – are seen to some extent as setting the benchmarks for Muslims' religious comportment amid non-Muslims. As Somalis rethink the practice of their religion in the West, they take into account, and give great weight to, the positions of the Islamists.

The Islamists' influence is obvious in the very way that the practice of Islam has evolved for diaspora Somalis. The old religious symbolism – the local Sufi shaykh, the dhikr, the token Qur'anic memorization – has given way to a sense of Islam as a vital force in understanding how to live in this new world, a force that might require more blatant identification (via, for instance, a beard or the hijab) or personal study (a parallel with the Jewish *yeshiva* might be made here). While diaspora Somalis may accept or reject one or other Islamist group's interpretation of doctrine or prescription for action, they share the sense of the religion's vitality that is the Islamists' driving force.

Beyond that shared sense of vitality, there is plenty of room for disagreement or variation in how diaspora Somalis have redefined their practice of Islam. They have, as the point has been continually made, woven both a renewed religious sense and a willingness to adapt (not conform) to Western society into the tapestries of their lives. If there is a common note, it is that religion is generally a matter of significance in their lives, however they then choose to define it and live by it.

The question that presents itself is what to call the phenomenon of developing diaspora Islam. Is it actually a 'new' Islam, standing in contrast to an 'old' Islam, or a geographically distinct Islam? To give it such a name is probably to overemphasize what is really a difference in practice. The practice of Islam has shifted; Islam itself has not. Islam has *evolved* in that it encompasses an ever-greater variation of practices and therefore interpretations of acceptable Muslim thought and behaviour. But it is the interpretations of Islam that have shifted, not the religion itself – perception, not the thing itself. Islam, like any other religion, is primarily what is made of it. Western Muslims – as the diaspora Somalis have become – may interpret aspects of doctrine differently from their co-religionists in Muslim-majority countries. They do not, however, see the religion that they practise as substantially different from the one practised in Mecca or Islamabad. This is an important point because, recalling James Piscatori's analysis of the *Satanic Verses* episode, we see that only while the veil of orthodoxy appears to be held tightly can variant interpretations be made – a characteristic as true of life as it is of literature.

And yet the implications of this shift in perception – of the broadening of the spectrum of religious perspectives – are immense. Diaspora Somalis do not see themselves as lesser Muslims for living in the West. They do not perceive themselves as lesser Muslims for redefining what constitutes a good practising Muslim. They see their religious interpretations as being every bit as valid as – and sometimes more so than – the interpretations of the established centres of Muslim orthodoxy.

These perceptions in turn contribute to the changing political geography of the Muslim world, to its 'decentring,' and to the fragmentation of religious authority to which Eickelman and Piscatori refer.[1] And this process in turn, over time, changes the very notion of 'diaspora.' As the validity of diaspora religious interpretation is increasingly accepted by Muslims living in non–Muslim-majority countries, the notion of what constitutes dar al-Islam shifts. Already, as the interviews demonstrated, there is justification for living in Britain and Canada. At the very least, knowledge and understanding of Islam are being spread in the non-Muslim world. At best, Muslims can live with 'more freedom' than in much of the Muslim-majority world. Whether this constitutes dar al-Islam, the neutral ground of dar al-'ahd, or, in the words of Shaykh Faisal Malawi, dar al da'wa, may be open to debate, but the seeds are sown for an increasing acceptance of this situation as justifiable and even beneficial from a doctrinal viewpoint.

Once that viewpoint has been accepted, it is not a radical shift, particularly for Somalis born in the West, or brought up there, to see themselves as Muslims who are *of* the West, and of Somali heredity. The increasingly accepted doctrinal justification for living outside Muslim-majority countries, in the context of a redefined practice of Islam, amounts to a powerful combination. While Mecca is always sacred ground, Muslim-majority countries are no longer the only places where acceptable Muslim interpretation is forged. Knowledgeable 'ulama are seen to live throughout the world, even in Muslim-minority countries and in the West. Where they are, where Muslims believe themselves to be capable of exercising *ijtihad* – the right of independent judgment, and therefore interpretation – becomes in its own right a nurturing centre of Islam. Such a centre may exist in London or Toronto as easily as in Mogadishu or Cairo.

Somalis are busy in Toronto and London creating Muslim space, to use Barbara Daly Metcalf's phrase,[2] as Vernon Schubel describes Shi'i Muslims doing in Toronto, with their recreation and observance of Karbala (the battleground on which the Prophet's grandson Hussein was killed) in Thornhill;[3] and as Pnina Werbner writes of Birmingham's Sufis 'stamping the earth with the name of Allah' in the course of Eid-Milad-un-Nabi celebrations.[4]

London or Toronto may come to be seen as a nurturing centre of Islam for the Muslims who live there, but – and here the argument comes full circle – it is in large part the political culture of the adoptive society that will determine the quality of the connection between Western Muslims and their non-Muslim compatriots. The dynamics at play in the Somali community, repeated in other Muslim diaspora communities, reveal the transformative potential of both the practice of Islam and its perception by Muslims. The nature of the relationship between the West and its Muslim communities depends as much on the West's perception as it does on the Muslims who make their home there.

In conclusion, it is worth reviewing the lines of inquiry as discussed in the Introduction: external integration, internal integration, political culture, absorption of the immigrant culture, and Islam's compatibility with the West.

External Integration

From an external, societal standpoint, Somalis are not fully integrated into either Canada or Britain. As we saw in chapter 7, barriers exist to their being able to move socially, politically, and economically without regard to their ethnicity, and institutions are not always sensitive to their cultural and religious needs. Barriers include temporary difficulties such as language and the lack of recognition of education and professional qualifications. Harder to overcome are the barriers of colour and cultural racism.

Political culture has a direct and clear impact on how external integration progresses. The ability of members of an ethnic group to be economically, politically, or socially mobile, without ethnicity being at issue, depends on society's willingness to accommodate that ethnicity where needed or desired and equally on its willingness to grant legitimacy of place and participation to the members of an ethnic group. Britain's political culture has yet to accept that immigrants and ethnic minorities are a part of the British polity and should play a role in British cultural and political life. Somalis in Britain spoke overwhelmingly of being alienated and kept at a distance by British society.

Colour racism appears to be more of an institutional and endemic problem in Britain than it is in Canada, as the interviews indicate and as portrayed in chapter 6. Cultural racism is a problem for Muslims in both countries. Although Canada's political culture would appear to grant legitimacy of place to ethnic minorities more effectively than Britain's (see chapter 6), this legitimacy is compromised where Muslims are concerned. Although colour, and other markers of ethnicity, are not widely seen as indicators of essential Otherness in Canada, Islam as a religion is widely regarded with ignorance and distrust, an attitude fostered and reinforced by its portrayal in the media. Somalis in Canada therefore encounter an attitudinal contradiction: respect for their right to be different and suspicion of the religion to which they adhere. Somalis in London, in contrast, experience further alienation as British political culture is reinforced by a negative, confrontational media portrayal of Islam.

As the interviews of chapter 3 indicate, Somalis have found that, with some inconveniences and adjustments, it is possible to practise Islam as desired in both London and Toronto. As the availability of halal meat increases and institutional sensitivity to Muslim needs rises, as more mosques are built and prayer rooms become accessible, the logistical concerns diminish. There are two significant exceptions to this: the ability of Muslims to attend communal prayers on Fridays and the ability of women to obtain employment if they wear the hijab. The solution to the first requires flexibility on the part of employers and employees, as well as willingness to accommodate employee's concerns. The second is, however, attributable to cultural racism.

Internal Integration

The process of internal integration is a distinct but related process, which is propelled by its own inner dynamic. Somalis began the process of weaving their birth- and adopted cultures together, in a variety of ways, from the moment of their arrival in Canada or Britain, as seen from the interviews in chapter 5, and further discussed in chapter 7. Internal integration – or cultural weaving of birth- and adopted cultures – is the inevitable result of making daily choices that require judgments based on past and present influences and experiences.

Somalis have generally become more religious on migrating into the diaspora. They are reading and studying the Qur'an and hadiths in the light of exile, many for the first time, and they are challenging the received oral understandings of their upbringings. As they renegotiate their identities in the West, they also redefine the practice of Islam and their own understandings of what it is to be a good Muslim.

For some, the process of being a good Muslim in the West involves building walls around their community and finding relative isolation from mainstream society. For most, however, the process involves a gradual accommodation of traditional customs to those of the new society, without losing what they consider to be essential to themselves as Muslims. While they worry about the values of their children, their own cultural renegotiations, as well as those of their teenagers, indicate that a redefined identity is not necessarily one that is less Muslim (see the interviews in chapters 4 and 5). Quite to the contrary, Somalis have generally combined accommodation to the West with a stronger identification with Islam and 'Muslimness.'

Internal integration occurs separately from external integration, but the two processes are interconnected. The quality of internal integration is affected by the environment in which it takes place. Even the most private and personal decision has its public aspect, and it is here that external acceptance, or lack of it, becomes an element in decisions – conscious or unconscious – of how to integrate. Therefore, although the integration of Somalis in both Toronto and London involves an accommodation of traditional culture to new, interviews with Londoners point to an element of awareness of societal hostility that is lacking in their Toronto counterparts. This awareness affects the decisions that they make, even if it is not the determining factor in their deciding what stand to take on female circumcision, on veiling, on extramarital sex, and so on.

Political Culture

Political culture directly affects the degree to which external integration can occur, by shaping public attitudes towards immigrants and ethnic minorities and the extent to which they are accepted as legitimate members of the collective. But it also affects the quality of internal integration, because no decision – no matter how personal – is made without an awareness of its public aspect. Therefore harmonious integration can be said to be facilitated by a political culture that creates a legitimate space for the immigrant Other. Such a political culture tends to enhance the flexibility of ostensibly disparate cultures, as opposed to a hostile one, which will encourage displays of rigidity.

A comparison of the schools issue in Canada and Britain will serve to illustrate this point. In Ontario, only Roman Catholic schools are publicly funded (in addition to the non-denominational public schools). In the hundred and thirty years since the signing of the British North America Act, Protestant schools have evolved into public, non-denominational schools where religion is de-emphasized. All Protestant, Jewish, and Muslim parents alike must fund schools privately if they are unhappy with the way religion is treated in the public system. In Alberta, where the equivalent of Britain's voluntary-aided status is obtainable, it is available to all groups equally – Protestant, Jewish, and Muslim. In both provinces, all groups have equal access to government funding and appear to be treated equally. In Britain, in contrast, it was the *apparent* discrimination against Muslim applicants that created the impression that regardless of how their application for government funding is presented it would be rejected. Muslims had come to believe that they would not be treated on an equal footing with non-Muslims, and counter-institutions such as the Muslim Parliament are the manifestation of that frustration. British political culture has yet to allow immigrants and ethnic minorities to feel that Britain is theirs to help shape, yet clearly there is movement, as is evident in the recent granting of state funding to two Muslim schools. It is a gradual process, however, and Somalis experience this resistance to sharing the shaping of the collective imagination as rejection and alienation.

Anglophone Canadian political culture has created, almost inadvertently, a space within which ethnic minorities and immigrants are granted a legitimacy within the Canadian political system. Interviews with Somalis demonstrate that, at present, they experience a degree of comfort and acceptance in Canada that allows them to integrate without the expectation of hostility that their British counterparts expressed. It is this legitimacy that was undermined by the federal government's apparent minimization of the significance of the transgression of the armed forces in Somalia, as underlined by the discussion in chapter 6. That legitimacy is rendered tenuous and fragile, in fact, by the very lack of understanding of the importance of the role of political culture in aiding harmonious integration. Canadian acceptance of ethnic minorities' legitimacy is also compromised, but not eradicated, by widespread suspicion of Islam as a religion, resulting in the attitudinal contradiction that many Somalis encounter. British resistance to ethnic-minority legitimacy is compounded by hostility to Islam and its practitioners. This means that integration in either Britain or Canada is an inevitable, but not straightforward affair.

The Absorption of Immigrant Culture by the Wider Society

I suggested above that the creation of the political culture of a country is an ongoing exercise, contributed to by all the citizens and inhabitants of the country. I suggested also that integration is a two-way street and that, as surely as individual immigrants weave the traditions of their birth- and adopted cultures together, so too, over time, does an immigrant-receiving country weave the combined cultures of its various immigrants into its tapestry. Chapter 2 argued that, while this shift on the part of the wider culture and political culture is a slow one, it is demonstrable in the cases of the United States and Canada, both of which have been immigrant-receiving societies since their inceptions.

It is too early for Somali culture or Islam to have woven its way significantly into the tapestries of Canada or Britain. On the continuum of centre-to-periphery discussed in chapter 2, Somalis are still on the fringes. It would not be possible for it to be otherwise, given that the rawness of migration has yet to wear off. Yet even at this early stage, it is possible to see the beginnings of the process, not least because Somalis belong to the larger Muslim community that is having an impact on Canadian and British society. Consider again the following examples: the two Muslim schools finally granted state funding in Britain; the British bank that gives its employees the option of wearing uniforms in traditional Muslim clothing styles; schools that have accepted the hijab, ensure that non-pork meals are available, and provide prayer facilities for students as a matter of course; cemeteries that permit Muslim burial practices; Somalis who have affected the religious and social practices of Muslims in the wider community in both Toronto and London; the workplaces in both cities that make accommodations for prayer for their employees; the increasing number of streets where a woman in the hijab is no longer an object of curiosity; the hospital in Toronto that has organized awareness seminars to limit cultural misunderstandings with Somali patients; the stocking of halal meat by an Ontario-wide supermarket chain. As nascent as these efforts are, they represent the beginnings of a process in which, over time, Somalis and even Islam will move closer to the 'centres' of both British and Cana-

dian society. Clearly this is a long-term process, which is hindered by
the essentialist, confrontational view of Islam that is propagated by the
popular media and given credence by some academic writing.

Islam's Compatibility with the West

As the analysis of chapter 7 shows, Islam is not a monolithic entity, and
its core values – however defined – are determined by cultural factors
as much as by the raw material of the religion (Qur'an and hadiths).
Migration and the cataclysm that caused it have forced a confrontation
for Somalis; they have by and large been unable to continue to accept
inchoate understandings of who and what they are. Unwelcome in the
Arab world, they are critical of Middle Eastern interpretations of the
umma and the lack of responsiveness shown by Arab nations to fellow
Muslims in need. They are critical of the racism encountered by Somalis who have sojourned in Arab lands. Although they all believe that
Islam demands modest dress on the part of both women and men, they
differ in their interpretation of what modesty calls for in terms of
female attire, and many object to cultural models that dictate the societal seclusion of women. The interviews demonstrate that many Somalis believe that respect for other monotheists allows them to live
cooperatively with non-Muslims, and many interpret this to mean that
it is possible to live in a way that contravenes the core values neither of
Islam nor of their adopted cultures, however defined. Moreover, as
chapter 7 indicates, they increasingly believe that they have the qualifications and knowledge to redefine practices, and to rework traditions,
as religious Western Muslims.

This study has argued that the degree of complexity of interpretation
and flexibility shown by Somali Muslims would indicate that Western
fears of the essential Otherness of Muslims are groundless. While exacerbated by sensationalist media coverage, these fears have at their base
an ignorance that is not effectively confronted, and is even encouraged,
by analytical popular writing and academic journals (see chapter 7).

In both Canada and Britain, as in other Western nations, Islam continues to be viewed as having alien, essentially incompatible values.
While on an internal level integration and redefinition continue all the
time, the hostility that an individual faces in society determines his or
her connection to that society. If a society treats members of an ethnic/
religious group as marginalized, that marginalization will be reflected,
to some extent, in their attitudes.

This study has contended that there is diversity and flexibility to be seen in the attitudes of recent Somali immigrants, the majority of whom have declared themselves to be more, not less Muslim since migrating westward. This diversity and flexibility indicate that there is every reason to believe that they will integrate successfully over time into Western political systems and societies and that this process will be facilitated if they are not artificially marginalized and alienated. It is an important conclusion: Muslims do not need to become less Muslim in order to integrate successfully into the West. Once Islam is understood to be diverse and complex and capable of being interpreted in a multitude of ways, it becomes clear that it cannot be cast in any 'essential' form and is therefore capable of flexibility and adaptation.

Somalis have been scattered into the diaspora, which is an unfamiliar and initially frightening place. But if one understands how it is that people weave their cultures together, the 'interface' between cultures and religions does not appear rigid and unforgiving. Rather, it is a place of accommodation and compromise. The country whose political culture understands this is one whose absorption of immigrants and ethnic groups is relatively smooth. For those who choose exile or are forced into it, and likewise for those who receive them, this is a vital understanding.

Notes

Introduction: Challenges in the Diaspora

1 Jamal Gabobe is a Somali refugee now living in Seattle, Washington. These stanzas were drawn from his book of poems, *Love and Memory*.

2 Political culture is generally defined as that portion of a society's culture that determines how its political system (the state apparatus and its procedures) actually work in its own context. Chapter 5 below explores this in further detail.

3 'Direct interpersonal communication is a complex circular process of initiation and response that can provide information with a kind of integration difficult to achieve by other means' Rhoda Métraux, 'Informants in Group Research,' in Mead and Métraux, eds., *The Study of Culture at a Distance*, 143–4. See also Modood, Beishon, and Virdee, *Changing Ethnic Identities*, 9–10. Modood *et al.* cite the following two sources in support of the approach: M. Hammersley and P. Atkinson, *Ethnography: Principles in Practice* (London: Tavistock, 1983); and R.G. Burgess, *In the Field: An Introduction to Field Research* (London: Allen and Unwin, 1984). Qualitative studies are increasingly recognized even in medical research; see 'Papers That Go beyond Numbers,' *British Medical Journal* (Oct. 1997), 740–3.

4 This technique is sometimes called 'snowballing.' See Modood, Beishon, and Virdee, *Changing Ethnic Identities*, 9.

5 'Mythic centre' refers to emotional, as opposed to actual, geography. For many Somalis therefore the mythic centre of their culture and religion includes the Arab world as well as their homeland. Others may consider it more narrowly – depending on their orientation, in terms either of Mecca or of Mogadishu.

Chapter One: Context

1 Many books are available on the breakdown of civil order in Somalia and its effects on civilians. See, for example, Gassem, *Hostages*. Written first in Italian and translated by the author into English, this study combines an account of political and social events with interviews with the victims of clan violence. The Barre government's attack on northern Somalia is recorded in Africa Watch, *Somalia*. Other accounts of the Somali tragedy can be found in Omar's *The Road to Zero* and Drysdale's *Whatever Happened to Somalia?* Ahmed Omar Askar has written a book of short stories intended to capture some of the events that led to civil war in *Sharks and Soldiers*. Also see Samatar, *The Somali Challenge*.
2 I.M. Lewis puts the number at five million, while Said Samatar estimates six to seven million; see his *Understanding Somalia*, 9; and Said Samatar, 6.
3 UNHCR, *UNHCR Update*.
4 This estimate is based on a combination of immigration statistics and the estimates of community leaders, researchers, and immigrant and refugee agencies, but it is impossible to be accurate. Estimates of Britain's Somali population, for instance, begin as low as 25,000 in the whole of Britain: the Refugee Council (1994), cited in Rutter, *Refugee Children in the Classroom*, 14. (Most Somalis in Britain are refugees.) On the high end are estimates such as that of the *Independent* (29 Sept.1994), as cited in *British Muslims Monthly Survey (BMMS)* (Birmingham: Centre for the Study of Islam and Christian–Muslim Relations, Selly Oak Colleges), 2 no. 9 (Sept. 1994) 18, which put the number in London alone at 65,000.
5 For articles and information on the resettlement of the Somali community in London, see El-Solh, 'Somalis in London's East End'; Somali Relief Association, *The Somalis*; El-Solh, '"Be True to Your Culture"'; Dench, *Fighting with Numbers*; Warner, ed., *Voices from Somalia*; Shamis Hussein, 'Somalis in London,' in Merriman, ed., The Peopling of London; and a video, Oxford House, *Somali Lives*.
  For information on Somali resettlement in Toronto, see: Opoku-Dapaah, *Somali Refugees in Toronto*; Kellerman, ed., *Somalia*; Ladan Caafi, 'The Somali Crisis in Canada: The Single Mother Phenomenon,' in *Hal-Abuur* 1 no. 4 (spring 1995), 31–5.
  Also worth reading on Somalia after the crisis and diaspora Somalis are Adam and Ford, eds., *Mending Rips in the Sky*, and a novel by Maria Molteno about the Somali refugee community in London entitled *A Shield of Coolest Air*. The Somali novelist Maxamed Daahir Afrax began editing and publishing a journal of Somali literature and culture, *Hal-Abuur*, in London

in 1993. Among other objectives, *Hal-Abuur* is intended to address 'the desperate need of the Somalis in the diaspora for literary material in their mother tongue reflecting their feelings and their issues of interest back home. The general exodus of Somali people, who have been forced to flee their homeland ... has resulted in the existence of a huge number of Somali refugees in Europe, North America and elsewhere in the world, where they face [a] new set of serious problems, such as multiple exile and cultural alienation.' Maxamad D. Afrax, 'Why *Hal-Abuur?*,' *Hal-Abuur* 1 no. 1 (summer 1993), 6.

6 Conditions in these refugee camps have been documented as horrific, not just because of inadequate food, housing, and hygiene, but also because of widespread murder, torture, and rape at the hands of brigands and the Kenyan security forces. Some Somalis have made their way to relatives in Mombasa or Nairobi, but Kenya is not anxious to add to its own ethnic Somali population and has been hostile to the refugees. See, for example, African Rights, *The Nightmare Continues*. Many Somalis interviewed in Toronto spoke of having spent two to three years in Kenya (in camps and/or cities) before making their way to Canada, usually via a brief sojourn in the United States.

7 See, for instance, Robinson, ed., *The International Refugee Crisis*; Bhabha and Shutter, *Women's Movement*; Matas, *Closing the Doors*; M. Louise Pirouet, 'The Rights of Refugees in the United Kingdom,' in Institute of Commonwealth Studies, *Multiculturalism and the State*, vol. I, 1–10; and UNHCR, *The State of the World's Refugees*.

8 See 'Ministers Suffer Another Setback on Asylum Claims,' *Electronic Telegraph*, 18 Feb. 1997, issue 634; also see *BMMS* 4 no. 1 (Jan. 1996) and 3 no. 12 (Dec. 1995).

9 The British merchant navy employed Somalis to work in the engine rooms of steamships. While the ships were docked in London, the seamen stayed in lodgings in the east end, where a small transient community gradually built up. Similar communities grew in Cardiff, Liverpool, and South Shields. Shamis Hussein, 'Somalis in London,' in Merriman, ed., *The Peopling of London*, 163.

10 For an examination of a related community, also initially composed of men who worked on British merchant ships, see Halliday's *Arabs in Exile*; Lawless, *From Ta'izz to Tyneside*.

11 Between 1980 and 1984, fewer than one hundred adult Somali refugees arrived in London. This number increased to between two hundred and four hundred refugee applications annually from 1984 to 1988 and then jumped dramatically during 1989 to over two thousand adult applications

annually, after war broke out in northern Somalia. Association of Metropolitan Authorities, *A Strategy for Housing Refugees.*

12 Dench, *Fighting with Numbers*, 36.

13 Opoku-Dapaah, *Somali Refugees in Toronto*, 14.

14 Ibid., 13.

15 Dench, *Fighting with Numbers*, 61.

16 See Elmi, 'Khat'; Kalix, 'Khat,' 1–6.

17 The leaf is flown daily into London, predominantly from Kenya. It loses its stimulant powers if not chewed when fresh. Britain considers its primary active ingredient – cathinone – to be a drug in distilled form but has not made the leaf illegal. See Kenneth Harris, *Khat (Qat, Chat).* Canada bans the unlicensed import of all agricultural products, including qat, and in June 1996 passed a bill that made sale of it illegal. Anecdotal evidence suggests that Canadian Somalis obtain theirs primarily via the United States, which does not stringently enforce its ban on the leaf. The leaf is flown into the United States from Kenya, Egypt, and the Middle East. See New York State Office, '*Khat* Street Advisory.'

Qat is chewed by members of the Yemeni community as well, although they prefer the milder Ethiopian variety. A debate over public policy on *qat* was held in Britain in the 1980s, as police, the medical community, and the press, as well as community members themselves, argued the danger of the leaf. In the end it was decided that the effects of chewing it were not serious or widespread enough to warrant antagonizing the community. See Halliday, *Arabs in Exile*, 121–8.

18 Cassanelli, 'The Role of Somali Diaspora Communities.'

19 See, for instance, Cassanelli, *Victims and Vulnerable Groups.*

20 This has been well documented. See, for instance, Human Rights Watch, Africa, *Somalia Faces the Future.* Africa Watch, *Somalia*; Drysdale, *Whatever Happened to Somalia?*; Omar, *The Road to Zero*; Cassanelli, *Victims and Vulnerable Groups.*

21 Abdi I. Samatar, 'Agrarian Political Economy in Transition,' in Samatar, ed., *The Somali Challenge*, 65–92.

22 I.M. Lewis, 'Sufism in Somaliland: A Study in Tribal Islam,' in Ahmed and Hart, eds., *Islam in Tribal Societies*, 129. Also I.M. Lewis, *Blood and Bone*, 95–111.

23 Cassanelli, *Victims and Vulnerable Groups*; also Ahmed, ed., *The Invention of Somalia.*

24 Cassanelli, *The Shaping of Somali Society*, 23–4.

25 Ahmed, *The Invention of Somalia*, Preface; also Lee Cassanelli, 'History and Identity.'

26 Ali Mazrui, 'On Race and Performance,' in Ali Mazrui, *Cultural Forces in World Politics* (London: James Currey, 1990), 140.
27 Cassanelli, 'History and Identity,' 6; also Mohamed Haji Mukhtar, 'Islam in Somali History: Fact and Fiction,' in Ahmed, ed., *The Invention of Somalia*, 21.
28 Interview, Roda, London, 25 May, 1995.
29 Conversation, Naomi Emmett, principal, Kingsview Village Junior School, Etobicoke, 4 Dec. 1995.
30 Local governments in Britain account for almost a quarter of total public spending and deliver important services such as housing and education. However, local authorities have few legislative authorities, and these may be changed by Parliament at will. They collect money from three sources: a central grant, service charges, and a form of local property tax called the council tax. See Kavanagh, *British Politics: Continuities and Change*, 257–77; and Norton, *The British Polity*, 221. In areas that absorb large numbers of refugees, resources are particularly scarce. Housing, for example, is meant to be provided to anyone in need, including refugees and people granted exceptional leave to remain, but the lack of suitable housing and lengthy waiting lists result in a perceived competition for places among needy groups. See Refugee Council, *Advice on Housing*; also Association of Metropolitan Authorities, *A Strategy for Housing Refugees*. The latter's foreword reads: 'The system, such as it is, is on the point of breakdown. Councils will inevitably refuse to house refugees, even those in "vulnerable" categories. They will have, simply, nowhere to go ... Many [refugees have] found themselves occupying already overcrowded accommodation and, in some cases, squatting.' See also Dench, *Fighting with Numbers*, 27, who writes of groups within the Somali community in Tower Hamlets who are pressing local government to provide the community with financial support commensurate with their numbers. Support for this approach 'lies in resentment of and competition with the local Bangladeshi community, which is large and growing in confidence and has exercised something of a stranglehold on the local political conscience; and which, moreover, has been conspicuously successful in getting resources generated to meet their special needs.'
31 The 1991 Canadian census reported the number of Muslims in Ontario as 146,000. It gave Canada a total Muslim population of just over a quarter-million. These estimates are generally considered fairly low, both because of under-reporting and because the 1990s have seen significant Muslim immigration. The Muslim World League estimates the number of Muslims in Canada to be closer to 400,000, a number also estimated by academic researchers.

32 The British census does not question respondents about religion, so the numbers of Muslims in Britain are estimated from questions on birthplace. The Office of National Statistics considered and rejected the inclusion of a question on religious affiliation in the 2001 census; *BMMS* 4 no. 8 (20 Sept. 1996), 8. This decision did not please many Muslims, who would prefer to be known as a religious, not a racial group; *Muslim News*, 30 Aug. 1996. Jorgen Nielsen corrects the 1991 census numbers for Muslims upward – primarily to account for under-enumeration – to between 1.25 and 1.5 million; Nielsen, *Muslims in Western Europe*, 41.
33 Philip Lewis, *Islamic Britain*.
34 Modood, *Racial Equality*, 7.
35 The publication *Gay News* was successfully prosecuted for printing a poem suggesting that Jesus Christ had been a homosexual.
36 Nielsen, *Muslims in Western Europe*, 58.
37 UK Action Committee on Islamic Affairs, *Muslims and the Law in Multi-Faith Britain*.
38 For instance, see John Rex, *Race and Ethnicity*.
39 Bhikhu Parekh, Introduction, also 'Britain and the Social Logic of Pluralism,' in Parekh, ed., *Britain*, 60–73.
40 Interview, Imam Abdulle Hakim, Toronto, 16 Feb. 1995.
41 Michael Valpy, 'The Hurt Felt by Somali Youngsters,' *Globe and Mail*, 23 Feb. 1996, A17.
42 For a sense of the controversy surrounding the role of ethnicity, see, for instance, Richler, 'A Clear and Present Danger'; also Asselin Charles, 'Why Immigrants and Minorities Feel Discomfort in Quebec,' *Globe and Mail*, 17 Oct. 1995, A19.
43 'Canadians Allege Violation of Religious Freedom,' *Washington Report on Middle East Affairs* (Washington, DC: Nov./Dec. 1994), 83.
44 'Educators outside Quebec Mystified by Hijab Ban,' *Globe and Mail*, 13 Dec. 1994, A1.
45 Hersi, 'The Arab Factor in Somali History,' 113; also Mukhtar, 'Islam in Somali History,' in Ahmed, ed., *The Invention of Somalia*, 8.
46 Hersi, 'The Arab Factor,' 113.
47 According to Mohamed Haji Mukhtar, certain Omani tribes – who refused to pay the *zakat* in opposition to the caliphate of Abu Bakr and were consequently severely persecuted and forced to flee – may have been the earliest wave of Muslim immigrants to the Somali coast. He cites Hassan Ibrahim Hassan, *Intishar al-Islam wa-al-Urubah Fima yali al-Sahra al-Kubra Sharq al-Qarra al-Ifriqiyyah wa-Gharbiha* (Cairo: Matba'at Lujnat al-Bayan al-Arabi, Cairo, 1957), 127. Mukhtar, 'Islam in Somali History Fact and Fiction,' in Ahmed, ed., *The Invention of Somalia*, 5.

48 Hersi, 'The Arab Factor,' 114–16; Mukhtar, 'Islam in Somali History,' 5.
49 Hersi, 'The Arab Factor,' 117.
50 Ibid., 115.
51 Mukhtar, 'Islam in Somali History,' 7.
52 Cassanelli, *The Shaping of Somali Society,* 98.
53 Hersi, 'The Arab Factor,' 121.
54 I.M. Lewis as quoted in ibid., 122.
55 Ahmed, 'God, Anti-Colonialism and Drums,' 98.
56 I.M. Lewis, *Blood and Bone,* 104–5. Lewis continues, 'Although the particular genealogical claims they make seem completely untenable, they nevertheless record a tradition which is true – that of long historical contact between Somaliland and Arabia.'
57 Ibid., 97.
58 Mukhtar, 'Islam in Somali History,' 20; Cassanelli, *The Shaping of Somali Society,* 28; Cassanelli, 'History and Identity.'
59 Trimingham, *Islam in Ethiopia,* 214–15.
60 Adam, 'Islam and Politics in Somalia,' 190.
61 Cassanelli, *The Shaping of Somali Society,* 124.
62 Meaning 'visitation,' *ziyara* refers to visits to gravesites to pray for the dead. The Prophet had initially forbidden such visits because of the exaggerated emphasis that was placed on them but subsequently recommended them. Muslim jurists are divided, however, on the permissibility of women participating. Maliki and some Hanafi jurists deem it acceptable, but Hanbali jurists decree it *makruh* (reprehensible), in part because women are deemed less capable of handling grief than men. The Wahhabiya of Saudi Arabia take this position further, absolutely forbidding the visitation of gravesites by Muslims. The Wahhabiyah regard ziyara as equivalent to 'saint veneration' and thus to the serious sin of *shirk* – anointing the dead with divinity. In this, the Wahhabiya diverge from all others in the Sunni community. See Abdulaziz Sachedina, in Esposito, ed., *The Oxford Encyclopedia of the Modern Islamic World,* vol. IV, 375–6. Otherwise, ziyara is regarded as a venerable Islamic tradition. See Eickelman and Piscatori, eds., *Muslim Travellers* – for example, 5, 204, 210, and 236–54.
63 Cassanelli, *The Shaping of Somali Society,* 124.
64 Andzrejewski, *Islamic Literature of Somalia,* 2.
65 Cassanelli, *The Shaping of Somali Society,* 194.
66 Lewis, 'Sufism in Somaliland,' 159.
67 Trimingham, *The Sufi Orders in Islam,* 40.
68 I.M. Lewis, *Peoples of the Horn of Africa,* 141.
69 Trimingham, *The Sufi Orders in Islam,* 41; also Jacqueline Chabbi, 'Abd al-Kadir al-Djilani, personnage historique,' *Studia Islamica* 38 (1973), 75–106;

cited in Bradford G. Martin, 'Qadiriyah,' in Esposito, ed., *Oxford Encyclopedia*, vol. III, 375–9.

70 Trimingham, *The Sufi Orders in Islam*, 42.

71 Ibid., 43; Lewis, 'Sufism in Somaliland,' 141. The order was introduced into Harar by Sherif Abu Bakr ibn 'Abd Allah al-'Aydarus.

72 Trimingham, *Islam in Ethiopia*, 234–5. The Ahmadiyya (Trimingham refers to it as the Idrisiyya) of northeast Africa should not be confused with the Ahmadiyya of India – a controversial, messianic movement founded in 1889 by Mirza Ghulam Ahmad and believed not to be authentically Muslim by many because of its claim of prophetic status for its founder. See Yohanan Friedman in Esposito, ed., *Oxford Encyclopedia*, vol. I, 56–7.

73 Trimingham, *The Sufi Orders in Islam*, 105–6.

74 Trimingham notes that there is an important distinction to be drawn between the ziyara as carried out by the 'genuine' Sufi and that of the lay public. The mystic's purpose was spritual communion (*muraqaba*) with the saint, but the popular notion developed that intercession can be sought with the saint because his soul lingers near his tomb. *The Sufi Orders in Islam*, 26. The notion of intercession is what would have angered the reformists as doctrinally impure. This development was accompanied by another: the notion that the saint's spiritual power (*baraka*) can be inherited by his successors and associates.

75 Ibid., 115.

76 Ibid., 120–1.

77 Cassanelli, *The Shaping of Somali Society*, 196.

78 Sheik-Abdi, *Divine Madness*, 47.

79 Ibid., 59.

80 Ahmed, 'God, Anti-Colonialism and Drums,' 107 and 111.

81 Sheik-Abdi, *Divine Madness*, 58.

82 Ibid., 58–9.

83 Cassanelli, *The Shaping of Somali Society*, 195.

84 Ibid., 136–7.

85 Ibid., 137.

86 Ibid., 141.

87 I.M. Lewis, *Blood and Bone*, 150–65.

88 Abdullahi, 'Tribalism, Nationalism and Islam,' 112.

89 The Islamic Movement has been defined by Kalim Siddiqui, former director of the Muslim Institute in London, as consisting of 'all those Muslims who, through individual or organized effort of whatever nature sanctioned by Islam, are trying to contribute towards the eventual establishment of one or more Islamic states under a *khalifah/imam* anywhere in the world.'

See *Challenge* 3 no. 1 (London: Muslim Parliament Network, 1995), cited in Greaves, 'The Reproduction of Jamaat-i Islami in Britain,' 207. Islamists in Western countries, in contrast, tend to concentrate on creating an environment in which Muslims can practise as they see fit and in encouraging Muslims to maintain an Islamic life (however this is interpreted).

90 For one exploration of their development, see Adam, 'Islam and Politics in Islam,' 189–221.

91 Interview, London, 8 Aug. 1995.

92 Shaykh Mohamed Sheikh Osman attributed the design to a Syrian scholar by the name of Shaykh Nasir Din al-Bani. Interview, London, 8 Aug. 1995.

93 See Fadwa El Guindi, 'Hijab,' in Esposito, ed., *Oxford Encyclopedia*, vol. II, 108–11.

94 This approach stood in marked contrast to that of the group of intellectuals and professionals who issued a document entitled 'The Islamic Call' in October 1990. The document called for an Islamic (*shura*) democracy, arrived at via non-violent means. See Adam, 'Islam and Politics in Somalia,' 215.

95 Aqli, 'Historical Development of Islamic Movements in the Horn of Africa.'

96 Abdullahi, 'Tribalism, Nationalism and Islam,' 115.

97 Ibid., 8–10. The group has been reported to have links with Hassan Turabi's National Islamic Front: *Sunday Times*, 20 Dec. 1992, as cited in Amnesty International's *Sudan Update* 4 no. 7 (Jan. 1993).

98 Abdullahi, 'Tribalism, Nationalism and Islam,' 114; Aqli, 'Historical Development of Islamic Movements,' 8.

99 The majority of contemporary Muslim writers invoke a Golden Age of Islam that covers the period of the Rightly Guided Caliphs (632–661), from the death of the Prophet through the death of 'Ali. Shaykh Mohamed Sheikh Osman, however, said in an interview that the Prophet is understood to have said that the best of his followers would be the first three generations. Consequently, al-Ittihad reckons the best years of Islam, during which the faith was practised correctly, as the ten remaining years of the Prophet's life after the hijra, followed by the three subsequent generations of the umma. Counting a generation as seventy years, this gives a figure of 220 years. Interview, London, 8 Aug. 1995. See also Shaykh Muhammad al-Saleh al-Uthaimin, *Muslim's Belief* (Medina: Islamic University, 1992), 23: 'We believe that the best among the Muslim *umma* are the Prophet's Companions, then their followers, and those who followed them. We also believe that a group of this *umma* will always remain victorious on the right path, unharmed by those who let them down or those who oppose them, until the Day of Judgement.' It is the practice of this period in Islamic history that al-Ittihad strives to reproduce.

100 Abdullahi, 'Tribalism, Nationalism and Islam,' 114–15.
101 Ibid.
102 Interview, Ahmed, Toronto, 31 Jan. 1995.
103 Interview, Ali, London, 17 July 1995, among other respondents.
104 Abdullahi, 'Tribalism, Nationalism and Islam,' 91–101.
105 Interview, Hamud, London, 23 May 1995.
106 Interview, Abdullahi, London, 29 July 1995.
107 John Eade, 'The Islamization of Space in London,' in Metcalfe, ed., *Making Muslim Space in North America and Europe*, 219.
108 Philip Lewis, *Islamic Britain*, 36–40.
109 Interview, London, 8 Aug. 1995.
110 While Somali tradition has dictated an inferior social position for women vis-à-vis men and justified it by reference to Islam, the nomadic way of life has precluded seclusion. See Janice Boddy's afterword to Aman, *Aman*, 309–10.
111 See, for example, Ahmed, *Women and Gender in Islam*; Mernissi, *Beyond the Veil*; Moghadam, ed., *Identity Politics and Women*; Robert A. Fernea and Elizabeth W. Fernea, 'Variation in Religious Observance among Islamic Women,' in Keddie, ed., *Scholars, Saints, and Sufis*, 385–401; Engineer, *The Rights of Women in Islam*; Afkhami, ed., *Faith and Freedom*; El-Solh and Mabro, eds., *Muslim Women's Choices*; and Yamani, ed., *Feminism and Islam*.
112 Debate on Internet Newsgroup 'soc.culture.somalia.'
113 Amnesty International, *Somalia – Update on a Disaster*, 30 April 1995 (AI Index: AFR 52/01/93), 6; and Amnesty International British Section, *Refugee Bulletin* issue 01/95 (Jan. 1995), 2; also Human Rights Watch, Africa, *Somalia Faces the Future*, 30–3.
114 Interview, Yusuf, Toronto, 6 March 1995, among other respondents.
115 Interview, Saida, London, 14 July 1995, among other respondents.
116 Interview, Ali, London, 17 July 1995.

Chapter Two: Cultural Integration

1 From the first page of the editors' preface to Glazer and Moynihan, eds., *Beyond the Melting Pot*.
2 Ibid.
3 Ibid., 16.
4 Ibid., 17.
5 Harold Isaacs, 'Idols of the Tribe,' in Glazer and Moynihan, eds., *Ethnicity*, 31–5.

6 Geertz, *The Interpretation of Cultures*, 259–60.
7 Barth, *Ethnic Groups and Boundaries*, 14.
8 Ibid., 14.
9 Isajiw, *Definitions of Ethnicity*, 21.
10 See Eliezer Ben-Rafael's discussion of the various approaches to ethnicity, in his *Emergence of Ethnicity*, 7–8.
11 Isajiw, *Definitions of Ethnicity*, 21–2.
12 Glazer and Moynihan, eds., *Ethnicity*, 7.
13 Bell, 'Ethnicity and Social Change,' in ibid., 169.
14 Ibid., 171.
15 Smith, *The Ethnic Revival in the Modern World*, 4.
16 *Ethnic Identities in a Transnational World*, 7.
17 John Porter, 'Ethnic Pluralism in Canada,' in Glazer and Moynihan, eds., *Ethnicity*, 295.
18 See Reitz and Breton, *The Illusion of Difference*.
19 Gordon, *Assimilation in American Life*.
20 Ibid., 91.
21 Ibid., 94.
22 Ibid., 118.
23 Ibid., 120.
24 Ibid., 122.
25 Ibid., 142–3.
26 Ibid., 71.
27 Ibid., 159. Gordon updated the book in an article in Glazer and Moynihan's *Ethnicity* detailing the behaviour of ethnic groups vis-à-vis one another, particularly as competitors for limited economic gain, but not altering his basic thesis on assimilation.
28 J.S. Furnivall, *Netherland India: A Study of a Plural Economy* (Cambridge, 1939), as cited in John Rex, 'The Political Sociology of a Multi-cultural Society,' in Institute of Commonwealth Studies, *Multiculturalism and the State*, vol. I, 26–35.
29 Bernard as quoted in Gordon, *Assimilation in American Life*, 68.
30 Ibid., 72–3.
31 Breton, Isajiw, Kalbach, and Reitz, *Ethnic Identity and Equality*.
32 Ibid., 20.
33 Ibid., 21.
34 Ibid.
35 This point is made as well by Spinner in *The Boundaries of Citizenship*, 51.
36 *Journal of Muslim Minority Affairs* 17 no. 1 (April 1997), 153–66.
37 Ibid., 160.

38 'Ethnic minorities' account for a quarter of the American population, and that percentage is increasing. See Young, ed., *The Rising Tide of Cultural Pluralism*, 17. In 1986, the non-British, non-French population of Toronto was 44.5 per cent; in Vancouver it was 37.4 per cent; and in Montreal it was 21.1 per cent: David Morrison, 'Human Rights, Religion and Multiculturalism,' in Institute of Commonwealth Studies, *Multiculturalism and the State*, vol. I, 42.

39 Hnatyshn was of Ukrainian background.

40 Spinner, *The Boundaries of Citizenship*, 77.

41 Cited in Gordon, *Assimilation in American Life*, 68.

42 Spinner, *The Boundaries of Citizenship*, 39–45.

43 Soysal, *Limits of Citizenship*. 29–30.

44 Ibid.

45 Almond and Powell, *Comparative Politics*, 50. Almond described political culture first in a paper presented at the Conference on the Comparative Method in the Study of Politics at Princeton University in 1955, and it was subsequently published as 'Comparative Political Systems.'

46 Pye, *Aspects of Political Development*, 104.

47 Before the term 'political culture' came into use, Max Weber noted the role of culture in allowing for the development of capitalism, for instance in his remarking on the significance of Judaism's responsibility for Christianity's hostility to magic – 'one of the most serious obstructions to the rationalisation of economic life.' See J.E.T. Eldridge, ed., *Max Weber*, 284. Seymour Lipset notes that Weber recognized how a significant event occurring in one society at one time could have a completely different series of consequences were it to occur in a different society at a different time: Max Weber, *Methodology of the Social Sciences*, 182–5, cited in Lipset, *Continental Divide*, 16. Giambattista Vico, the eighteenth-century Italian philosopher, lamented the presumption, created by Cartesian thought, that observable science is more essential to knowledge than human cultural creations, precisely because the importance of the latter is consequently obscured. Verene, *Vico's Science of Imagination*, 193–221.

48 See, for instance: Almond and Powell, *Comparative Politics*; Pye, *Aspects of Political Development*; also Pye and Verba, eds., *Political Culture and Political Development*.

49 Samuel Huntington, 'The Goals of Development,' in Huntington and Weiner, eds., *Understanding Political Development*, 28.

50 Pye, *Aspects of Political Development*, 105.

51 Geertz, *The Interpretation of Cultures*, 259–60.

52 Verba, 'Conclusion: Comparative Political Culture,' in Verba and Pye, eds.,

Political Culture and Political Development, 529–56.

53 Ibid., 533.

54 This is beginning to change. See, for instance, Tariq Modood's introduction to Modood and Werbner, eds., *The Politics of Multiculturalism in the New Europe*, 1–25.

55 Quoted by Taylor, *Multiculturalism and 'The Politics of Recognition'*, 65, and other commentators on the subject.

56 The authors cited here are not equally critical of this view. Bernstein's *Dictatorship of Virtue* attacks the conviction as muddle-headed and dictatorially equalizing. Taylor's essay discusses the philosophical underpinnings of the belief, concluding that while it may tend to equalize culture and achievement without consideration of merit, it need not have such a draconian end.

57 Canadian Multiculturalism Act, 1988.

58 See David Bell's *The Roots of Disunity*; Bibby's *Mosaic Madness*; and Bissoondath's *Selling Illusions*. For a contrary view, see Kymlicka, *Multicultural Citizenship*.

59 Although they may have been there initially not as explorers or farmers but as slaves, the presence in large numbers of African Americans from the early days of the 'American empire' is critical to their descendants' understanding of a need to renegotiate or re-understand their own identities. These discussions are separate yet again from those of the place of Aboriginal peoples in either the United States or Canada and their role in the rest of society.

60 Prince of Wales, *Islam and the West*.

61 Parekh emphasizes that he does not intend the sort of pluralism described by Furnival and applied to societies consisting of more than one ethnic group, in which political or economic power is divided, frequently uneasily, between the groups, so that it has a connotation of separateness of ethnic groups that is not descriptive of immigrant-absorbing Western liberal democracies. See Furnivall, *Colonial Policy and Practice*, and also Banton, *Racial and Ethnic Competition*. Parekh is quoted here in 'Britain and the Social Logic of Pluralism,' in his edited *Britain*, 60–1.

62 See, for instance, Nira Yuval-Davis, 'Ethnicity, Gender and Multiculturalism,' in Werbner and Modood, eds., *Debating Cultural Hybridity*, 193–208.

63 See, for example, and in addition to the references noted elsewhere, the following: Holmes, *A Tolerant Country?*; Henry-Layton, *The Politics of Immigration*; Banton, 'The Race Relations Problematic,' *British Journal of Sociology* 42 no. 1 (1991), 115–30; Banton, *Race Relations*; and Gilroy, *There Ain't No Black in the Union Jack*.

64 Rex, *Race and Ethnicity.*
65 See Parekh, *Britain*; or Modood, Beishon, and Virdee, *Changing Ethnic Identities.*
66 Modood, Beishon, and Virdee, *Changing Ethnic Identities*, 5.
67 Tariq Modood, 'The Limits of America: Rethinking Equality in the Changing Context of British Race Relations,' in Ward and Badger, eds., *The Making of Martin Luther King and the Civil Rights Movement*, 131–49. Also see Stephen Small's 'Unravelling Racialised Relations in the United States of America and the United States of Europe,' in Solomos and Wrench, eds., *Racism and Migration in Western Europe*, 233–50.
68 This is illuminated precisely by Parekh's collection of essays by black British intellectuals on their experiences of living in, and integrating into, Britain, in *Colour, Culture and Consciousness*; see especially his 'Postscript,' 220–43.
69 *Race and Racism* (London: Routledge, 1943), 97, cited in Solomos, *Race and Racism in Britain*, 17.
70 See Miles, in *Racism after 'Race Relations'*, for a broad discussion of the approach and its challenges.
71 Cited in Ben-Tovim Gabriel, Law, and Stredder, *The Local Politics of Race*, 17.
72 *Today*, 21 April 1990, cited in Solomos, *Race and Racism in Britain*, 229.
73 *Electronic Telegraph*, 9 Oct. 1997, issue 868.
74 *The Times*, 5 July 1989, cited in Solomos, *Race and Racism in Britain*, 225.
75 The *Daily Telegraph*, for instance, titled an editorial 'Races Apart,' 17 May 1989, cited in Solomos, *Race and Racism in Britain*, 224.
76 Solomos, *Race and Racism in Britain*, 225; Miles, *Racism after 'Race Relations'*, 4–5.
77 Modood, *Not Easy Being British*; the quotation may be found on 53, but see 47–59.
78 Modood, *Racial Equality*, 12.
79 Miles, *Racism after 'Race Relations,'* 135.
80 Philip Cohen, 'The Perversions of Inheritance: Studies in the Making of Multi-Racist Britain,' in Cohen and Bains, eds., *Multi-Racist Britain*, 15.
81 A. Sivanandan, 'The New Racism,' *New Statesman and Society* (Nov. 1988), 8–9, cited in Miles, *Racism after 'Race Relations'*, 18. Also Rich, *Prospero's Return?* 24: 'The protracted civil war in the former Yugoslavia suggests that modern forms of racism have expanded beyond defence of pigmentation and race into defence of "culture," however variously this can be described.' Stavenhagen, in *The Ethnic Question*, 127, writes that the key to the 'new racism' is not biological difference but 'behaviour, economic activity, cultural values, social relations, and so forth.' See also Robert Miles's discussion in 'The Articulation of Racism and Nationalism: Reflections on European History,'

in Solomos and Wrench, *Racism and Migration in Western Europe*, 35–52. See also Tariq Modood, '"Difference," Cultural Racism and Anti-Racism,' in Werbner and Modood, eds., *Debating Cultural Hybridity*, 154–72.

82 This was President George Bush's response to Iraq's aggression against Kuwait, cited in Ali Mazrui, 'Race and Religion in the New World Order,' in Ismael and Ismael, eds., *The Gulf War and the New World Order*, 533.

83 Ibid., 521–35.

84 Ibid., 534. Also see Mazrui, 'Towards Cultural Realignment,' in Mazrui, *Cultural Forces in World Politics*, 250 7.

85 Peter Jackson, 'The Idea of "Race" and the Geography of Racism,' in Jackson, ed., *Race and 'Racism'*, 12.

86 Miles, *Racism after 'Race Relations'*, 101.

87 Modood, *Racial Equality*, 6.

88 Nash, *The Cauldron of Ethnicity*, 4.

Chapter Three: Islam in London and Toronto

1 Interview, Toronto, 31 Jan. 1995.

2 See chapter 2.

3 Interview, Toronto, 31 Jan. 1995.

4 Interview, 21 March 1995.

5 Yusuf and his wife divorced shortly thereafter, owing, he maintained, to different religious orientations. He subsequently remarried a devout Somali who wears the jilbab.

6 Interview, London, 17 July 1995.

7 Interview, Toronto, 31 Jan. 1995.

8 Interview, London, 20 May 1995.

9 Although Abdullahi understood my questions, he gave his answers in Somali, and they were translated by Nur. The interview was held in London, 29 July 1995.

10 Interview, Toronto, 6 March 1995.

11 Interview, Toronto, 26 April 1995.

12 Interview, London, 17 May 1995.

13 Interviews, Toronto, 11 May 1995.

14 Interview, 26 July 1995.

15 Interview, 6 June 1995.

16 Interview, 18 July 1995.

17 Interview, London, 21 May 1995.

18 Interview, London, 16 May 1995.

19 Interview, Toronto, 9 May 1995.

20 Interview, translated, London, 20 July 1995.
21 Interview, Toronto, 7 March 1995.
22 Interview, London, 18 May 1995.
23 Interview, Toronto, 24 March 1995.
24 Ibid.
25 Interview, London, 19 May 1995.
26 Interview, London, 4 Aug. 1995.
27 Interview, London, 26 July 1995.
28 Interview, Toronto, 5 June 1995.
29 Interview, London, 14 July 1995.
30 Interview, London, 24 May 1995.
31 Some respondents, particularly among the Isaaq, referred to the members of the Islamic movements as al-Wahada.
32 Interview, London, 21 May 1995.
33 Interview, Toronto, 28 June 1995.
34 Interview with Aden Ibrahim, 28 June 1995.
35 'Media Watch,' *Codka Jaaliyadda* 1 issue 5 (Dec. 1994), 1.
36 Interview, Hassan Mohamud, 7 June 1995; also SOYAT, *Mission Statement*.
37 Privately, Hassan is a supporter of al-Islah. SOYAT as an organization takes no stand.
38 Interview, 7 June 1995.
39 Among the sources it uses is a slim booklet: al-Uthaimin, *Muslim's Belief*.
40 Interview, London, 20 July 1995.
41 The family was advised that the fetus should be buried like any other person. There is no national policy in Britain on burying fetuses, so procedure varies from local authority to local authority. In one case in Sheffield, for instance, a Muslim family resorted to burying a miscarried fetus in their own garden because the Sheffield council's cemeteries would bury only fetuses of twenty-four weeks' gestation or more. The family would not agree to the normal procedure of disposal by cremation. *BMMS* 2 no. 7 (July 1994), 12.
42 Parekh, 'The Concept of Fundamentalism,' in Aleksandras Shtromas, ed., *The End of 'Isms'?* 113–21.
43 Ibid., 111.
44 Ibid., 109.

Chapter Four: Transfer of Values

1 On some of the issues surrounding schooling, see: Joly, *Ethnic Minorities and Education in Britain*; also Nielsen, *Muslims in Western Europe*, 53–9; and Dwyer and Meyer, 'The Institutionalisation of Islam.'

2 In Britain, in 1991, there were a total of fifteen privately-funded Muslim schools. See Parker-Jenkins, 'Muslim Matters,' 570. The Islamiah School, for instance, with eighty students, cost parents £1,000 per year in fees. There was a fund for subsidies for parents who could not afford the fees, but in 1993 the school had a 1,000-name waiting list. 'Muslims Stand Their Ground,' *Guardian Education*, 23 March 1993, 6–7. The *Muslim News* put the number of Muslim independent schools in Britain at forty-five by early 1996: no. 82, 16 Feb. 1996, 3.

In 1995 there were a total of twelve such schools in Canada, two of which were in Toronto and both of which covered only the elementary grades. The Islamic Foundation School, for instance, with 155 pupils, charged $2,500 in annual fees.

3 'Muslims Test Patten's Faith in Education Diversity,' *The Times*, 23 March 1993, 4.

4 'Time for Pluralism: Muslims Should Be Allowed Their Own State Schools,' *The Times*, 22 Feb. 1993, 17. The application was denied in August of that year.

Refused British government funding, the Islamiah Schools Trust had been relying on funds from Saudi Arabia, which diminished after the Gulf War and reportedly were endangered altogether when Yusuf Islam sent a letter to the Saudi ambassador inquiring about the arrest of certain Islamic scholars and government opponents: *Muslim News* no. 80, 22 Dec. 1995, 3.

5 'Tories Arouse Fundamental Anger,' *Observer*, 22 Aug. 1993, 6. The *Economist*, three years later, argued that 'if state-financed Christian schools are to stay then it follows that state-financed Muslim schools must also be allowed. To rule otherwise would be patently unfair.' 'All God's Children: The British Government Should Bow to Demands That It Pay for Muslim Schools,' 30 April 1996, 14.

6 *The Times* Internet Edition, 10 Jan. 1998, British News.

7 Education is a provincial matter according to the constitution, and Alberta has funded a number of 'Charter' schools along the voluntary-aided idea. These include Christian and Muslim institutions.

8 Sections 28 and 29 of Ontario Regulation 262, made under the Education Act, 1981, of the Province of Ontario.

9 Toronto Board of Education, *Readings and Prayers*, covers various traditions, including the beliefs of secular humanists and 'people of native ancestry,' as well as Christians, Jews, Muslims, Sikhs, Hindus, Jainists, Baha'is, Zoroastrians, and Confucianists.

10 Alan Borovoy, general counsel, Canadian Civil Liberties Association, on CBC Newsworld. 'The Fourth 'R': Religion in the Classroom,' *Toronto Star*, 14 Sept. 1996, C4.

11 Supreme Court of Canada, *Adler v. Ontario*, 21 Nov. 1996.

12 Section 7 of the Education Reform Act, 1988, cited in Parker-Jenkins, 'Muslim Matters,' 572.

13 Joly, *Ethnic Minorities and Education in Britain*, 13.

14 Akhtar, *The Muslim Parents Handbook*, 29. The *Handbook* urges that parents insist that any school with a majority of Muslim pupils allocate time and place for Friday communal prayer (30).

15 George Orwell School in Islington, for instance, is a public school of roughly 550 students, two-thirds of whom do not speak English as a mother tongue and one-third of whom are refugees. An introduction to the school has been prepared for parents of new arrivals and translated into Somali. It reads, in part, 'The school provides all the subjects of the National Curriculum, plus Religious Education, which helps children to understand many different religions but does not favour any particular one. Many students in the school benefit from the opportunity to attend their own mosque within the school, run by students.' George Orwell School,' *Induction Programme*, 2.

16 Nielsen, *Muslims in Western Europe*, 56.

17 Akhtar, *The Muslim Parents Handbook*, 29.

18 *Muslim News* no. 81, 26 Jan. 1996, 1.

19 Ibid., 16 Feb. 1996, 1.

20 Jeff Spinner, *The Boundaries of Citizenship*, 40–1.

21 See Stephen William Barton, 'The Qur'an School,' in his monograph, *The Bengali Muslims of Bradford*, 150–74.

22 Sarwar, *British Muslims and Schools*, 14.

23 Ibid., 15.

24 Interview, Asha, Toronto, 27 March 1995.

25 Sarwar, *Sex Education*, update insert, 1–2.

26 Interview, Layla, London, 25 July 1995, among other respondents.

27 See Nielsen, *Muslims in Western Europe*, 54. Over time, rules governing uniforms were relaxed to permit the wearing of the hijab, and either vegetarian or halal meals were provided as an alternative.

28 As noted by Toronto imam Abdulle Hakim, the reaction of schools in Etobicoke to the influx of Somali refugees was to ask local 'ulama for help in determining the needs of the new students. Interview, Imam Abdulle Hakim, 16 Feb. 1995. Uniforms are not worn in Canadian public schools, and school cafeterias regularly provide vegetarian meals.

29 Interview, Toronto, 5 June 1995.

30 Interview, Toronto, 6 Feb. 1995.

31 Interview, Toronto, 26 April 1995.

32 Interview, Toronto, 14 March 1995.
33 Interview, Toronto, 31 Jan. 1995.
34 Interview, Toronto, 26 April 1995.
35 Interview, London, 25 May 1995.
36 Interview, London, 18 May 1995.
37 Tension between Asians and Somalis stems in part from the perceived com-
    petition for limited resources by immigrant and ethnic communities. See
    El-Solh, 'Somalis in London's East End,' 28; 'Simmering Hatred That
    Threatens a Melting Pot,' *Independent*, 26 May 1991.
38 Interview, London, 26 May 1995.
39 Interview, London, 29 July 1995.
40 Interview, London, 29 July 1995.
41 Interview, Toronto, 11 June 1995.
42 Interview, London, 25 May 1995.
43 Interview, Toronto, 21 March 1995.
44 Interview, Toronto, 5 June 1995.
45 Interview, London, 24 May 1995.
46 Interview, London, 14 July 1995.
47 Interview, Toronto, 27 March 1995.
48 Interview, London, 20 July 1995.
49 Interview, London, 25 July 1995.
50 Interview, Toronto, 23 March 1995.
51 A soft drink.
52 See the quotation from Sahra in chapter 5.
53 See Eleanor Abdella Doumato, 'Marriage and Divorce: Modern Practice,' in
    Esposito, ed., *Oxford Encyclopedia*, vol. III, 52. Many consider even the mar-
    riage of a Muslim to a kitabiyya woman to be *makruh* (disapproved), espe-
    cially outside dar al-Islam, where the influence of her religion is likely to be
    greater on the children. See Doi, *Women in Shari'ah*, 44–9.
54 Interview, London, 21 July 1995.
55 Interview, Toronto, 7 April 1995.
56 Interview, Toronto, 27 March 1995.
57 Interview, London, 2 Aug. 1995.
58 Interview, Imam Abdul Hakim, Toronto, Jan. 1995. Also Michael Valpy,
    'The Hurt Felt by Somali Youngsters,' *Globe and Mail*, 23 Feb. 1996, A17.
59 Interview, Toronto, 23 March 1995.
60 Interview, Toronto, 24 March 1995.
61 Interview, Toronto, 28 March 1995.
62 Interview, London, 2 Aug. 1995.
63 Interview, London, 4 Aug. 1995.

Chapter Five: Bridging Two Worlds: Weaving Two Cultures

1 Interview, Said, Toronto, 6 June 1995.
2 Interview, Yusuf, Toronto, 21 March 1995.
3 Interview, Safiya, Toronto, 5 June 1995.
4 Interview, Amina, Toronto, 7 March 1995.
5 Interview, Hibaq, London, 19 May 1995.
6 Interview, Nura, London, 26 July 1995.
7 Interview, Roda, London, 25 May 1995.
8 Interview, Warsame, Toronto, 24 March 1995.
9 Interview, Rashid, Toronto, 26 April 1995.
10 Interview, Nasra, Toronto, 20 April 1995.
11 Interview, Farhia, Toronto, 5 June 1995.
12 Interview, Anab, London, 18 May 1995.
13 Interview, Layla, London, 25 July 1995.
14 Donna Lee Bowen, 'Family Planning,' in Esposito, ed., *Oxford Encyclopedia*, vol. I, 464–465.
15 Musallam, *Sex and Society in Islam*, notably chap. 1, 'Why Islam Permitted Contraception,' 10–38.
16 Bowen, in Esposito, ed., *Oxford Encyclopedia*, vol. I, 464–5.
17 Interview, Ibrahim Sheikh Mohamed, London, 20 July 1995.
18 Interview, Fawziya, London, 21 July 1995.
19 Interview, Abdurahman, London, 26 July 1995.
20 Interview, Ayaan, London, 4 Aug. 1995.
21 This is because of the infibulations.
22 Interview, Nura, thirties, London, 26 July 1995.
23 Interview, Layla, eighteen, London, 25 July 1995.
24 Muslim jurists uniformly denounce abortion, on the basis of the value placed by the Qur'an on the preservation of life, and on hadiths that emphasize Muhammad's concern for the same. The only exception is where the mother's health is endangered. Although the fetus's right to life is seen to be equal to the mother's after 120 days (when ensoulment is said to occur), in the event that only one of the two lives can be saved, the preference is given to the mother on the grounds that she is the origin of the fetus and has responsibilities and duties to other family members as well. See Abul Fadl Mohsin Ebrahim, 'Abortion,' in Esposito, ed., *Oxford Encyclopedia*, vol. I, 17–19.
25 Interview, Ismail, Toronto, 31 Jan. 1995.
26 Interview, Ahmed, Toronto, 31 Jan. 1995.
27 Interview, Fathia, London, 26 May 1995.

28 Interview, Nura, London, 26 July 1995.
29 Interview, Fawziya, London, 21 July 1995.
30 Interview, Sahra, Toronto, 23 March 1995.
31 Interview, Aman and Hawa, Toronto, 7 April 1995.
32 Interview, Osman, Toronto, 21 April 1995.
33 Interview, Hamud, London, 20 July 1995.
34 Interview, Hamud, London, 23 May 1995.
35 Interview, Osob, Toronto, 14 March 1995.
36 Interview, Roda, London, 25 May 1995.
37 Interview, Kalima, Toronto, 4 July 1995.
38 Interview, Jewahir, Toronto, 19 Feb. 1995.
39 Interview, Nasra, Toronto, 20 April 1995.
40 Gallo and Abdisamed, 'Female Circumcision in Somalia: Anthropological Traits.'
41 Ismail, 'Female Circumcision,' 218.
42 See, for instance, Boddy, 'Womb as Oasis'; Toubia, *Female Genital Mutilation*; and Raqiya Haji Dualeh Abdalla, *Sisters in Affliction*. Other sources include: Dorkenoo, *Cutting the Rose*; Lightfoot-Klein, *Prisoners of Ritual*; Fran Hosken, *The Hosken Report*; El Dareer, *Woman, Why Do You Weep?*; Gallo, *La circoncisione femminile in Somalia*; and Koso-Thomas, *The Circumcision of Women*.
43 In addition to sources previously mentioned, see FORWARD, *Report on the First National Conference on Female Genital Mutilation*; van der Kwaak, 'Female Circumcision and Gender Identity'; Lamb, 'Female Excision'; Hale, 'A Question of Subjects'; and RAINBO, *Battlefields of Women's Bodies*.
44 A similar decision was taken for the first time in the United States in June 1996. *New York Times*, 14 June 1996, 1.
45 The Jordanian daily *al-Ra'i*, Sunday, 9 July 1995, 24; I am grateful to Nadia Taher for her translation.
46 Personal communication with Nadia Taher, researcher and lecturer in the Development Planning Unit of London University, 13 Aug. 1995. Taher was in Egypt at the time of the conference, when Shaykh Sha'rawi's speech was widely reported.
47 'Judge Rules in Favor of Islamic Lawyers,' *Middle East Times*, 27 June–3 July 1997.
48 'Religious Leader Reaffirms Opposition to Female Circumcision,' *Africa News Online*, All Africa Press Service, 4 Aug. 1997.
49 *Al-Ahram*, 3 June 1995, and *Rose El-Yousef*, July 1996; translation: Ford Foundation, Cairo.
50 *Globe and Mail*, 29 Dec. 1997, A10.

51 Hicks, *Infibulation.*

52 An example of this was a *Rough Cuts* documentary presented on the CBC Newsworld channel that featured interviews with Somali teenagers at a Toronto high school on female circumcision. The premise of the show was that female genital mutilation (FGM), graphically demonstrated, is a prevalent and growing problem for Canadians. The interviewer had promised the girls that their faces would be blacked out when the interview was televised, but the angry face of one teenager was clearly shown as she declared that FGM was the only way to keep girls from the dangers of sexual experimentation and that she was in favour of it. Both the community and the school felt betrayed by the interviewer and the program. Kim Harris, 'Our Daughters' Pain.'

53 Interview, Hibaq, London, 19 May 1995.

54 Interview, Roda, London, 25 May 1995.

55 Interview, Ayaan, London, 4 Aug. 1995.

56 Interview, Fawziya and Kinsi, London, 21 July 1995.

57 Interview, Ibrahim Sheikh Mohamed, London, 20 July 1995.

58 This informant implies that female circumcision is sanctioned traditionally, but not necessarily obligatory.

59 Interview, Saida, London, 14 July 1995.

60 Interview, Zeinab, Toronto, 5 June 1995.

61 Interview, Said, Toronto, 6 June 1995.

62 Interview, Anab, London, 18 May 1995.

63 Interview, Fathia, London, 26 May 1995.

64 Interview, Sadia, Toronto, 27 March 1995.

65 Interview, Qassim, Toronto, 23 March 1995.

66 Interview, Amina, Toronto, 7 March 1995.

67 Interview, Jewahir, Toronto, 19 Feb. 1995.

68 Interview, Farhia, Toronto, 5 June 1995.

69 Interview, Warsame, Toronto, 24 March 1995.

70 Interview, Toronto, 9 May 1995.

71 Interview, Osob, Toronto, 14 March 1995.

72 Interview, Sahra, Toronto, 23 March 1995.

73 Interview, Mubarek, London, 2 Aug. 1995.

74 Interview, Abdikarim, Toronto, 23 March 1995.

75 Interview, Amir, London, 2 Aug. 1995.

76 Interview, Nur, London, 29 July 1995.

77 Interview, Abdurahman, London, 26 July 1995.

78 Interview, Layla, London, 25 July 1995.

79 Interview, Ismail, Toronto, 31 Jan. 1995.

Chapter Six: London and Toronto

1 The politician in question is the Newfoundlander John Crosbie, in the run-up to the 1984 federal election. He lost the nomination to Brian Mulroney, a fluently bilingual Quebecer.

2 *Globe and Mail*, 18 Feb. 1998, A1.

3 The Loyalists were Americans who remained faithful to the crown throughout the American War of Independence and either chose to or were forced to flee to British territories when it became clear the tide had turned against them.

4 On the subject of Canadian political culture, and the differences between Canada and the United States, see the following: Horowitz, *Canadian Labour in Politics*, chap. 1; Lipset, *Revolution and Counter-Revolution* and *Continental Divide*, as well as Hartz, *Founding of New Societies*.

5 Morton Weinfeld, attempting to explain the persistence of ethnic group identification in 1981, noted that the Canadian multicultural model may be attractive to Canadians precisely because of their 'frustration in identifying a uniquely Canadian culture. In the absence of any consensus on the substance of Canadian identity or culture, multiculturalism fills a void.' 'Myth and Reality,' 94.

6 See Chong, *The Concubine's Children*.

7 Abella and Troper, *None Is Too Many*, preface.

8 Pierre Antcil, 'Interlude of Hostility: Judeo–Christian Relations in Quebec in the Interwar Period, 1919–1939,' in Davies, ed., *Antisemitism in Canada*, 142–4.

9 *Two Solitudes* is the title of a Quebec-based novel written by Hugh McLennan in 1945. The phrase has come to encapsulate the notion of two peoples that continually miscommunicate with one another. It is a poetic rendition of the famous phrase of the British aristocrat Lord Durham, whose 1839 report recommended complete cultural and linguistic assimilation of Quebec's French population. He introduced the report by regretting the fact that history had been such that he had arrived in British North America to find 'two nations warring in the bosom of a single state.' C.P. Lucas, ed., *Lord Durham's Report on the Affairs of British North America* (London: 1912), 16, cited in Lower, *Colony to Nation*, 218.

10 See Reitz and Breton, *The Illusion of Difference*, which examines the disparity between belief and reality in the Canadian and American absorption of immigrants. Although Canadians believe that they encourage 'cultural retention' more than Americans do, the study found that immigrants do not retain their birth culture more readily in Canada than in the United States.

11 Ibid., 88.
12 Anderson, *Imagined Communities*.
13 Poutine is a popular Quebec street food: french fries and cheese curds covered with gravy; tortière is a meat pie.
14 Arendt, *The Human Condition*, 22–78.
15 Kopytoff, 'Public Culture'; quotations from 14 and 15, respectively.
16 Spinner, *The Boundaries of Citizenship*, 75.
17 'Parking Snag May Jeopardize Mosque,' *Toronto Star*, 29 Sept. 1995, A6. The mosque was eventually approved, after modifications were made to the plans, some months later. 'Mosque Finally Wins Go-Ahead,' *Toronto Star*, 20 Feb. 1995, A1.
18 As promised by the Parti Québécois provincial government, a referendum was held on 30 October 1995, in order to ascertain whether Quebecers wanted their government to negotiate independence from the rest of Canada. The sovereigntists lost the vote by a margin of less than a percentage point. Anglophone and 'allophone' voters (those whose mother tongue was neither English nor French) voted overwhelmingly in favour of remaining in Canada.
19 Mackey, 'Postmodernism and Cultural Politics in a Multicultural Nation.'
20 Public attitude testing by the B'nai Brith League for Human Rights indicates that roughly 70 per cent of Canadians support 'diversity' and 'multiculturalism' and the respect for difference that those terms imply. Dr Karen Mock, national director, interviewed on *Metro Morning*, CBC Radio, 15 March 1996, 7:15 a.m.
21 CBC Radio, *CBO Morning*, interview with Melinda Courmier, community relations officer at the Etobicoke General Hospital, and Abdullahi Eo, from Dejinta Beesha, 2 April 1996, 7:15 a.m.
22 Meech Lake was a 1989 attempt to bring Quebec back formally into the Canadian fold by belatedly including its signature on the constitution. It included a number of constitutional changes that were vigorously debated and widely opposed.
23 Bell, *The Roots of Disunity*, 4.
24 The Reform party, a new organization with a regional western Canadian base, has stated that its intention is to do away with Multicultural policy. None the less, the party consistently gets itself into difficulty over its stand on ethnicity, and this element of its platform has virtually no constituency in Ontario or eastern Canada.
25 See Rich, *Prospero's Return?*, 7–26, for a discussion of the English sense of identity, in particular its present conception, which dates from the late nineteenth century and encompasses nostalgia for a pastoral, pre-industrial (non-urban) time and place.

26 Cohen, *Multi-Racist Britain*, 34: 'The working class "goes racist" when and wherever the presence of immigrants or ethnic minorities threatens to expose the ideological structures which it has erected to protect itself from recognising its real conditions of subordination. It is not because immigrants are actually undermining their standard of living, but because their entry into and across the local labour or housing market signifies the fact that the working class does not, in fact, own or control either jobs or neighbourhoods, that the immigrant presence is found intolerable.'

27 Prince of Wales, *Islam and the West*, 22.

28 Ray Honeyford was a school headteacher in Bradford who in 1984 published an article in a right-wing journal arguing that concessions to Muslim parents were wrong-headed and undermined a cohesive British sense of identity. The resulting tumult ended in his early retirement in December 1985.

29 'Judges Get Lessons in Gender Awareness,' *The Times*, 21 June 1996, Internet Edition.

30 Parekh, *Britain*, 71–3.

31 Ibid., 75. The tone of his comments parallels another proposal in John Rex's *Race and Ethnicity*, where Rex discusses the possible benefits to Britain of a policy of multiculturalism as ethnic legitimacy but recognizes that he is discussing an ideal, a world of 'ought,' not 'is'; 119–35.

32 John Rex, 'The Political Sociology of a Multi-Cultural Society,' in Institute of Commonwealth Studies, *Multiculturalism and the State*, vol. I, 26–35.

33 Spinner, *The Boundaries of Citizenship*, 39–45.

34 Ibid., 74–5.

35 *BMMS* 2 no. 11 (Nov. 1994), 14.

36 Ibid. 2 no. 6 (June 1994), 1.

37 *Electronic Telegraph*, 9 Oct. 1997, Issue no. 868.

38 Submission to the United Nations Committee on the Elmination of all Forms of Racial Discrimination, 1995, quoted in *Islamophobia: A Challenge for Us All* (London: 1997, Runnymede Trust), 31.

39 *BMMS* 3 no. 8 (Aug. 1995), 11.

40 Ibid. 2 no. 10 (Oct. 1994), 15.

41 Ibid. 2 no. 9 (Sept. 1994), 16; also 4 no. 2 (20 March 1996), 12.

42 'Oxford Colleges Oppose Plan for Islamic Minaret,' *Electronic Telegraph*, 10 May 1997, issue 715; 'Islamic Centre "Too Big" for Oxford,' ibid. 27 June 1997, issue 763.

43 Miles, *Racism after 'Race Relations'*, 5–6.

44 The issue was raised again when a Jewish woman was rejected for a job as a food taster at Marks & Spencer because she would not eat pork. Her only recourse was to claim that the company was guilty of racial discrimination

– a claim that was supported before an industrial tribunal by the Commission for Racial Equality. 'M&S Rejects Food Taster Who Refuses to Eat Pork,' *Daily Telegraph*, 4 June 1996, 3.
45 *Guardian*, 27 Sept. 1996, 12.
46 Commission on British Muslims and Islamophobia, *Islamophobia*.
47 'Religious Bias Could Be Outlawed,' *Electronic Telegraph*, 30 July 1997, issue 796.
48 *Muslim News*, 31 Oct. 1997, 1.
49 Verba, in *Political Culture and Political Development*, 532.
50 Parekh, 'Minority Practices and Principles of Toleration.'
51 Ibid., 259.
52 Ibid., 261.
53 For useful books on the affair, see: Appignanese and Maitland, eds., *The Rushdie File*; Malise Ruthven, *A Satanic Affair*; and Akhtar, *Be Careful with Muhammad!* Rushdie's response to the affair can be found in his *In Good Faith*.
54 Modood, *Racial Equality*, 7.
55 Piscatori, 'The Rushdie Affair and the Politics of Ambiguity.'
56 Ibid., 774.
57 Ibid., 776.
58 Ibid., 781–5.
59 'The Satanic Verses Controversy, A Brief Introduction,' in Horton, ed., *Liberalism, Multiculturalism and Toleration*, 104–13.
60 See, for instance Pipes, *The Rushdie Affair*, 214–23.
61 Peter Jones, 'Respecting Beliefs and Rebuking Rushdie,' in Horton, ed., *Liberalism, Multiculturalism and Toleration*, 131.
62 Ibid., 131.
63 There were of course Muslims for whom it was very much an issue of concern. Among these were the contributors to a volume of essays in support of Rushdie, entitled, in its English translation, *For Rushdie* (New York: George Braziller, 1994).
64 Tariq Modood, 'Muslims, Incitement to Hatred and the Law,' in Horton, ed., *Liberalism, Multiculturalism and Toleration*, reprinted in UK Action Committee on Islamic Affairs, *Muslims and the Law in Multi-faith Britain*, 72.
65 Ibid., 74.
66 Ibid., 75.
67 Nielsen, *Muslims in Western Europe*, 163.
68 Sardar and Wyn Davies, *Distorted Imagination*, 201–3.
69 Jim Keegstra was an Alberta highschool teacher who was deprived of his job for teaching anti-semitic views to his students. The province of Alberta

was supported in its actions by the Supreme Court of Canada in December 1990 and again, after a second appeal, in 1996. On both occasions, the high court upheld the constitutionality of criminal code provisions against promoting hatred. *Globe and Mail*, 29 Feb. 1996, A9.

70 Kepel, *À l'ouest d'Allah*, 121–34.
71 Piscatori, 'The Rushdie Affair,' 786.
72 Greaves, 'The Reproduction of Jamaat-i Islami in Britain,' 187–210.
73 Interview, Farhia, twenty-three, Toronto, 5 June 1995.
74 Interview, Saida, thirty-four, London, 14 July 1995.
75 Interview, Hersi, forties, Toronto, 15 March 1995.
76 Interview, Rashid, forties, Toronto, 26 April 1995.
77 Interview, Shugri, twenty-eight, London, 17 May, 1995.
78 Interview, Nasra, Toronto, 20 April 1995.
79 Interview, Ismail, thirty-four, Toronto, 31 Jan. 1995.
80 Interview, Said, forties, Toronto, 6 June 1995.
81 Interview, Zeinab, fifties, 5 June 1995.
82 Interview, Nura, thirties, London, 26 July 1995.
83 Interview, Hamud, London, 23 May 1995.
84 Interview, Hibaq, twenty-nine, London, 19 May 1995.
85 Interview, Farah, seventeen, Toronto, 28 March 1995.
86 Interview, Warsame, eighteen, Toronto, 24 March 1995.
87 Ali Mazrui, cited in Sardar and Davies, *Distorted Imagination*, 204–5.
88 Interview, Yusuf, thirty-four, Toronto, 6 March 1995.
89 Interview, Ahmed, thirties, Toronto, 31 Jan. 1995.
90 Interview, Roda, twenty-five, London, 25 May 1995.
91 Interview, Hassan, twenty-two, Toronto, 6 March 1995.
92 Interview, Abdurahman, twenty-seven, London, 26 July 1995.
93 Interview, Fathia, thirties, London, 26 May 1995.
94 Interview, Ayaan, twenty-three, London, 4 Aug. 1995.
95 Interview, Aboker, forties, London, 20 July 1995.
96 Interview, Fawziya, thirties, London, 21 July 1995.
97 Interview, Kalima, thirties, London, 21 July 1995.
98 Interview, Rashid, Toronto, 26 April 1995.
99 Interview, Yusuf, Toronto, 6 March 1995.
100 Interview, Zeinab, Toronto, 5 June 1995.
101 Interview, Nasra, Toronto, 20 April 1995.
102 Interview, Sahra, Toronto, 23 March 1995.
103 Interview, translator, Somali Women's and Children's Network, 9 May 1995.
104 Interview, Hassan, Toronto, 6 March 1995.

105 Interview, Farah, Toronto, 28 March 1995.

106 Interview, Jama, Toronto, 6 June 1995.

107 Interview, Daud, Toronto, 11 June 1995.

108 Interview, Nasir, Toronto, 10 April 1995.

109 Interview, Hassan Ali Mohamud, Toronto, 7 June 1995.

110 Interview, Samira, London, 24 May 1995. Kim Campbell was minister of defence in the Mulroney government at the time that Canadian peacekeepers in Somalia killed a Somali intruder into their camp. A commission was set up to investigate the incident and the armed forces' handling of it. The peacekeeping unit involved was disbanded, and the repercussions for the armed forces were significant: officers lost their jobs and/or were publicly embarrassed. For immigrant Somalis, the fact of the killing was less important than how it was handled in Canada. See discussion this chapter.

111 Interview, Fawziya, London, 21 July 1995.

112 Interview, Layla, London, 25 July 1995.

113 Interview, Amir, London, 2 Aug. 1995.

114 Interview, Nura, London, 26 July 1995.

115 Interview, Ayaan, London, 4 Aug. 1995.

116 Interview, Fathia, London, 26 May 1995.

117 Interview, Hibaq, London, 19 May 1995.

118 Interview, Khatara, London, 21 July 1995.

119 Interview, Abdullahi, London, 29 July 1995.

120 Interview, Roda, London, 25 May 1995.

121 Interview, Saida, London, 14 July 1995.

122 Interview, Anab, London, 18 May 1995.

123 Differences lie in how overt racism is and how it manifests itself. See the discussion below in this chapter.

124 *The Globe and Mail*, 14 Nov. 1996, A10.

125 M. Louise Pirouet, 'The Rights of Refugees in the United Kingdom,' in Institute of Commonwealth Studies, *Multiculturalism and the State*, vol. I, 1–2.

126 Pye, *Aspects of Political Development*, 105.

127 Bhikhu Parekh, 'Hannah Arendt,' in Parekh, *Contemporary Political Thinkers*, 12–13. Also Parekh, *Hannah Arendt and the Search for a New Political Philosophy*, 131–7.

128 Ibid., 134.

129 Parekh, *Colour, Culture and Consciousness*, 230–1.

130 *Dishonoured Legacy: The Lessons of the Somalia Affair* (Ottawa: Minister of Public Works and Government Services Canada, 1997), executive summary, 1.

131 *Globe and Mail*, 3 July 1997, A4.

132 Discussions about racism in Ontario, for instance, involve relatively subtle questions such as the discretionary decisions routinely made by police, prosecutors, and judges: 'Black Community Gets Data to Back Up Racism Complaints: Study Finds Ontario Justice System Riddled with Prejudice,' *Globe and Mail*, 17 Jan. 1996, A5. Racism in Britain is documented by books such as Satnam's *Racial Violence and Harassment* (London: Policy Studies Institute, 1995) and Commission for Racial Equality, *Living in Terror*.

133 See, for instance, Philip, *Frontiers*, 12.

134 For further works on racism in Canada, see: Bolaria and Li, *Racial Oppression in Canada*; Pizanias and Frideres, *Freedom within the Margins: The Politics of Exclusion*; Ruggles and Rovinescu, *Outsider Blues*; and Berdichewsky, *Racism, Ethnicity and Multiculturalism*.

135 See Commission on British Muslims and Islamophobia, *Islamophobia*, 5. One of the characteristics of a 'closed' view of Islam is the assumption that 'anti-Muslim hostility [is] accepted as natural and "normal."'

136 See, for instance, Eickelman and Piscatori, *Muslim Politics*, 81–2.

137 Arendt, *The Human Condition*.

138 Eickelman and Piscatori, *Muslim Politics*, 81–9.

139 Akhtar, *The Muslim Parents Handbook*, 33.

140 Interview, Hibaq, London, 19 May 1995.

141 Interview, Abdullahi, London, 29 July 1995.

142 Interview, Faduma, London, 21 May 1995.

143 The United Nations Habitat II conference in June 1996 recognized Toronto's efforts at integrating Somali immigrants with a 'Best Practices' Award of Excellence on the grounds that racial tolerance is a crucial element of development worldwide. '"Best Practices": Canada: "I'm Working for My Son's Future,"' *Turkish Daily News*, 4 June 1996, A8.

Chapter Seven: Integration

1 Although assimilation is no longer broadly used as an explanation for the integration process, its assumptions are still widely adhered to, as Shaheen Azmi maintains in 'Canadian Social Service Provision and the Muslim Community in Metropolitan Toronto.'

2 'Cajun' is the name given to the originally French population of Louisiana. The word 'Cajun' is derived from 'acadien.' The Cajuns were forcibly removed from Nova Scotia (Acadia) to the French-owned region in 1755 because they would not swear allegiance to the British crown.

3 Geertz, *The Interpretation of Cultures* 259.

4 See discussion and definition of racism, chapter 1, especially of Miles, in his *Racism after 'Race Relations'*. Also Parekh, *Colour, Culture and Consciousness*, 220–43.

5 Commission on British Muslims and Islamophobia, *Islamophobia*. The commission did not coin the term 'Islamophobia,' which it says was first used in an American periodical article in 1991 and had since been adopted by members of the American and British Muslim communities.

6 Ibid., 4–5.

7 See, for instance: Nielsen, *Muslims in Western Europe*; Bernard Lewis and Schnapper, eds., *Muslims in Europe*; Abedin and Sardar, *Muslim Minorities in the West*; Vertovec and Peach, eds., *Islam in Europe*; Enoch, 'The Intolerance of a Tolerant People'; Gerholm and Lithman, *The New Islamic Presence in Western Europe*; Islamic Council of Europe, *Muslim Communities in Non-Muslim States*; Nielsen, *Religion and Citizenship in Europe and the Arab World*; Peach and Glebe, 'Muslim Minorities in Western Europe'; Shadid, 'The Integration of Muslim Minorities in the Netherlands'; Shadid and Van Koningsveld, *Religious Freedom and the Position of Islam in Western Europe*.

8 Friedrich Heckmann, 'Nation, Nation-state and Policy towards Ethnic Minorities,' in Lewis and Schnapper, eds., *Muslims in Europe*, 116–29.

9 Kepel, *Les banlieues de l'Islam*, 381; the translation is my own.

10 Kepel, *À l'ouest d'Allah*, 272.

11 In addition to the books on Muslims in Europe mentioned above, among the many works available on British Muslims are the following: Philip Lewis, *Islamic Britain*; Raza, *Muslims in Britain*; Barton, *The Bengali Muslims of Bradford*; Halliday, *Arabs in Exile*; Pnina Werbner, 'Diaspora and Millennium: British Pakistani Global–Local Fabulations of the Gulf War,' in Ahmed and Donnan, eds., *Islam, Globalization and Postmodernity*, 213–36; and Scantlebury, 'Muslims in Manchester.' See also books on the Rushdie affair, as cited above in chapter 5, and Modood, *Not Easy Being British*.

12 Ironically, though it was largely ignored in the ruckus, *The Satanic Verses* was concerned precisely with the predicament facing migrant South Asian Muslims in Britain, but Rushdie is not the only author to have addressed the theme. Hanif Kureishi has explored the territory in film (*My Beautiful Launderette*, screenplay published) and in fiction, with *The Black Album*.

13 On Muslims in North America, see, for instance: Haddad and Smith, eds., *Muslim Communities in North America*; Waugh, Abu-Laban, and Qureshi, eds., *The Muslim Community in North America*; McCloud, *African American Islam*; and Lee, *The Nation of Islam*.

14 Kepel, *À l'ouest d'Allah*, 272.

15 See, for instance, Piscatori, *Islam in a World of Nation-States*, 105–6; also

Yvonne Y. Haddad, 'Sayyid Qutb: Ideologue of Islamic Revival,' in
Esposito, ed., *Voices of Resurgent Islam*, 67–98; Charles Tripp, 'Sayyid Qutb:
The Political Vision,' in Rahnema, ed., *Pioneers of Islamic Revival*, 154–80.

16 Pipes, '"The World is Political!!,"' 41.
17 *Week in Review,* Sunday, 21 Jan. 1996, section 4, 1.
18 *Foreign Affairs* (summer 1993), 22–49.
19 Ibid., 30.
20 Ibid., 40.
21 Cited in Hourani, *Islam in European Thought*, 11.
22 Friedrich Schliermacher, *The Christian Faith* (Edinburgh, 1928), 37, cited in
ibid., 24.
23 Ernst Renan, 'L'islamisme et la science,' in *Oeuvres complètes*, vol. I (Paris,
1942), 946, cited in Hourani, *Islam in European Thought*, 30.
24 John Esposito lists a number of headlines in Europe and America that further illustrate the diversity and frequency of these stories. Included among
them are: 'Don't Look for Moderates in the Islamist Revolution,' *International Herald Tribune*, 4 Jan. 1995; 'Focus: Islamic Terror: Global Suicide
Squad,' *Sunday Telegraph*, 1 Jan. 1995; 'France Back on the Rack: As Algeria's Rage Targets Its Tormented Former Oppressor the Rest of Europe
Could Be in Its Sights,' *Guardian*, 28 Dec. 1994; and 'A Holy War Heads Our
Way,' *Reader's Digest*, Jan. 1995. These are cited in Esposito, *Islamic Threat:
Myth or Reality*, 2nd ed. (Oxford: Oxford University Press, 1995), 194–5. See
also the discussion on media portrayal of Islam and Muslims in Commission on British Muslims and Islamophobia, *Islamophobia*.
25 *Globe and Mail*, 29 April 1994, D1.
26 See also Said's *Covering Islam*.
27 Journalists, and media sociologists, debate constantly over the ability of the
media to present arguments objectively. While objectivity is understood to
be an elusive ideal, it is generally accepted that there are certain techniques
that conscientious journalists should undertake in order to approach the
ideal as much as possible. Prime among these is independent verification of
charges or claims made by sources, since it is understood that to quote
sources without checking the veracity of their statements is to grant them a
credibility they may not merit. Merely finding an opposing source to dis-
credit the statement of the first is not considered independent verification.
28 Halliday, *Islam and the Myth of Confrontation*, 147–8.
29 Ibid. See especially chapter 6, 'Anti-Muslimism and Contemporary Politics:
One Ideology or Many?'
30 Ibid., 164–5.
31 See Pipes, *The Rushdie Affair*, 214–23.

32 Imtiyaz Yusuf, 'Hijrah,' in Esposito, ed., *The Oxford Encyclopedia*, vol. II, 111–12.
33 'Muslim Populations under Non-Muslim Rule,' in Lewis and Schnapper, eds., *Muslims in Europe*, 12.
34 Ibid., 17.
35 Muhammad Khalid Masud, 'The Obligation to Migrate: The Doctrine of *Hijra* in Islamic Law,' in Eickelman and Piscatori, eds., *Muslim Travellers*, 40.
36 Ibid., 42.
37 Ibid., 43.
38 Shadid and Van Koningsveld, *The Integration of Islam and Hinduism in Western Europe*, 229.
39 Ibrahim Sheikh Mohamed, Nur Ul-Islam, interview, London, 20 July 20 1995.
40 See Daniel Pipes, for instance. 'As Muslim critics are the first to admit, their coreligionists fare poorly almost without regard to the index one chooses. Whether one considers material well-being, social equity, military power, public hygiene or cultural originality, Muslims have done badly compared to others. While this array of problems is obviously too complex to be cured by a single solution, it is also clear that the severe limitations on personal freedom under which most Muslim peoples toil has crucial importance.' *The Rushdie Affair*, 248. For Pipes, progress for Muslim countries, and successful integration into the West, comes at a price: 'This means, for instance, no pressure on the government to pay for Muslim schools, no attempts to get Islamic law accepted in courts, and no extension of blasphemy laws to cover Islamic topics. To integrate into the West, Muslims need not forego their faith, but they must accept the supremacy of civil law – and freedom of speech is a critical element of that law' (247). It was not only Western observers who analysed the affair this way. In an example of what Halliday means when he writes that Islamists often use the language of confrontation to make their own points, Kalim Siddiqui, director of the Muslim Institute in London, begins *The Implications of the Rushdie Affair for Muslims in Britain* with the following sentence: 'The Rushdie affair may well go down in history as the issue that finally brought the Western civilization and the civilization of Islam into a head-on global confrontation.'
41 For an analysis that separates the apparent from the pith in this affair of high sentiment and political confusion, see Piscatori's 'The Rushdie Affair and the Politics of Ambiguity.'
42 Some writers were driven to zealous condemnation of Islam over their defence of Rushdie. Doris Lessing, for instance, called Islam in Britain an 'incomprehensible, alien force.' See 'On Salman Rushdie: A Communica-

tion,' *Partisan Review* 56 no. 3 (summer 1989), 407–8, cited in ibid., 779. Many writers who wrote in Rushdie's defence, however, were Muslim themselves. See Abdallah et al., *For Rushdie: Essays by Arab and Muslim Writers in Defense of Free Speech.*

Other writers were equally zealous in their condemnation of Rushdie. Germaine Greer, for example, called Rushdie 'a megalomaniac'; John Le Carré declared that Rushdie, in refusing to withdraw the book, 'has nothing more to prove except his own insensitivity.' See Halliday, 'The Fundamental Lesson of the Fatwa,' 16.

43 Michael Gilsenan has defined Islam as 'a word that identifies varying relations of practice, representation, symbol, concept, and worldview within the same society and between different societies. There are patterns in these relations, and they have changed in very important ways over time.' *Recognizing Islam*, 19.

44 Interview, Kalima, Toronto, 4 July 1995.

45 Eickelman and Piscatori, *Muslim Politics*, 38.

46 Ibid.

47 Ibid., 68–79 and 131–5.

48 Ibid., 72.

49 Ibid., 71.

50 Ibid., 28–9.

51 Interview, Deeqa, Toronto, 24 March 1995.

Conclusion: Transformative Islam

1 Eickelman and Piscatori, *Muslim Politics*, chap. 6 and elsewhere.

2 Metcalf, ed., *Making Muslim Space in North America and Europe.*

3 Vernon James Schubel, 'Karbala as Sacred Space,' in ibid., 186–203.

4 Werbner, 'Stamping the Earth with the Name of Allah.'

References

Abdalla, Raqiya Haji Dualeh. *Sisters in Affliction: Circumcision and Infibulation of Women in Africa*. London: Zed Books, 1982.

Abdallah, Anouar, et al. *For Rushdie: Essays by Arab and Muslim Writers in Defense of Free Speech*. New York: George Braziller, 1994.

Abdullahi, Abdurahman. 'Tribalism, Nationalism and Islam: The Crisis of Political Loyalty in Somalia.' MA thesis, McGill University, 1992.

Abedin, Syed Z. 'The *Ummah* and the Predicament of Muslim Minorities.' *Islamic Culture* 64 no. 4 (Oct. 1990), 1–27.

Abedin, Syed, and Sardar, Ziauddin. *Muslim Minorities in the West*. London: Grey Seal Books, 1995.

Abella, Irving, and Troper, Harold. *None Is Too Many*. Toronto: Lester & Orpen Dennys, 1982.

Abu-Sahlieh, Sami A. Aldeeb. 'The Islamic Conception of Migration.' *International Migration Review* 30 no. 1 (spring 1996), 37–57.

Adam, Hussein M. 'Islam and Politics in Somalia.' *Journal of Islamic Studies* 6 no. 2 (July 1995), 189–221.

Adam, Hussein M., and Ford, Richard, eds. *Mending Rips in the Sky: Options for Somali Communities in the Twenty-first Century*. Lawrenceville, NJ: Red Sea Press, 1997.

Afkhami, Mahnaz, ed. *Faith and Freedom: Women's Human Rights in the Muslim World*. London: I.B. Tauris, 1995.

Afrah, M.M. *The Somali Tragedy*. Mombasa: Mohamed Printers, 1994.

Africa Watch. *Somalia: A Government at War with Its Own People: Testimonies about the Killings and the Conflict in the North*. London: Africa Watch, 1990.

African Rights. *The Nightmare Continues ... Abuses against Somali Refugees in Kenya*. London: African Rights, 1993.

Ahmed, Ali Jimale. *Daybreak Is Near: Literature, Clans and the Nation-State in Somalia*. Lawrenceville, NJ: Red Sea Press, 1996.

– ed. *The Invention of Somalia*. Lawrenceville, NJ: Red Sea Press, 1995.

Ahmed, Akbar S., and Hart, David M. *Islam in Tribal Societies: From the Atlas to the Indies*. London and Boston: Routledge & Kegan Paul, 1984.

Ahmed, Akbar S., and Donnan, Hastings, eds. *Islam, Globalization and Postmodernity*. London and New York: Routledge, 1994.

Ahmed, Leila. *Women and Gender in Islam: Historical Roots of a Modern Debate*. New Haven, Conn.: Yale University Press, 1992.

Ahmed, Christine Choi. 'God, Anti-Colonialism and Drums: Sheikh Uways and the Uwaysiyya.' *Ufuhamu* (Journal of the African Activist Association, University of California) 17 no. 11 (spring 1989), 96–117.

Ajami, Fouad. 'In Europe's Shadows: The Tragedy of Bosnia, and the Long, Troubled History of Islam in the Balkans.' *New Republic*, 21 Nov. 1994, 29–37.

Akhtar, Shabbir. *Be Careful with Muhammad! The Salman Rushdie Affair*. London: Bellew Publishing, 1989.

– *The Muslim Parents Handbook*. London: Ta-Ha Publishers, 1993.

Ali, Ibrahim. *The Origin and History of the Somali People*. Cardiff: Ibrahim Ali, 1993.

Alladin, Ibrahim. *Multiculturalism in the 1990s: Policies, Practices and Implications*. Edmonton: EISA Publishers, 1993.

Allen, Tim, ed. *In Search of Cool Ground: Flight and Homecoming in Northeast Africa*. Trenton, NJ: Africa World Press, 1996.

Almond, Gabriel, and Powell, G. Bingham., Jr. *Comparative Politics: A Developmental Approach*. Boston: Little, Brown & Co., 1966.

Almond, Gabriel, and Verba, Sidney. *The Civic Culture: Political Attitudes and Democracy in Five Nations*. Boston: Little, Brown & Co., 1965.

Almond, Gabriel. 'Comparative Political Systems.' *Journal of Politics* 18 (1956), 391–409.

Alund, Aleksandra, and Schierup, Carl-Ulrik. *Paradoxes of Multiculturalism*. Aldershot: Avebury, 1991.

al-Uthaimin, Shaikh Muhammad al-Saleh. *Muslim's Belief [Aqidat Ahl al-Sunna wa'l Jama'a]*. Trans. Dr Maneh Hammad al-Johani. Medina: Islamic University.

Aman. *Aman: The Story of a Somali Girl*. Toronto: Knopf Canada, 1994.

Anderson, Benedict. *Imagined Communities*. London: Verso, 1983.

Andrzejewski, B.W. *Islamic Literature of Somalia*. Bloomington: Indiana University, 1983.

Anwar, Muhammad. *Race and Politics*. London: Tavistock Publications, 1986.

– *Young Muslims in a Multi-Cultural Society*. London: Islamic Foundation, 1982.

Appadurai, Arjun, and Breckenridge, Carol. 'Why Public Culture?' *Public Culture Bulletin* 1 no. 1 (fall 1988), 5–9.

Appiah, Anthony. '"But Would That Still Be Me?" Notes on Gender, "Race," Ethnicity, as Sources of "Identity."' *Journal of Philosophy* 87 no. 10 (Oct. 1990), 493–9.

Appignanesi, Lisa, and Maitland, Sara, eds. *The Rushdie File*. London: Fourth Estate, 1989.

Aqli, Abdirisaq. 'Historical Development of Islamic Movements in the Horn of Africa.' Paper presented to the First Conference of the European Association of Somali Studies, London, 1993.

Arendt, Hannah. *The Human Condition*. Chicago: University of Chicago Press, 1958.

Askar, Ahmed Omar. *Sharks and Soldiers*. Jarvenpaa, Finland: Ahmed Omar Askar, 1992.

Association of Metropolitan Authorities. *A Strategy for Housing Refugees*. London: Association of Metropolitan Authorities, 1991.

Azmi, Shaheen. 'Canadian Social Service Provision and the Muslim Community in Metropolitan Toronto.' *Journal of Muslim Minority Affairs* 17 no. 1 (April 1997), 153–66.

Back, Les, and Nayak, Anoop. *Invisible Europeans? Black People in the New Europe*. Birmingham: AFFOR, 1993.

Ballard, Roger, ed. *Desh Pardesh: South Asian Settlers in Britain*. London: C. Hurst & Co., 1992.

Banton, Michael. *Race Relations*. London: Tavistock, 1967.

– *Racial and Ethnic Competition*. Cambridge: Cambridge University Press, 1983.

Barth, Frederic. *Ethnic Groups and Boundaries*. Boston: Little, Brown & Co., 1969.

Barton, Stephen William. *The Bengali Muslims of Bradford*. Leeds: University of Leeds, 1986.

Bedford, Carmel. *Fiction, Fact and the Fatwa: 2,000 Days of Censorship*. London: Article 19, 1994.

Bell, David. *The Roots of Disunity: A Study of Canadian Political Culture*. Rev. ed. Toronto: Oxford University Press, 1992.

Ben-Rafael, Eliezer. *The Emergence of Ethnicity: Cultural Groups and Social Conflict in Israel*. Westport, Conn.: Greenwood Press, 1982.

Ben-Rafael, Eliezer, and Sharot, Stephen. *Ethnicity, Religion and Class in Israeli Society*. Cambridge: Cambridge University Press, 1991.

Ben-Tovim, G., Gabriel, J., Law, I., and Stredder, K. *The Local Politics of Race*. London: MacMillan, 1986.

Bentley, G. Carter. 'Ethnicity and Practice.' *Comparative Studies in Sociology and History* 29 (1987), 24–55.

Berdichewsky, Bernardo. *Racism, Ethnicity and Multiculturalism*. Vancouver: Future Publications, 1994.

Berlin, Myrna, et al. 'The Story of Kipling.' Toronto: Kipling Collegiate Institute, 1994.

Bernstein, Richard. *Dictatorship of Virtue*. New York: Alfred A. Knopf, 1994.

Berrington, Ann. 'Marriage and Family Formation among the White and Ethnic Minority Populations in Britain.' *Ethnic and Racial Studies* 17 no. 3 (July 1994), 517–43.

Bhabha, Jacqueline, and Shutter, Sue. *Women's Movements: Women Under Immigration, Nationality and Refugee Law*. London: Trentham Books, 1994.

Bhat, Ashok, Carr-Hill, R., and Ohri, S. *Britain's Black Population*. Aldershot: Gower Publishing, 1988.

Bibby, Reginald W. *Mosaic Madness*. Toronto: Stoddart, 1990.

Bissoondath, Neil. *Selling Illusions: The Cult of Multiculturalism in Canada*. Toronto: Penguin Books, 1994.

Black, C.E. *The Dynamics of Modernization: A Study in Comparative History*. New York: Harper & Row, 1966.

Boddy, Janice. 'Womb as Oasis: The Symbolic Context of Pharaonic Circumcision in Northern Sudan.' *American Ethnologist* 9 no. 4 (Nov. 1982), 682–98.

Bolaria, B. Singh, and Li, Peter S. *Racial Oppression in Canada*. Toronto: Garamond Press, 1988.

Bottomley, Gillian. *From Another Place*. Cambridge: Cambridge University Press, 1992.

Bourne, Bill, Eichler, Udi, and Herman, D, eds. *Writers and Politics: Voices from the Channel 4 Television Series*. Nottingham: Spokesman, 1987.

Brass, Paul. *Ethnic Groups and the State*. London: Croom Helm, 1985.

Bratt, James D. 'God, Tribe, and Nation: Ethno-Religious History at Middle Age.' *Comparative Studies in Sociology and Religion* 33 (Jan. 1991), 176–86.

Breton, R., Isajiw, W., Kalbach, W., and Reitz, J. *Ethnic Identity and Equality: Varieties of Experience in a Canadian City*. Toronto: University of Toronto Press, 1990.

Burgess, Sue, and Loeb, Deborah. *Promoting Health and Well-Being: Report on a Pilot Project in Tower Hamlets*. London: Tower Hamlets Well-Being Project, 1994.

Burton, Richard F. *First Footsteps in East Africa*. New York: Dover Publications, 1987.

Carey-Wood, Jenny, Duke, Karen, Karn, Valerie, and Marshall, Tony. *The Settlement of Refugees in Britain*. Home Office Research Study No. 141. London, 1995.

– *The Shaping of Somali Society: Reconstructing the History of a Pastoral People*. Philadelphia: University of Pennsylvania Press, 1982.

Cassanelli, Lee. 'History and Identity Among Somali Refugees: A Recent

Example from Coastal Kenya.' Revised version of a paper presented to the Folklore Seminar, University of Pennsylvania, Jan. 1994.

– 'Oversimplifying the "Lessons" of American Intervention.' Unpublished paper, University of Pennsylvania, Philadelphia.

– 'The Role of Somali Diaspora Communities in Homeland Politics.' Revised version of a paper presented to the Workshop on Ethnic Group Conflict, Woodrow Wilson International Center for Scholars, Washington, DC, 1994.

– *Victims and Vulnerable Groups in Southern Somalia.* Occasional paper. Ottawa: Immigration and Refugee Board, 1995.

Castles, Stephen. 'How Nation-States Respond to Immigration and Ethnic Diversity.' *New Community* 21 no. 3 (July 1995), 293–308.

CBC Newsworld. 'Should Government Fund Religious Schools?' *On the Line.* Videotaped program. Toronto: Canadian Broadcasting Corporation, 25 Feb. 1995.

CBC Television. 'A Place Called Dixon.' *CBC Prime Time News*, 24 Aug. 1994. Transcript. Toronto: Canadian Broadcasting Corporation, 1994.

Centre for the Study of Islam and Muslim–Christian Relations. *British Muslims Monthly Survey.* Birmingham: Selly Oak Colleges, multiple volumes.

– *The Rushdie Affair: A Documentation.* Research Papers, Muslims in Europe, No. 42. Birmingham: Selly Oak Colleges, 1989.

Cesari, Jocelyne. *Être Musulman en France.* Paris: Éditions Karthala et Ireman, 1994.

Chong, Denise. *The Concubine's Children.* Toronto: Penguin Books, 1995.

Church, Jenny, and Summerfield, Carol, eds. *Social Focus on Ethnic Minorities.* London: Office for National Statistics, 1996.

Codka Jaaliyadda (Community Voice). Monthly Newsletter of the Somali Islamic Society of Canada. Toronto: SISCA, multiple volumes.

Cohen, Philip, and Bains, Harwant, eds., *Multi-Racist Britain.* London: Macmillan, 1988.

Commission for Racial Equality (CRE). *Living in Terror: A Report on Racial Violence and Harassment in Housing.* London: CRE, 1987.

Commission on British Muslims and Islamophobia. *Islamophobia: A Challenge for Us All.* London: Runnymede Trust, 1997.

Connor, Walker. 'Beyond Reason: The Nature of the Ethnonational Bond.' *Ethnic and Racial Studies* 16 no. 3 (July 1993), 373–89.

Craig, Gerald M. *Upper Canada: The Formative Years.* Toronto: McClelland & Stewart, 1965.

Crown Prince El Hassan Bin Talal of the Hashemite Kingdom of Jordan. *The Europe of Religions.* Address to an International Conference organized by the Institute for Human Sciences. Vienna, Nov. 1994.

Davies, Alan, ed. *Antisemitism in Canada*. Waterloo: Wilfrid Laurier University Press, 1992.

Dench, Geoff. *Fighting with Numbers: Strategies of Somali Refugees in East London*. London: Centre for Community Studies, 1993.

– *Minorities in the Open Society: Prisoners of Ambivalence*. London: Routledge & Kegan Paul, 1986.

Dennis, Ferdinand. *Behind the Frontlines: Journey into Afro-Britain*. London: Victor Gollancz Ltd., 1988.

Deutsch, Karl W. *Nationalism and Social Communication*. Cambridge, Mass.: The MIT Press, 1953.

Diawara, Manthia. 'Black British Cinema: Spectatorship and Identity Formation in "Territories."' *Public Culture* 3 no. 1 (fall 1990), 33–47.

Doi, 'Abdul Rahman I. *Woman in Shari'ah*. London: Ta-Ha Publishers, 1989.

Donner, Fred. *The Early Islamic Conquests*. Princeton, NJ: Princeton University Press, 1981.

Dorkenoo, Efua. *Cutting the Rose. Female Genital Mutilation, the Practice and Its Prevention*. London: Minority Rights Publication, 1994.

Drysdale, John. *Whatever Happened to Somalia?* London: Haan Associates, 1994.

Duke, Karen. 'The Resettlement Experiences of Refugees in the UK: Main Findings from an Interview Study." *New Community* 22 no. 3 (July 1996), 461–78.

Dwyer, Claire, and Meyer, Astrid. 'The Institutionalism of Islam in the Netherlands and in the UK: The case of Islamic Schools.' *New Community* 21 no. 1 (Jan. 1995), 37–54.

Edmundson, Mark. 'Prophet of a New Postmodernism: The Greater Challenge of Salman Rushdie.' *Harper's Magazine* (Dec. 1989), 62–71.

Eickelman, Dale, and Piscatori, James. *Muslim Politics*. Princeton, NJ: Princeton University Press, 1996.

– *Muslim Travellers: Pilgrimage, Migration, and the Religious Imagination*. London: Routledge, 1990.

El Dareer, Asma. *Woman, Why Do You Weep? Circumcision and Its Consequences*. London: Zed Books, 1982.

Elmi, Abdullahi Sheikh. 'Khat: History, Spreading and Problems in Somalia.' *Proceedings of the Second International Congress of Somali Studies*. Vol. IV, 271–83. Hamburg, Aug. 1993.

El-Solh, Camillia Fawzi. '"Be True to Your Culture": Gender Tensions among Somali Muslims in Britain.' *Immigrants and Minorities* 12 no. 1 (March 1993), 21–46.

– 'Somalis in London's East End: A Community Striving for Recognition.' *New Community* 17 no. 4 (July 1991), 539–52.

El-Solh, Camillia Fawzi, and Mabro, Judy, eds. *Muslim Women's Choices: Religious Belief and Social Reality.* Oxford: Berg Publishers, 1994.

Eldridge, J.E.T. ed. *Max Weber: The Interpretation of Social Reality.* London: Thomas Nelson & Sons, 1971.

Enew, Judith, and Milne, B. *The Next Generation: Lives of Third World Children.* London: Zed Books, 1989.

Engineer, Ashghar Ali. *The Rights of Women in Islam.* New York: St Martin's Press, 1992.

Eno, Omar. 'The Historical Roots of the Somali Tragedy and the Vulnerable Minority Groups, Particularly the Bantu/Jarer." Paper presented to the African Studies Association, Orlando, Fla., Nov. 1995.

– 'Suggestions for Conflict Resolution in Somalia: Minority Rights.' Paper presented to the Post-Convention Symposium for the Fifth Congress for Somali Studies, Boston, June 1995.

– 'The Untold Apartheid in Somalia Imposed on Bantu/Jareer People.' Paper presented to the Fifth Congress for Somali Studies, Boston, Nov. 1993.

Enoch, Yael. 'The Intolerance of a Tolerant People: Ethnic Relations in Denmark.' *Ethnic and Racial Studies* 17 no. 2 (April 1994), 282–300.

Esposito, John. *Islam and Politics*, 3rd ed. Syracuse: Syracuse University Press, 1991.

– *Islam: The Straight Path.* Oxford and New York: Oxford University Press, 1988.

– *The Islamic Threat: Myth or Reality?* Rev. ed. Oxford: Oxford University Press, 1995.

– ed. *The Oxford Encylopedia of the Modern Islamic World.* 4 vols. Oxford: Oxford University Press, 1995.

– ed. *Voices of Resurgent Islam.* London and New York: Oxford University Press, 1983.

Ferguson, Marjorie. 'Invisible Divides: Communication and Identity in Canada and the U.S.' *Journal of Communication* 43 no. 2 (spring 1993), 42–57.

Foley, Conor, and Shutter, Sue. *The Last Resort: Violations of the Human Rights of Migrants, Refugees and Asylum Seekers.* London: National Council for Civil Liberties, 1995.

Foundation for Women's Health Research and Development (FORWARD). *Report on the First National Conference on Female Genital Mutilation: Unsettled Issues for Health and Social Workers in the U.K.* London: FORWARD, 1989.

Friesen, John W. *When Cultures Clash*, 2nd ed. Calgary: University of Calgary, 1993.

Furnivall, J.S. *Colonial Policy and Practice.* New York: New York University Press, 1956.

Gabobe, Jamal. *Love and Memory.* Seattle: Cune Publishing, 1997.

Gallo, Pia Grassivaro. *La circoncisione femminile in somalia*. Milan: Franco Angeli, 1986.

Gallo, Pia Crassivaro, and Abdisamed, Marian. 'Female Circumcision in Somalia: Anthropological Traits.' *Anthropoligisher Anzeiger* 43 no. 4 (Dec. 1985), 311–26.

Garnham, Nicholas. 'The Mass Media, Cultural Identity, and the Public Sphere in the Modern World.' *Public Culture* 5 (1993), 251–65.

Gassem, Mariam Arif. *Hostages*. Nairobi: Central Graphics Services, 1994.

Gebresellasie, Yohannes. 'Canada's Response to Black African Immigrants.' *Refuge* 13 no. 1 (1993), 2–5.

Geertz, Clifford. *The Interpretation of Cultures*. New York: Fontana Press, 1993.

Gellner, Ernest. *Postmodernism, Reason and Religion*. London: Routledge, 1992.

George Orwell School. *Induction Programme: George Orwell School*. Narration script for introductory lecture to new parents. London: George Orwell School, Islington, 1995.

Gerholm, Tomas, and Lithman, Yngve Georg. *The New Islamic Presence in Western Europe*. London: Mansell Publishing Ltd, 1988.

Gilad, Lisa. *The Northern Route*. St John's, Nfld: Memorial University, 1990.

Gilroy, Paul. *The Empire Strikes Back*. London: Hutchinson & Co., 1982.

– *Small Acts*. London: Serpent's Tail, 1993.

– *There Ain't No Black in the Union Jack*. London: Hutchinson & Co., 1987.

Gilsenan, Michael. *Recognizing Islam: Religion and Society in the Modern Arab World*. New York: Pantheon Books, 1982.

Glazer, Nathan, and Moynihan, Daniel Patrick. *Beyond the Melting Pot: The Negroes, Puerto Ricans, Jews, Italians, and Irish of New York*. Cambridge, Mass.: MIT Press and Harvard University Press, 1963.

– eds. *Ethnicity: Theory and Experience*. Cambridge, Mass.: Harvard University Press, 1975.

Gordon, Paul. *Citizenship for Some? Race and Government Policy 1979–1989*. London: Runnymede Trust, 1989.

Gordon, Milton M. *Assimilation in American Life*. Oxford: Oxford University Press, 1964.

Goulbourne, Harry. 'Varieties of Pluralism: The Notion of a Pluralist Post-Imperial Britain.' *New Community* 17 no. 2 (Jan. 1991), 211–27.

Goulbourne, Harry. *Black Politics in Britain*. Aldershot: Avebury, 1990.

Gozlan, Martine. *L'Islam et la Republique: Des Musulmans de France contre l'inté-grisme*. Paris: Belfond, 1994.

Greaves, R.A. 'The Reproduction of Jamaat-i Islami in Britain.' *Islam and Christian–Muslim Relations* 6 no. 2 (Dec. 1995), 187–210.

Greeley, Andrew. 'The Rediscovery of Diversity.' *Antioch Review* (fall 1972), 130–3.

Greenhalgh, Trisha, and Taylor, Rod. 'Papers That Go beyond Numbers (Qualitative Research).' *British Medical Journal* (Oct. 1997), 740–3.

Gundara, Jagdish S., and Duffield, Ian, eds. *Essays on the History of Blacks in Britain*. Aldershot: Avebury, 1992.

Haddad, Yvonne Hazbeck, and Smith, Jane Idleman. *Muslim Communities in North America*. Albany: State University of New York, 1994.

Haddad, Yvonne Yazbeck. 'Islamist Depictions of Christianity in the Twentieth Century: The Pluralism Debate and the Depiction of the Other.' *Islam and Christian–Muslim Relations* 7 no. 1 (1996), 75–93.

Hal-Abuur. Journal of Somali Literature and Culture. Periodical. London: multiple volumes.

Hale, Sondra. 'A Question of Subjects: The "Female Circumcision" Controversy and the Politics of Knowledge.' *Ufahamu* 22 no. 3 (1994), 26–35.

Halliday, Fred. *Arabs in Exile: Yemeni Migrants in Urban Britain*. London: I.B. Tauris, 1992.

– *Islam and the Myth of Confrontation*. London: I.B. Tauris, 1995.

– 'The Fundamental Lesson of the Fatwa.' *New Statesman and Society* 6 no. 239, 12 Feb. 1993, 16–20.

Hammond, Phillip. 'Religion and the Persistence of Identity.' *Journal for the Scientific Study of Religion* 27 no. 1 (1988), 1–11.

Hanley, Gerald. *Warriors*. London: Eland, 1971.

Harris, Kenneth. Home Office Newham Drugs Prevention Team. *Khat (Qat, Chat)*. Information Sheet. London: Institute for the Study of Drug Dependence, 1994.

Harris, Kim. 'Our Daughters' Pain.' *Rough Cuts*. Television documentary. CBC Newsworld, Toronto, 1 April 1995.

Harrow, Kenneth. *Faces of Islam in African Literature*. London: James Currey Ltd, 1991.

Hartz, Louis. *The Founding of New Societies*. New York: Harcourt, Brace & World, Inc., 1964.

Healthy Islington. *Islington Somali Community Survey Report*. London: Healthy Islington, 1993.

Hersi, Ali Abdirahman. 'The Arab Factor in Somali History: The Origins and the Development of Arab Enterprise and Cultural Influences in the Somali Peninsula.' PhD thesis, University of California, Los Angeles, 1977.

Hewitt, Ibrahim B. *What Does Islam Say About ... ?* London: Muslim Educational Trust, 1993.

Hicks, Esther, K. *Infibulation: Female Mutilation in Islamic Northeastern Africa*. New Brunswick, NJ: Transaction Publishers, 1993.

Hiro, Dilip. *Black British, White British*. London: Grafton Books, 1991.

Hiskett, Mervyn. *The Course of Islam in Africa*. Edinburgh: Edinburgh University Press, 1994.

Hofstader, Richard, and Lipset, Seymour Martin. *Turner and the Sociology of the Frontier*. New York: Basic Books Inc., 1968.

Holmes, Colin, ed. *Immigrants and Minorities in British Society*. London: George Allen & Unwin, 1978.

– *A Tolerant Country? Immigrants, Refugees and Minorities in Britain*. London: Faber & Faber, 1991.

Home Office. *Control of Immigration: Statistics, United Kingdom, 1993*. London: HMSO, 1994.

Horowitz, Gad. *Canadian Labour in Politics*. Toronto: University of Toronto Press, 1968.

Horton, John, ed. *Liberalism, Multiculturalism and Toleration*. London: Macmillan, 1993.

Hosken, Fran. *The Hosken Report: Genital and Sexual Mutilation of Females*. Lexington, Mass: Women's International Network News, 1979.

Hourani, Albert. *Islam in European Thought*. Cambridge: Cambridge University Press, 1991.

– *Western Attitudes towards Islam*. Southampton: University of Southampton, 1974.

House of Commons of Canada. Bill C-93: An Act for the Preservation and Enhancement of Multiculturalism in Canada. Ottawa: House of Commons, 1988.

Human Rights Watch, Africa. *Somalia Faces the Future: Human Rights in a Fragmented Society*. New York: Human Rights Watch, Africa, 1995.

Huntington, Samuel P., and Weiner, Myron, eds. *Understanding Political Development*. Boston: Little, Brown & Co., 1987.

Huntington, Samuel P. 'The Clash of Civilizations?' *Foreign Affairs* 72 no. 3 (summer 1993), 22–49.

Husaini, Zohra. *Muslims in the Canadian Mosaic*. Edmonton: Muslim Research Foundation, 1990.

Ibn Battuta. *Travels in Asia and Africa, 1325–1354*. Trans. and selected by H.A.R. Gibb. New Delhi: Saeed International, 1990.

Ibrahim, Ali Ahmed. 'Inter-Riverine Somalia: A Nomad Licensed to Kill.' Paper presented to the First Inter-Riverine Studies Convention, Toronto, Nov. 1994.

Ignatieff, Michael. *Blood and Belonging: Journeys into the New Nationalism*. Toronto: Penguin Books, 1994.

Institute of Commonwealth Studies. *Multiculturalism and the State*, Vol. I. London: University of London, 1994.

Internet Newsgroup. 'soc.culture.somalia.' June and July 1995.

Isajiw, W. Wsevelod. *Definitions of Ethnicity.* Toronto: Multicultural History Society of Ontario, 1979.

Islamic Council of Europe. *Muslim Communities in Non-Muslim States.* London: Islamic Council of Europe, 1980.

Ismail, Edna Adan. 'Female Circumcision.' *Proceedings of the Second International Congress of Somali Studies.* Vol. IV, 217–21. Hamburg, 1983.

Ismael, Tareq, and Ismael, Jacqueline, eds. *The Gulf War and the New World Order.* Gainesville: University Press of Florida, 1994.

Issa-Salwe, Abdisalam. *The Collapse of the Somali State: The Impact of the Colonial Legacy.* London: Haan Associates, 1994.

Jackson, Peter. *Race and 'Racism': Essays in Social Geography.* London: Allen & Unwin, 1987.

Jacobs, Brian D. *Racism in Britain.* London: Christopher Helm, 1988.

Joly, Daniele. *Britannia's Crescent: Making a Place for Muslims in British Society.* Aldershot: Avebury, 1995.

– *Ethnic Minorities and Education in Britain: Interaction between the Muslim Community and Birmingham Schools.* Birmingham: Centre for the Study of Islam and Christian–Muslim Relations, Selly Oak Colleges, 1989.

– *Haven or Hell? Asylum Policies and Refugees in Europe.* New York: St Martin's Press, 1996.

– *Refugees in Europe.* Nottingham: Russell Press Ltd, 1990.

Jones, Bill and Kavanagh, Dennis. *British Politics Today,* 5th ed. Manchester: Manchester University Press, 1994.

Jones, Trevor. *Britain's Ethnic Minorities.* London: Policy Studies Institute, 1993.

Journal of the Anglo–Somali Society. Periodical. London: Multiple volumes.

Kalix, Peter. 'Khat: A Plant with Amphetamine Effects.' *Journal of Substance Abuse Treatment* 5 (1988), 163–9.

Kallen, Evelyn. *Ethnicity and Human Rights in Canada,* 2nd ed. Toronto: Oxford University Press, 1995.

Kavanagh, Dennis. *British Politics: Continuities and Change.* 2nd ed. Oxford: Oxford University Press, 1990.

Kaye, Ronald. 'The Politics of Religious Slaughter of Animals: Strategies for Ethno-Religious Political Action.' *New Community* 19 no. 2 (Jan. 1993), 235–50.

Keddie, Nikki R. ed., *Scholars, Saints, and Sufis.* Berkeley: University of California Press, 1972.

Kedourie, Elie. *Nationalism.* London: Hutchinson University Library, 1960.

Kellerman, Maureen, ed. *Somalia: A Cultural Profile.* Ottawa: Catholic Immigration Centre, 1989.

Kepel, Gilles. *À l'ouest d'Allah.* Paris: Éditions de Seuil, 1994.

– *Les banlieues de l'Islam: naissance d'une religion en France*. Paris: Éditions de Seuil, 1987.

Khadduri, Majid. *War and Peace in the Law of Islam*. Baltimore: The Johns Hopkins Press, 1955.

King, Michael. *God's Law versus State Law: The Construction of an Islamic Identity in Western Europe*. London: Grey Seal Books, 1995.

Kopytoff, Igor. 'Public Culture: A Durkheimian Genealogy.' *Public Culture Bulletin* 1 no. 1 (fall 1988), 11–16.

Kose, Ali. 'Post-Conversion Experiences of Native British Converts to Islam.' *Islam and Christian–Muslim Relations* 5 no. 2 (1994), 195–206.

Koser, Khalid. 'European Migration Report.' *New Community* 22 no. 1 (Jan. 1996), 151–8.

Koso-Thomas, Olayinka. *The Circumcision of Women*. London: Zed Books, 1987.

Kriegel, Leonard. 'Writers and Ethnicity.' *Partisan Review* 54 (Winter 1987), 115–20.

Kureishi, Hanif. *The Black Album*. New York: Scribner, 1995.

– *The Buddha of Suburbia*. London: Faber & Faber, 1990.

– *My Beautiful Launderette and Others*. London: Faber & Faber, 1997.

Kutty, Faisal. 'Islamic Movements and the West: Coexistence or Confrontation?' *Muslim Voice* 2 no. 6 (March 1995), 1–2.

Kymlicka, Will. *Multicultural Citizenship*. Oxford: Oxford University Press, 1995.

Laitin, David D. *Politics, Language, and Thought: The Somali Experience*. Chicago: University of Chicago Press, 1977.

Laitin, David D., and Samatar, Said S. *Somalia: Nation in Search of a State*. Boulder, Col.: Westview, 1987.

Lamb, Claire. 'Female Excision: The Feminist Conundrum.' *Ufahamu* 20 no. 3 (1992), 13–31.

Lambert, Wallace, and Taylor, Donald. *Coping with Cultural and Racial Diversity in Urban America*. New York: Praeger, 1990.

Laurence, Margaret. *The Prophet's Camel Bell*. London: Macmillan & Co., 1963.

– collector and trans. *A Tree for Poverty: Somali Poetry and Prose*. Toronto: McClelland & Stewart, 1970.

Lawless, Richard. *From Ta'izz to Tyneside: An Arab Community in the North-East of England during the Early Twentieth Century*. Exeter: University of Exeter Press, 1995.

– 'Religion and Politics among Arab Seafarers in Britain in the Early Twentieth Century.' *Islam and Christian–Muslim Relations* 5 no. 1 (1994), 35–56.

Layton-Henry, Zig. *The Politics of Immigration*. Oxford: Blackwell, 1992.

Lee, Martha F. *The Nation of Islam: An American Millenarian Movement*. Syracuse, NY: Syracuse University Press, 1996.

Leveau, Remy, and Kepel, Gilles, eds. *Les Musulmans dans la societé française.* Paris: Presses de la fondation nationale des sciences politiques, 1988.

Lewis, Bernard. *Cultures in Conflict: Christians, Muslims, and Jews in the Age of Discovery.* New York: Oxford University Press, 1995.

Lewis, Bernard, and Schnapper, Dominique. *Muslims in Europe.* London: Pinter Publishers, 1994.

Lewis, I.M. *Blood and Bone: The Call of Kinship in Somali Society.* Lawrenceville, NJ: Red Sea Press, 1994.

– *Marriage and the Family in Northern Somaliland.* Kampala, Uganda: East African Institute of Social Research, 1962.

– *A Modern History of Somalia,* 3rd ed. Boulder, Col.: Westview Press, 1988.

– *A Pastoral Democracy.* Oxford: Oxford University Press, 1961.

– *Peoples of the Horn of Africa.* London: International African Institute, 1955.

– *Understanding Somalia.* London: Haan Associates, 1993.

Lewis, I.M., Mayall, James, et al. *A Study of Decentralised Political Structures for Somalia: A Menu of Options.* Report prepared by consultants from the London School of Economics and Political Science. London, 1995.

Lewis, Philip. 'Christian–Muslim Relations in a Cold Climate.' *Month,* 2nd series, 24 nos. 9 & 10 (Sept.–Oct. 1991), 405–11.

– *Islamic Britain: Religion, Politics and Identity among British Muslims.* London: I.B. Tauris, 1994.

Liebkind, Karmela, ed. *New Identities in Europe: Immigrant Ancestry and the Ethnic Identity of Youth.* London: Gower Publishing Company, 1989.

Lightfoot-Klein, Hanny. *Prisoners of Ritual: An Odyssey into Female Genital Circumcision in Africa.* New York: Harrington Park Press, 1989.

Lipset, S.M. *Continental Divide: The Values and Institutions of the United States and Canada.* Toronto and Washington, DC: Canadian–American Committee, 1989.

– *Revolution and Counter-Revolution.* New York: Basic Books, 1968.

Lower, A.R.M. *Colony to Nation: A History of Canada.* Toronto: McClelland & Stewart, 1977.

MacDonald, Ian A., and Blake, Nicholas J. *Immigration Law and Practice in the United Kingdom,* 3rd ed. London: Butterworths, 1991.

MacDonogh, Steve, ed. *The Rushdie Letters.* Lincoln: University of Nebraska Press, 1993.

MacEwen, Martin. 'Anti-Discrimination Law in Great Britain.' *New Community* 20 no. 3 (April 1994), 353–70.

Mackey, Eva. 'Postmodernism and Cultural Politics in a Multicultural Nation: Contests over Truth in the "Into the Heart of Africa" Controversy.' *Public Culture* 7 (1995), 403–31.

Mallon, Elias. *Neighbors: Muslims in North America*. New York: Friendship Press, 1989.

Mata, Fernando. 'The Multiculturalism Act and Refugee Integration in Canada.' *Refuge*, 13 no. 9 (Feb. 1994), 17–20.

Matas, David with Simon, Ilana. *Closing the Doors: The Failure of Refugee Protection*. Toronto: Summerhill Press, 1989.

Mazrui, Ali. *Cultural Forces in World Politics*. London: James Currey, 1990.

– 'Islamic and Western Values." *Foreign Affairs* 76 no. 5 (Sept.–Oct. 1997), 118–32.

McKenna, Ian B. 'Legal Protection against Racial Discrimination in Canada.' *New Community* 20 no. 3 (April 1994), 415–36.

McLellan, Janet, and Richmond, Anthony H. 'Multiculturalism in Crisis: A Postmodern Perspective on Canada.' *Ethnic and Racial Studies* 17 no. 4 (Oct. 1994), 662–83.

McLoud, Beverly Aminah. *African American Islam*. New York: Routledge, 1995.

Mead, Margaret, and Métraux, Rhoda, eds. *The Study of Culture at a Distance*. Chicago: University of Chicago Press, 1953.

Mernissi, Fatima. *Beyond the Veil: Male–Female Dynamics in Muslim Society*. London: Al-Saqi Books, 1985.

Merriman, Nick, ed. *The Peopling of London: Fifteen Thousand Years of Settlement from Overseas*. London: Museum of London, 1993.

Metcalf, Barbara Daly, ed. *Making Muslim Space in North America and Europe*. Berkeley: University of California Press, 1996.

Miles, Robert. *Racism after 'Race Relations'*. London: Routledge, 1993.

Ministry of National Planning. *Somalia in Figures*. Mogadishu: Ministry of National Planning, 1985.

Modood, Tariq. 'Ethno-Religious Minorities, Secularism and the British State.' Paper presented to the conference 'Religion in the Common European Home,' St Mary's College, London, 1992.

– *Muslims, Race and Equality in Britain: Some Post–Rushdie Affair Reflections*. Birmingham: Centre for the Study of Islam and Christian–Muslim Relations, Selly Oak Colleges, 1990.

– 'Muslim Views on Religious Identity and Racial Equality.' *New Community* 19 no. 3 (April 1993), 513–19.

– *Racial Equality: Colour, Culture and Justice*. London: Institute for Public Policy Research, 1994.

Modood, Tariq, Beishon, Sharon, and Virdee, Satnam. *Changing Ethnic Identities*. London: Policy Studies Institute, 1994.

– *Not Easy Being British: Colour, Culture and Citizenship*. London: Runnymede Trust and Trentham Books, 1992.

Modood, Tariq, and Werbner, Pnina, eds. *The Politics of Multiculturalism in the New Europe: Racism, Identity and Community.* London: Zed Books, 1997.

Moghadam, Valentine, ed. *Identity Politics and Women: Cultural Reassertions and Feminisms in International Perspective.* Boulder, Col.: Westview Press, 1994.

Mohamed, Hassan A. 'Refugee Exodus from Somalia: Revisiting the Causes.' *Refuge* 14 no. 1 (April 1994), 6–10.

Molteno, Marion. *A Shield of Coolest Air.* London: Shola Books, 1993.

Moore, Sally Falk. 'The Production of Cultural Pluralism as a Process.' *Public Culture* 1 no. 2 (spring 1989), 27–48.

Morris, Brian. *Anthropological Studies of Religion.* Cambridge: Cambridge University Press, 1987.

Moynihan, Daniel Patrick. *Pandaemonium: Ethnicity in International Politics.* Oxford: Oxford University Press, 1993.

Musallam, Basim. *Sex and Society in Islam.* Cambridge: Cambridge University Press, 1983.

Muslim Educational Trust. *Comments on the Government White Paper, Choice and Diversity.* London: MET, 1992.

Muslim News. Monthly newspaper. London: Multiple Volumes.

Muslim Voice. Monthly newspaper. Multiple volumes. Toronto: Muslim Students Association, University of Toronto.

Naseer, Syed M. 'Living as Muslims in the West: In This Global Village, We Cannot Shut Ourselves to the Winds of Dialogue.' *Message* (monthly publication of the Islamic Circle of North America) 19 no. 9 (Feb. 1995), 25.

Nash, Manning. *The Cauldron of Ethnicity in the Modern World.* Chicago: University of Chicago Press, 1989.

New York State Office of Alcoholism and Substance Abuse Services. 'Khat, Street Advisory.' *Prevline* (Albany) 4 no. 318. 15 Aug. 1993.

Newsweek. 'Muslim Europe: How Will a Rising Islamic Population Change the Continent?' *Newsweek,* 29 May 1995, 12–19.

Nielsen, Jorgen. *Muslims in Western Europe.* 2nd ed. Edinburgh: Edinburgh University Press, 1995.

– 'Muslims in Britain: Searching for an Identity.' *New Community* 13 no. 3 (spring 1987), 384–94.

– *Religion and Citizenship in Europe and the Arab World.* London: Grey Seal, 1992.

– 'Family Law and Multi-Cultural Britain.' *Newsletter of the Centre for the Study of Islam and Christian–Muslim Relations* 14 (Nov. 1985), 15–18.

Norton, Philip. *The British Polity.* 3rd ed. New York: Longman, 1994.

Nyang, Sulayman S. *Islam, Christianity and African Identity.* Battleboro, Vt.: Amana Books, 1984.

O'Brien, Conor Cruise. 'American Identities.' *Partisan Review* 61 no. 3 (1994), 485–92.

Omar, Mohamed Osman. *The Road to Zero: Somalia's Self-Destruction*. London: Haan Associates, 1992.

Opoku-Dapaah, Edward. *Somali Refugees in Toronto: A Profile*. Toronto: York University Centre for Refugee Studies, 1994.

Oxford House. *Somali Lives: Culture in Exile*. Video. London: London Fields, 1993.

Panayi, Panikos. 'The Historiography of Immigrants and Ethnic Minorities: Britain Compared with the USA.' *Ethnic and Racial Studies* 19 no. 4 (Oct. 1996), 823–840.

Parekh, Bhikhu. *Britain: A Plural Society*. London: Commission for Racial Equality and the Runnymede Trust, 1989.

– ed. *Colour, Culture and Consciousness: Immigrant Intellectuals in Britain*. London: George Allen & Unwin Ltd., 1974.

– *Contemporary Political Thinkers*. Oxford: Martin Robertson, 1982.

– 'The Concept of National Identity.' *New Community* 21 no. 2 (April 1995), 255–68.

– *Hannah Arendt and the Search for a New Political Philosophy*. London: Macmillan Press Ltd, 1981.

– 'Minority Practices and Principles of Toleration. *International Migration Review* 30 no. 1 (1996), 251–84.

Parker-Jenkins, Marie. 'Muslim Matters: The Educational Needs of the Muslim Child.' *New Community* 17 no. 4 (July 1991), 569–582.

Parrinder, Geoffrey. *Africa's Three Religions*. London: Sheldon Press, 1969.

Peach, Ceri. 'The Muslim Population of Great Britain.' *Ethnic and Racial Studies* 13 no. 3 (July 1990), 414–19.

Peach, Ceri, and Glebe, Gunther. 'Muslim Minorities in Western Europe.' *Ethnic and Racial Studies* 18 no. 1 (Jan. 1995), 26–45.

Philip, Marlene Nourbese. *Frontiers: Essays and Writings on Racism and Culture*. Stratford: Mercury Press, 1992.

Pipes, Daniel. *The Rushdie Affair: The Novel, the Ayatollah, and the West*. New York: Birch Lane Press, 1990.

– '"The World is Political!!" The Islamic Revival of the Seventies.' *Orbis* (spring 1980), 9–41.

Piscatori, James P. 'The Rushdie Affair and the Politics of Ambiguity.' *International Affairs* 66 no. 4 (1990), 767–789.

– *Islam in a World of Nation-States*. London: Royal Institute of International Affairs, 1986.

– ed. *Islam in the Political Process*. Cambridge: Cambridge University Press, 1983.

– ed. *Islamic Fundamentalisms and the Gulf Crisis*. Chicago: American Academy of Arts and Sciences and the Fundamentalism Project, 1991.

Pizanias, Caterina, and Frideres, James. *Freedom within the Margins: The Politics of Exclusion*. Calgary: Detselig Enterprises Ltd, 1995.

Political Office of the Presidency, Women's Section. *Somali Women in Socialist Construction: International Women's Year, 1975*. Mogadishu: Office of the Presidency, 1975.

Poulter, Sebastian. 'The Significance of Ethnic Minority Customs and Traditions in English Criminal Law.' *New Community* 16 no. 1 (Oct. 1989), 121–8.

Pouwels, Randall. *Horn and Crescent: Cultural Change and Traditional Islam on the East African Coast*. Cambridge: Cambridge University Press, 1987.

Prince of Wales. *Islam and the West*. A lecture given in the Sheldonian Theatre, Oxford, 27 Oct. 1993. Oxford: Oxford Centre for Islamic Studies, 1993.

Pryor, Edward T., Goldmann, Gustave J., Sheridan, Michael J., and White, Pamela M. 'Measuring Ethnicity: Is "Canadian" an Evolving Indigenous Category?' *Ethnic and Racial Studies* 15 no. 2 (April 1992), 212–35.

Pye, Lucian W., and Verba, Sidney. *Political Culture and Political Development*. Princeton, NJ: Princeton University Press, 1965.

– *Aspects of Political Development*. Boston: Little, Brown & Co., 1966.

– *Asian Power and Politics: The Cultural Dimensions of Authority*. Cambridge, Mass.: Harvard University Press, 1985.

Qureshi, Shoaib, and Khan, Javed. *The Politics of Satanic Verses: Unmasking Western Attitudes*. Leicester: Muslim Community Surveys, 1989.

Rahnema, Ali, ed. *Pioneers of Islamic Revival*. London: Zed Books, 1994.

Ratcliffe, Peter, ed. *'Race,' Ethnicity and Nation*. London: UCL Press, 1994.

Rath, Jan, Groenendijk, Kees, and Penninx, Rinus. 'The Institutionalisation of Islam.' *New Community* 18 no. 1 (Oct. 1991), 101–114.

Raza, Mohammad. *Islam in Britain*. Leicester: Volcano Press, 1991.

Read, Mel, and Simpson, Alan. *Against a Rising Tide: Racism, Europe and 1992*. Nottingham: Spokesman, 1991.

Refugee Council. *Advice on Housing*. London: Refugee Council, 1994.

– *Advice on How to Claim Income Support*. London: Refugee Council, 1995.

Reitz, Jeffrey, and Breton, Raymond. *The Illusion of Difference: Realities of Ethnicity in Canada and the United States*. Ottawa: C.D. Howe Institute, 1994.

Research, Action and Information Network for Bodily Integrity of Women (RAINBO). *Battlefields of Women's Bodies: The Political Controversy over FGM in Egypt*. New York: RAINBO, 1995.

Rex, John. *Ethnic Identity and Ethnic Mobilisation in Britain*. Coventry: Centre for Research in Ethnic Relations, 1991.

– *Race and Ethnicity*. Buckingham: Open University Press, 1986.

Rex, John, and Drury, Beatrice. *Ethnic Mobilistion in a Multi-Cultural Europe.* Aldershot: Avebury, 1994.

Rich, Paul. *Prospero's Return? Historical Essays on Race, Culture and British Society.* London: Hansib, 1994.

Richler, Mordecai. 'A Clear and Present Danger.' *Saturday Night* (Feb. 1996), 50–5.

Richmond, Anthony. 'Socio-Cultural Adaptation and Conflict in Immigrant-Receiving Countries.' *International Social Science Journal* 36 no. 3 (1984), 519–36.

Robinson, Vaughan, ed. *The International Refugee Crisis: British and Canadian Responses.* Oxford: University of Oxford and Macmillan Press, Ltd., 1993.

Rogge, John R. *The Displaced Population in South and Central Somalia and Preliminary Proposals for Their Re-Integration and Rehabilitation: A Report to the United Nations Development Programme.* Winnipeg: University of Manitoba, 1993.

– *Rehabilitation and Reconstruction Needs for Displaced Persons in Somalia: With Special Reference to the Northern Regions and to the Juba Valley: A Report to the United Nations Development Programme.* Winnipeg: University of Manitoba, 1993.

Rotberg, Robert, ed. *The Mixing of Peoples.* Stamford, Conn.: Greylock, 1978.

Rothschild, Joseph. *Ethnopolitics: A Conceptual Framework.* New York: Columbia University Press, 1981.

Ruggles, Clifton, and Rovinescu, Olivia. *Outsider Blues: A Voice from the Shadows.* Halifax: Fernwood Publishing, 1996.

Rushdie, Salman. *In Good Faith.* London: Granta, 1990.

– *The Satanic Verses.* New York: Viking Penguin, 1988.

Ruthven, Malise. *A Satanic Affair: Salman Rushdie and the Rage of Islam.* London: Chatto & Windus, 1990.

Rutter, Jill. *Refugee Children in the Classroom.* London: Trentham Books, 1994.

Said, Abdul, and Simmons, Luiz R. *Ethnicity in an International Context.* New Brunswick, NJ: Transaction Books, 1976.

Said, Edward. *Covering Islam.* Rev. ed. New York: Vintage Books, 1997.

– *Orientalism.* New York: Vintage Books, 1979.

Samatar, Ahmed I. *Socialist Somalia: Rhetoric and Reality.* London: Zed Books, 1988.

– ed. *The Somali Challenge: From Catastrophe to Renewal?* Boulder, Col.: Lynne Reinner Publishers, 1994.

Samatar, Said S., ed. *In the Shadow of Conquest: Islam in Colonial Northeast Africa.* Lawrenceville, NJ: Red Sea Press, 1992.

– *Somalia: A Nation in Turmoil.* London: Minority Rights Group, 1991.

Sardar, Ziauddin, and Wyn Davies, Merryl. *Distorted Imagination: Lessons from the Rushdie Affair.* London: Grey Seal, 1990.

Sarwar, Ghulam. *British Muslims and Schools: Proposals for Progress.* London: Muslim Educational Trust, 1991; rev. ed., 1994.

– *Education Reform Act, 1988: What Can Muslims Do?* London: Muslim Educational Trust, 1988.

– *Sex Education: The Muslim Perspective.* London: Muslim Educational Trust, 1992 (and 1994 update).

Scantlebury, Elizabeth. 'Muslims in Manchester: The Depiction of a Religious Community.' *New Community,* 21 no. 3 (July 1995), 425–35.

Shadid, W.A. 'The Integration of Muslim Minorities in the Netherlands.' *International Migration Review* 25 no. 2 (1991), 355–73.

Shadid, W.A.R., and Van Koningsveld, P.S. 'Islam in the Netherlands: Constitutional Law and Islamic Organizations.' *Journal of Muslim Minority Affairs* 16 no. 1 (1996), 111–28.

– eds. *The Integration of Islam and Hinduism in Western Europe.* Kampen, Netherlands: Kok Pharos Publishing, 1991.

– *Muslims in the Margin.* Kampen, Netherlands: Kok Pharos Publishing, 1996.

– *Religious Freedom and the Position of Islam in Western Europe.* Kampen, Netherlands: Kok Pharos Publishing, 1995.

Sharma, Satya P., Ervin, Alexander M., and Meintel, Deirdre. *Immigrants and Refugees in Canada.* Saskatoon: University of Saskatchewan, 1991.

Sheik-Abdi, Abdi. *Divine Madness: Mohammed Abdulle Hassan (1856–1920).* London: Zed Books, 1993.

– *Tales of Punt: Somali Folktales.* Macomb, Illi.: Dr Leisure, 1993.

Shtromas, Alexsandras. *The End of 'Isms'? Reflections on the Fate of Ideological Politics after Communism's Collapse.* Oxford: Blackwell Publishers, 1994.

Siddiqui, Kalim. *The Implications of the Rushdie Affair for Muslims in Britain.* Speech given April 1989. London: Muslim Institute, 1989.

Siemerling, Winfried. *Writing Ethnicity: Cross-Cultural Consciousness in Canadian and Quebecois Literature.* Toronto: ECW Press, 1996.

Skellington, Richard. *'Race' in Britain Today.* London: Sage Publications, 1992.

Smith, Anthony D. *The Ethnic Revival in the Modern World.* Cambridge: Cambridge University Press, 1981.

– ed. *Ethnicity and Nationalism.* Leiden: E.J. Brill, 1992.

– 'The Origins of Nations.' *Ethnic and Racial Studies* 12 no. 3 (July 1989), 340–67.

– *Theories of Nationalism.* London: Duckworth, 1971.

Smolicz, J.J. 'Tradition, Core Values and Intercultural Development in Plural Societies.' *Ethnic and Racial Studies* 11 no. 4 (Nov. 1988), 387–410.

Sniderman, Paul, et al. *Working Paper on Anti-Semitism in Quebec.* Toronto: York University, 1992.

Solomos, John. *Race and Racism in Britain*. 2nd ed. London: Macmillan Press Ltd., 1993.

Solomos, John, and Back, Les. *Race, Politics and Social Change*. London: Routledge, 1995.

Solomos, John, and Wrench, John. *Racism and Migration in Western Europe*. Oxford: Berg Publishers, 1993.

Somali Community Information Centre. *Annual Report*. London: SCIC, 1994.

Somali Press. Monthly newspaper. Multiple volumes. Toronto.

Somali Relief Association (UK). *The Somalis: An Invisible Community in Crisis*. London: Haan Associates, 1992.

Somali Youth Association of Toronto (SOYAT). *Mission Statement*. Toronto: SOYAT, Aug. 1993.

Soysal, Yasemin Nuhoglu. *Limits of Citizenship: Migrants and Postnational Membership in Europe*. Chicago: University of Chicago Press, 1994.

Spinner, Jeff. *The Boundaries of Citizenship: Race, Ethnicity, and Nationality in the Liberal State*. Baltimore: Johns Hopkins University Press, 1994.

Stack, John F., ed., *Ethnic Identities in a Transnational World*. Westport, Conn.: Greenwood Press, 1981.

– *The Primordial Challenge: Ethnicity in the Contemporary World*. New York: Greenwood Press, 1986.

Stavenhagen, Rodolfo. *The Ethnic Question: Conflicts, Development, and Human Rights*. Tokyo: United Nations University Press, 1990.

Steward, Julian H. 'Levels of Sociocultural Integration: An Operational Concept.' *Journal of Anthropological Research* 42 (fall 1986), 337–353.

Taylor, Charles. *Multiculturalism and 'The Politics of Recognition.'* Princeton, NJ: Princeton University Press, 1992.

Tomlinson, Sally. *Home and School in Multicultural Britain*. London: Batsford Academic and Educational Books Ltd, 1984.

Toronto Board of Education. *Readings and Prayers*. Toronto: Board of Education for the City of Toronto, 1985.

Toubia, Nahid. *Female Genital Mutilation: A Call for Global Action*. New York: Nahid Toubia, 1993.

Trimingham, John. *Islam in East Africa*. Oxford: Clarendon Press, 1964.

– *Islam in Ethiopia*. London: Frank Cass & Co., 1965.

– *The Sufi Orders in Islam*. Oxford: Clarendon Press, 1971.

UK Action Committee on Islamic Affairs (UKACIA). *Muslims and the Law in MultiFaith Britain: Need for Reform*. Memorandum to the Home Secretary. London: UKACIA, 1993.

United Nations High Commissioner for Refugees (UNHCR). *The State of the World's Refugees: In Search of Solutions*. Oxford: Oxford University Press, 1995.

– *UNHCR Update on Refugee Developments in Africa.* Geneva: United Nations High Commissioner for Refugees, 21 Aug. 1992.

Urban Mozaik. Periodical (Toronto). 1 no. 1 (winter 1997).

Van den Berghe, P. *Race and Ethnicity.* New York: Basic Books, 1970.

Van der Kwaak, Anke. 'Female Circumcision and Gender Identity: A Questionable Alliance.' *Journal of Social Science and Medicine* 35 no. 6 (1992), 777–87.

Verene, Donald. *Vico's Science of Imagination.* Ithaca, NY: Cornell University Press, 1981.

Vertovec, Steven, and Peach, Ceri. *Islam in Europe: The Politics of Religion and Community.* London: Macmillan Press Ltd, 1997.

Virdee, Satnam. *Racial Violence and Harassment.* London: Policy Studies Institute, 1995.

Waldron, Sidney, and Hasci, Naomi. *Somali Refugees in the Horn of Africa.* Oxford: Queen Elizabeth House, Oxford University, 1995.

Walker, Alice, and Parmar, Pratibha. *Warrior Marks: Female Genital Mutilation and the Sexual Blinding of Women.* New York: Harcourt Brace & Company, 1993.

Ward, B., and Badger, T. eds. *The Making of Martin Luther King and the Civil Rights Movement.* Birmingham, England: Macmillan, 1995.

Warner, Rachel, ed. *Voices from Somalia.* London: Minority Rights Group, 1991.

Waugh, Earle, Abu-Laban, Baha, and Qureshi, Regula, eds. *The Muslim Community in North America.* Edmonton: University of Alberta Press, 1983.

Weber, Max. *The Methodology of the Social Sciences.* Trans. Edward Shils. New York: Free Press, 1949.

Weinfeld, Morton. 'Myth and Reality in the Canadian Mosaic: "Affective Ethnicity."' *Canadian Ethnic Studies* 13 no. 3 (1981), 80–95.

Weingrod, Alex, ed. *Studies in Israeli Ethnicity: After the Ingathering.* New York: Gordon and Breach, 1985.

Werbner, Pnina. 'Sealing the Koran: Offering and Sacrifice among Pakistani Labour Migrants.' *Cultural Dynamics* 1 no. 1 (1988), 77–97.

– 'Stamping the Earth with the Name of Allah: Zikr and the Sacralizing of Space among British Muslims." *Cultural Anthropology* 11 no. 3 (Aug. 1996), 309–38.

Werbner, Pnina, and Modood, Tariq, eds. *Debating Cultural Hybridity: Multi-Cultural Identities and the Politics of Anti-Racism.* London: Zed Books, 1997.

Werbner, Pnina, and Anwar, Muhammad, eds. *Black and Ethnic Leaderships: The Cultural Dimensions of Political Action.* London: Routledge, 1991.

Wimmer, Andreas. 'Explaining Xenophobia and Racism: A Critical Review of Current Research Approaches.' *Ethnic and Racial Studies* 20 no. 1 (Jan. 1997), 17–41.

Yamani, Mai. *Feminism and Islam: Legal and Literary Perspectives.* New York: New York University Press, 1996.

Young, Crawford, ed. *The Rising Tide of Cultural Pluralism: The Nation-State at Bay?* Madison, Wisc.: University of Wisconsin Press, 1993.

Yousif, Ahmad F. *Muslims in Canada: A Question of Identity.* Toronto: Legas, 1993.

Zebiri, Kate. 'Relations between Muslims and Non-Muslims in the Thought of Western-Educated Muslim Intellectuals.' *Islam and Christian–Muslim Relations* 6 no. 2 (1995), 255–77.

Index

Fadumo, 89–90
Farah, 130, 178–9, 182
Farhia, 86, 113, 141, 153–4, 177
al-Fasi, Sayyid Ahmad Ibn Idris al-
Fasi, 30–1
fasting (during Ramadan), 87, 114
Fathia, 110, 144, 152–3, 180, 185
Fawziya, 143, 144, 151, 180, 184
female circumcision, 9, 142, 148–56,
157, 193, 194, 215; in Egypt, 149;
historical reasons for, 150; Islamic
position on, 149; legality in West,
149; *sunna* form of, 149
Feversham College, 102
Finsbury Park mosque, 71
fiqh, 142
five pillars, 29, 73
France, 50; Islam in, 206–7
Free Trade Agreement (Canada–
United States), 162–4
Friday communal prayers, 70, 72, 74,
126, 128, 208, 209, 232
Furnivall, J.S., 50

Gabobe, Jamal, 3, 239 n. 1
Gadabuursi, 28
garbasaar, 39, 85
Geertz, Clifford, 44, 59, 205
gender relations, 17–18, 72–3, 75–6,
91, 93, 98, 100, 122–3, 138, 139, 158,
209, 224; pre-marital, 124, 127–8,
129–30, 131, 133
genealogy (*abtirsiinyo*), 28–9
Germany, 50; Islam in, 206
al-Ghazali, Abu Hamid, 142
Glazer, Nathan, 43
Golder's Green, 112
Gordon, Milton, 47, 49–50, 56

Habar Gedir, 41

hadiths, 34–5, 38, 40, 73, 98, 127, 208,
225, 233
hajj, 73, 87, 137, 225
Hal-Abuur, 241 n. 5
halal food, 17, 23, 25, 74, 79, 87, 92,
114, 116, 119, 121, 124, 127, 131, 132,
166, 170, 232
Halimo, 80
Halliday, Fred, 219, 242 n. 17
Hamda, 115
Hamud, 37, 145–6, 178, 210
Hanafi jurisprudence, 38
Hanbali jurisprudence, 30
al-Haq, Shaykh Gad al-Haq Ali,
149
haram, 91
Hargeisa, 22, 40
Hashi, 77, 98
Hassan, 74, 180, 182
Hassan, Sayyid Mohammed Abdulle
Hassan (the 'Mad Mullah'),
31–2
Hawa, 121–3, 133, 145
Hawaardle, 41
Hawiye, 20, 21, 23, 37, 41
heer (*xeer*), 29
Hersi, 177
Hibaq, 83, 138, 151, 178, 185, 195,
209–10
Hicks, Esther, 150
hijab, 25, 26, 32, 35, 38–9, 72, 78, 79, 80,
81, 82–3, 84, 85–6, 89, 91, 93, 95, 96,
105, 114, 115, 118, 122–3, 123–4, 133,
203, 224, 232, 235
hijra, 27, 95, 220–1
Hiraan, 41
Hnatyshyn, Ray, 54
homosexuality, 138, 141–2
Honeyford, Ray, 24, 168, 263 n. 28
Horton, John, 173